MW00333842

Self-determination of peoples

Titles published in the Hersch Lauterpacht Memorial Lecture Series

Self-determination of peoples

A legal reappraisal

ANTONIO CASSESE

A GROTIUS PUBLICATION

CAMBRIDGE
UNIVERSITY PRESS

Published by the Press Syndicate of the University of Cambridge
The Pitt Building, Trumpington Street, Cambridge CB2 1RP
40 West 20th Street, New York, NY 10011–4211, USA
10 Stamford Road, Oakleigh, Melbourne 3166, Australia

© Cambridge University Press 1995

First published 1995
Reprinted 1996, twice

Printed in Great Britain at the University Press, Cambridge

A catalogue record for this book is available from the British Library

Library of Congress cataloguing in publication data

Cassese, Antonio
Self-determination of peoples: a legal reappraisal/
Antonio Cassese
p.   cm.
Includes bibliographical references and index.
ISBN 0 521 48187 2 (hc)
1. Self-determination, National. I. Title.
JX4054.C32 1995
341.26—dc20 94—32490 CIP

ISBN 0 521 48187 2 hardback

Contents

Contents

Contents

Contents

Contents

Preface

My first inquiry into the international legal status of the principle of self-determination dates back to 1957, the year I began working towards my LL. M at Pisa University. In those days, I was intrigued by the potential far-reaching ramifications of the principle, as well as by the problems and challenges posed by its inherent ambiguities. Since that time, I have been wrestling with this topic, although admittedly in fits and starts, and indeed have returned to it on many occasions, tracing the gradual process by which the principle has gained a foothold in the body of international legal rules. Like all inquiries into areas straddling the border between politics and law, discussing self-determination's maturation from a political concept to an international legal norm has proved extremely difficult. Thus, after thirty-odd years of thinking about the matter, I decided I ought to take stock of my prior work in the area and rethink problems previously examined. My hope was to develop an over-arching perspective on the principle. I have thus reached a number of conclusions that are markedly different from those expressed in my earlier writings. Although I have changed my mind on many points, I have of course drawn upon my previous research and made use of it in the course of the present reappraisal. This should account for the frequent references to my past writings: they are simply intended to indicate where I have dwelt more extensively on the matter at hand, and should not be seen as a manifestation of that narcissistic bent that all too often befalls aging scholars, making them so prone to self-citation.

I am aware, of course, that this book cannot exhaust the topic, which is indeed immense. I hope, however, that it offers a fairly readable survey of the subject, thereby contributing to a better understanding of the interplay of politics and law in the world community.

As time goes by, I have become more and more persuaded that even we international lawyers should write short essays or small books consisting of brief chapters: the international reality has become so complicated, multi-faceted and evasive that the bent for 'esprit de système' should give way to quick scholarly forays into small fragments of reality; after all, 'the devil is in the detail'. Why do we not take as a model the short, pithy and profound stories or essays of J.L. Borges? Alas, in writing this ponderous book, once again I have been unable to live up to my own design. My frustration will probably be passed over to the reader, to whom I therefore owe an apology; however, to make up partially for my failings, I have drafted a final chapter, where he or she can at least find a thumb-nail sketch of my long analysis.

I would not have set about both rethinking the whole range of questions relating to self-determination and undertaking the extensive research work that was needed without the powerful incentive given by the invitation to deliver the H. Lauterpacht Memorial Lectures in Cambridge. I am most grateful to E. Lauterpacht both for the honour of kindly including me among the Cambridge lecturers and for the great forbearance he showed in waiting for my typescript.

I am also greatly indebted to a number of colleagues and friends who were generous enough to read the last draft but one and make helpful comments. In addition to E. Lauterpacht, I should mention R. Barsotti (Florence University), L. Condorelli (Geneva University), R. Higgins (London School of Economics), S. Marks (Cambridge University), M. Shaw (Leicester University). In particular, I owe my friend J. H. H. Weiler (Harvard Law School) a great deal for his many insightful comments and generous input. It goes without saying that I alone bear full responsibility for any misapprehensions or gaps that might still exist in spite of the many critical and constructive suggestions from which I have benefited.

I am also beholden to Melanie Stein who, with great competence, helped me prepare a first draft and to Cyril Adjei, who adroitly polished up the last three drafts and compiled the indexes. Evie Zaccardelli, as usual, showed great care and consideration in preparing the final typescript; Julia Valerio skilfully attended to proof-reading and Jean Field undertook the copy-editing with admirable competence. To all of them I would like to express my deep appreciation.

Abbreviations

AEL	Collected Courses of the Academy of European Law
AF	*Annuaire Français de Droit International*
AFDI	*Annuaire Français de Droit International*
AJICL	*African Journal of International and Comparative Law*
AJIL	*American Journal of International Law*
ASDI	*Annuaire Suisse de Droit International*
AVR	*Archiv des Völkerrechts*
AYIL	*Australian Yearbook of International Law*
BYIL	*British Yearbook of International Law*
Case WRJIL	*Case Western Reserve Journal of International Law*
CSCE	Conference on Security and Cooperation in Europe
CYIL	*Canadian Yearbook of International Law*
Dept. St. Bul.	*Department of State Bulletin*
EC	European Community
EG	*Enciclopedia Giuridica*
EJIL	*European Journal of International Law*
Encyclopedia	R. Bernhard (ed.), *Encyclopedia of Public International Law*
EPC Bul.	*European Political Cooperation Bulletin*
FA	Foreign Affairs
Fest.	*Festschrift*
GA	General Assembly
GAOR	General Assembly Official Records
GYIL	*German Yearbook of International Law*
HILJ	*Harvard International Law Journal*
HR	*Hague Recueil*
ICJ	International Court of Justice
ICLQ	*International and Comparative Law Quarterly*

IJIL	*Indian Journal of International Law*
ILC	International Law Commission
ILM	International Legal Materials
ILR	International Law Reports
Israel L.Rev.	*Israel Law Review*
IYHR	*Israel Yearbook of Human Rights*
Keesing's	*Keesing's Contemporary Archives*, later *Keesing's Record of World Events*
NILR	*Netherlands International Law Review*
NTIR	*Nordisk Tidsskrift for International Ret (Acta Scandinavia Juris Gentium)*
NYIL	*Netherlands Yearbook of International Law*
NYUJILP	*New York University Journal of International Law and Politics*
OAS	Organisation of American States
OAU	Organisation of African Unity
Proceedings ASIL	*Proceedings of the American Society of International Law*
PYIL	*Palestinian Yearbook of International Law*
RBDI	*Revue Belge de Droit International*
RDI	*Rivista di Diritto Internazionale*
RDILC	*Revue de droit international et de législation comparé*
RDP	*Revue de droit public*
Repertório	A. A. Cançado Trindade (ed.), *Repertório da prática brasileira do direito internacional público, Período 1941–1960* (Brasilia 1984), *Período 1961–1981* (Brasilia 1984)
Res.	Resolution
RGDIP	*Revue Générale de Droit International Public*
SAJIL	*South African Journal of International Law*
SC	Security Council
SCOR	Security Council Official Records
Stanford JIL	*Stanford Journal of International Law*
UN	United Nations
UNCIO	United Nations Conference on International Organisation
UNTS	United Nations Treaty Series
UN Ybk	*Yearbook of the United Nations*
US Digest	*Digest of US Practice in International Law*
VJIL	*Virginia Journal of International Law*
Zeit.	*Zeitschrift für ausländisches öffentliches Recht und Völkerrecht*

1

Introduction

The significance of self-determination

Self-determination has been one of the most important driving forces in the new international community. It has set in motion a restructuring and redefinition of the world community's basic 'rules of the game'. At the same time, its ideological origins render it a multifaceted but also an extremely ambiguous concept. This concept is emblematic of international law in the twentieth century. *Historically*, it is associated with, and has been instrumental in, the principal tremors, even quakes, of contemporary international relations. Tracing the evolution of self-determination in theory and practice thus becomes a way of narrating an important part of our present world history. *Politically*, it is a concept which is, at one and the same time, both boldly radical and deeply subversive. This captures some of the deep ambivalence of States towards the international legal order. Self-determination is also significant *jurisprudentially*. From this vantage point, self-determination is a powerful expression of the underlying tensions and contradictions of international legal theory: it perfectly reflects the cyclical oscillation between positivism and natural law, between an emphasis on consent, that is, voluntarism, and an emphasis on binding 'objective' legal principles, between a 'statist' and a communitarian vision of world order.

To explore self-determination, as this book will do, is therefore a way of opening a window towards a multifaceted, hugely important phenomenon. It is also a way of opening a veritable Pandora's box. In every corner of the globe peoples are claiming the right to self-determination. Consider the most celebrated cases: Palestine, Western Sahara, South Africa, East Timor, Quebec. Add to these the Kurds; the Basques; the indigenous populations of Australia, Guatemala, the United States and Canada; the Armenians; the inhabitants of Gibraltar and the Falkland/Malvinas Islands. Which of these peoples actually have a *right* to self-determination under international law? Moreover, what is the scope of the right possessed? More generally, to what extent have international law-makers accepted the political postulate of self-determination in the realm of legal rules? To put it differently, to what extent have they permitted the principle to reshape international relations? If it is undisputed that the principle has by now gained a foothold in the international community, does it have a major impact on traditional international institutions, or does it only have an effect at the margin? These are the major questions I shall set out to answer.

The approach chosen

There has been no dearth of writings on self-determination in its variety of dimensions. This is not surprising. What is, perhaps, surprising, as we approach the end of the century, is the strange absence of a comprehensive legal account of the concept. It is suggested that such an account is badly needed, especially in an area as sensitive as this, where we are faced with confusing State practice, deceptively complex or contradictory resolutions from international organizations and scant and reticent views of courts, not to mention publicists. The core of my research is, thus, unashamedly doctrinal: its by-word is *lex lata*. In other words, this book is about the right to self-determination as it exists in international law. After carefully reading the immense literature on self-determination I have come to these three conclusions. First, there is still some need for a sober legal assessment of the matter. Second, this assessment must be based on a close scrutiny of State practice (to the extent that it can be gleaned from national digests or UN proceedings). Third, there is need for a reappraisal of self-determination against the background of the whole body of international law, with a view to pinpointing the bearing, if any, of the principle on the various segments of traditional international law. In this book I shall therefore endeavour, as much as possible, to look at the whole range of problems from a strictly legal viewpoint, on the assumption that such an approach can bear more fruit in this so highly politicized area.

In keeping with my general outlook as a lawyer, I shall, however, also try to go *beyond* the realm of law. Indeed, a modern doctrinal account should not closet itself in the lawyer's hermetically sealed chamber.

This study is therefore committed to a *contextual approach* to law in which history, politics, and jurisprudence are all employed in the service of legal elucidation.

The case for a historical approach is easily made. A still photograph of the current state of law would be incomprehensible – how could one understand the way the law is today if one does not study its evolution into its current state? Can we understand a human being without delving into his or her biography? Can we understand a polity without exploring its history? How, then, can we hope to understand the legal parameters of self-determination at the end of the century if we do not trace its antecedents at the beginning? Equally important, how can one conceive of the law of tomorrow without understanding how it was yesterday? The reader will thus be invited to arrive at the current state of law via a comprehensive historical survey.

Likewise, to discuss self-determination without extensive reference to the political context in which the law has developed is to perpetrate, or revive, a fiction which should once and for all be interred. I do not adopt the position that law is politics. But it seems obvious, indeed trite, that the two are intimately connected.

Finally, although my orientation is positivist – a commitment to the 'is' – it would be foolhardy, especially in the area of self-determination, to mask the deep challenges that emerge from time to time – and more forcefully in recent years – to the positivist approach to international law, to the very ability of lawyers to define rules that constrain behaviour. Consequently, besides inquiring into the present parameters of the right, I shall also discuss its failings and the direction in which the international community's conception of the right seems to be moving: where does self-determination, in both theory and practice, fall short? In which ways is the international community prepared to 'reinvent' the right and ensure it a wider applicability?

The principal postulates of this inquiry

It may be useful, in this brief introduction, to set out some of my key premises, since they will inform the discussion in the text – though normally as a backdrop and rarely taking front stage.

First, the *historical perspective*. Arguably, in this century decisive turning-points have occurred in the wake of the First World War, the Second World War and the Cold War. Self-determination was a key concept in articulating these changes. The First World War brought to an end a

3

long period in the history of the law of nations which was dominated by a Eurocentric, largely homogeneous, small club of the old Powers and which continued to equate national sovereignty excessively with political rulers, more particularly the Head of State. This old order was forever shattered both with the emergence of the Soviet Union and a radical and new willingness to undermine the 'dogma' of State sovereignty and cater internationally for peoples – although in the 'fall-back formula' of 'protection of minorities'. It is not yet possible to talk of self-determination as positive international law in this period, but it clearly was the animating *political ideal*, which encapsulated the new post-war order. The debate about self-determination in that period is fundamental to an understanding of its key ideological and political components. The period immediately after the First World War will thus provide the context for understanding the *idea* itself.

The First World War may, in some respects, be seen as a general rehearsal of the Second World War, but this second conflagration was a far more devastating and traumatic event in its impact and, consequently, far more vigorous in the ensuing legal transformations. The First World War ushered in a turn towards fledgling institutions (e.g. the League of Nations), fledgling norms (e.g. the Kellogg–Briand Pact of 1928 designed to outlaw resort to war 'as an instrument of national policy' and a means 'for the solution of international controversies') and, in the present context, the *idea* of self-determination. The Second World War, on the other hand, brought about the far more ambitious and robust United Nations Organization, the unequivocal outlawing of the use of force, and the relentless drive to transform self-determination from an idea into a legally binding principle (it was also accompanied by the enfranchisement of the Third World, brought about by vociferous insistence on self-determination as an anticolonial standard). The period immediately after the First World War, and the Charter framework, will provide the context for understanding the maturing of self-determination from a political concept to an international legal norm.

The end of the Cold War – a period in which violence was conducted by satellites of the Superpowers all over the world and which saw a cumulative death toll in the millions and a military expenditure higher than any previous conflict – saw another revival of self-determination, but again with a new twist. If, in the past, self-determination used the coin of 'progress', in its third apparition it has come to be seen increasingly as fuelling the currency of ethno-national intolerance, rivalry, tribalism, xenophobia, and worse: a Golem turned on its Creators. The post-Cold

War period and the subsequent New International Order will be the context for understanding the limits and dangers of the concept.

A note of warning must, however, be sounded. The three historical epochs – reflected respectively in Chapters 2, 3, and 10–11 – are as explained a context in which to understand the respective cluster of ideas, legal concepts, and their political ramifications. I will provide this context but it is for the reader to construct his or her own understanding.

This very same invitation to the involved reader applies to the second contextual element concerning the *politics of self-determination*. The key idea in this respect is the Janus-like nature of self-determination. The concept of self-determination is both radical, progressive, alluring and, at the same time, subversive and threatening. This 'Janus quality' has brought about a deep ambivalence towards self-determination which, in turn, may explain the difficulties the international community experiences in trying to articulate the idea in a palatable way, in transforming it – in an acceptable manner – into a set of legally binding standards, and dealing with its limits and dangers in a consistent fashion.

Let us consider, for a moment, the contradictory nature of self-determination. *Internally*, self-determination could be used and has been used as a vehicle for enfranchisement, for ever expanding circles of citizens against all manner of *ancien régimes*. On this score, the 'self' of the nation has shifted: it is no longer embodied in a Monarch ruling over a State but in the citizens of the State. Self-determination is thus the reflection in international law of a movement that began with the American and French Revolutions and reached its climax in twentieth-century notions of universal suffrage.

Externally, self-determination has been no less of a challenge to established authority – that of the small circle of 'civilized nations' which constituted the international legal order. As I have already noted, self-determination was the vehicle through which this international *ancien régime* could be challenged by the admittance of new members. One of the major developments of twentieth-century international law has been the expansion of the family of nations to include, sometimes after bloody conflict, States of the so-called Third World – a development in which the notion of self-determination was at the conceptual centre.

But it is in this very allure – which has been employed, using different terminology, by the American and French Revolutions and by countless other States ever since – that the subversion lurks. The dynamic is simple: self-determination is attractive so long as it has not been attained; alternatively, it is attractive so long as it is applied to others. Once realized,

5

enthusiasm dies fast, since henceforth it can only be used to undermine perceived internal and external stability. In the hands of would-be States, self-determination is the key to opening the door and entering into that coveted club of statehood. For existing States, self-determination is the key for locking the door against the undesirable from within and outside the realm.

This *in-built ambivalence* will constitute one, if not the, principal explanatory 'golden thread' running through the historical–doctrinal narrative of this book. At the level of political ideas in the epoch after the First World War, we will find, to give but one example, the strange alliance of Wilson and Lenin, both espousing self-determination – except as applied to themselves. In the Charter after the Second World War, we will continually confront in such documents as the 1970 UN Declaration on Friendly Relations, formulations which characterize self-determination with the flowery and loose rhetoric of freedom and liberation and yet couch its operative terms in the dry and tight language of legal disclaimers, substantially excluding any secession from existing States. Here too we find strange bedfellows: with First, Second, and Third Worlds transcending their ideological differences and uniting around texts which are carefully drafted so as not to rattle any skeletons in their respective cupboards.

The same in-built ambivalence towards self-determination also offers some explanation of the pathologies of the post-Cold War epoch. On the one hand, both internal democracy and external liberation have, arguably, matured – or, at least, are in the process of maturing – into universal standards: the transition in South Africa, the reaction of the world community to the situation in Haiti, and the startling transformation in the former Soviet Union and its erstwhile empire can be seen as examples. However, at the same time, one can observe in the old First World an indecisive vacillation between endorsing independence or instead favouring a revival of minority regimes; of preaching to the new Eastern European States a gospel of tolerance and multi-culturalism, while practising the opposite – as in France or Germany – in one's own back yard. In the Third World we see an increasing number of States, notably in Africa, to whom self-determination acted as midwife at their birth into the international community, which are now engaged in the wholesale destruction of any semblance of either internal or external commitment to that concept.

To be sure, this in-built ambivalence, this combination of radicalness and subversion, is not the only explanatory principle. But as the reader proceeds through the vicissitudes of doctrinal development, he or she will surely find in the endless variations of this ambivalence a powerful tool of analysis.

Finally, let me hint at the *jurisprudential dimension*. As I explained above, this book is not about legal theory: it does not try to construct a 'theory' of self-determination. But the approach adopted – the eye to history and politics and, at the same time, a commitment to the somewhat traditional habits of tracing State practice, interpreting case-law and resolutions and comparing one with the other – will expose the elements which in turn highlight several of the deep jurisprudential conundrums surrounding this concept. Let me set forth some of the questions which the reader should keep in mind in this regard: Has international law really come up with a workable formula of how to define the 'self' entitled to 'determination'? Are the rules on self-determination which have gained international acceptance and consent more than a mere consecration of decolonization? Are they operational in the new era of post-colonialism and post-Cold War? Can it be said that the practice of States – in, say, recognizing Bangladesh and not recognizing the Turkish Republic of Northern Cyprus – followed the law, or has law, in this area, always followed practice? How does the story of self-determination, as told in this book, contribute to the perennial argument on the extent to which international law actually constrains State behaviour or, instead, simply provides a 'structure of justification' for that behaviour? These questions are not the focus of the book, but they hover over almost every page. I shall consequently return to them in the conclusion.

PART I

The historical background

2

Self-determination as an international political postulate

The French Revolution

The origin of the principle of self-determination can be traced back to the American Declaration of Independence (1776) and the French Revolution (1789), which marked the demise of the notion that individuals and peoples, as subjects of the King, were objects to be transferred, alienated, ceded, or protected in accordance with the interests of the monarch. The core of the principle lies in the American and French insistence that the government be responsible to the people.

In France, self-determination was first propounded as a standard concerning the *transfer of territory*. Although it was proclaimed as early as 1790, it was formally enshrined in Article 2 of Title XIII of the Draft Constitution presented by Condorcet to the National Convention on 15 February 1793:

[La République française] renonce solennellement à réunir à son territoire des contrées étrangères, sinon d'après le voeu librement émis de la majorité des habitants, et dans le cas seulement où les contrées qui solliciteront cette réunion ne seront pas incorporées et unies à une autre nation, en vertu d'un pacte social, exprimé dans une constitution antérieure et librement consentie.[1]

---

[1] Text in R. Redslob, 'Völkerrechtliche Ideen der französischen Revolution', in *Festgabe für Otto Mayer*, Tübingen 1916, 293. Article 53(3) of the French Constitution of 1958 crystallizes the rule which formed Title XIII of the 1793 draft constitution: 'Nulle cession, nul échange, nulle adjonction de territoire n'est valable sans le consentement des populations intéressées.' See the bibliography cited in A. Cassese, 'La diffusion des idées révolutionnaires et l'evolution du droit international', in Société française de droit international, *Révolution et droit international*, Paris 1990, 299, n. 2. See also R. J. Dupuy, 'La Révolution française et le droit international actuel', 214 HR, 1989-II, 25–6. See generally, F. Ermacora, 'Ursprung und Wesen des Selbstbestimmungsrechts der Völker

11

However, although the French leaders, in drafting Article 2, proclaimed a lofty principle, they misapplied it in actual practice. More specifically, they used the text to justify the annexation of lands belonging to other sovereigns. As long as the results of a plebiscite tilted in France's favour, annexation was 'legal'. For example, on 28 October 1790, Merlin de Douai, citing the Alsatian population's desire to be joined with France, asserted that Alsace was French and ought no longer to be ruled by the German princes who claimed sovereignty over the region under the Treaty of Westphalia. According to him, the desires of the Alsatians prevailed over the Treaty. Commenting on Merlin de Douai's claim, the historian Droz rightly notes:

'Aux engagements de souverain à souverain, l'Assemblée substituait ainsi un nouveau droit international public en vertu duquel il était possible d'annexer pacifiquement les pays révoltés contre leur souverain légitime.[2]

Revolutionary France's alleged adherence to the principle of self-determination paved the way for the 1791 annexation of the territory of Avignon and the 1793 annexation of Belgium and the Palatinate. Plebiscites were held and the territories were annexed in accordance with the populations' express desire to unite with France. The right to self-determination was not, however, uniformly applied. Plebiscites were only valid if the vote was pro-French.[3]

The discriminatory implementation of the principle was not the only problem. There was an 'internal' limitation on the principle as well. The principle embodied in Title XIII of the 1793 Draft was significantly limited in scope. It was to be applied only to changes in States' borders. Colonial peoples were not deemed to have a right to self-determination; neither were minorities or ethnic, religious or cultural groups. Moreover, the principle did not explicitly refer to the peoples' right freely to choose their own rulers, what we today call the right to 'internal' self-determination (self-determination as a criterion for the democratic legitimation of a State).

---

und seine Entwicklung bis zum zweiten Weltkrieg', in K. Rabl (ed.), *Inhalt, Wesen und gegenwärtige praktische Bedentung des Selbstbestimmungsrechts der Völker*, Munich 1964, 50–75.

[2] J. Droz, *Histoire diplomatique de 1648 à 1919*, 3rd edn, Paris 1972, 178–9.

[3] On these plebiscites, see S. Wambaugh, *A Monograph on Plebiscites*, New York 1920, 4–10 and 33–57. See generally, W. von Blittersdorff, *Das Internationale Plebiszit. Praktische Fragen der Verwirklichung des Selbstbestimmungsrechts*, Hamburg and Frankfurt/Main 1965.

Whatever their limitations and flaws, the importance of the late-eighteenth century French proclamations concerning self-determination should not be belittled. The right devolved implicitly from the profoundly anti-despotic democratic spirit that inspired the French revolutionaries in the years 1789–92. The modern-day right of peoples to external self-determination has its origins in this early principle, which was primarily conceived and proclaimed as permitting States to justify allocations of territories to one State as opposed to another.

Once the concept of self-determination was born, it was destined to play a major role in the development of the international community. The concept first spread from France to neighbouring Italy, where in the nineteenth century Giuseppe Mazzini invoked it – in the form of a political postulate demanding that all *nations* be allowed freely to choose their status – in his push for the unification of Italy,[4] and the Italian politician and jurist P. S. Mancini made it a focal point of his work under the guise of the principle of *nationality*.[5] Then, with the advent of the First World War and the Bolshevik Revolution, it emerged on the international scene. For US President Woodrow Wilson it was the key to lasting peace in Europe. For V. I. Lenin it was a means of realizing the dream of world-wide socialism.

---

[4] Mazzini wrote that 'God . . . divided Humanity into distinct groups upon the face of our globe, and thus planted the seeds of nations. Bad governments have disfigured the design of God, which you may see clearly marked out . . . by the courses of the great rivers, by the lines of the lofty mountains, and by other geographical conditions . . . The divine design will infallibly be fulfilled. Natural divisions . . . will replace the arbitrary divisions sanctioned by bad governments. The map of Europe will be remade. The Countries of the People will rise, defined by the voice of the free, upon the ruins of the countries of the Kings and privileged castes. Between these Countries there will be harmony and brotherhood', quoted by D. E. D. Beales, 'Mazzini and the Revolutionary Nationalism', in D. Thomson (ed.), *Political Ideas*, London 1969, 146.

[5] See P. S. Mancini, 'Della Nazionalità come fondamento del diritto delle Genti' (1851), in 32 *Diritto internazionale*, 1978, 1 ff.; 'Dei Progressi del diritto nella società, nella legislazione e nella scienza' (1858–9), *ibid.*, 155 ff.; 'La Vita dei popoli nell'Umanità' (1872), *ibid.*, 182 ff. In general, see R. Redslob, *Le principe des nationalités*, Paris 1930, especially 1–38; C. Curcio, *Nazione e Autodecisione dei popoli – Due idee nella storia*, Milan 1977, 53 ff. See also, D. Anzilotti, *Corso di diritto internazionale* (1928), 4th edn, Padua 1955, 116–17; J. F. Guilhaudis, *Le droit des peuples à disposer d'eux-mêmes*, Grenoble 1976, 40–2. The principle of nationality was concisely set out by the leading German lawyer J. C. Bluntschli as follows: 'Jede Nation ein Staat, jeder Staat ein nationales Wesen' (*Allgemeine Staatslehre*, Stuttgart 1875, 107).

Lenin and Wilson

Lenin

Lenin was the first to insist, to the international community, that the right of self-determination be established as a general criterion for the liberation of peoples. To be sure, before him self-determination had been championed at the political level by a number of conventions originating from various leftist parties[6] and in 1913 Stalin had written a detailed pamphlet on the matter[7] – a pamphlet, it should be stressed, ignored by

---

[6] For instance, the Programme of the 'Russian Social Democratic Labour Party' adopted in 1903, at its Second Congress, a programme, which proclaimed at point 9: 'The right of self-determination for all nations forming part of the State.' For the (German) text of various political resolutions adopted between 1896 and 1919 by the II and III 'International', see K. Rabl, *Das Selbstbestimmungsrecht der Völker*, 2nd edn, Cologne and Vienna 1973, 514–24.

[7] J. Stalin, *Marxism and the National Question* (1913), in J. Stalin, *Marxism and the National and Colonial Question, A Collection of Articles and Speeches*, London 1941, 3–67. After propounding a broad definition of 'nation' ('It is therefore clear that there is in fact no *single* distinguishing characteristic of a nation. There is only a sum total of characteristics, of which, when nations are compared, one characteristic (national character), or another (language), or a third (territory, economic conditions) stands out in sharper relief. A nation constitutes the combination of all these characteristics taken together', *ibid.*, at 11), Stalin pointed out the following: 'The right to self-determination means that only the nation itself has the right to determine its destiny, that no one has the right *forcibly* to interfere in the life of the nation, to *destroy* its schools and other institutions, to *violate* its habits and customs, to *repress* its language, or *curtail* its rights'(*ibid.*, at 18). 'The right to self-determination means that a nation can arrange its life according to its own will. It has the right to arrange its life on the basis of autonomy. It has the right to complete secession. Nations are sovereign and all nations are equal' (*ibid.*, at 19).

Stalin also raised the question of how to implement self-determination. He observed the following: 'A nation has the right freely to determine its own destiny. It has the right to arrange its life as it sees fit, without, of course, stamping on the rights of other nations. That is beyond dispute.

But *how* exactly should it arrange its own life, *what forms* should its future constitution take, if the interests of the majority of the nation and, above all, of the proletariat, are to be borne in mind?

A nation has the right to arrange its life on autonomous lines. It even has the right to secede. But this does not mean that it should do so under all circumstances, that autonomy, or separation, will everywhere and always be advantageous for a nation, i.e., for the majority of its population, i.e., for the toiling strata . . .

But what solution would be most compatible with the interests of the toiling masses? Autonomy, federation or separation?

All these are problems the solution to which will depend on the concrete historical conditions in which the given nation finds itself.

Nay, more. Conditions, like everything else, change, and a decision which is correct at one particular time may prove to be entirely unsuitable at another' (20–1).

'socialist' scholars[8] and to which, instead, a learned commentator rightly drew attention some years ago.[9] Nevertheless, the first forceful proponent of the concept at the international level was Lenin.[10]

As the American historian Arno Mayer has pointed out, Lenin fully developed his ideas on the subject between 1915 and July 1916 while he was writing his book *On Imperialism*. The principle of self-determination was, in the words of Mayer, 'the political extension of Lenin's primarily economic analysis of imperialism'.[11] It was to lead to the liberation of oppressed peoples which was, in turn, to contribute to the success of the socialist revolution.[12]

Lenin's *Theses on the Socialist Revolution and the Right of Nations to Self-Determination*, published in March 1916, contains the first compelling enunciation of the principle.[13] Many other Soviet proclamations of self-

---

[8] See for example: G. B. Starushenko, *The Principle of National Self-Determination in Soviet Foreign Policy*, Moscow 1964, especially 13–86; R. Arzinger, *Das Selbstbestimmungsrecht der Völker im allgemeinen Völkerrecht der Gegenwart*, Berlin 1966.

[9] I. Brownlie, 'An Essay in the History of the Principle of Self-Determination', in *Grotian Society Papers 1968, Studies in the History of the Law of Nations*, edited by C. H. Alexandrowicz, The Hague 1968, 93. Stalin's works are also cited by H. Raschhofer, *Das Selbstbestimmungsrecht – sein Ursprung und seine Bedeutung*, 2nd edn, Bonn 1960, 13–14, and Rabl, *Das Selbstbestimmungsrecht der Völker*, 64, 66, 97–8.

[10] On Lenin's concept of self-determination, see, in particular, Starushenko, *The Principle of National Self-Determination*, 41–86; Arzinger, *Das Selbstbestimmungsrecht im allgemeinen Völkerrecht der Gegenwart*, 44–57; P. A. Steiniger, *Oktoberrevolution und Völkerrecht*, Berlin 1967, 42 ff.; D. Berndt, 'Entwicklung und Konzeption der Selbstbestimmungsrechts der Völker bei Lenin', PhD thesis, University of Münster, 1971, 88 ff.; H. Kröger (ed.), *Völkerrecht*, vol. I, Berlin 1981, 86–93. One of the most searching analyses of Lenin's contribution to self-determination is that by H. Carrère d'Encausse, 'Unité prolétarienne et diversité nationale. Lénine et la théorie de l'autodétermination', 21 *Revue française de science politique*, 1971, 221–55.

[11] A. J. Mayer, *Wilson vs. Lenin. Political Origins of the New Diplomacy, 1917–1918*, Cleveland and New York 1964, 298. A different approach to Lenin's views is taken by S. W. Page, 'Lenin and Self-Determination', 28 *The Slavonic Review*, 1949–50, 342–58, who traces Lenin's doctrine back to the so-called 'National Question' in the history of Russian Social-democracy but also points out Lenin's disagreements with social-democratic tenets.

[12] See Lenin's 'The Socialist Revolution and the Right of Nations to Self-Determination' (January–February 1916), in V.I. Lenin, *Selected Works*, London, 1969, 159 ff., 167. See also 'Report on Peace' (8 November 1917), in V. I. Lenin, *On the Foreign Policy of the Soviet State*, Moscow 1968, 11–15 and 'Lenin's Marginal Notes on a Letter from G. V. Chicherin' (10 March 1922) in Lenin, *On the Foreign Policy*, 421 ff. In addition, see 'Socialism and War' (August 1915) in V. I. Lenin, *Collected Works*, vol. XVIII, New York 1930, 235–6, and 'The Revolutionary Proletariat and the Right of Nations to Self-Determination' (November 1915), *ibid.*, 367–73.

[13] Lenin, *Selected Works*, 157.

determination followed soon thereafter, the most notable being the famous 26 October 1917 Decree on Peace.[14]

Looking at the various Soviet declarations from that era, one is forced to conclude that Lenin and the other Soviet political leaders envisioned self-determination as having *three components*. First, it could be invoked by ethnic or national groups intent on deciding their own destiny freely. Second, it was a principle to be applied during the aftermath of military conflicts between sovereign States, for the allocation of territories to one or another Power. Third, it was an anti-colonial postulate designed to lead to the liberation of all colonial countries. The second component, which prohibited territorial annexations against the will of the peoples concerned, was, for the most part, a reiteration of the principle of self-determination proclaimed by the French Revolutionaries of the late eighteenth century. The first and third components, in contrast, were to a large extent novel.

Under the first component of the principle of self-determination, which granted ethnic or national groups the right to decide their destiny freely, all ethnic groups – not just those living under colonial rule – were to have the right to choose whether to secede from the Power to which they were attached or, alternatively, to demand autonomy while remaining part of the larger structure. Several Soviet texts published during and immediately after the First World War stressed the latter principle; for instance, the 1918 Soviet Constitution explicitly granted a right to self-determination and recognized the Union Republics' right to secede.

Self-determination as an anti-colonial postulate meant that peoples under colonial domination would be able to gain their independence. In 1922, Soviet Foreign Minister Chicherin wrote a letter to Lenin describing the problems that the principle, in its anti-colonial mode, aimed to solve:

The World War has resulted in the intensification of the liberation movement of all oppressed and colonial peoples. World States are coming apart at the seams. Our international programme must bring all oppressed colonial peoples into the international scheme. The right of all peoples to secession or to home rule must be recognized . . . The novelty of our plan must be that the Negro and all other colonial peoples participate on an equal footing with European peoples in the conferences and commissions and have the right to prevent interference in their internal affairs.[15]

Plainly, the political philosophy underpinning this conception of self-

---

[14] See Lenin, *Foreign Policy*, 11 ff.   [15] Published in Lenin, *Foreign Policy*, 421 ff.

determination was socialism. As Lenin forcefully stated in his *Theses*, 'victorious socialism' necessarily means 'full democracy'. Now, socialism and democracy were to go hand in hand, on the international level, with the 'full equality of nations' and 'the right of the oppressed nations to self-determination, i.e. the right to free political separation'.[16] To be fully consistent, socialism and democracy in one State necessarily called for freedom and equality of all nations on the world level. We shall soon see, however, that the implication of the ideological motivation of Lenin's view of self-determination was also to act as a strong limit on the application of the principle.

Emphasis should be laid on the way of implementing self-determination that was advocated by Lenin. For him, the self-determination of nations living in sovereign States was to be primarily realized through secession. Secession, however, was not necessarily to be carried out by forcible means, but could result from the free expression of a popular vote.[17] In the case of territorial changes, self-determination of peoples could be implemented by a 'vote', that is, a plebiscite or referendum,[18] whereas to attain self-determination, that is to say, political independence and international status, colonial peoples were entitled to engage in armed violence. However, for Lenin the attainment of independence by a nation or a people was not to be regarded as the ultimate goal. Stressing the dangers of 'separation, fragmentation and the formation of small States' and, by the same token, the 'indisputable advantages' of 'big States', Lenin emphasized the advantages of federation as opposed to independent nations. Federation, in its turn, was not the final objective, for in his view the most appropriate way of setting up State structures that met the requirement of respect for peoples and centralism, lay in the 'inevitable integration of nations', of course in a socialist world.[19] As Lenin put it:

In the same way as mankind can arrive at the abolition of classes only through a transition period of the dictatorship of the oppressed class, it can arrive at the inevitable integration of nations only through a transition period of the complete emancipation of all oppressed nations, i.e. their freedom to secede.[20]

---

[16] Lenin, 'Theses', in *Selected Works*, 157.
[17] For Lenin self-determination meant 'complete freedom to agitate for secession and for a referendum on secession by the seceding nation', 'Theses', 159.
[18] See 'Decree on Peace', in Lenin, *Foreign Policy*, 12.
[19] See Lenin, 'Socialism and War', 235; 'The Revolutionary Proletariat and the Right of Nations to Self-Determination', 370–3; 'Theses', 159.
[20] 'Theses', 160. See on this point the apposite remarks of C. Hill, *Lenin and the Russian Revolution*, London 1957, 141.

Let us now dwell on the major feature and, indeed, flaw of Lenin's conception of self-determination. Like the eighteenth-century French politicians, the Soviet leader championed self-determination more to further his ideological and political objectives than to safeguard peoples. The socialist cause and the interests of the Revolution always took priority over the principle. This concept was enunciated by Lenin as early as 1916 in his famous *Theses*, when he emphasized 'the necessity to *subordinate* the struggle for the demand under discussion [i.e. self-determination] and for all the basic demands of political democracy, directly to the revolutionary mass struggle for the overthrow of the bourgeois governments and for the achievement of socialism'.[21] The concept was spelled out even more clearly in an article Lenin wrote in favour of the conclusion of a peace treaty with Germany, which appeared in *Pravda* on 21 February 1918. Arguing that the Soviet government had to conclude a peace treaty (the Brest-Litovsk Treaty that Russia signed with Germany, Austria-Hungary, Bulgaria, and Turkey, on 3 March 1918) in order for socialism to thrive and triumph, Lenin was forced to address the fact that yielding Poland, Lithuania, part of Latvia, Estonia, and Byelorussia to Germany would mean a betrayal of their peoples and would constitute an abandonment of the principle of self-determination. 'Which should be put first, the right of nations to self-determination, or socialism?' he asked rhetorically. His answer was: 'Socialism.'[22] The principle of self-determination was championed only in so far as it furthered the class struggle. The philosophical ideal was employed as a strategic tool.

Whilst the subsequent record reveals a marked consistency in the USSR's and other socialist States' views in respect of anti-colonialism – this component of the principle conformed with their political and ideological interests – there is little mention of, and no support for the first and second components: those governing internal political processes and border changes. The October Revolution, an expression of 'the people's will', led to a *de facto* denial of the principle of self-determination as regards both the annexation of foreign territories – consideration may also be had to what happened in 1940 in Latvia, Estonia, and Lithuania – and the right of ethnic and national groups to choose their destiny.

Ultimately, Lenin and the other Soviet leaders were more interested in the self-determination of the working class in each State than in the

---

[21] 'Theses', 167. My italics.   [22] *Ibid.*, 37.

self-determination of populations in their entirety. However, despite the principle's subordinated position, the Soviet focus on the right to self-determination, particularly regarding anti-colonialism, had an enormous influence on the foreign policy of the various States and the corpus of international law. It is largely due to the efforts of the Soviet Union that the principle was incorporated into the United Nations Charter and then gradually developed into a general principle of international law.

Wilson

At the same time as Lenin was championing self-determination with an eye towards a worldwide socialist revolution, US President Woodrow Wilson was developing his own thoughts on the subject.[23] While the Leninist conception was of course based on socialist political philosophy, Wilsonian self-determination originated from typically Western democratic theory. For the US President, self-determination was the logical corollary of popular sovereignty; it was synonymous with the principle that governments must be based on 'the consent of the governed'. In other words, for Wilson self-determination basically consisted of the right of peoples freely to choose their government. Thus, Wilson substantially advocated a *fourth potential formulation* of self-determination not considered by Lenin: that the principle required that peoples of each State be granted the right freely to select State authorities and political leaders. Self-determination meant self-government.

However, as the First World War progressed, Wilsonian self-determination took on 'external' dimensions. Peoples were to be free to choose their sovereign. People were no longer to be, in the words of

---

[23] On W. Wilson's concept of self-determination, see in particular: T. S. Woolsey, 'Self-Determination', 13 AJIL, 1919, 302–5 ff.; A. Cobban, *National Self-Determination*, London, New York and Toronto, 1945, 13–22, 27–9, 65; G. Decker, *Das Selbstbestimmungsrecht der Nationen*, Göttingen 1955, 109 ff.; M. Bourquin, 'Regards sur l'oeuvre de W. Wilson', *Fest. J. Spiropoulos*, Bonn 1957, 62–6; R. Isaak, 'Wilson: The Nation State and International Organization', in R. Isaak (ed.), *Individuals and World Politics*, 2nd edn, Monterey, Calif., 1981, 65 ff.; 165 ff., 179; M. Pomerance, 'The United States and Self-Determination: Perspectives on the Wilsonian Conception', 70 AJIL, 1976, 1–27; Pomerance, *Self-Determination in Law and Practice*, The Hague, Boston and London, 1982, 1–7; A. Walworth, *Wilson and his Peacemakers – American Diplomacy at the Paris Peace Conference, 1919*, New York and London 1986, 468–518. See also H. Foley, *Woodrow Wilson's Case for the League of Nations*, Princeton 1923, 34–51.

Wilson, 'bartered about from sovereignty to sovereignty as if they were mere chattels and pawns in a game'.[24]

On the international level Wilson thus propounded *four different variants of self-determination*. First, he advocated the right of each people to choose the form of government under which it would live. This concept, which was alluded to in Point 6 of Wilson's speech of 8 January 1918 on the 'Fourteen Points',[25] was however the one on which the US President laid the least emphasis; actually, after having strongly asserted it, he gradually played it down.[26]

The second version of self-determination was that relating to the restructuring of the States of central Europe in accordance with national desires. Believing that if the principle of self-determination were implemented correctly the risk of renewed global conflict would be significantly reduced, Wilson insisted that self-determination should be the guiding principle when it came to dividing the Ottoman and Austro-Hungarian empires and redrawing the map of Europe.[27]

Third, Wilson championed self-determination as a criterion governing territorial change. As he stated in the third Principle of his speech of 11 February 1918 on 'The Four Principles',

every territorial settlement in this war must be made in the interest and for the benefit of the populations concerned, and not as a part of any mere adjustment or compromise of claims amongst rival States.[28]

---

[24] Wilson's speech of 11 February 1918 in W. Wilson, *War and Peace, Presidential Messages, Addresses and Public Papers (1917–1924)*, ed. R. S. Baker and W. E. Dodd, vol. I, New York and London 1927, 182.

[25] '*Six*. The evacuation of all Russian territory, and such a settlement of all questions affecting Russia as will secure the best and freest cooperation of the other nations of the world in obtaining for her an unhampered and unembarrassed opportunity for the independent determination of her own political development and national policy, and assure her of a sincere welcome into the society of free nations under institutions of her own choosing, and more than a welcome, assistance also of every kind that she may need and may herself desire' (*ibid.*, 159–60).

[26] However, in his speech at Billings (Montana) on 11 September 1919, speaking of the League of Nations' Covenant, Wilson stated that: 'The fundamental principle of this treaty is a principle never acknowledged before, a principle which had its birth and has had its growth in this country: that the countries of the world belong to the people who live in them, and that they have a right to determine their own destiny and their own form of government and their own policy, and that no body of statesmen, sitting anywhere, no matter whether they represent the overwhelming physical force of the world or not, has the right to assign any great people to a sovereignty under which it does not care to live.' (Text in S. K. Padover (ed.), *Wilson's Ideals*, Washington DC 1942, at 109.)

[27] See Points 9, 10, 11, 12, and 13 of the Fourteen Points, *ibid.*, 160–1.   [28] *Ibid.*, 183.

Fourth, Wilson took self-determination into account for the purpose of settling colonial claims. However, in his view self-determination should not be the sole or even the paramount yardstick in this area, but must be reconciled with the interests of colonial Powers.[29]

It is apparent that Lenin and Wilson's views differed in three respects. First, the different political and ideological underpinnings of their theory of self-determination; second, the upholding by Wilson, also on the international level (albeit in a very moderate manner), of the essentially 'domestic' and internal dimension of the principle (self-determination as freedom of democratic choice of one's own government); third, the differing way of implementing self-determination suggested by the two leaders. It is worth concentrating on this last point, which is indeed crucial.

Wilson did not envision self-determination as giving rise to a right to wage violent revolutions. Whereas Lenin called for the immediate liberation of those living under colonial rule, Wilson championed 'orderly liberal reformism'.[30] For example, as I have just pointed out, Point 5, which addressed the rights of colonial peoples, made the right to self-determination contingent on Western interests. The aspirations of colonial peoples were to be taken into account without radically undermining existing power structures.

Lenin saw self-determination as a revolutionary principle for radically (and, if necessary, by force of arms) redistributing power within existing States or granting independence both to those nationalities oppressed by central governments and peoples subject to colonialism. This conception called into question not only the internal structure of States but also that of the international community since it granted recognition at the international level to nations and peoples governed by 'oppressive structures'. In contrast, Wilson envisaged self-determination as a principle to be implemented in an orderly, non-violent fashion under the guidance of international law. In Europe, 'well-defined national aspirations' were to be 'accorded the utmost satisfaction' (so stated Principle IV of the Speech of 11 February 1918). In other words, self-determination was to be realized through plebiscites and in conformity with reports issued by international

---

[29] See Point 5 of the Speech of 8 January 1918 ('A free, open-minded, and absolutely impartial adjustment of colonial claims, based upon a strict observance of the principle that in determining all such questions of sovereignty the interests of the populations concerned must have equal weight with the equitable claims of the Government whose title is to be determined') *ibid.*, 159.

[30] N. Gordon Levin, Jr, *Woodrow Wilson and World Politics: America's Response to War and Revolution*, New York 1968, 247.

commissions of experts assigned to study border disputes. In Africa, the Far East, and the Middle East it was to be achieved more gradually, in accordance with the programme for the League of Nations Mandates.

Four main objections have been rightly raised against Wilson's conception of self-determination. First, it was too loose and indeterminate, besides proposing, as shown above, solutions expressed in vague and all-encompassing terms. This point was sharply made as early as 1918 by one of the President's closest associates, namely Secretary of State Robert Lansing. In a note of 20 December 1918, he set out some critical remarks, the value of which cannot be disputed.[31] Second, Wilson was not aware of all the implications of his theory, when he so forcefully and eloquently proposed it in the international arena; in other words, he naively under-estimated the consequences that his ideas would produce on the world scene. Again, this point was forcefully made by Lansing[32] and subsequently Wilson himself was to acknowledge this as a serious mistake[33] – a mistake that, with hindsight and from a contemporary ideological viewpoint that is favourable to self-determination, can no doubt be regarded as a *felix culpa*. Third, Wilson's concepts were advanced for *foreign* consumption, but were not intended to apply to the American scene: as a matter of fact, he rejected

[31] R. Lansing wrote: 'When the President talks of "self-determination" what unit has he in mind? Does he mean a race, a territorial area, or a community? Without a definite unit which is practical, application of this principle is dangerous to peace and stability', R. Lansing, *The Peace Negotiations – A Personal Narrative*, New York and Boston 1921, 97.

[32] In a note of 30 December 1918 he wrote the following: 'The more I think about the President's declaration as to the right of 'self-determination', the more convinced I am of the danger of putting such ideas into the minds of certain races. It is bound to be the basis of impossible demands on the Peace Congress and create trouble in many lands.

What effect will it have on the Irish, the Indians, the Egyptians, and the nationalists among the Boers? Will it not breed discontent, disorder, and rebellion? Will not the Mohammedans of Syria and Palestine and possibly of Morocco and Tripoli rely on it? How can it be harmonized with Zionism, to which the President is practically committed?

The phrase is simply loaded with dynamite. It will raise hopes which can never be realized. It will, I fear, cost thousands of lives. In the end it is bound to be discredited, to be called the dream of an idealist who failed to realize the danger until too late to check those who attempt to put the principle in force. What a calamity that the phrase was ever uttered! What misery it will cause!' (*ibid.*, 97 ff.).

[33] In a speech to the Committee of Foreign Relations of the Senate made on 19 August 1919, he said: 'When I gave utterance to those words [concerning self-determination] I said them without the knowledge that nationalities existed, which are coming to us day after day . . . You do now know and cannot appreciate the anxieties that I have experienced as a result of many millions of people having their hopes raised by what I have said' (in H. M. V. Temperley, *A History of the Peace Conference of Paris*, vol. IV, London, New York and Toronto 1969, 429).

the application of internal self-determination – conceived as a way of protecting and safeguarding minority or ethnic groups – to the United States.[34] Fourth, at the international level Wilson did not, or rather was unable to, consistently pursue his ideas so as to have them accepted by other statesmen. As we shall soon see, neither the Peace Treaties following the First World War, nor the Covenant of the League of Nations upheld Wilson's ideas or, if the Treaties did, those ideas were implemented in very peripheral areas.

Wilson somewhat naively believed that under the guidance of the League of Nations the old imperialist system would gradually be replaced by a new liberal order. However, his draft provision on self-determination, which coupled the principle of territorial integrity with the concept that territorial adjustments must be made in the interest of the peoples concerned,[35] was not included in the final text of the Covenant, possibly because of doubts within the US delegation itself, and in any case on account of the strong opposition of Great Britain.[36]

The aftermath of the First World War

From the outset of the Allies' war against Austria-Hungary, Germany, Bulgaria, and the Ottoman Empire, self-determination maintained a high

---

[34] Wilson stated that 'America does not consist of groups. A man who thinks of himself as belonging to a particular national group in America has not yet become an American' (quoted in I. L. Claude, Jr, *National Minorities: An International Problem*, Cambridge, Mass., 1955, at 81).

[35] Wilson's original draft of a Covenant included Article 3, which read as follows: 'The Contracting Powers unite in guaranteeing to each other political independence and territorial integrity; but it is understood between them that such territorial readjustments, if any, as may in the future become necessary by reason of changes in present racial conditions and aspirations or present social and political relationships, pursuant to the principle of self-determination, and also such territorial readjustments as may in the judgment of three-fourths of the Delegates be demanded by the welfare and manifest interest of the peoples concerned, may be effected if agreeable to those peoples; and that territorial changes may in equity involve material compensation. The Contracting Powers accept without reservation the principle that the peace of the world is superior in importance to every question of political jurisdiction or boundary' (text in Lansing, *The Peace Negotiations*, 283. In the revised draft, which Wilson laid before the Commission on the League of Nations at its first session, Article 3 became Article 7 ('The High Contracting Parties undertake to respect and preserve as against external aggression the territorial integrity and existing political independence of all States members of the League.')

[36] On the British opposition, see Lansing, *The Peace Negotiations*, 94 ff. See also Cobban, *National Self-determination*', 11 ff. For the various positions of States, see Temperley, *A History of the Peace Conference of Paris*, vol. IV, 429–43.

profile. Indeed, most of the Allies claimed that the primary purpose of their war effort was the realization of the principle of nationality and of the right of peoples to decide their own destiny. Austria and Germany had an easy task when they objected, in a note of 11 January 1917,[37] that the Allied governments had little title, if any, for such claims, in view of the manner in which they treated minorities, nationalities, and peoples in their own countries and colonies (explicit mention was made of the Irish and Finnish peoples, the Boer Republics, and the North African colonies under British, French or Italian rule, as well as 'the violence brought to bear on Greece, for which there is no precedent in history').

It should therefore not be surprising that the principle was to a very large extent subordinated to other concerns when it came to making the peace treaties with the vanquished[38] (as for the Treaty of Brest-Litovsk between Russia and Germany, I have already mentioned above that Lenin explicitly stated that overriding political reasons, as well as the need to fight for socialism in Russia, had compelled Russia to set aside self-determination when deciding upon the cession of territories and nations to Germany). Thus, the Treaty of Versailles of 28 June 1919, with Germany, transferred territories to the new States of Poland and Czechoslovakia without any consultation with the relevant population and, in a similar fashion, Japan was given control over the Chinese territory of Kiaochow. Plebiscites were only rarely provided for, and then only with regard to small portions of territory.[39] Similarly, the treaty of peace with Austria (made at Saint Germain on 10 September 1919) allocated South Tyrol/Alto Adige to Italy without any plebiscite,[40] provided for the cession

---

[37] See J. B. Scott (ed.), *Official Statements of War Aims and Peace Proposals, December 1916 to November 1918*, Washington 1921, 44.

[38] On the application of self-determination in the peace treaties see in particular Cobban, *National Self-Determination*, 16–34. On the role of the principle of self-determination at the Versailles Conference, see in particular Decker, *Das Selbstbestimmungsrecht der Nationen*, 115–25; Rabl, *Das Selbstbestimmungsrecht der Völker*, 1973, 55–95.

[39] The Treaty provided for plebiscites for Upper Silesia, for the southern part of Eastern Prussia (the regions of Allenstein and Marienweder), for Northern Schleswig and for Saarland (for this last territory a plebiscite was to be held fifteen years after the conclusion of the peace treaty).

[40] The question of South Tyrol/Alto Adige is particularly enlightening. The area belonged to Austria by virtue of the Treaty of Vienna of 9 June 1815. After the outbreak of the First World War, in exchange for fighting on the Allies' side against the Habsburg Empire and Germany, Italy was promised by the Allies (by means of the Treaty of London of 26 April 1915: Article 4) the award of the Southwest Austrian provinces of South Tyrol in the event of a final victory for the Allies. In January 1918, in his Fourteen Points, W. Wilson stated that 'a readjustment of Italian frontiers will have to

to Poland and Romania of territories formerly belonging to Austria, and, in addition, banned Austria from joining Germany.[41] Similar cessions of territories without any prior consultation with the populations concerned were provided for in the Treaty of Neuilly, of 27 November 1919, with Bulgaria, whereas the Treaty of Lausanne with the Ottoman Empire, of 24 July 1923 (which superseded the Treaty of Sèvres of 11 August 1920), no longer envisaged an independent State for the Armenians and large autonomy for Kurdistan, but merely made provision for an exchange of populations (the Greeks living in Turkey were to move to Greece and the Turks settled in Greece were to be transferred to Turkey).

Thus, on the whole, self-determination was deemed irrelevant where the people's will was certain to run counter to the victors' geopolitical, economic, and strategic interests. Where the conducting of a plebiscite was

be made along a clearly recognizable demarcation line between nationalities'. In spite of its loose wording (cf. C. Seymour, 'Woodrow Wilson and Self-determination in the Tyrol', 2 *Virginia Quarterly Review*, 1962, 571) this statement clearly referred to a decision based on the principle of self-determination or respect for nationalities. This reference was however watered down and indeed emasculated by Wilson's personal envoy, Colonel Edward House, in his comment on the Fourteen Points, drafted in response to criticisms of the American President's programme (see the interesting comments on Point IX in House's telegram to Lansing of 29 October 1918 in *Papers Relating to the Foreign Relations of the United States*, Washington, DC 1918, Suppl. I, vol. I, 1933, 410). During the peace negotiations Austria insisted on respect for the principle of self-determination and the consequent need for a plebiscite; see the two Austrian memorandums, one of 10 July 1919 (text in N. Almond and R. Lutz, *The Treaty of St. Germain*, Stanford 1935, 299–309) the other of 9 August 1919 (*ibid.*, 310–25). However, this request was not complied with by the Allies (Great Britain, France, and Russia), and the Treaty of Saint Germain of 10 September 1919 allocated South Tyrol/Alto Adige to Italy without the holding of any plebiscite. Thus, the security requirements on which Italy had so strongly insisted with the Allies eventually prevailed over the principle of respect for the wishes of the populations concerned.

For the general historical background to this question, see in particular W. Wengler, 'Die Neuregelung der Südtiroler Frage', 3 AVR, 1952, 319–22; Rabl, *Das Selbstbestimmungsrecht der Völker*, 649–60; A. E. Alcock, *The History of the South Tyrol Question*, M. Joseph Ltd, Publisher for the Graduate Institute of International Studies, Geneva 1970; F. Ermacora, *Die Selbstbestimmungsidee-Ihre Entwicklung von 1918–1974*, Vienna 1974, 35–9 and, more extensively, M. Toscano, *Alto Adige – South Tyrol*, Baltimore and London 1975, 1–14. See also A. Fenet, *La question du Tyrol du Sud. Un problème de droit international*, Paris 1968; F. Ermacora, 'Ueber die Innere Selbstbestimmung', in *Menschenrechte, Volksgruppen, Regionalismus, Festgabe für T. Veiter*, Vienna 1982, 36–7; F. Ermacora, 'The Protection of Minorities before the United Nations', 182 HR, 1983-IV, 282–3, 332–3; H. Hannum, *Autonomy, Sovereignty and Self-Determination*, Philadelphia 1990, 432–40; D. Schindler, 'South Tyrol', in 12 *Encyclopedia* 1990, 348–50.

[41] The Treaty with Austria provided for quite a few plebiscites, essentially in Klagenfurt, Teschen, and Burgenland.

considered inappropriate, or the interests of the Allies were likely to be imperilled, the resident populations were not consulted. Wilson was right when he bitterly admitted in a speech given on 17 September 1919 in San Francisco, that:

It was not within the privilege of the conference of peace to act upon the right of self-determination of any peoples except those which had been included in the territories of the defeated empires.[42]

Although the rhetoric surrounding the principle did result in a number of plebiscites, the arbitrary manner in which the Allies decided which populations were entitled to determine their fate defeats any suggestion that a 'right' to self-determination existed. This contention is further supported by the fact that the Allies did not insist that the new States that emerged out of the peace process should adopt a democratic form of government. They were not required to rule with 'the consent of the governed'. However, some of the States were forced to guarantee minority rights,[43] since it was felt that granting protection to minorities was an attenuated and 'realistic' way of taking account of the rights of groups without going to the length of recognizing their right to self-determination.[44] The League's minority rights system was ultimately marred by two major flaws: firstly, it was simply a fall-back solution resorted to as a result of the unwillingness to apply self-determination; and secondly, it was extremely selective, for it only applied to Central and Eastern European States but not to the Great Powers and, more generally, to Western States.

---

[42] See Wilson, *War and Peace*, vol. II, New York and London 1927, 244.

[43] Formal guarantees of minority rights were provided by the treaties the Great Powers concluded with Poland, Czechoslovakia, Yugoslavia, and Romania. Minorities were also protected under the peace treaty concluded with Austria, Hungary, Bulgaria and Turkey and the Polish-German Convention of 1922. For the text of the minorities treaties, see Temperley, *Peace Conference of Paris*, vol. V, 432 ff. For the background to the treaties, see N. Feinberg, 'La question des minorités à la Conférence de la Paix de 1919–1920 et l'action juive en faveur de la protection internationale des minorités', in C. Seymour and E. House (eds.), *What Really Happened at Paris*, New York 1921, 204 ff. See also H. Rosting, 'Protection of Minorities by the League of Nations', 17 AJIL 1923, 641–60; J. Stone, *International Guarantees of Minority Rights*, London 1932; I. L. Claude, Jr, *National Minorities – An International Problem*, Cambridge, Mass., 6–50. For a discussion of the Permanent Court of International Justice judgments on minority rights, see N. Feinberg, 'La juridiction et la jurisprudence de la Cour Permanente de Justice Internationale en matière de minorités,' 59 HR, 1937-I, 587 ff.

[44] The link between self-determination and the protection of minorities was emphasized by the International Committee of Jurists, set up in 1920 by the Council of the League of Nations to advise on the question of the Aaland Islands (see below, pp. 27–33).

Another major setback for the principle of self-determination was that it was not incorporated into the Covenant of the League of Nations, as was noted above. However, the drafters of the Covenant, while rejecting the proposal put forward by Wilson to proclaim self-determination, were keen to retain the rhetoric attached to the principle, by insisting that the new Organization be called the 'League of *Nations*' and not of 'States', as had been suggested by the Portuguese and Brazilian delegates in 1919.[45]

All this confirms that which was stated in 1920 by the Committee of Jurists appointed by the Council of the League of Nations to study the Aaland Islands situation: in the era after the First World War self-determination, although in vogue as a political postulate and a rhetorical slogan (chiefly in the Wilsonian version), was not a part of the body of international legal norms.

The Aaland Islands case

In July 1920, the Council of the League of Nations appointed a commission of three jurists to examine whether, under international law, the inhabitants of the Aaland Islands (situated in the Baltic Sea, off the Swedish coast) were free to secede from Finland and join the Kingdom of Sweden.[46] According to Sweden, the principle of self-determination

[45] In the first meeting of the 'Commission on the League of Nations', held in February 1919, the Portuguese delegate 'suggested calling the organization a "Society of States" rather than of nations'. But the British delegate answered that 'the difference between the words "Nations" and "States" was a very small one' (in D. H. Miller, *The Drafting of the Covenant*, vol. I, New York and London 1928, 135). In the second meeting of the Commission, held on 4 February 1919, the Brazilian delegate repeated the proposal previously made by the Portuguese delegate, but it was once again rejected, although no specific reasons for the rejection were given (see *ibid.*, 141–2, as well as vol. II, 256). It should, however, not be overlooked that Great Britain may have been prompted to prefer the word 'nations' for another reason: to enable the British Dominions to become members of the League. This explanation could be borne out by the British insistence on substituting the words 'Members of the League' for the words 'States' or 'States which are members of the League' in various provisions of the Covenant (see Miller, *The Drafting of the Covenant*, vol. I, 477–83).

[46] On the Aaland Islands question, see in particular: P. M. Brown, 'The Aaland Islands Question', 15 AJIL, 1921, 268–72; A. J. Toynbee, 'Self-Determination', 494 *The Quarterly Review*, 1925, 330 ff.; F. de Visscher, 'La question des Iles d'Aaland', 2 RDILC, 1921, 35–56, 243–84; R. Boursot, *La question des Iles Aaland. Esquisse d'une théorie du droit des peuples à disposer d'eux-mêmes*, Dijon 1923; Redslob, *Le principe des nationalités*, 133–43; N. J. Padelford and K. G. A. Andersson, 'The Aaland Islands Question', 33 AJIL, 1939, 465–87; J. Barros, *The Aaland Islands Question: Its Settlement by the League of Nations*, New Haven 1968 (which mainly focuses on the historical and diplomatic aspects); see especially 268–334; J. H. W. Verzijl, *International Law in Historical Perspective*, Leiden

guaranteed the Aaland Islanders the opportunity, by way of a plebiscite, to register their wish to unify with Sweden. According to Finland, the case presented by Sweden to the Council dealt with a question which, under international law, ought to be left to the Finnish domestic jurisdiction.[47]

Ultimately there were not one, but two, League reports concerning the legal aspects of the dispute. The first report, issued by an International Committee of Jurists called upon to determine whether the Aaland Islands question fell within the competence of the League of Nations or was a purely domestic concern, started off by pointing out that although the concept of self-determination had been promoted with zeal during the war, it could not be considered an international legal norm. Specifically, it noted that although the principle was an integral part of 'modern political thought', it was not mentioned in the Covenant of the League of Nations and its recognition 'in a certain number of international treaties [could] not be considered as sufficient to put it upon the same footing as a positive rule of the Law of Nations'. The Report continued:

Positive International Law does not recognize the right of national groups, as such, to separate themselves from the State of which they form part by the simple expression of a wish, any more than it recognizes the right of other States to claim such a separation. Generally speaking, the grant or refusal of the right to a portion of its population of determining its own political fate by plebiscite or by some other method, is, exclusively, an attribute of the sovereignty of every State which is definitively constituted. A dispute between two States concerning such a question, under normal conditions therefore, bears upon a question which International Law leaves entirely to the domestic jurisdiction of one of the States concerned. Any other solution would amount to an infringement of [the] sovereign rights of a State and would involve the risk of creating difficulties and a lack of stability which

---

1968, vol. I, 328–32; H. Raschhofer, *Selbstbestimmungsrecht und Völkerbund – Das Juristengutachten im Aalandstreit vom 5. September 1920*, Cologne 1969, especially 9–34; T. Modeen, 'Völkerrechtliche Probleme der Aaland-Inseln', 37 *Zeit.*, 1977, 604–18; E. Gayim, *The Principle of Self-Determination – A Study of its Historical and Contemporary Legal Evolution*, Oslo 1990, 15–18. See also S. Calogeropoulos-Stratis, *Le droit des peuples à disposer d'eux-mêmes*, Brussels 1973, 54–9; F. Seyersted, 'The Aaland Autonomy and International Law', 51 NTIR, 1982, 23–8; Hannum, *Autonomy, Sovereignty and Self-Determination*, 370–5.

[47] Under Paragraph 8 of Article 15 of the Covenant of the League of Nations, if one of the parties to a dispute brought to the Council of the League of Nations maintained that, under international law, the dispute referred to a question falling solely within the domestic jurisdiction of the party, and the Council deemed the objecting party correct, the Council was required to record the fact in a report and refrain from recommending a solution.

would not only be contrary to the very idea embodied in the term 'State', but would also endanger the interests of the international community.[48]

Thus, the International Committee of Jurists clearly upheld the Finnish position that under positive international law 'it pertains exclusively to the sovereignty of any definitely constituted State to grant to, or withhold from, a fraction of its population the right of deciding its own political destiny by means of a plebiscite, or in any other way'.[49] Nevertheless, according to the Committee, the Aaland Islands dispute fell within the jurisdiction of the League of Nations. This was not because of any alleged 'right' to self-determination which outweighed issues of State sovereignty but because Finland, only recently liberated from Russian control, in the International Committee of Jurists' opinion, 'had not yet acquired the character of a definitively constituted State' and was not an independent member of the international community.[50] In other words, the principle of self-determination of peoples was called into play not because the population of the Islands had a right that superseded State interests, but because Finland was purportedly still in flux.

Having adopted the Jurists' view that the League was competent to decide the Aaland Islands question,[51] the Council appointed a Commission of Rapporteurs to recommend a programme of action. Their report, issued several months later,[52] recommended that the Aaland Islands remain under the sovereignty of Finland but that this country be obliged to increase the guarantees granted to the Islands by the Autonomy Law of 7 May 1920.[53]

Legal commentators usually confine themselves to drawing attention to the aforementioned statement of the International Commission of Jurists,

---

[48] 'Report of the International Committee of Jurists Entrusted by the Council of the League of Nations with the Task of Giving an Advisory Opinion upon the Legal Aspects of the Aaland Islands Question', *Official Journal of the League of Nations*, Special Supplement No. 3, October 1920, 5.

[49] 'Preliminary Observations by the Finnish Minister on the Report of the Committee of Jurists', *ibid.*, January/February 1921, 66.

[50] 'Report of the Committee of Jurists', 14 (see also 5).

[51] The Council only adopted the conclusions, not the report of the Jurists as a whole. See 'Minutes of the Twelfth Meeting of the Council', 23 June 1920, *Official Journal of the League of Nations*, September 1921, 692.

[52] See League of Nations, *Report presented to the Council of the League by the Commission of Rapporteurs*, Council Doc. B7/21/68/106, 16 April 1921, especially 21 ff.

[53] For the text of the Swedish–Finnish Agreement laying down special guarantees for the Aaland islanders, see *Official Journal of the League of Nations*, September 1921, 701–2.

echoed by the Commission of Rapporteurs,[54] to the effect that in 1919–20 self-determination was not part of positive international law. However, there are two further points made by these bodies that deserve attention, for they signal developments that the world community could and indeed did follow – at least to some extent – in subsequent years. The two bodies did not limit themselves to a dismissal of the view that customary rules on self-determination had emerged. One of them also delved into the link between self-determination and minority protection and both delineated, on the basis of general principles of law and justice,[55] *policy lines* that the international community ought to adopt, in their view.

First, the Commission of Jurists discussed the relationship between self-determination and the protection of minorities. On this issue, that body took the view that the protection of minorities was a sort of fall-back solution in case, for a number of extra-legal reasons, peoples could not be granted the right to attain independent statehood or to choose between two existing States. The Commission of Jurists held that the principle of self-determination and that of the protection of minorities had both a common ground and a common object ('to assure to some national Group the maintenance and free development of its social, ethnical or religious characteristics'). However, whenever 'geographical, economic or other similar considerations' prevented resort to self-determination, 'a solution in the nature of a compromise' lay in the protection of minorities.[56]

---

[54] See League of Nations, *Report*, 27.

[55] The Commission of Rapporteurs stated twice that the principle of self-determination embodied 'the idea of justice and liberty', *ibid.*, 27, 28.

[56] 'The principle recognising the rights of peoples to determine their political fate may be applied in various ways; the most important of these are, on the one hand the formation of an independent State, and on the other hand the right of choice between two existing States. This principle, however, must be brought into line with that of the protection of minorities, both have a common object – to assure to some national Group the maintenance and free development of its social, ethnical or religious characteristics.

The protection of minorities is already provided for, to a very varying extent, in a fairly large number of constitutions. This principle appears to be one of the essential characteristics of liberty at the present time. Under certain circumstances, however, it has been thought necessary to go further, and to guarantee, by international treaties, some particular situation to certain racial or religious minorities. Thus, in some recent treaties a special legal regime, under the control and guarantee of the League of Nations, has been established for certain sections of the population of a State.

The fact must, however, not be lost sight of that the principle that nations must have the right of self-determination is not the only one to be taken into account. Even though it be regarded as the most important of the principles governing the formation of States, geographical, economic and other similar considerations may put obstacles in the way of its complete recognition. Under such circumstances, a solution in the nature of a

The second point on which both League of Nations bodies insisted, and to a large extent agreed, is even more important. They took the view that while the protection of minorities was the only rational and sensible solution for providing safeguards to ethnic or religious groups without disrupting the territorial integrity of States, there might however be cases where minority protection could not be regarded as sufficient. Both bodies asserted that such cases arose when the State at issue manifestly abused its authority to the detriment of the minority, by oppressing or persecuting its members, or else proved to be utterly powerless to implement the safeguards protecting the minority. In such cases, according to the Commission of Jurists, one must regard the dispute as no longer coming within the purview of domestic jurisdiction (and one may wonder whether the Commission also thought that in such cases one should also make allowance for some form of resort to self-determination).[57] On the same issue, the Commission of Rapporteurs took a bolder view and stated that, when confronted with the cases at issue, one ought exceptionally to admit the right of 'separation' of the minority from the State.[58]

compromise, based on an extensive grant of liberty to minorities, may appear necessary according to international legal conception [*sic*] and may even be dictated by the interests of peace' (*ibid.*, 6).

[57] 'The Commission, in affirming these principles, does not give an opinion concerning the question as to whether a manifest and continued abuse of sovereign power, to the detriment of a section of the population of a State, would, if such circumstances arose, give to an international dispute, arising therefrom, such a character that its object should be considered as one which is not confined to the domestic jurisdiction of the State concerned, but comes within the sphere of action of the League of Nations. Such a supposition certainly does not apply to the case under consideration, and has not been put forward by either of the parties to the dispute' (*ibid.*, 5).

[58] The Commission stated the following: 'What reasons would there be for allowing a minority to separate itself from the State to which it is united, if this State gives it the guarantees which it is within its rights in demanding, for the preservation of its social, ethnical or religious character? Such indulgence, apart from every political consideration, would be supremely unjust to the State prepared to make these concessions.

The separation of a minority from the State of which it forms a part and its incorporation in another State can only be considered as an altogether exceptional solution, a last resort when the State lacks either the will or the power to enact and apply just and effective guarantees' (*ibid.*, 28). The Commission then applied this concept to the question under discussion and stated that the Aalanders had no right to secession, for they had not been oppressed: 'There is another consideration which excludes the analogy which it is wished to establish between the Finnish people and the Aaland population. Finland has been oppressed and persecuted, her tenderest feelings have been wounded by the disloyal and brutal conduct of Russia. The Aalanders have neither been persecuted nor oppressed by Finland' (*ibid.*, 28). It then observed: 'We recognise that the Aaland population, by reason of its insular position and its strong

31

Concluding remarks

Since it was first formulated around the second half of the eighteenth century, the principle of self-determination of peoples has been put forward in *political philosophy* in varying senses. It has been understood in turn as: (i) a criterion to be used in the event of territorial changes of sovereign States (interested populations should through plebiscites have the right to choose which State to belong to); (ii) a democratic principle legitimizing the governments of modern States (the people should have the possibility of choosing their own rulers); (iii) an anti-colonialist postulate (peoples subject to colonial rule should have the right to secure independence or at any rate freely to choose their international status); (iv) a principle of freedom for 'nations' or ethnic or religious groups constituting minorities in sovereign States (these groups should have the right to create an independent State or to join groups existing in another State).[59]

It was the French Revolution that proclaimed the principle, though mainly as a ban on territorial annexations or changes ignoring the wishes of the populations concerned, as well as, to a lesser extent, a criterion of democratic legitimation of governments. It was however the French

tradition, forms a group apart in Finland, not only distinct from the Finnish population, but also in certain respects distinct from the Swedish-speaking population. They deserve all the more protection and support in that they are, because of their great remoteness from the Finnish mainland, left to themselves, so to speak, in their struggle for the preservation of their ethnical heritage. We admit also that the fear fostered by the Aalanders of being little by little submerged by the Finnish invasion has good grounds, and that effective measures should be taken with a view to eliminating this danger. If it were true that incorporation with Sweden was the only means of preserving its Swedish language for Aaland, we should not have hesitated to consider this solution. But such is not the case. There is no need for a separation. The Finnish State is ready to grant the inhabitants satisfactory guarantees and faithfully to observe the engagement which it will enter into with them: of this we have no doubt. To take the Aaland Islands away from Finland in these circumstances would be the more unjust inasmuch as from the point of view of history, geography and politics, all the arguments militate in favour of the *status quo*' (*ibid.*, 28–9).

[59] D. Ronen, *The Quest for Self-Determination*, New Haven and London 1979, 9–12 and 24–52, identifies 'five types of quests for self-determination' in history and political philosophy: (1) *national* self-determination (1830s–1880s); (2) *class* self-determination (propounded by Marxism in the mid-nineteenth century); (3) *minorities'* self-determination (chiefly advocated by W. Wilson between 1916 and the 1920s); (4) *racial* self-determination (proclaimed by colonial peoples from 1945 to the 1960s); (5) *ethnic* self-determination (mid 1960s onwards); major instances are: Quebec, Biafra, Scotland, Bangladesh). See also D. Thürer, *Das Selbstbestimmungsrecht der Völker – Mit einem Exkurs zur Jurafrage*, Berne 1976, 15 ff.; D. Thürer, 'Das Selbstbestimmungsrecht der Völker – Ein Ueberblick' in 22 AVR, 1984, 114–17

Revolution itself that first, and in several cases, trod the principle underfoot. It was only around 1917 that the principle was proclaimed anew, by two leading statesmen: Lenin and Wilson. The former conceived of it primarily as an anti-colonialist postulate; the latter advocated self-determination essentially as a standard of democracy and a regulatory criterion for the break up of the empires defeated at the end of the First World War (chiefly the Austro-Hungarian and Ottoman Empires).

Despite the numerous wartime proclamations concerning a right of peoples to self-determination, at the close of the First World War self-determination was to a very large extent disregarded. Plebiscites afforded some populations the opportunity to determine border changes, but one could not substantiate a claim that border changes were illegal due to the lack of elections, by reference to positive law. Similarly, although the principle of self-determination led to autonomous local government in the Aaland Islands and was – to some extent – the basis for the formal minority guarantees included in the treaties between the Great Powers and the new States emerging out of the peace treaties, peoples had no legal right to demand representative government or local rule. Regardless of what Wilson or Lenin or any other statesman said, self-determination remained a political principle, nothing more. State sovereignty and territorial integrity remained of paramount importance.

In spite of these failings, it should not be forgotten that the two bodies of the League of Nations called upon to study the Aaland Islands question clearly perceived and emphasized the political importance of self-determination. Furthermore, they envisaged the possible resort to self-determination in cases where the alternative solution to its implementation, namely protection of minorities, should prove absolutely unworkable because of the oppressive attitude of a State towards minority groups. Thus, a *policy line* was put forward which the world community, to some extent, took up and, indeed, which might yield even more fruit in the future.

PART II

Self-determination becomes an international legal standard

3

Treaty law

The United Nations Charter

During the Second World War, as early as 1941, the US and the UK proclaimed self-determination as one of the objectives to be attained and put into practice at the end of the conflict. The Atlantic Charter drafted by President F. D. Roosevelt and Winston Churchill, and made public on 14 August 1941, proclaimed self-determination as a general standard governing territorial changes, as well as a principle concerning the free choice of rulers in every sovereign State (internal self-determination).[1] However, Churchill hastened to place a restrictive interpretation on the Atlantic Charter: on 9 September 1941 he clearly stated to the House of Commons that the principle of self-determination proclaimed in the Charter did not apply to colonial peoples (in particular, to India, Burma, and other parts of the British Empire) but only aimed at restoring 'the sovereignty, self-government and national life of the States and nations of Europe under the Nazi yoke', besides providing for 'any alterations in the territorial boundaries which may have to be made'.[2]

---

[1] '*Second*, they [the two drafters of the Declaration] desire to see no territorial changes that do not accord with the freely expressed wishes of the peoples concerned; *third*, they respect the right of all peoples to choose the form of government under which they will live; and they wish to see sovereign rights and self-government restored to those who have been forcibly deprived of them.' Text in J. A. S. Grenville, *The Major International Treaties: 1914–1973 – A History and Guide with Texts*, London 1974, 198 ff.

[2] Parliamentary Debates, Fifth Series, vol. 374, *House of Commons, Official Report*, eighth vol. of Session 1940–41, 68–69. Churchill's statement is mentioned by E. R. Stettinius, Jr, *Roosevelt and the Russians – The Yalta Conference*, Garden City, New York 1949, 244 ff. See also R. C. Hula, 'National Self-Determination Reconsidered', 10 *Social Research*,

In 1944, representatives of the US, the UK, the Soviet Union, and China entered into secret and informal negotiations with the aim of setting the foundations for a world organization. They emerged from the talks at Dumbarton Oaks with several proposals for a UN Charter. However, despite the fact that the Allies had embraced the principle of self-determination in several policy documents adopted between 1941 and 1944,[3] it did not appear anywhere in the draft Charter, which however included a provision, although somewhat weak, on human rights.[4] It seemed that the UN Charter was destined, like the League of Nations Covenant, to be silent with regard to the rights of peoples.

By the end of April 1945, when the United Nations Conference on International Organization met in San Francisco, the Four Powers had, however, reconsidered the issue at the insistence of the USSR.[5] Thus, among the amendments renegotiated and presented in San Francisco was a provision stating that the Organization aimed 'to develop friendly relations among nations based on respect for the principle of equal rights and self-determination of peoples, and to take other appropriate measures to strengthen universal peace'.[6] Although the Four Powers had not devised an effective means for the use and expansion of the principle, they had at least identified self-determination as a major objective of the new world organization.

In the relevant body of the San Francisco Conference (Committee I of Commission I) several States approved of the new provision, the Philippines, Egypt, the Ukraine, Iran, Syria, and Yugoslavia among

---

1943, 1–21. On the Atlantic Charter and self-determination, see generally G. Decker, *Das Selbstbestimmungsrecht der Nationen*, 177–86; K. J. Partsch, 'Fundamental Principles of Human Rights: Self-Determination, Equality and Non-Discrimination', in K. Vasak (ed.), *The International Dimensions of Human Rights*, vol. I, Paris 1982, 64–5.

[3] For a discussion of these documents, which include the Atlantic Charter, see in particular Brownlie, 'An Essay in the History of the Principle of Self-Determination', 96–8. See also A. Cassese, 'Political Self-Determination – Old Concepts and New Developments', in A. Cassese (ed.), *U.N. Law – Fundamental Rights: Two Topics in International Law*, Alphen aan der Rijn 1979, 161, note 2.

[4] For the text of the Dumbarton Oaks Proposals, see *Postwar Foreign Policy Preparation 1939–1945*, Department of State Publication 3580, Washington, DC, Government Printing Office, 1949, 611 ff.

[5] On the role of the Soviet Union in insisting on the proclamation of the right to self-determination, see R.B. Russel, *A History of the United Nations Charter*, Washington 1958, 62 ff., 810; G. Starushenko, *The Principle of National Self-Determination in Soviet Foreign Policy*, 142–7; Brownlie, 'An Essay in the History', 98.

[6] See UNCIO, vol. VI, 1945, 296.

them.[7] However, not all of the States were amenable to the idea that self-determination ought to be included in the Charter. Some, most notably Belgium, were in fact very critical. The Belgian representative, the distinguished international lawyer H. Rolin, issued a brief memorandum containing two major criticisms, both focusing on the provision's departure from the traditional State-oriented approach. He first asserted that the provision referring to self-determination had been founded on 'confusion'; and he pointed out that 'one speaks generally of the equality of *States*' not of peoples. His second argument was:

It would be dangerous to put forth the peoples' right of self-determination as a basis for the friendly relations *between the nations*. This would open the door to inadmissible interventions if, as seems probable, one wishes to take inspiration from the peoples' right of self-determination in the action of the Organization and not in the relations between the peoples.[8]

After stressing that the world was still far from full self-determination, the Belgian delegate raised several important concerns. Specifically, he wondered whether in the case where a national minority in a given country claimed the right to self-determination, the Organization would be expected to step in and other States would feel duty-bound to intervene on the strength of the concept of 'friendly relations'. Rolin then proposed that the entire provision be withdrawn.[9]

It would seem that the Belgian delegate did not take into account self-determination as an anti-colonial principle. He only perceived it as a criterion for protecting *nationalities* or *minorities* but even from this angle he dismissed it. In its place, Belgium put forward counter-proposals aimed at strengthening the protection of human rights[10] but later withdrew them.

Other States also expressed doubts about the proposed Charter provision, mostly out of fear that a provision on self-determination would foster civil strife and secessionist movements. Venezuela voiced concern.[11] Colombia formally declared:

If it [self-determination] means self-government, the right of a country to provide its own government, yes, we would certainly like it to be included; but if it were to

---

[7] See the microfilmed minutes (unpublished) of the debates of the First Committee of the First Commission of the San Francisco Conference, 14–15 May and 1 and 11 June, 1945, Library of the Palais des Nations, Geneva [hereinafter Debates].

[8] UNCIO, vol. VI, 300.

[9] See Debates, 14 May (afternoon session), 12 and 14.

[10] Debates, 14 May, 13. See also UNCIO, vol. VI, 640.

[11] Debates, 15 May (morning session), 14.

be interpreted, on the other hand, as connoting a withdrawal, the *right of withdrawal or secession*, then we should regard that as tantamount to *international anarchy*, and we should not desire that it should be included in the text of the Charter.[12]

Fomenting secessionist movements was not, however, the only fear. The potential misuse of the principle of self-determination was also raised. For example, Egypt, making a veiled reference to Germany and Italy, observed that the principle lent itself to manipulation. Politicians could easily invoke the principle – as did Hitler – to justify military invasions and annexations. This led the Syrian delegate to point out that the principle of self-determination contemplates free expression; if a people is unable to express its genuine will, self-determination cannot be considered to have been achieved.[13]

Subsequently, the Committee responsible for the drafting of the relevant provision agreed on four points. First, 'this principle corresponded closely to the will and desires of peoples everywhere and should be clearly enunciated in the Chapter [of the UN Charter]'.[14] Second, 'the principle conformed to the purposes of the Charter only insofar as it implied the right of self-government of peoples and not the right of secession'.[15] Third, it was agreed that the principle of self-determination 'as one whole extends as a general basic conception to a possible amalgamation of nationalities if they so freely choose'.[16] Fourth, it was agreed that 'an essential element of the principle [of self-determination] is free and genuine expression of the will of the people, which avoids cases of the alleged expression of the popular will, such as those used for their own ends by Germany and Italy in later years'.[17]

This last passage might be construed to mean that the framers of the Charter – intent on emphasizing that many authoritarian governments which claim the support of the 'popular will' do not in fact rule with the 'free and genuine' will of the people – considered the realization of self-determination to be coterminous with 'freedom of political expression and from authoritarian government'. However, a careful examination of the unpublished minutes of the debates that led to the adoption of the passage

[12] Debates, 15 May, 20 (my italics).
[13] Debates, 14 May, 24 ff. (Egypt); 15 May (morning session), 12 (Syria).
[14] See UNCIO, vol. VI, 296.
[15] *Ibid.* The French text was as follows: 'On a déclaré que ce principe n'était compatible avec les buts de la Charte que dans la mesure où il impliquait, pour les peuples, le droit de s'administrer eux-mêmes, mais non pas le droit de sécession', *ibid.*, 298.
[16] *Ibid.*, 704.
[17] UNCIO, vol. VI, 455.

quoted warns against such a conclusion. The preparatory work suggests that the Wilsonian dream of representative governments for all was not contemplated. The emphasis on the need for a 'genuine' choice was only intended to stress that where a people is afforded the right to express its views, it must truly be free to do so.[18]

The final text of UN Charter does not confine itself to the political 'rhetoric' of self-determination of the League of Nations' Covenant (the name of the new Organization also includes the word 'Nations', and the preamble starts with the well-known, rather hypocritical and misleading sentence 'We the peoples of the United Nations . . . '). The UN Charter goes beyond that and includes Article 1(2), which provides that one of the purposes of the United Nations is:

to develop friendly relations among nations based on respect for the principle of equal rights and self-determination of peoples, and to take other appropriate measures to strengthen universal peace.[19]

The lively debate on self-determination and the Syrian Rapporteur's report to the Commission[20] suggest that four main features characterize the concept eventually proclaimed in Article 1(2).[21]

---

[18] See Cassese, 'Political Self-determination', 139 and notes 5 and 6.

[19] See also Articles 55 and 56 of the UN Charter. Article 55 provides that: 'With a view to the creation of conditions of stability and well-being which are necessary for peaceful and friendly relations among nations based on respect for the principle of equal rights and self-determination of peoples, the United Nations shall promote: (a) higher standards of living, full employment, and conditions of economic and social progress and development; (b) solutions of international economic, social, health, and related problems; and international cultural and educational co-operation; and (c) universal respect for, and observance of, human rights and fundamental freedoms for all without distinction as to race, sex, language, or religion.' Article 56 provides that: 'All Members pledge themselves to take joint and separate action in co-operation with the Organization for the achievement of the purposes set forth in Article 55.'

[20] UNCIO, vol. VI, 455 and 714 ff.

[21] On Articles 1(2), 55–6, 73 and 76, in addition to the classic commentaries on the UN Charter, see, among others, S. Calogeropoulos-Stratis, *Le droit des peuples à disposer d'eux-mêmes*, 108–15, 263–5; Guilhaudis, *Le droit des peuples à disposer d'eux-mêmes*, 168–73; K. Doehring, 'Das Selbstbestimmungsrecht der deutschen Nation', in *Recht und Staat im sozialen Wandeln. Fest. für H. U. Scupin*, Berlin 1983, 555–60; Thürer, 'Das Selbstbestimmungsrecht der Völker. Ein Ueberblick', 118–19; D. Thürer, 'Self-Determination' in *Encyclopedia*, vol. VIII, 1985 at 471–2; F. Lattanzi, 'Autodeterminazione dei popoli', in *Digesto delle Discipline Pubblicistiche*, vol. II, Turin 1987, 5–9; G. Arangio-Ruiz, 'Autodeterminazione (diritto dei popoli alla)', in *Enciclopedia Giuridica*, vol. IV, Rome 1988, 2–3; E. Gayim, *The Principle of Self-Determination – A Study of its Historical and Contemporary Legal Evolution*, Oslo 1990, 21–6; M. Bedjaoui, in J. P. Cot and A. Pellet (eds.), *La Charte des Nations Unies*, 2nd edn, Paris 1991, 1070–83; K. J. Partsch

First, States were unable positively to define self-determination. The concept of self-determination upheld in the Charter can only be negatively inferred from the debate preceding the adoption of Article 1(2). Self-determination *did not mean* (a) the right of a minority or an ethnic or national group to secede from a sovereign country; (b) the right of a colonial people to achieve political independence; for these peoples self-determination could only mean 'self-government' (this conclusion can be drawn from the clear agreement reached when drafting the provision to the effect that self-determination only meant 'self-government' and also from the fact that Article 76 of the UN Charter, laying down the basic objectives of the trusteeship system, contemplated 'their progressive development towards self-government or independence'; a systematic interpretation of the Charter would thus warrant the conclusion that, by implication, 'self-government' did not mean 'independence'); (c) the right of the people of a sovereign State freely to choose its rulers through regular, democratic and free elections; for these peoples also self-determination only meant 'self-government'; (d) the right of two or more nations belonging either to a sovereign country or two sovereign countries to merge; this right is ruled out by the ban on secession (plainly, the right at issue would imply that nations belonging to one or more States could secede, in order to achieve the 'possible amalgamation of nationalities' referred to by the Syrian Rapporteur).[22]

It follows that the principle enshrined in the UN Charter boils down to very little; it is only a principle suggesting that States should grant *self-government* as much as possible to the communities over which they exercise jurisdiction.[23]

'Selbstbestimmung' in R. Wolfrum (ed.), *Handbuch der Vereinten Nationen*, Munich 1991, 745–52; K. Doehring, in B. Simma (ed.), *Charta der Vereinten Nationen – Ein Kommentar*, Munich 1991, 15–32; B. Driessen, *A Concept of Nation in International Law*, The Hague 1992, 118–24.

[22] Consequently, the reference to 'amalgamation' can only be taken to mean the merger of two sovereign countries based on the same nationality (think, for instance, of the unification of the two German States, which actually took place in recent years).

[23] Cf. UNCIO, vol. VI, 296. The Charter's other provisions, Chapters XII and XIII and Article 73 in particular, support the thesis that Article 1(2) enshrined the moderate version of self-determination. Chapters XII and XIII ensured that there was no radical break with the colonial system by providing for an international trusteeship system. Article 73 provided for colonial power rule the so-called 'non-self-governing territories'. Article 76 imposed upon the colonial powers the rather vague obligation 'to develop *self-government*' in the non-self-governing territories. Article 76, part of the trusteeship programme, was more pointed; 'the basic objectives' of the trusteeship system included,

So much for the *notion* of self-determination. As for the second feature of the principle in the UN Charter, it should be stressed that Article 1(2) merely laid down one of many lofty *goals of the Organization*. The threat to State interests was thus minimized.

The third feature of the principle is that self-determination, conceived of as a postulate deeply rooted in the concept of the equal rights of peoples or, as explained by the Philippine delegate, in the 'equality of races',[24] was considered to be a means of furthering the development of *friendly relations among States*: it would foster universal peace. This last qualifier, *a fortiori*, limited the power of the principle. Since self-determination was not considered to have a value independent of its use as an instrument of peace, it could easily be set aside when its fulfilment raised the possibility of conflicts between States.

Fourthly, since self-determination was envisaged primarily as a programme or aim of the Organization, and since the UN Charter neither defined self-determination precisely nor distinguished between 'external' and 'internal' self-determination, the Charter *did not impose direct and immediate legal obligations on Member States* in this area (the obligation laid down in Article 56 of the Charter is very loose and in any case does not impose the taking of direct and specific action by each Member State of the UN).

In spite of all these limitations and shortcomings, the fact remains that this was the first time that self-determination had been laid down in a multilateral treaty – a treaty, one should add, that had been conceived of as one of the major pieces of legislation of the new world community. Thus, the adoption of the UN Charter marks an important turning-point; it signals the maturing of the political postulate of self-determination into a legal standard of behaviour. In 1945 this legal standard was primarily intended to guide the action of the Organization. Over the years Member States of the UN gradually turned that standard into a precept that was also directly binding on States.

in addition to 'self-government', 'independence'. Thus, although the level of self-government afforded was to be 'appropriate to the particular circumstances of each territory and its peoples and the freely expressed wishes of the peoples concerned, and as may be provided by the terms of each trusteeship agreement', Chapter XIII actually afforded peoples greater rights than Article 1(2) (the general provision on self-determination) — or at least offered a limited class of dependent peoples greater rights.

[24] UNCIO, vol. VI, 704.

Political attitudes in the era after the Second World War

In the decades immediately following the Second World War, the principle embedded in Article 1(2) of the United Nations Charter evolved in a manner which those who drafted it could not have foreseen. The predominance of the socialist doctrine of self-determination and the momentum generated by the anti-colonialist movement at the Bandung Conference in 1955 shifted the emphasis from peaceful relations among sovereign States to independence from colonial rule.

The socialist countries – soon joined, at least at the political level, by an increasing number of freshly independent Third World countries[25] – were the most active advocates of anti-colonial self-determination. They adopted and developed Lenin's thesis that self-determination should first and foremost be a postulate of anti-colonialism. Side by side with political doctrine, Eastern European legal literature strongly advocated this concept. The Soviet international lawyers G. B. Starushenko and G. Tunkin, and three of their East German counterparts, Arzinger, Steiniger, and Graefrath underlined that, above all else, self-determination meant the liberation of peoples subject to racist regimes (like that of South Africa) and colonial domination and its 'after-effects'.[26] Their emphasis

---

[25] On the African approach to self-determination, see M.V. Krishnan, 'African Contribution to the Development of the Principle of Self-Determination', 5 *Africa Quarterly*, 1966, 312–23; C.C. Mojekwu, 'Self-Determination: The African Perspective', in Y. Alexander and R.A. Friedlander (eds.), *Self-Determination: National, Regional and Global Dimensions*, Boulder, Col. 1980, 221–39. On the Latin American approach, see N. Lerner, 'Self-Determination: The Latin American Perspective', *ibid.*, 63–78. See also M. Bennouna, 'Tiers Monde et autodétermination', *Le droit à l'autodétermination*, 83 ff.

[26] Starushenko, *The Principle of National Self-Determination in Soviet Foreign Policy*; G. Tunkin, *Theory of International Law*, transl. W. E. Butler, London 1973, 7–14, 60–9, 262–5; B. Graefrath, *Die Vereinten Nationen und die Menschenrechte*, Berlin 1956, 54 ff.; R. Arzinger, *Das Selbstbestimmungsrecht im allgemeinen Volkerrecht der Gegenwart*, Berlin 1966, especially 112–25; P. A. Steiniger, *Oktoberrevolution und Volkerrecht*, Berlin 1967; G. Tunkin, *Theory of International Law*, London 1974, 7 ff., 60 ff., 262 ff. and *passim*; B. Graefrath, 'A Necessary Dispute on the Contents of the Peoples' Right to Self-determination – Rejection of an Old Concept in a New Guise,' *Bulletin of the GDR Committee for Human Rights*, 1981, no. 1, 11. See also H. Kröger (ed.), *Völkerrecht*, vol. I, Berlin 1981, 121–4.

On the Soviet attitude to self-determination see also: E. R. Goodman, The Cry of National Liberation: Recent Soviet Attitudes Towards National Self-Determination, 14 *International Organization*, 1960, 92–106; B. Meissner, *Sowjetunion und Selbstbestimmungsrecht*, Cologne 1962, 32–80 (see also the extremely important documentary section, at 151–338); M. Wannow, *Das Selbstbestimmungsrecht im Sowjetischen Völkerrechtsdenken*, Göttingen 1965; I. Levkov, 'Self-Determination in Soviet Politics', in Alexander and Friedlander, *Self-Determination*, 133–90; Charvin, 'Le droit à l'autodétermination dans les régimes marxistes', *Le droit à l'autodétermination*, 65–82; A. Bohlmann, 'Sowjetische

was on the right to external self-determination. They insisted that peoples have a right freely to choose their international status. This is not to say, however, that issues relating to internal self-determination were wholly ignored. On the contrary, the socialist jurists argued that in a sovereign State internal self-determination, that is, the right of a people to freely choose their rulers, meant the right to choose a socialist government. In other words, they addressed issues of internal self-determination but they did so in an extremely ideological manner. Implicit in their arguments was the notion that self-determination could only be fully realized in a socialist country.[27]

A second main undercurrent of socialist statements and writings after the Second World War is the link between self-determination and the principles of sovereign equality of States and non-interference in domestic affairs. In the Eastern Bloc conception, self-determination in its 'external' dimension amounted to 'the right to exist as a State'[28] but once this right had been won the principles of sovereign equality and non-intervention took over. Only then would the State arising from the expression of the people's will be adequately protected.[29]

The Third World countries' approach to self-determination was both less carefully developed and more linear. For these States, self-determination mainly meant three things: (1) the fight against colonialism and racism; (2) the struggle against the domination of any alien oppressor illegally occupying a territory (an idea that was furthered largely due to the insistence of the Arab States, after 1967, with the case of Palestine in mind);

Nationalitätenpolitik und deutsches Volkstum in der UdSSR', *Menschenrechte, Volksgruppen, Regionalismus - Festgabe für T. Veiter*, Vienna 1982, 129–34; H. Graf Huyn, 'Selbstbestimmungsrecht als Grundlage der Freiheit', in *Menschenrechte und Freiheit - Voraussetzung für den Frieden*, Berne 1987, 13–20; E. Loebl, 'Das Selbstbestimmungsrecht im Westen und Osten', *ibid.*, 39–46; F. Przetacznik, 'The Basic Collective Human Right to Self-Determination of Peoples and Nations as a Prerequisite for Peace: Its Philosophical Background and Practical Application', 69 *Revue droit international et des sciences diplomatiques et politiques*, 1991, 301–4.

For recent developments in the legal literature of the former Soviet Union, see T. Schweisfurth, 'The New Approach to the Law of Peaceful Coexistence', in R. Lefeber, M. Fitzmaurice and E. W. Vierdag (eds.), *The Changing Political Structure of Europe - Aspects of International Law*, Dordrecht, Boston, and London 1991, at 47.

[27] See Graefrath, 'A Necessary Dispute', 14.

[28] Graefrath, *Die Vereinten Nationen*, 56.

[29] The view that, if applied to States, self-determination amounts to the right to non-interference (or non-intervention) is also shared by J. J. A. Salmon, 'Le droit des peuples à disposer d'eux-mêmes - Aspects juridiques et politiques', in *Le Nationalisme*, Brussels 1972, 359–62, Guilhaudis, *Le droit des peuples à disposer d'eux-mêmes*, 118–26 and Thürer, 'Das Selbstbestimmungsrecht der Völker', at 473.

(3) the struggle against all manifestations of neocolonialism and in particular the exploitation by alien Powers of the natural resources of developing countries. Ethnic and tribal conflicts being rife in many developing countries, the Third World group ignored or even explicitly denied the rights of minorities or nationalities living within sovereign States. For the most part, the Third World championed 'external', not 'internal' self-determination, with external self-determination being granted only to limited categories of peoples.

As for the Western States, their initial strategy mainly consisted of opposing the new formulation of the principle (which targeted colonialism) put forward by the socialist and Third World States.[30] The West initially spent the majority of its time insisting that Article 1(2) of the Charter merely set out broad guidelines for the Organization as such and therefore did not impose any specific obligation on Member States of the UN. Only after the socialist and Third World countries had made inroads in the battle against colonialism did the Western States take the offensive. At that point, they began emphasizing that the principle ought to be interpreted as the right of the peoples of every State freely to choose a system of government that fully meets the aspirations of the people. According to the Western States, the principle of self-determination enshrined in the UN Charter contemplated (1) *internal* self-determination and (2) *universality* of application.[31] The Western States also linked the principle to human rights but in a different sense than that advocated by the socialist countries. For the West, self-determination was the quintessence of democratic freedom or, in other words, the synthesis of the civil and political rights of every

---

[30] See generally: W. Barbour, 'The Concept of Self-Determination in American Thought', 31 *Dept. St. Bul.*, 1954, 576–9; E. S. Efrat, 'Self-Determination: Canadian Perspectives', in Alexander and Friedlander, *Self-Determination: National, Regional and Global Dimensions*, 21–41; J. F. Murphy, 'Self-Determination: United States Perspectives', *ibid.*, 43–61; H. S. Johnson, 'Self-Determination: Western European Perspectives, *ibid.*, 81–96; T. H. Hachey, 'Self-Determination: British Perspectives, *ibid.*, 97–131. See also H. Raschhofer, 'The Right of Self-Determination from the Western Viewpoint', 7 *Internationales Recht und Diplomatie*, 1962, 25–36.

[31] The Western position was aptly summarized by the US delegate in his statement of 31 March 1952 in the UN Economic and Social Council (ECOSOC). He repeatedly emphasized that self-government meant the 'promotion of self-government' (27 *Dept. St. Bul.*, 18 August 1952, 269) and also stressed that 'the problem of self-determination is a universal one – one of significance for all States and not only States administering non-self-governing territories' (*ibid.*, 271). That self-determination 'is universal in scope' was reaffirmed on 12 November 1955 by US Deputy Under-Secretary of State J.F. Murphy ('The Principle of Self-Determination in International Relations' in 33 *Dept. St. Bul.*, 28 November 1955, at 894).

people. In brief, the principle was conceived as the fundamental criterion for the democratic legitimization of governments.[32]

The 1966 International Covenants on Human Rights

Introductory remarks

It is well known that even before the adoption of the Universal Declaration of Human Rights, in 1948, the Member States of the UN intended gradually to turn the few provisions of the UN Charter into a set of legally binding treaty provisions specifying the general principle of respect for human rights laid down in the Charter. The Universal Declaration was the first step in this direction. As early as 1950 the Commission on Human Rights decided that the Declaration should be followed by a treaty setting out in legally binding terms the rights proclaimed in the Declaration. Later on, in 1954, it was decided rather that these should be two distinct treaties: one dealing with civil and political rights, the other covering social, economic, and cultural rights.

In the course of the drafting process, Western countries put forward the view that the two Covenants on Human Rights should only lay down the fundamental rights and freedoms of individuals. By contrast, the Soviet Union strongly advocated the need for both Covenants formally to enshrine the right of peoples to self-determination, which, in the Soviet view, was a precondition for the respect of individual rights.

As we shall see, in the event it was the Soviet view that prevailed, thanks to the strong support of developing countries.[33]

---

[32] As the US delegate to the Third Committee of the General Assembly stated in 1972: 'Freedom of choice is indispensable to the exercise of the right of self-determination. For this freedom of choice to be meaningful, there must be corresponding freedom of thought, conscience, expression, movement and association. Self-determination entails legitimate, lively dissent and testing at the ballot box with frequent regularity', 50 *Dept. St. Bul.*, 25 December 1972, 1748. In 1955, the US Deputy Under Secretary of State Murphy had pointed out that the essence of the concept of self-determination 'may be simply stated as follows: Peoples and nations should have an opportunity freely to choose their own national destiny without restraints, coercion or intimidation. Perhaps the essence of the concept lies in "freedom of choice"' (33 *Dept. St. Bul.*, 28 November 1955, at 890).

[33] On Article 1, see the bibliography cited in my paper 'The Self-Determination of Peoples', in L. Henkin (ed.), *The International Bill of Rights – The Covenant on Civil and Political Rights*, New York 1981, 418–19, n. 20. In addition, see C. Y. Hu, *Das Selbstbestimmungsrecht als eine Vorbedingung des völligen Genusses aller Menschenrechts Konventionen vom 16. Dez. 1966*, Zürcher Dissertation, Zurich 1972, especially 217–74; Ermacora, *Die*

The origin of the Article on self-determination

In 1950, in the Third Committee of the General Assembly, the Soviet Union proposed that a provision dealing with self-determination be included in the Covenant on Human Rights. The primary concern was the right of self-determination of colonial peoples. The secondary consideration was the rights of minorities.[34]

The Third Committee rejected the Soviet proposal, voting against the initial operative paragraph without addressing each provision on its individual merits.[35] Afghanistan and Saudi Arabia subsequently took up the subject, introducing a procedural draft resolution inviting the Commission on Human Rights 'to study ways and means which would ensure the right of peoples and nations to self-determination and to prepare recommendations for consideration by the General Assembly'. Notably, the proponents of this draft did not confine themselves to the issue of colonial peoples. While Saudi Arabia and a number of other Third World countries focused on colonial peoples,[36] Afghanistan and other Asian, African, and Latin American countries, as well as a few Western

Selbstbestimmungsidee, 15–16 and M. Potocny, 'Le principe de l'autodétermination des peuples (les articles premiers des Pactes relatifs aux droits de l'homme)', 24 *Bulletin de droit tchecoslovaque*, 1967, 356–71 (essentially on the Czechoslovak draft Article 1 – A/AC.125/L.16, Section VI – and the draft submitted by ten Third World countries – A/AC.125/L.31 – as well as the socialist view of self-determination) and Calogeropoulos-Stratis, *Le droit des peuples à disposer d'eux-mêmes*, 134–7.

See also D. Blumenwitz, 'Die Menschenrechtspakte der Vereinten Nationen und das Selbstbestimmungsrecht der Völker', in F. Ermacora (ed.), *Menschenrechte und Selbstbestimmung*, Vienna 1980, 21 ff.; E. Klein, 'Das Selbstbestimmungsrecht – Ideen und Aufgaben', 34 *Politische Studien*, 1983, 637–8; D. Thürer, 'Das Selbstbestimmungsrecht der Völker – Ein Ueberblick', 22 AVR, 1984, 121–3; J. A. de Obieta Chalband, *El derecho humano de la autodeterminación de los pueblos*, Madrid 1985, 78–80; Lattanzi, 'Autodeterminazione dei popoli', 17; Arangio-Ruiz, 'Autodeterminazione (diritto dei popoli alla)', 4.

34 'Every people and every nation shall have the right to national self-determination. States which have responsibilities for the administration of Non-Self-Governing territories shall promote the fulfilment of this right, guided by the aims and principles of the United Nations in relation to the peoples of such Territories. The State shall ensure to national minorities the right to use their native tongue and to possess their national school, museums and other cultural and educational institutions.' UN Doc., 1950, Annexes, A/C.3/L.96, 17.

35 UN Doc., A/1559, 28.

36 UN Doc., 1951, Mexico (A/C.3/SR.310, paras. 7–11; SR.311, paras. 29–32); Syria (*ibid.*, SR.311, paras. 7–8) Saudi Arabia (A/C.3/SR.309, paras. 56–7, SR.310, para. 3; SR.367, para. 42; SR.398, paras. 32–34; SR.403, para. 85; SR.563, para. 12); Liberia (A/C.3/SR.366, para. 25; SR.400, para. 9).

States, emphasized that the right in question should apply to other peoples as well, namely, peoples oppressed by despotic governments.[37]

Although the Soviet Union immediately rallied round the Asian and Arab States, she continued to insist that self-determination should only afford a right to colonial peoples. Repeatedly endeavouring to narrow the scope of the principle, the Soviet representative introduced several proposals to that effect: the first one in the General Assembly in 1951, the second in the Commission on Human Rights in 1952.[38] The majority of States, however, became increasingly adamant in their insistence that the article on self-determination have a wider scope and not merely be limited to colonial situations.

In 1952, Chile, in the Commission on Human Rights, proposed an important addition to the draft article on self-determination. It moved that a paragraph should be added which stated that self-determination encompasses the right to control natural resources. This proposal, one of the first steps taken in the United Nations to change international rules governing expropriation and nationalization, was immediately endorsed by all the socialist States and a wide array of Third World countries.

As for Western States, their strategy was to oppose any provision on self-determination. The staunchest opponents were the United Kingdom, France, and Belgium, those most concerned about retaining control over their colonies. Other States, such as the United States, Canada, the Scandinavian countries, and Brazil, took a rather cautious stand. They claimed to support the principle of self-determination but not the Third World initiative, which, in their view presented a number of legal and

---

[37] UN Doc., 1951, Afghanistan (A./C.3/SR.309, para. 53; *ibid.* SR.362, para. 11); India (SR.399, para. 4). The same stand was taken in 1955 by various countries: Afghanistan (A/C.3/SR.644, para. 10), El Salvador (SR.645, para. 24), Lebanon (SR.649, paras. 29–30, 34), India (SR.651, para. 4), Egypt (SR.651, para. 332), Afghanistan (SR.652, para. 3, SR.654, para. 37, SR.677, para. 27). As for Western countries supporting this view, mention can be made of the statement by the US delegate in 1951 (A/C.3/SR.364, para. 19). In 1955 the same stand was taken by New Zealand (A/C.3/SR.649, para. 9), the UK (SR.652, para. 24) and Denmark (SR.677, para. 27).

[38] In 1952 the Soviet Union submitted a draft proposal to the Commission on Human Rights which only mentioned dependent territories (E/CN.4/L.21). Egypt called for an amendment 'aimed at making good' (E/CN.4/L.23 Rev.1) the omission of the Soviet draft by the inclusion of a paragraph 'referring to all countries without exception' (E/CN.4/SR.255, 10). The Egyptian amendment was subsequently adopted.

procedural obstacles.[39] However, a few Western countries showed themselves to be rather more flexible, co-operating at certain stages in the improvement of the provision. The US, in 1952, even voted in favour of the bulk of the draft Article in the Commission on Human Rights, although it cast a negative vote on the paragraph concerning natural resources.

By and large, it can be contended that Western countries opposed the provision on self-determination either on account of their colonial interests, or out of fear that the paragraph relating to the free disposition of natural resources imperilled foreign investments and enterprises in developing countries.[40] They expressed their opposition by putting forward a number of 'technical' arguments. Thus, they repeatedly insisted that self-determination was a political principle, not a justiciable right.[41] It was, in their view, too nebulous and vague to be included in an international treaty.[42] In addition, they argued that self-determination did not

[39] The United States stated that the promotion of the principle of self-determination was the responsibility of the Trusteeship Council and the Fourth Committee, which was a view shared by Canada (UN Doc., A/C.3/SR.310, paras. 28, 32). Brazil pointed out that the proposed article was inappropriate because the principle was already stated in Article 1(2) of the UN Charter (*ibid.*, para. 30 and SR.360, para. 6).

[40] In January 1952, in the Third Committee, Resolution 545(VI), requesting, *inter alia*, the Commission on Human Rights to include in the Covenant an article on self-determination, was supported by the majority of Third World and socialist countries. Australia, Belgium, Canada, France, The Netherlands, New Zealand, Turkey, the United Kingdom, and the United States voted against the article. Chile, China, Colombia, Cuba, Denmark, Ecuador, Israel, Norway, Peru, and Sweden abstained (UN Doc., A/C.3/SR.403, para. 58). In 1952, the article on self-determination was adopted by the Commission on Human Rights by 13 votes to 4, with one abstention. Belgium, the UK, Australia, and France voted against the article. The United States voted in favour, but reserved the right to propose changes or additions when it came up for discussion in the General Assembly. In addition, the United States voted against the Chilean proposal relating to the present paragraph 2. In 1955, the article was adopted in the Third Committee by 33 votes to 12 (France, Luxemburg, The Netherlands, New Zealand, Norway, Sweden, Turkey, the UK, the USA, Australia, Belgium, Canada), with 13 abstentions (Cuba, Denmark, Dominican Republic, Ethiopia, Honduras, Iceland, Iran, Israel, Panama, Paraguay, Brazil, Burma, China) (UN Doc., A/C.3/SR.676, para. 27).

[41] See, for instance, the British statement of 2 July 1955, UN Doc., A/2910/Add.1, Xth Session, 1955, Annexes, 5, as well as the statement made by the UK representative in the Third Committee (A/C.3/SR.642, para. 11); see also the Australian statement of 20 July 1955 and The Netherlands statement of 29 August 1955 (*ibid.*, 11 and 14).

[42] See Belgium (UN Doc., A/C.3/SR.361, para. 10, SR.643, para. 9); Sweden (*ibid.*, A/C.3/SR.641, paras. 13, 18); Denmark (*ibid.*, SR.644, para. 2); Australia (*ibid.*, SR.647, para. 17).

fit into the Covenant because it was a collective right; the Covenant, concerned with the rights and freedoms of individuals, might even be jeopardized by the inclusion of the principle.[43] The States opposing the principle also set forth a host of other arguments: the implementation system laid down that the Covenant could not be applied to self-determination;[44] self-determination was of necessity a slow and gradual process which would not be furthered by including a provision on the subject in an international treaty;[45] since Article 1(2) of the UN Charter addressed self-determination, there was no need to make reference to the principle in the Covenant;[46] since it was impossible to speak of the right to self-determination without also providing for the right of secession, the implementation of the former right might involve the multiplication of frontiers and barriers among nations.[47] Finally, objections were raised on the procedural plane, with several States contending that the Third Committee of the General Assembly and the Commission on Human Rights did not have jurisdiction over the matter.[48]

However, the Western States did not limit themselves to defensive arguments; they also engaged in 'offensive' tactics. They stressed the dangers that the proposed provision might pose for the territorial integrity of sovereign States harbouring minorities. In addition, they insisted that if the right to self-determination were incorporated in the Covenant, it should also apply to the peoples of sovereign States oppressed by their own governments.

By the time the Article on self-determination was finally adopted in 1955 only a few States still maintained that it should be limited to colonial situations.[49] These States feared that if the provision were not so limited, it might be interpreted as conferring rights on national minorities, which would disrupt sovereign States. However, their fear was misplaced: the

---

[43] See, e.g., Sweden, UN Doc. A/C.3/SR.641, para. 13.

[44] See, e.g., Denmark, UN Doc. A/C.3/SR.644, para. 3.

[45] See, e.g., UK, UN Doc. A/C.3/SR.309, para. 59.

[46] See, e.g., Brazil, UN Doc. A/C.3/SR.310, para. 30.

[47] See, e.g., Belgium, UN Doc. A/C.3/SR.361, paras. 10, 13; Australia, SR.363, para. 39; France, SR.399, para. 314.

[48] See, e.g., UK, UN Doc. A/C.3/SR.309, para. 58; France, *ibid.*, paras. 62–3; SR.399, paras. 27 and 29; US, SR.310, para. 28; Canada, *ibid.*, para. 32; Turkey, *ibid.*, para. 49; Nicaragua, SR.312, para. 5; Peru, *ibid.*, para. 7.

[49] See, for example, Greece (UN Doc., A/C.3/SR.572, para. 32); Saudi Arabia (*ibid.* A/C.3/SR.580, paras. 21–3, SR.582, paras. 75–6, SR.648, para. 15); Liberia (*ibid.*, SR.644, para. 33); Syria (*ibid.*, SR.648, paras. 7–9, SR.672, para. 25); Lebanon (*ibid.*, SR.654, para. 39); Pakistan (*ibid.*, SR.671, para. 23).

overwhelming majority of countries had already explicitly stated that the provision was not intended to cover such minorities.

In the end, the debate was between the developing and socialist countries, who favoured the inclusion of the principle of self-determination, and Western States (plus some pro-Western States such as Brazil) who were for the most part against it. Obviously the former group won. Ironically, however, it was the losing camp's strategies which did the most to broaden the principle of self-determination. By endorsing the view that self-determination, if included in the Covenant, must not be limited to colonial situations, the West markedly contributed to the widening of the scope of the Article. Moreover, the Western States were instrumental in ensuring that the rule, once agreed upon, was properly worded. By raising a number of technical objections to proposed drafts of the Article, the Western States prompted the Article's main supporters to play closer attention to the language used.

The content of self-determination as laid down in the Covenants

Article 1 of both the UN Covenant on Economic, Social and Cultural Rights and the UN Covenant on Civil and Political Rights provides as follows:

All peoples have the right of self-determination. By virtue of that right they freely determine their political status and freely pursue their economic, social and cultural development.

All peoples may, for their own ends, freely dispose of their natural wealth and resources without prejudice to any obligations arising out of international economic cooperation, based upon the principle of mutual benefit, and international law. In no case may a people be deprived of its own means of subsistence.

The States Parties to the present Covenant, including those having responsibility for the administration of Non-Self-Governing and Trust Territories, shall promote the realization of the right of self-determination, and shall respect that right, in conformity with the provisions of the Charter of the United Nations.

SELF-DETERMINATION AS A CONTINUING RIGHT: EXPRESSION OF THE POPULAR WILL

Article 1(1) provides that peoples, by virtue of the right to self-determination, are entitled to 'freely determine' the political, economic, social, and cultural policies of the State. The choice of the word 'freely' is instructive, and its meaning twofold.

First – and here lies the primary significance of the provision – Article 1(1) requires that the people choose their legislators and political leaders free from any manipulation or undue influence from the *domestic* authorities themselves. In this respect, in order to understand the exact parameters of internal self-determination one must refer to the other provisions of the Covenant on Civil and Political Rights. Internal self-determination presupposes that all members of a population be allowed to exercise those rights and freedoms which permit the expression of the popular will. Thus, internal self-determination is best explained as a manifestation of the totality of rights embodied in the Covenant, with particular reference to: freedom of expression (Article 19); the right of peaceful assembly (Article 21); the right to freedom of association (Article 22); the right to vote (Article 25 b); and, more generally, the right to take part in the conduct of public affairs, directly or through freely chosen representatives (Article 25 a). Only when individuals are afforded these rights can it be said that the whole people enjoys the right of internal self-determination. Consequently, one can claim a breach of Article 1 of the Covenant if a State abuses or gravely disregards the limitations on civil and political rights authorized by the Covenant.

Linking self-determination with individual rights is not, however, without negative ramifications. Once we accept that the key to assessing a people's enjoyment of internal self-determination lies in its ability to exercise the political and civil rights enumerated in the Covenant, we must also accept that the right to full self-determination is not absolute, that is, it can be exceptionally curtailed in cases of derogations made under Article 4 of the Covenant.[50] To be accurate, by virtue of Article 4, Article 1 can be derogated from in two ways. First, *directly*, where a State explicitly declares under Article 4(3) that it intends to derogate from the provision on self-determination. Second, *indirectly* (and this realistically seems a more probable occurrence), when a State avails itself of the right of derogation with regard to those provisions of the Covenant which flesh out self-determination, that is, the aforementioned Articles on political freedoms.

---

[50] Article 4(1) provides as follows: 'In time of public emergency which threatens the life of the nation and the existence of which is officially proclaimed, the States Parties to the present Covenant may take measures derogating from their obligations under the present Covenant to the extent strictly required by the exigencies of the situation, provided that such measures are not inconsistent with their other obligations under international law and do not involve discrimination solely on the ground of race, colour, sex, language, religion or social origin.'

Thus, although Article 1, unlike other provisions of the Covenant, is couched in absolute terms (in that it does not include any 'escape clause' granting Contracting States the power to restrict the exercise of the right to self-determination), it is subject to the same limitations incorporated in the Covenant's other provisions. Indeed, the Article is marred by the same defect which *may* render the Covenant's other provisions somewhat ineffective: loopholes which leave too much discretion to contracting States.

An even greater shortcoming lies in the fact that the Covenant's provisions on the democratic process are rather loose. In other words, the *democratic model* outlined in the Covenant is so generic that States can easily contend that they live up to it, and hence accord political self-determination, although they in actual fact do not really allow the whole people to make a genuine choice concerning the political regime. Thus, for instance, Article 25, on the right to take part in the conduct of public affairs and in 'genuine periodic elections' is so sweeping and vague that it can easily permit single-party systems (provided they make allowance for periodic – indeed, ritualistic – elections), thus denying in actual fact a genuine exercise of the right to self-determination. Similarly, Article 21 (on the right of peaceful assembly) and 22 (on freedom of association) may be subjected to so many restrictions that States may easily justify serious curtailments of those rights, thus *de facto* stultifying one of the basic preconditions of political self-determination.

However, despite these flaws, Article 1 has been a major impetus to self-determination's development into a legal principle encompassing the *internal* decision-making process, for it is Article 1(1) which established a permanent link between self-determination and civil and political rights. Since the advent of Article 1, the issue of whether a State has respected its peoples' right to self-determination cannot be resolved without an inquiry into the State's decision-making process. In short, there is no self-determination without democratic decision-making.

This leads to an important point: the right to self-determination provided for in the Covenants is a *continuing right*. The language of Article 1 and the attendant preparatory work compel such a conclusion. Although the draft of Article 1 proclaimed, 'all peoples *shall have* the right to self-determination', the final text reads, 'all peoples *have* the right to self-determination'. This change was intended 'to emphasize the fact that the right referred to is a *permanent* one'.[51]

---

[51] Comment made by the Chairman of the Working Party of the Third Committee when presenting the draft to the Third Committee (UN Doc., A/C.3/SR.668, para. 3).

In short, the drafters of Article 1 advanced a broad approach to self-determination, one to a very large extent different from the political doctrine which had evolved in the years immediately following the Second World War. As we have seen above, in the era immediately after the Second World War, the majority of States equated the achievement of independent status by colonial countries with the final realization of self-determination (we will see that an exception was then made for racist States). Under the Covenant, however, the right to self-determination does not end with independence. The issue of whether the government of a sovereign State is in compliance with Article 1 is a legitimate question, with reference to any State, at any point in time.

SELF-DETERMINATION AS A CONTINUING RIGHT: FREEDOM FROM OUTSIDE INTERFERENCE

The second meaning of the word 'freely' in Article 1(1) is less explicit than the first one but no less important. Article 1(1) requires that a State's domestic political institutions must be free from outside interference. It therefore prohibits States from meddling in the affairs of another contracting State, in a manner that seriously infringes upon the right of that State 'freely to determine [its] political status and economic, social and cultural development'. It follows, first, that the Covenants reinforce the duty incumbent upon every State under customary international law to respect every other State's political independence and territorial integrity. Second, they also prohibit contracting States from invading and occupying the territory of other contracting States in such a manner as to deprive the people living there of their right of self-determination. Thus, military occupation and, *a fortiori*, annexation of a foreign territory amounts to a grave breach of Article 1(1) (such action is not in conflict with Article 1(1) if it is justified by Article 51 of the UN Charter and, therefore, being restricted to the need to repel an act of aggression, is limited in duration).

THE RIGHT OVER NATURAL WEALTH AND RESOURCES

Given that the people of every sovereign State have a permanent right to choose by whom they are to be governed, it is only logical that they should have the right to demand that the chosen central authorities exploit the territory's natural resources so as to benefit the people. Herein enters Article 1(2), which provides that the right to control and benefit from a territory's natural resources lies with the inhabitants of that territory. This right, and the corresponding duty of the central government to use the resources in a manner which coincides with the interests of the people, is the natural consequence of the right to political self-determination.

The problem lies not in understanding the nature of the right but in ensuring State compliance. Decisions concerning the exploitation of natural resources require a wide measure of discretionary power and generally turn on a host of technical and economic factors. Therefore it is often hard for peoples to police their governments. Nevertheless, Article 1(2) can have an impact in extreme situations, where it is relatively easy to demonstrate that a government is exploiting the natural resources in the exclusive interest of a small segment of the population and is thereby disregarding the needs of the vast majority of its nationals. Similarly, it may be invoked with some success where it is apparent that a government has surrendered control over its natural resources to another State or to foreign private corporations without ensuring that the people will be the primary beneficiaries of such an arrangement. Either of these situations would constitute a clear violation of Article 1(2) of the Covenants.

One must note, however, that the right of peoples to have control over their natural resources is subject to a major limitation: the free disposition of the natural wealth and resources must neither impair, nor conflict with, international treaties or agreements which aim to promote international economic co-operation; nor may it violate international customary rules protecting the rights of foreign investors. This limitation, written into paragraph 2 at the behest of the industrialized States, was motivated by two considerations. First, and most obviously, the industrialized States wanted to ensure that the expropriation or nationalization of foreign investments would be adequately compensated.[52] Second, they wanted to discourage developing States from abandoning foreign investment programmes in the name of economic self-determination.[53] Relying on the then-existing consensus that States had a duty effectively and promptly to compensate foreign investors in cases of expropriation or nationalization, the drafters of paragraph 2 inserted a reference to international law in order to ensure prompt, adequate, and effective compensation if either of the two situations occurred. The reference to international law was intended to vitiate the more severe aspects of the provision granting

[52] See, e.g., remarks made by the US (E/CN.4/SR.257, 6 and A/C.3/SR.646, paras. 34–5), and by the UK (A/C.3.SR.642, para. 19).
[53] See, e.g., France (E/CN.4/SR.257, p. 5); the USA (*ibid.*, 6); Lebanon (*ibid.*, 10); Australia (E/CN.4/SR.647, para. 24); Panama (E/CN.4/SR.650, para. 28).

sovereign States (or the administering authority of dependent territories) the right to disregard international treaties and agreements which do not benefit the people.[54]

It should, however, be added that both Covenants also include a provision whereby 'Nothing in the present Covenant shall be interpreted as impairing the inherent right of all peoples to enjoy and utilize fully and freely their natural wealth and resources' (Article 47 of the Covenant on Civil and Political Rights and Article 25 of the other Covenant). These provisions were inserted in the Covenants much later than Article 1(2) and were aimed at 'rectifying' Article 1(2) in order to meet new demands in the wake of the evolution of international politics and law that had taken place in the meantime. It follows that in cases of the expropriation or nationalization of the natural resources of a people, the duty to pay compensation, if any, is governed by the rules of customary international law currently in force.[55]

SELF-DETERMINATION OF DEPENDENT PEOPLES

Article 1(3) grants peoples of dependent territories (non-self-governing and trust territories) the right freely to decide their international status, in other words, whether to form a State or to associate with an existing sovereign

---

[54] What the drafters were unable to foresee was the extent to which the international norms governing compensation were soon to change. Throughout the 1960s and 1970s the Third World and the socialist States consistently challenged the international rules on compensation, arguing that States need not compensate investors who, for prolonged periods, drew excessive profits at the expense of the host State. In addition, they asserted that even if compensation was due, it need not be prompt and, in some instances, need not be paid in full. These challenges to the pre-1955 rule of prompt and adequate compensation to some extent modified the traditional international rules on compensation. A new principle, enshrined in UN resolutions on the 'new economic order' was advocated with a view to replacing the old norm; compensation need not be paid in every case, and furthermore, where compensation is required, it is the legal norms of the expropriating State which are applicable (see, for instance, Article 2(c) of the Charter of Economic Rights and Duties of States. See also, G. Elian, 'Le principe de la souveraineté sur les ressources nationales et les incidences juridiques sur le commerce international', 149 HR, 1976-I, 7 ff.; M. Bedjaoui, 'Non-alignment et droit international', 151 HR, 1976-III, 431 ff.)

[55] See on this point the arguments I developed in my paper in Henkin, *The International Bill of Rights*, 103–7. According to a number of authors, Article 47 was actually intended to override Article 1(2): K. P. Saskena, 'International Covenants on Human Rights', 15–16 IJIL, 1970, 602; Y. Dinstein, 'Collective Rights of Peoples and Minorities', 25 ICLQ 1976, 110–11. See also D. Halperin, 'Human Rights and Natural Resources', 9 *William and Mary Law Review*, 1968, 770–87.

State. Under this provision – now almost completely outdated on account of the fact that almost all colonial people have achieved independence – those States that are Parties to the Covenants and which were responsible for the administration of dependent territories are obliged 'to promote the realization of the right of self-determination . . . in conformity with the provisions of the Charter of the United Nations'. By reason of this latter provision, the drafters of the Covenants imposed on contracting States responsible for the administration of dependent territories a duty not explicitly provided for in the Charter, namely, the duty to grant self-determination to the peoples of dependent territories. Although Article 76 of the Charter cites 'independence' as one of the basic objectives of the trusteeship system, neither Chapter 11 (on non-self-governing territories), nor Chapter 12 (on the trusteeship system) specifically employs the term 'self-determination'. Article 1(3) of the Covenant compensates for this lacuna; since it is to be read in conjunction with Chapters 11 and 12 of the UN Charter, it actually writes the principle of self-determination into the chapters governing dependent territories (although, of course, technically speaking it cannot amend those Chapters but only supplement them for those Member States of the UN which have ratified the Covenants).[56] In this way, the Covenants give teeth to the Charter's general principle of self-determination, which some considered as having no application with respect to the governance of dependent territories.[57]

[56] That Article 1 of the Covenant goes further than the UN Charter is borne out by the reservation made by the UK at the time of signature of the Covenant and confirmed upon ratification ('The Government of the United Kingdom declare their understanding that, by virtue of Art.103 of the Charter of the UN, in the event of any conflict between their obligations under Art.1 of the Covenant and their obligations under the Charter (in particular, under Articles 1, 2 and 73 thereof) their obligations under the Charter shall prevail' (in UN, *Human Rights, Status of International Instruments*, New York 1987, 46–7).

It should be recalled that in 1991, on the occasion of the discussion in the UN Human Rights Committee of the 3rd British report on the implementation of the Covenant on Civil and Political Rights, the UK delegate noted that: 'The Government's declaration in connection with article 1 of the Covenant did not constitute a reservation and had been made at a time when the right of self-determination was less clearly defined than was now the case. It merely stated that in the event of a conflict between the United Kingdom's obligations under article 1 of the Covenant and those of the Charter, the latter would prevail (*Report of the Human Rights Committee to the G.A.*, 1991, UN Doc. A/46/40, para. 360).

[57] Article 1(3) is not, however, the first gloss on Chapters XI and XII. As early as 1960 the UN General Assembly had already adopted the famous Resolution 1514(XV). This resolution proclaimed that dependent peoples have a 'right to complete independence' with the Administering Power being obliged to take 'immediate steps . . . to transfer all

THE PEOPLES REFERRED TO IN ARTICLE I

According to many commentators, the text of Article 1 of the 1966 Covenants raises far more questions than it answers. Which peoples are afforded a right under Article 1? What is the scope of the right granted? How is the right to be implemented? This section addresses the first two of these issues (the third one will be dealt with in Chapter 5).[58]

In the author's view, the general spirit and context of Article 1, combined with the preparatory work, lead to the conclusion that Article 1 applies to: (1) entire populations living in independent and sovereign States, (2) entire populations of territories that have yet to attain independence, and (3) populations living under foreign military occupation. It is thus apparent that the existence of a right to self-determination is not necessarily determined by reference to a territory's international political status.

The right of peoples to be free from any outside interference has already been discussed above, with particular reference to colonial domination and military occupation. The focus will now be on two main issues that are especially problematic: (1) peoples living in sovereign states and (2) minority groups.

As far as the internal self-determination of *peoples living in sovereign States* was concerned, the drafting history of Article 1 shows that self-

---

powers', as distinct from the Administering Power merely having a duty to 'promote the realisation of' and 'respect' the 'right to self-determination'. Although it is always difficult to draw a watertight distinction between customary and treaty law, arguably at treaty level it was only in 1966 that the UN Chapter was supplemented. As, of course, Resolution 1514(XV) was a powerful impetus to the crystallization of a customary rule (see below, Chapter 4, pp. 69–70), it could be contended that perhaps in late 1960 the two Chapters of the UN Charter were in the process of being supplemented at both normative levels.

58 Obviously, the question of what is meant by 'people' will be answered only with regard to the Covenants. For a different notion, enshrined in a different international text, see R.N. Kiwanuka, 'The Meaning of 'People' in the African Charter on Human and Peoples' Rights', 82 AJIL, 80–101. On the notion of 'peoples' see also the apposite remarks by H. Thierry, 'L'évolution du droit international – Cours Général de Droit International Public', 222 HR, 1990-III, 162–3. More generally, see G. Héraud, 'Le droit des petits peuples à disposer d'eux-mêmes', *Menschenrechte, Volksgruppen, Regionalismus, Festgabe für T. Veiter*, 81–95; H. Rumpf, 'Das Subjekt des Selbstbestimmungrechts', in D. Blumenwitz and B. Meissner (eds.), *Das Selbstbestimmungsrecht der Völker und die deutsche Frage*, Cologne 1983, 47 ff.; D. Murswiek, 'Offensives und Defensives Selbstbestimmungsrecht. Zum Subjekt des Selbstbestimmungsrecht der Völker', 23 *Der Staat-Zeit. für Staatslehre, öffentliches Recht und Verfassungsgeschichte*, 1984, 524–48.

determination was generally considered to afford a right to be free from an authoritarian regime. This view was, of course, forcefully propounded by Western States such as the US, the UK, Greece, New Zealand, and Denmark, once they realized that they could not oppose a provision on self-determination.[59] Surprisingly, the same view was also advocated by a number of developing countries. Thus, in 1950, the Indian delegate stated that:

Individual and political rights could not be implemented if the people to whom they had been granted lived under a despotic regime. As has been recognized in Article 21, paragraph 3 of the [Universal] Declaration [of Human Rights], the will of the people should be the basis of the authority of government.[60]

In the same vein the delegate of Syria pointed out that from a domestic point of view the principle at issue took the form of self-government, that is to say a people's right to adopt representative institutions and be able freely to choose the form of government which it wished to adopt.[61]

This concept was echoed by the representatives of Pakistan, Lebanon, and Egypt.[62] In 1954, the representative from Egypt stated that the right of self-determination was to be implemented, 'in practice by means of elections and plebiscites through which the individual expressed his wishes'.[63]

In addition, India's reservation to Article 1, surprisingly entered upon ratification of the Covenants, and the other States' response to it lend credence to the thesis that peoples living in sovereign States are within its scope. On ratifying the Covenants, India made a reservation to the effect that the right of self-determination pertains only to 'peoples under foreign domination': it is not relevant with regard 'to sovereign independent States or to a section of a people or nation – which is the essence of national integrity'.[64] The fact that India considered it necessary to enter such a reservation signals that the consensus must have been leaning in the other direction. The responses of France, the Federal Republic of Germany, and the Netherlands support this view. All three States objected to the reservation on the grounds that the right of self-determination applies

---

[59] See above, pp. 50–1.
[60] UN Doc. A/C.3/SR.310 para. 14, 1950.
[61] UN Doc. A/C.3/SR.397 para. 5, 1950.
[62] UN Doc. A/C.3/SR.253, 13 (Pakistan); SR.254, 9 (Lebanon); A/C.3/SR.571, para. 4 (Egypt).
[63] UN Doc. A/C.3/SR.571, para. 4, 1954.
[64] For the text of this reservation, see UN, *Human Rights, Status of International Instruments*, UN Doc. ST/HR/5, 1987, 9.

to *all* peoples[65] (India, however, has subsequently insisted on her reservation).[66]

Let us now turn to the question of *minority groups*. Does Article 1 confer on minorities living in sovereign States the right, under international law, to free themselves from majority rule? To answer this question we must refer to Article 27 of the Covenant on Civil and Political Rights, which grants persons who are members of ethnic, religious or linguistic minorities the right to enjoy their own culture, to profess and practice their own religion, and to use their own language. Examining Article 27, two things must be noted. First, it addresses itself to individual, as opposed to group rights. It is the individual members of a minority group, not the group itself, who are the holders of the rights conferred. Second, Article 27 does not contemplate political, economic or social autonomy. The enumerated rights only refer to cultural, religious and linguistic freedoms, that is, the rights needed to guarantee that a minority is able to maintain its identity.[67]

An examination limited to the texts of the Covenants may well lead to the conclusion that minorities are entitled to more than the rights enumerated in Article 27. It may, after all, be claimed that the provisions might be cumulative. In other words, minorities might be entitled to the right of political, economic and social self-determination provided for in Article 1 *and* the rights provided for in Article 27. The entire body of preparatory work, however, compels the opposite conclusion.

In 1950, Afghanistan and Saudi Arabia, the authors of a draft resolution regarding the article on self-determination, deleted the word 'peoples' from their draft 'at the suggestion of delegations which feared that its inclusion might encourage minorities within a State to ask for the right to self-determination'.[68] Upon the request of Mexico 'peoples' was reintroduced, but only on the clear understanding that it was not intended to refer to minorities. An examination of the 1951 debates in the Third Committee and the 1952 discussions in the Commission of Human Rights

---

[65] *Ibid.*, 18 ff. The original text of the German objection can be read in 42 *Zeit.*, 1982, 532.

[66] See India's initial report on the implementation of the UN Covenant on Civil and Political Rights, submitted in 1983, *Addendum*, UN Doc. CCPR/C/10/Add. 8, at 9 (paras. 28 ff.), as well as her Second Report, submitted in 1989, *Addendum*, UN Doc. CCPR/37/Add.13, at 5, paras. 8–11, and the debate that took place in the Human Rights Committee in 1991 (UN Doc. CCPR/C./SR.1039, para. 33; SR.1040, paras. 3–5).

[67] On Article 27 see L. B. Sohn, 'The Right of Minorities', in Henkin, *The International Bill of Rights*, 270–89, and the bibliography cited there, at 470, note 1.

[68] UN Doc. A/C.3/SR.310, para. 3.

makes it even more clear that the majority of States did not intend 'peoples' to encompass minorities.[69] It was feared that granting minorities a legal right to self-determination would create havoc in sovereign States.

Thus, in answer to the query 'Are the limitations of Article 27 to be read into Article 1?', a positive response must be made. This has far-reaching implications. It necessitates a conclusion which contradicts the political claims of a broad range of ethnic groups currently vying for 'self-determination', because under the Covenants these minority groups are not entitled to self-determination.

The practice of the UN Human Rights Committee[70]

It seems that initially the Committee has tended to take a restrictive view of self-determination. This has manifested itself in various forms. First, the Committee has primarily emphasized the *external* dimension of self-determination. Thus, in 1984, the Committee pointed out that contracting States must take '*positive action* to facilitate realization of and respect for the right of peoples to self-determination', adding however that in so far as sovereign States were concerned, this action for the promotion of self-determination 'must be consistent with the States' obligations under the Charter of the UN and under international law: in particular, States must refrain from interfering in the internal affairs of other States and thereby

---

69 See, e.g., statements made in the Third Committee by Liberia (A/C.3/SR.366, para. 29); China (A/C.3/SR.369, para. 13: 'the problem at issue is that of national majorities and not of minorities') and India (A/C.3/SR.399, paras. 5–6: '[T]he problem of minorities, which is completely different, should not be raised in connection with its [viz. right of self-determination] implementation. The sponsors of the draft resolution would never allow the article which they requested to be inserted in the Covenant to be invoked in an attempt to destroy the unity of a nation or to impede the creation of such unity. Any such attempt would be contrary to the purpose of the sponsors of the draft resolution, who recognize the basic principle of national sovereignty.') See also statements made in 1952 in the Commission of Human Rights by India (E/CN.4/SR.253, 13, SR.256, 15); Lebanon (*ibid.*, SR.254, 9); Uruguay (*ibid.*, SR.259, 5) and in the General Assembly in 1954 by China (A/C.3/SR.570, para. 16) and Greece (*ibid.*, SR.572, para. 32, SR.577, para. 8). Finally, see generally the records of the 1955 General Assembly debates (A/C.3/SR.642–75), for statements made by China, Canada, Iran, Venezuela, Greece, Colombia, Saudi Arabia, India, the United Kingdom, Ecuador, Iraq, Pakistan, Syria, and Egypt.

70 See generally D. McGoldrick, *The Human Rights Committee*, Oxford 1991, 247–68; M. Novak, 'Minderheitenschutz und Selbstbestimmungsrecht in der Praxis des UNO-Ausschusses für Menschenrechte', in F. Ermacora, H. Tretter and A. Pelzl (eds.), *Volksgruppen im Spannungsfeld von Recht und Souveranität in Mittel- und Osteuropa*, Vienna 1993, 204–17.

adversely affecting the exercise of the right to self-determination'.[71] Thus, not only was the internal dimension of self-determination somewhat neglected, but it was added that contracting States were debarred by the principle of non-interference from inquiring as to whether internal self-determination was being implemented in other States. Actually, it is apparent from contracting States' reports, as well as the comments of Committee members, that emphasis was laid on external self-determination[72] although in some instances mention was also made of the internal dimension.[73]

Second, and consistently with the general trend just pointed out, the Committee tended at the outset to uphold a loose interpretation of the various provisions of the Covenant on Civil and Political Rights concerning the democratic process, chiefly Article 22 (freedom of association) and 25 (the right to take part in elections and the conduct of public affairs). Under this interpretation a single-party system was regarded as compatible with the concept of representative democracy: in particular, pluralism and the rule of law were not always considered as indispensable elements of true democracy. It followed that the test for verifying whether internal (political) self-determination was implemented in Contracting States was ultimately rather loose and at any event not particularly exacting.[74]

---

[71] See Report of the Human Rights Committee to the GA, UN Doc. A/39/40, 1984, at 143, para. 6.

[72] See, e.g., the debate in the Committee in 1984 on Canada (*Report of the Human Rights Committee to the G.A.* 1985, UN Doc. A/40/40, para. 195), USSR (*ibid.*, paras. 260–1, and 263), the Dominican Republic (*ibid.*, para. 386), New Zealand (Cook Islands) (*ibid.*, 434 and 449), the UK (*ibid.*, paras. 536–8); in 1985 on Luxembourg (*Report* . . . , UN Doc. A/41/40, paras. 57 and 78), Sweden (*ibid.*, paras. 109–10), Finland (*ibid.*, paras. 175–6), the Federal Republic of Germany (*ibid.*, paras. 267–9), Czechoslovakia (*ibid.*, paras. 318, 324); in 1987 on Tunisia (*Report* . . . , UN Doc. A/42/40, paras. 112–13), Senegal (*ibid.*, para. 191), Denmark (*Report* . . . , UN Doc. A/43/40, para. 157); in 1988 on Ecuador (*ibid.*, paras. 319–20), France (*ibid.*, paras. 370–5), Australia (*ibid.*, paras. 426–7), Japan (*ibid.*, para. 595), Norway (*Report* . . . ., UN Doc. A/44/40, para. 60), Mexico (*ibid.*, para. 104), The Netherlands (*ibid.*, paras. 199–200); in 1989 on Uruguay (*ibid.*, para. 281), New Zealand (*ibid.*, paras. 373–5), Mauritius (*ibid.*, paras. 494–7).

[73] See, e.g., the debate in 1984 on the USSR (*Report of the Human Rights Committee to the G.A.*, UN Doc. A/40/40), para. 266; Spain (*ibid.*, para. 479), the UK (*ibid.*, paras. 539–40); in 1985 on Finland (*Report* . . . , UN Doc. A/41/40, para. 177); in 1987 on Senegal (*Report* . . . , UN Doc. A/42/40, paras. 190–1), Iraq (*ibid.*, paras. 352–3), Denmark (see *Report* . . . , UN Doc. A/43/40, paras. 154–6), Australia (*ibid.*, para. 428); in 1989 on Bolivia (*Report* . . . , UN Doc. A/44/40, paras. 410 and 432).

[74] See, e.g., the debate on Romania in 1979 (*Report of the Human Rights Committee to the G.A.*, 1980, UN Doc. A/36/40, para. 178), on Hungary in 1980 (*ibid.*, paras. 310–11), on Tanzania in 1981 (*Report of the Human Rights Committee to the G.A.*, 1981, UN Doc.

Third, the Committee has consistently taken the view that under the Optional Protocol only individuals can lodge 'communications', and consequently peoples or peoples' representatives have no right to invoke Article 1 of the Covenant on Civil and Political Rights. This interpretation has been justified by arguing that the Optional Protocol permits individuals to file complaints with the Committee only in cases where a Contracting State has allegedly violated a right to which he or she is entitled under the Covenant; since the right to self-determination is a *collective* right, individuals do not have standing to complain of its alleged breach.[75]

The more recent practice of the Committee shows, however, that the Committee is increasingly turning its attention to internal self-determination. This goes hand in hand with its insistence that political pluralism is not only a basic hallmark of democracy but also one of its necessary preconditions; with the consequence that now the Committee seems to consider non-multi-party systems as scarcely compatible with the democratic model outlined in the Covenant.[76] It follows that now Committee members and, consequently, States, tend to lay greater emphasis on the importance of internal self-determination as a truly

---

4/37/40, paras. 216–24), on Mali (*ibid.*, paras. 239 and 249), on the USSR in 1985 (*Report of the Human Rights Committee to the G.A.*, 1985, UN Doc. A/40/40, paras. 258 and 269), on Zaire in 1987 (*Report of the Human Rights Committee to the G.A.*, 1987, UN Doc. A/42/40, paras. 271 and 286); see also the debate on Romania (*ibid.*, paras. 295, 298, 339–40). Furthermore, see the debate on Togo in 1989 (*Report of the Human Rights Committee to the G.A.*, UN Doc. A/44/40, paras. 251 and 267).

[75] See the Human Rights Committee's decision of 27 July 1988 on communication no. 197/1985 (*Ivan Kitok v. Sweden*), UN Doc. CCPR/C/33/D/197/1985, para. 6.3., as well as the decision of 26 March 1990 (*The Lubicon Lake Band v. Canada*), UN Doc. CCPR/C/38/D/167/1984, para. 32.1 and the decision of 30 April 1990 (*A.B. et alii v. Italy*), UN Doc. CCPR/C/40/D/413/1990, para. 3.2. A previous case brought by a Canadian who was a member of the Mikmaq tribe had been declared inadmissible on procedural grounds on 20 July 1984: Communication no. R.19/78, UN Doc. CCPR/C/22/R.19/78. Subsequently the Human Rights Committee declared as admissible a complaint by representatives of the Mikmaq tribe in so far as it raised questions covered by Article 25(a) of the Covenant; see decision of 4 November 1991 (*Grand Chief Donald Marshall et al. v. Canada*), UN Doc. CCPR/C/43/D/205/1986, paras. 5.1 and 6. See also the decision of 5 November 1991 (*R.L. et al. v. Canada*), in *Report of the Human Rights Committee to the G.A.*, UN Doc. A/47/40, 373, para. 6.2.

[76] See, e.g., the remarks made in 1990 by several Committee Members on pluralism in Zaire (CCPR/C/SR.995, paras. 43, 49, 54, 60). See also *Report of the UN Human Rights Committee to the G.A.*, 1990, UN Doc. A/45/40, paras. 542–6, 576–7. In addition, see the comments made in 1990 on Vietnam (*ibid.*, paras. 447 and 491). Furthermore, see the Committee's comments in 1991 on Sudan (*Report . . .* , UN Doc. 4/46/40, paras. 493, 504–5, 518) and on Ukraine (*ibid.*, paras. 220–1).

democratic decision-making process, offering the population of sovereign States a real and genuine choice between various economic and political options.[77]

Concluding remarks

It is apparent from the above that the political postulate of self-determination only entered the realm of international law in 1945, when it was proclaimed in Article 1(2) of the UN Charter. This multilateral treaty laid down the principle in a rather loose and weak form and this can be seen in two main respects: first, self-determination was only taken to mean *self-government*; second, it was to constitute a *goal* of the Organization and of its Member States; in other words, no specific and stringent legal obligation was imposed on States.

Things, however, were soon to change in the era after the Second World War. Article 1(2) had a snowball effect, for it lent moral and political force to the aspirations of colonial countries, strongly backed up by socialist States. Thus, Article 1(2) was eventually perceived and relied upon as a legal entitlement to decolonization. More importantly, the United Nations served as an international forum promoting and channelling the gradual crystallization of legal rules governing this amorphous subject.

At the legislative level this process culminated in the adoption, in 1966, of Article 1 common to the two UN Covenants on Human Rights. Strikingly, the Covenants did not fully reflect the *political* trends prevailing in the world community: indeed, while the majority of Member States of this community vociferously insisted on self-determination as an anti-colonial principle, at the *legislative* level *a much broader notion* of self-determination was upheld. More specifically, the Covenants represented a significant step forward in four respects.

First, they enshrined the right of the whole population of each contracting State to internal self-determination, that is, the right freely to choose their rulers. However loose and ambiguous the wording of Article 1 may be, there is no gainsaying the fact that this was the first time that an international legal rule proclaimed self-determination *qua* the right of a

---

[77] See, e.g., the remarks of the Soviet delegate in 1989 (*Report of the U.N. Human Rights Committee to the G.A.*, 1990, UN Doc. A/45/40, paras. 73, 83–7), the comments on Canada in 1990 (*Report* . . . , UN Doc. A/46/40, paras. 48, 50–1), Finland (*ibid.*, paras. 111–12), Spain (*ibid.*, para. 181), in 1991 on Madagascar (*ibid.*, para. 532), in 1992 on Colombia (*Report* etc., 1992, UN Doc. A/47/40, paras. 377, 382, 391), and Yugoslavia (*ibid.*, paras. 433–4, 438–40, 465).

whole people to democratic rule. Second, the Covenants laid down the obligation for each contracting State to refrain from interfering with the independence of other States, hence also from occupying a foreign territory in such a manner as to curtail the right of the foreign peoples to self-determination. Thus, external self-determination was proclaimed in a manner that was markedly different from the traditional approach to this subject (previously external self-determination was only conceived of as the right to achieve independent statehood). Third, the UN Charter provisions on dependent peoples were revitalized, in that they were now looked upon as part of the new perspective of self-determination (this, of course, only holds true for States parties to both the Charter and the Covenants). Fourth, a new dimension of self-determination was brought forward, namely the right to control natural resources; self-determination was no longer envisaged in merely a political dimension but was also seen to have economic ramifications.

It should be added that the increase in the number of States becoming parties to the UN Covenants has gradually strengthened the impact of Article 1. Furthermore, as we shall see, with the passage of time Article 1 has been increasingly invoked by Western States in international fora, regardless of whether or not the Covenants have been ratified. In other words, Article 1 has been relied upon *per se*, as sanctioning a value that should apply to any State, whether or not it has become a contracting party to the Covenants. Thus, Article 1 tends to be given a meaning and a weight which extends far beyond those strictly pertaining to a treaty provision.

4

The emergence of customary rules: external self-determination

Introductory remarks: two necessary caveats

The role of treaty rules in the customary process

Before tackling the question of the gradual evolution of customary rules on self-determination, it is imperative to draw attention to two important factors or caveats.

First of all, a powerful incentive to the crystallization of customary rules on the matter has been constituted by *treaty* provisions: Article 1(2) of the UN Charter and subsequently Article 1 common to the two 1966 Covenants. Treaty-making has contributed to the emergence and consolidation of general rules in two ways. Firstly, when the treaty rules were elaborated, Member States of the UN had an opportunity to take a stand, to voice their views and concerns as well as to react to the statements of other governments. All these pronouncements had an impact that went beyond their final result – the treaty provisions – because they stimulated much debate and prompted States to adopt positions that were conducive to their gradual acceptance of general standards on the matter. Treaty-making is also relevant in another respect. Once adopted, treaty rules had a significant spin-off effect, in that – together with the monitoring mechanisms overseeing their implementation – they led to contracting States being increasingly amenable to the adoption of the course of action dictated by the rules. As membership in the UN came practically to coincide with membership of the world community and the number of contracting Parties to the Covenants increased at a rapid pace, a growing number of States became bound by international legal standards on self-determination and consequently behaved as required by those standards.

This of course set the stage for the gradual formation of *general* norms on the matter – norms that, as we shall soon see, to a large extent coincide with treaty rules as far as their content is concerned.

The view is therefore warranted that treaty law has been a major factor that has contributed to the emergence of customary rules.[1] This should not be surprising. Treaty rules were worked out by the United Nations and it was again the United Nations that contributed to the gradual formation of general standards. In this area, as in similar ones, the World Organization has played a pivotal role:[2] on the basis of its Statute (Article 1(2)), it has first proclaimed new values, then gradually enshrined them in resolutions and subsequently promoted the hammering out of treaty rules and in addition monitored their observance. Furthermore, it has insisted on the general applicability of some concepts relating to self-determination, thus significantly stimulating the emergence of general standards.

It should be added that there are several reasons why treaty rules were not regarded as sufficient by States and the need was therefore felt to develop general norms. Firstly, the majority of States (chiefly the developing and the then socialist countries) thought that – because of Western reluctance or even opposition – it would not be possible to regulate by treaty, in a satisfactory way, the right of colonial peoples to self-determination. The best way they saw of achieving their political aims was in the laying down of political standards couched in legal terminology and enshrined in General Assembly resolutions: insistence on their importance and on the necessity for colonial Powers to act upon them would gradually turn those standards into legally binding norms of a general purport. Secondly, the same majority of States was not satisfied with the exceedingly concise way treaty provisions regulated external self-determination, in

---

[1] On the role of *bilateral* agreements in the emergence of customary law on self-determination, see M. Koteswara Rao, 'Right of Self-Determination in the Post-Colonial Era: A Survey of Juristic Opinion and State Practice', 28 IJIL, 1988, 69–71.

[2] The crucial importance of the UN for the development of the international law of self-determination is obvious and is linked to the fact that this principle could not emerge and take shape without UN *action* and *scrutiny*. To quote the perceptive remarks of H. Blix (*Sovereignty, Aggression and Neutrality*, Uppsala 1970, 13–14), '[The right of self-determination] is an example of a rule which, for its proper application to concrete cases, *requires international institutions*. Which people is entitled to self-determination? If, on the one hand, dangerous fragmentation of States is to be avoided, and, on the other, the rule is to have practical significance, there needs to be a third party to assess the concrete cases and apply the rule. While a political organ like the General Assembly may not be ideal in this role, it seems to be the only one which has assumed it for the time being' (my italics).

particular the right of peoples under foreign domination. Thirdly, the situation of the black populations of Southern Rhodesia and South Africa prompted the same majority of States to frame this situation as a question of the (internal) self-determination of the black population. As it was unthinkable – on account of Western opposition – for treaty rules to be agreed upon on these matters, the best way out was found in the gradual evolution of general standards. One of the advantages of these standards was that their relatively slow formation and their necessarily flexible content would make them more palatable to the West.

It follows from the above remarks that although in the next pages I shall primarily concentrate on UN practice and pronouncements of individual States for the purpose of ascertaining the content and import of general rules, this does in no way imply that treaty rules are excluded from the picture. It is only for the sake of clarity and a more precise exposition, that treaty rules and their implementation will not be mentioned again from this different angle – that is, *qua* part and parcel of the customary process.

The role of UN Resolutions in the crystallization of customary rules

A second caveat is necessary. The problem area we are discussing shows a distinct feature: although customary rules have resulted from the usual combination of *usus* and *opinio juris*, these two elements have not played the normal role that can be discerned in other – less political and more technical – areas of international relations. In these other areas, the first element that normally emerges is the repetition of conduct by an increasing number of States, accompanied at some stage by the belief that this conduct is not only dictated by practical (economic, military, political) reasons, but is also imposed by some sort of legal command. By contrast, in the case of self-determination – as in similar highly sensitive areas fraught with ideological and political dissension – the first push to the emergence of general standards has been given by the *political will* of the majority of Member States of the UN, which has then coalesced in the form of General Assembly resolutions. Strictly speaking, these resolutions are neither *opinio juris* nor *usus*. Rather they constitute the major factor triggering (a) the taking of a legal stand by many Member States of the UN (which thereby express their legal view on the matter)[3] and (b)

---

[3] In the *Nicaragua* case the International Court of Justice pointed out that '*opinio juris* may, though with all due caution, be deduced from, *inter alia*, . . . the attitude of States towards certain General Assembly resolutions, and particularly resolution 2625(XXV) [on

the gradual adoption by these States of attitudes consistent with the resolutions.

It follows that, when discussing customary international law in the area of self-determination, special emphasis will be placed here on two UN Documents: the 1960 Declaration Granting Independence to Colonial Countries and Peoples[4] and the 1970 Declaration on Principles of International Law Concerning Friendly Relations and Co-operation among States in Accordance with the Charter of the UN.[5] The former, in conjunction with the UN Charter, contributed to the gradual transformation of the 'principle' of self-determination into a legal right for non-self-governing peoples. The latter was instrumental in crystallizing a growing consensus concerning the extension of self-determination to other areas. Both are vital in developing an understanding of how general international law regulates self-determination.

These two documents, however, should not be looked at *per se*, but within the general context of their adoption. In other words, they are significant in that their elaboration prompted Member States of the UN to express their views and take a stand on self-determination. The pronouncements of States before, during, and after the adoption of the two Declarations, in conjunction with the actual behaviour of States in international dealings, constitute important elements of State practice. Together with statements made by individual States in other fora (for instance, declarations of government representatives in national parliaments) and rulings of international courts, they make up the bulk of *usus* and *opinio juris* in the matter.

For the sake of clarity, I shall analyse the formation of customary law in the area of 'external' and 'internal' self-determination[6] separately.

Friendly Relations]'. The Court went on to state the following: 'The effect of consent to the text of such resolutions cannot be understood as merely that of a "reiteration or elucidation" of the treaty commitment undertaken in the Charter. On the contrary, it may be understood as an acceptance of the validity of the rule or set of rules declared by the resolution by themselves' (ICJ, Reports 1986, 99–100, para. 188).

[4] GA Resolution 1514(XV), 14 December 1960.

[5] GA Resolution 2625(XXV), 24 October 1970.

[6] This distinction can already be found in W. Wengler, 'Le droit à la libre disposition des peuples comme principe de droit international', 10 *Revue hellénique de droit international*, 1957, 27, and W. Wengler, *Völkerrecht*, vol. II, Berlin 1964, 1032–3. It has been taken up by various authors, including A. V. Lombardi, *Bürgerkrieg und Völkerrecht*, Berlin 1976, 181, 335–9, 341–2. It would seem that A. Verdross and B. Simma, *Universelles Völkerrecht*, 3rd edn, Berlin 1984, at 320, erroneously attributed the distinction to Lombardi's work cited above.

External self-determination[7]

The self-determination of colonial peoples

THE EVOLVING OF GENERAL STANDARDS

Between the early 1950s and the 1960s, at the behest of socialist countries led by the Soviet Union, and with the strong support of the developing countries that had already achieved political independence, the principle of self-determination was vociferously invoked within the United Nations to legitimize the termination of colonial rule. When the initial reluctance of Western countries gradually gave way to grudging acceptance of the new trends, a wide measure of agreement evolved in the United Nations both about the idea that non-self-governing territories should have the opportunity freely to choose their international status and about the manner in which their right to self-determination would be implemented.

This general consent was reflected in two important resolutions adopted in 1960 by the UN General Assembly. The first was Resolution 1514(XV), passed on 14 December 1960 by a vote of 89 to 0, with 9 abstentions (Australia, Belgium, Dominican Republic, France, Portugal, Spain, Union of South Africa, UK, US). This resolution was called the 'Declaration on Granting Independence to Colonial Countries and Peoples'.[8] The other resolution, Resolution 1541(XV), was passed on 15 December 1960 by a vote of 69 to 2 (Portugal, Union of South Africa), with 21 abstentions (from socialist, as well as some Western countries).[9] The latter resolution included in its annex the 'Principles which should guide Members in determining whether or not an obligation exists to transmit the information called for in Article 73(*e*) of the Charter of the United Nations'.[10] Subsequently, the 1970 Declaration on Friendly Relations supplemented, in some respects, these two resolutions.

Close scrutiny of these General Assembly pronouncements,[11] of the statements made by States in the United Nations both before and after

---

[7] See, generally, C. Gusy, 'Von der Selbstbestimmung durch den Staat zur Selbstbestimmung im Staat', 30 AVR, 1992, 397–404.

[8] For the text of the resolution, see UN Ybk, 1960, 49 ff.

[9] For the list of the abstaining countries, *ibid.*, 1960, 509.

[10] For the text of the resolution, *ibid.*, 509 ff.

[11] On Resolution 1514, see in particular S. K. N. Blay, 'Self-Determination v. Territorial Integrity in Decolonization', 18 NYUJILP, 1986, 442–9.

their adoption, as well as the practice of the United Nations in the area of decolonization, warrants the conclusion that in the 1960s there evolved in the world community a set of general standards specifying the principle of self-determination enshrined in the UN Charter, with special regard to colonial peoples.

The legal position was best summarized in 1971 by the International Court of Justice in its Advisory Opinion on *Namibia*, when the Court, after considering the Mandates system, held that

The subsequent development of international law in regard to non-self-governing territories, as enshrined in the Charter of the United Nations, made the principle of self-determination applicable to all of them.[12]

The essential content of the standards concerning colonial peoples can be outlined as follows:

(1) all peoples subjected to colonial rule have a right to self-determination, that is, to 'freely determine their political status and freely pursue their economic, social and cultural development' (operative paragraph 2 of Resolution 1514(XV);

(2) this right only concerns external self-determination, that is, the choice of the international status of the people and the territory where it lives;

(3) the right belongs to the people as a whole: if the population of a colonial territory is divided up into various ethnic groups or nations, they are not at liberty to choose by themselves their external status. This is because the principle of territorial integrity should here play an overriding role. Indeed, under operative paragraph 6 of Resolution 1514(XV), 'Any attempt aimed at the partial or total disruption of the national unity and the territorial integrity of a country is incompatible with the purposes and principles of the Charter of the United Nations'. It is apparent, both from the text of this provision and from the preparatory work,[13] that developing countries, with the full support of socialist States and without any opposition from Western countries, firmly believed that colonial boundaries should not be modified, lest

[12] ICJ, Reports 1971, 31 (para. 52).

[13] Before the adoption of Resolution 1514(XV), Guatemala had proposed an addendum to the draft submitted by forty-three African and Asian States; according to this proposal, 'the principle of the self-determination of peoples may in no case impair the right of territorial integrity of any State or its right to the recovery of territory'. However, this proposal was later withdrawn at the request of Indonesia, which pointed out that the question was already covered by operative para. 6 of the 43-Power draft (the present operative para 6). See UN Ybk, 1960, 48.

this would trigger the disruption of many colonial countries, as well as serious disorder as a result of the carving up of old States into new. In short, the principle *uti possidetis* was regarded as paramount (see below, Chapter 8). These geopolitical considerations led States actually to deny the right of self-determination to individual ethnic groups within colonial territories;

(4) as for the procedures for realizing the right to self-determination, States ultimately made a distinction based on the final result of self-determination, that is, according to whether a colonial country would (i) end up as a sovereign independent State, or (ii) associate with an independent State or instead (iii) integrate into an independent State. For the first of these three cases, it was not formally required that the wishes of the population concerned should be ascertained by means of a plebiscite or referendum. On the contrary, for the other two cases Resolution 1541(XV) required that association or integration with an independent State 'should be the result of a free and voluntary choice by the peoples of the territory concerned expressed through informed and democratic processes' (in the case of integration even more stringent requirements were set out);[14]

(5) once a people has exercised its right to external self-determination, the right expires. This may be inferred from paragraph VI of the Principle on self-determination laid down in the Declaration on Friendly Relations, which states:

[T]he territory of a colony or other Non Self-Governing Territory has, under the Charter, a status separate and distinct from the territory of the State administering it; and such separate and distinct status under the Charter shall exist until the people of the colony or Non-Self-Governing Territory have exercised their right of self-determination in accordance with the Charter, and particularly its purposes and principles.

Under the Declaration, if a people chooses to associate or integrate with a sovereign country, it can subsequently only exercise the right to internal self-determination (as will be seen shortly, this is the case if the government denies the people access to government by way of racial discrimination). Once again, the peoples' right to external self-determination is seen to

---

[14] Principle IX(b) of Resolution 1541(XV), provides that: 'The integration should be the result of the freely expressed wishes of the territory's peoples acting with full knowledge of the change in their status, their wishes having been expressed through informed and democratic processes, impartially conducted and based on universal adult suffrage. The United Nations could, when it deems it necessary, supervise these processes.'

have been limited by the perceived need to safeguard territorial integrity and political unity.

Before analysing the manner in which the practice of the United Nations evolved, it should be emphasized that the legal regulation just mentioned manifested *three major flaws*.

Firstly, the internal self-determination of colonial peoples was totally disregarded, that is, their right freely to choose their form of government, their rulers, etc. Their liberation from colonial rule, in order to achieve independence (or association or integration with another State) was what was seen as important. Admittedly, it would have been historically difficult and, in practice, complicated to provide for free and democratic political elections so as to ensure respect for pluralistic democracy in those territories. The fact remains however that no attention was paid to this 'internal' dimension of self-determination.

Secondly, the norms that gradually evolved eventually gave pride of place to the territorial integrity of colonial territories, thus ruling out the possibility for ethnic groups that constituted a 'colonial people' freely to choose their international status. The resultant self-determination was therefore rather truncated in this second respect.

Thirdly, it was taken for granted that whenever it appeared that the people of a colonial territory wished to opt for independence, it was not necessary to establish this wish by means of a plebiscite or a referendum. In other words, it was felt that the wish for independence – however manifested or ascertained – did not need to be verified by resorting to the means that the practical implementation of self-determination normally required.

THE ACTUAL IMPLEMENTATION OF THE STANDARDS

An overview of UN practice with regard to colonial situations
The UN record in the field of decolonization is impressive.[15] According to a 1979 report prepared for the UN by Héctor Gros Espiell, the then

---

[15] On the role of self-determination in the process of decolonization, and the UN practice in this matter, see in particular: C. Eagleton, 'Excesses of Self-Determination', 31 FA, 1952–3, 592 ff., and 'Self-Determination in the United Nations', 47 AJIL, 1953, 88 ff.; R. Emerson, *Self-Determination Revisited in the Era of Decolonization*, Cambridge, Mass. 1964, 25 ff.; J. Kunz, 'The Principle of Self-Determination of Peoples, Particularly in the Practice of the United Nations', in K. Rabl (ed.), *Inhalt, Wesen und gegenwärtige praktische Bedeutung des Selbstbestimmungsrechts der Völker*, Munich 1964, 137–70; M. K. Nawaz, 'The Meaning and Range of the Principle of Self-Determination', 82 *Duke Law*

Special Rapporteur of the Sub-Commission on the Prevention of Discrimination and Protection of Minorities of the Commission on Human Rights, seventy territories achieved independence between 1945 and 1979.[16] In only a limited number of cases was the right of self-determination exercised and independence not achieved.[17] In the years following the publication of Gros Espiell's report, several territories included in his list of twenty-eight situations still to be resolved achieved independence.[18] Others on the list, South Africa and the territories occupied by Israel in particular, do not, it is submitted, come within the purview of 'colonial situations' included within the report. Thus, at present, there are approximately a dozen 'situations' still outstanding and

---

Journal, 1965, 82 ff.; D. W. Bowett, 'Self-Determination and Political Rights in the Developing Countries', 60 Proceedings ASIL, 1966, 129–35; R. Emerson, 'Self-Determination', *ibid.*, 135–41; W. B. Ofuatey-Kodjoe, *Self-Determination in International Law: Towards a Definition of the Principle*, PhD thesis, Columbia University 1970, 245–74; U. Umozurike, *Self-Determination in International Law*, Hamden, Conn. 1972; A. Rigo Sureda, *The Evolution of the Right of Self-Determination: A Study of the United Nations Practice*, Leiden, 1973; T. M. Franck and P. Hoffman, 'The Right of Self-Determination in Very Small Places', 8 NYUJILP, 1976, 331 ff.; W. Ofuatey-Kodjoe, *The Principle of Self-Determination in International Law*, New York 1977, 97–147; J. F. Engers, 'From Sacred Trust to Self-Determination', 24 NILR, 1977, 85 ff.; J. Crawford, *The Creation of States in International Law*, Oxford 1979, 89 ff.; anon., 'The Decolonization of Belize: Self-Determination v. Territorial Integrity', 22 *Virginia Journal of International Law* 1982, 849 ff.; Pomerance, *Self-Determination in Law and Practice*, 1982, 9–36; J. Charpentier, 'Autodétermination et décolonisation', in *Mélanges C. Chaumont*, Paris 1984, 117–33; O. Kimminich, 'Die Renaissance des Selbstbestimmungsrechts nach dern Ende des Kolonialismus', *Fest. für B. Meissner*, Berlin 1985, 601 ff.; M. Shaw, *Title to Territory in Africa*, Oxford 1986, 92–144; Z. Drnas de Clément, 'El derecho de libre determinacion de los pueblos: colonialismo formal, Neocolonialismo, colonialismo interno', 3 *Anuario Argentino de Derecho Internacional*, 1987–9, especially 214 ff.; Bennouna, 'Tiers Monde et autodétermination', in *Le droit à l'autodétermination*, 83–94; Lombardi, *Bürgerkrieg und Völkerrecht*, 189 ff.; Blay, 'Self-Determination versus Territorial Integrity in Decolonization', 441 ff.; T. M. Franck, *The Power of Legitimacy among Nations*, New York and Oxford 1990, 160 ff.

[16] H. Gros Espiell, Special Rapporteur, *Implementation of United Nations Resolutions Relating to the Right of Peoples under Colonial and Alien Domination to Self-Determination*, Study for the Sub-Commission on Prevention of Discrimination and Protection of Minorities of the Commission on Human Rights, United Nations, New York, 1980. Text originally issued under the symbol E/CN.4/Sub.2/405 (vols. I and II).

[17] West Irian became part of Indonesia; Ifni was incorporated into Morocco; the Mariana Islands became a free associated state with the US; and Niue achieved 'self-government in free association' with New Zealand.

[18] South Rhodesia, now called Zimbabwe; Belize; Brunei; Saint Christopher and Nevis; Saint Lucia; Saint Vincent and the Grenadines; and most recently, Namibia (however, as we shall see, to some extent the question of Namibia is not only a colonial question, but also an issue of foreign illegal occupation).

one case, that of East Timor (annexed by Indonesia in 1975), which was settled with total disregard for UN pronouncements and without UN approval.

Among the remaining situations, three stand out in particular, they being indicative of the inherent difficulties in resolving self-determination claims and the predicament the UN faces in the field: Gibraltar, the Falklands/Malvinas, and Western Sahara.

To what extent has the United Nations taken notice of the freely expressed will of colonial peoples?

The United Nations' practice has to a great extent upheld and applied the standards which have been referred to above. However, it has placed a liberal interpretation on them, in two respects.

Firstly the World Organization has sought to emphasize the requirement that self-determination should always be based on the freely expressed will of peoples. Accordingly, since 1954 the United Nations has organized, and often supervised, elections or plebiscites in non-self-governing territories, before their accession to independence or their association or integration with other countries.[19] Mention can be made of the plebiscites or elections held in the British Togoland Trust Territory in 1956,[20] French Togoland in 1958,[21] the British Northern Cameroons

[19] See M. Merle, 'Les plébiscites organisés par les Nations Unies', AFDI, 1961, 425–44. See also H. S. Johnson, *Self-Determination within the Community of Nations*, Leiden 1967, 59–98. It is interesting to note that in 1952 the US delegate in the UN Economic and Social Council (ECOSOC) criticized the practice of UN supervised plebiscites. In a statement of 31 July 1952, commenting on a draft resolution, he pointed out the following: 'The United States feels that the paragraph [of the draft resolution] unduly restricts the methods by which the wishes of non-self-governing people may be ascertained in the future by placing virtually sole reliance upon the UN supervised plebiscite. The adoption of the U.N. Charter does not require all nations to conduct *all* their foreign affairs through the United Nations; other means of international dealings have distinct advantages. Similarly, in the dealings between an administering country and the non-self-governing people, these people themselves may desire direct methods of contact which may not always be associated with the United Nations. For example, the United States recently arranged to determine the wishes of the people of Puerto Rico, Alaska and Hawaii, without a U.N. plebiscite' (30 *Dept. St. Bul.*, 1952, at 270).

[20] A plebiscite was held in British Togoland in May 1956 (upon the recommendation of the UN GA Res. 944(X) of 15 December 1955). The population voted in favour of the union of their territory with an independent Gold Coast (the other option being the separation of Togoland under British administration and continuance of a trusteeship pending a decision as regards independence). See UN Ybk, 1956, 368 ff.

[21] By virtue of Res. 1182(XII) the UN General Assembly accepted the invitation of the government of Togoland to supervise elections, which were held on 27 April 1958. On

in 1959[22] and the British Southern Cameroons in 1961,[23] Rwanda-Urundi in 1961,[24] Western Samoa in 1962,[25] the Cook Islands in 1965,[26] Equatorial Guinea in 1968,[27] Papua-New Guinea in 1972,[28] the New Zealand Territory of Niue in 1974,[29] the Ellice Islands in 1974 (the voters decided to become a separate territory under the name of Tuvalu),[30] the

23 October 1958 the Chamber of Deputies of Togoland voted in favour of independence. See UN Ybk, 1958, 355 ff.

[22] On 13 May 1959 the UN GA decided, by virtue of Res. 1350(XIII) to hold separate plebiscites under UN supervision in Northern and Southern Cameroons (under British administration). A plebiscite was held in Northern Cameroons on 7 November 1959 and people chose to postpone a decision (the alternative being that of joining Nigeria immediately). Arrangements were made for another referendum to be held in 1961. See UN Ybk, 1959, 361.

[23] UN supervised plebiscites were held in the two territories on 11 and 12 February 1961. Northern Cameroons decided to join Nigeria, Southern Cameroon decided to join the Republic of Cameroun. The results were later endorsed by the UN GA by virtue of Res.1608(XV) of 21 April 1961. See UN Ybk, 1961, 494 ff.

[24] The future of the monarchy in Rwanda was submitted to a UN supervised referendum (UN GA Res. 1580(XV)). The referendum was held in Rwanda on 25 September 1961 alongside the general elections. People voted against the monarchy and consequently a republic was proclaimed. See UN Ybk, 1961, 484 ff.

[25] A plebiscite was held on 9 May 1961 in order to ascertain the wishes of the inhabitants concerning their future (UN GA Res. 1569(XV) of 18 December 1960). The constitution adopted by the Constitutional Convention on 28 October 1960 was endorsed and it was decided that Western Samoa would become an independent State on the basis of that same constitution on 1 January 1962. See UN Ybk, 1961, 495 ff.

[26] On 18 February 1965 the UN GA (Res. 2005(XIX)) authorized the Secretary-General to appoint a UN representative to supervise general elections, which were held on the Cook Islands on 21 April 1965. See UN Ybk, 1965, 570 ff.

[27] A UN supervised referendum on the question of independence was held in Equatorial Guinea on 11 August 1968. The mission stayed on to supervise general elections, which were held on 22 and 29 September. See UN Ybk, 1968, 741.

[28] By virtue of Res. 2156(XXXVIII) of 18 June 1971 the Trusteeship Council decided to send a visiting mission to Papua-New Guinea to observe the elections to the House of Assembly. The mission visited the country from 15 February to 17 March 1972. See UN Ybk, 1972, 522.

[29] A referendum on self-determination was held in Niue in September 1974. The administering authority, New Zealand, invited the UN to send observers. The vote was in favour of self-government in free association with New Zealand. The results were endorsed by the G.A. by virtue of Res. 3285(XXIX) of 13 December 1974. See UN Ybk, 1974, 792 ff.

[30] On 12 November 1974 a UN visiting mission was sent to Ellice Island at the request of the United Kingdom, to supervise a referendum on separation from the Gilbert islands. Ellice islanders voted in favour of separation. By virtue of Res. 3288(XXIX) of 13 December 1974 the GA expressed their appreciation of the mission's work. See UN Ybk, 1974, 791.

Northern Marianas in 1975,[31] and the French Comores Islands in 1974 and 1976.[32] Only in few cases did the UN fail to organize such plebiscites or elections. According to a distinguished commentator,[33] the cases of Gibraltar, West Irian, and Western Sahara stand out in this respect.

Secondly, in at least two cases (Rwanda-Urundi and the British Cameroons) the United Nations did not give primacy to the principle of territorial integrity. In the case of Rwanda-Urundi (a Belgian-administered territory) between 1959 and 1962 the United Nations overcame strong resistance to the splitting of the territory on the part of many African States, which were convinced that the best future for the territory lay 'in the evolution of a single, united and composite State'. As UN visiting missions had found compelling evidence of a strong feeling among the population that the separate personalities of Rwanda and Burundi should be respected, the Organization set up and supervised free elections from which the will of the two peoples to separate became apparent. In 1962, the General Assembly, by Resolution 1746(XVI) thus agreed to let Rwanda and Burundi 'emerge as two independent and sovereign States'. In the case of the British Cameroons, the United Nations' visiting mission concluded that the people of the Northern Cameroons preferred integration into Nigeria to political independence as a sovereign State. As for the inhabitants of Southern Cameroons (also under British administration), it was not clear whether they wished independence or integration into Cameroun (a former French colony). The United Nations therefore decided to call for separate UN-supervised plebiscites. The result was that the people of the Northern Cameroons opted for union with Nigeria and those of the Southern Cameroons voted for integration with Cameroun. In this case too, the United Nations was thus instrumental in making the principle of self-determination prevail over that of territorial integrity.

This practice should not, however, be overemphasized. The first of the two trends referred to above merely shows that the UN endeavoured, as

---

[31] By virtue of Res. 2160(XLII) of 4 June 1975 the Trusteeship Council decided to send a visiting mission to observe the plebiscite in the Mariana Islands district of the Trust Territory of the Pacific Islands. See UN Ybk, 1975, 744.

[32] Plebiscites were held in the Comoro Islands in 1974 and in 1976. In 1974 the three main islands (Anjouan, Grande Comore, and Moheli) opted for independence, whereas the majority in Mayotte rejected independence. A special referendum was again held concerning Mayotte in 1976 and the vast majority voted in favour of remaining with France. See 22 AFDI, 1976, 964–7; D. Rouzié, 'Note', in 103 *Journal de Droit International*, 1976, 392–405. For the reactions to the referendum in Mayotte in the General Assembly and Security Council, see Pomerance, *Self-Determination in Law and Practice*, 30–1.

[33] T. M. Franck, 'The Stealing of the Sahara', 70 AJIL, 1976, 700 ff.

far as possible, to meet the basic requirements of the principle of self-determination. It is not clear, however, whether the States concerned regarded themselves as legally bound to hold a referendum or a plebiscite in each case of decolonization. As for the second of the trends above mentioned, it should be underlined that the two territories at issue were even at the time of colonization distinct and separate in many respects. We are therefore confronted here with cases where the setting up of one independent State would have been blatantly contrary to the history and wishes of the populations concerned. The practice followed by the UN in these two cases cannot however be transposed to other instances, such as that of a colonial people consisting of various ethnic groups artificially welded together by the colonial Power. Indeed in these cases, the United Nations did not inquire as to the possible wishes of the various groups but simply endorsed the achievement of independence by the colonial territory.

Cases where the principle of self-determination was blatantly set aside
Against this background of a fairly consistent implementation of self-determination in the colonial sphere, some instances of a gross disregard for the principle stand out; (i) India's annexation of the Portuguese enclaves within its territory of *Goa, Damao and Din*, in 1961; (ii) the annexation of *West Irian* by Indonesia in 1969; (iii) the occupation and subsequent annexation of *East Timor* by Indonesia in 1975. This last case will be the subject of closer scrutiny in Chapter 9 (pp. 223–30). Therefore, only the first two cases will be dealt with here. (Some commentators add to this list the territories of

---

[34] As is well known, under the Treaty of Nanking of 1842 and the Convention of Peking of 1860, Hong Kong islands and a part of the Kowloon Peninsula were ceded to Great Britain in perpetuity. The rest of the territory (the New Territories plus the rest of Kowloon) comprising 92 per cent of the total land area was leased to Great Britain for ninety-nine years under a third Treaty, the Convention of Peking executed in 1898. The Chinese government has consistently argued that the whole of Hong Kong is Chinese territory and that the aforementioned treaties were unequal. Recently, negotiations commenced between the two governments concerning the whole area (the 8 per cent of Hong Kong's land area would not be viable without the New Territories, which contain most of the territory's agriculture and industry, its power stations, airport and container port). In 1984 the two governments signed a Joint Declaration whereby Hong Kong would revert to China in 1997.

On a few occasions, in discussions before the UN Human Rights Committee on the British periodic reports on the Covenant on Civil and Political Rights, the British government has reported on measures taken to respect self-determination. Thus, in 1991, answering questions on self-determination in Hong Kong, the British delegate pointed out that: 'Following the signing of the Joint Declaration in 1984, an Assessment

Hong Kong[34] and Macao,[35] but this inclusion may be questionable, in view of the historical particularities of the territories; in any case, in the face of the lukewarm attitude taken by the UN,[36] it would seem that, at least in the case of Hong Kong, the two parties concerned have attached importance to the wishes of the population.)[37]

With regard to the three enclaves of Goa, Damao, and Din,[38] Portugal

Office had been established to evaluate the views of the people of Hong Kong, who were found to be largely in favour of the text. The Basic Law Drafting Committee consisted of 59 members, 23 of whom were from Hong Kong, and a Basic Law Consultative Committee, consisting exclusively of Hong Kong representatives, had been set up to determine public opinion in the Territory with regard to the draft Basic Law. The Hong Kong Government had issued a statement to the effect that it welcomed the intensive consultations which China had conducted with the people of Hong Kong during the drafting process and that efforts had been made to take account of the concerns expressed by Hong Kong during the consultation process' (see *Report of the Human Rights Committee to the General Assembly*, 1991, UN Doc. A/46/40, para. 367; see also paras. 354, 368–9). The issue had already been discussed in 1988 (see *Report of the Human Rights Committee to the General Assembly*, 1989, UN Doc. A/44/40, paras. 143, 152–4).

35 As for Macao, which will be returned by Portugal to China in 1999, see, *inter alia*, the discussion in 1990 on the Portuguese periodic report on the UN Covenant on Civil and Political Rights, before the Human Rights Committee: *Report of the Human Rights Committee to the General Assembly*, 1990, vol. I, UN Doc. A/45/40, paras. 124, 126.

36 It is worth recalling that in 1972 the United Nations, at the request of China, decided that Hong Kong and Macao and dependencies were 'part of Chinese territory occupied' respectively 'by the British and Portuguese authorities' and consequently must be removed from the list of non-self-governing Territories (see UN Ybk, 1972, 543, where mention is made of the Chinese request of 8 March 1972 and the subsequent decision of the Committee of 24). See also the endorsement by the General Assembly, in Resolution 2908(XXVII) (*ibid.*, 550–1; and cf. 625), which has the consequence that the exercise of reversionary rights by China will be carried out without any consultation of the population concerned. This position is accounted for by the political and military importance of China and the consequent fear, by other countries, that China might reclaim the territories in question by resort to force, without being checked by the UN Security Council. However, the particularities of the case that may have warranted the setting aside of self-determination include at least two important elements: (i) the population of the territory has remained to a very large extent Chinese; (ii) the transfer of the two territories to Great Britain was effected on the basis of a Treaty that provided for a lease and not a cession proper.

37 See below, Chapter 12.

38 On the question of Goa, see in particular Q. Wright, 'The Goa Incident', 56 AJIL, 1962, 617 ff.; I. Brownlie, *International Law and the Use of Force by States*, Oxford 1964, 349, 379–83; Higgins, *The Development of International Law, Through the Political Organs of the United Nations*, London 1963, 187–8; Blay, 'Self-Determination v. Territorial Integrity', 466–7; J. Crawford, *The Creation of States in International Law*, cit., 112–13; R. C. A. White, 'Self-Determination: Time for a Re-Assessment?', 28 NILR, 1981, 158; Emerson, *Self-Determination Revisited in the Era of Decolonization* 19–24; Rigo Sureda, *The Evolution of the Right of Self-Determination*, 172–7, 329–32; M. Shaw, *Title to Territory in Africa*, cit., 151.

was slow to put in motion the process of decolonization but India decided not to wait for a plebiscite or referendum and so invaded this territory on 12–13 December 1961. When the UN Security Council met at the request of Portugal, India, supported by Liberia, asserted that its armed action was justified because Portugal had no sovereign right over non-self-governing territories in Asia, its occupation of those territories was illegal, and furthermore 'the people of Goa are as much Indians as people of any other part of India'.[39] This view was rejected by some members of the Security Council, namely the US, the UK, France, Turkey, and China, who all put forward various arguments mainly related to the illegal use of force (but the US also mentioned, in passing, the principle of self-determination).[40] Two other States, namely Chile and Ecuador, also criticised the stand taken by India but explicitly referred to self-determination. Thus, the Chilean delegate pointed out the following:

In the present case, we think the parties should take into consideration the wishes of the inhabitants of Goa, Damao and Din. There is no doubt whatsoever that the Portuguese possessions in India are historical vestiges of a colonial past . . . Neither historical possessions [by Portugal] nor violent possessions [by India] should prevail, but the freely expressed wishes of the inhabitants of the disputed territories.[41]

The United Arab Republic (as it then was) and Ceylon also relied on self-determination but their conclusion was different to that of Chile and Ecuador. According to them, since the people of the enclaves had not been allowed by Portugal to exercise their right to self-determination, India's resort to force did not amount to an act of aggression.[42]

The formal outcome of this situation is well known. A draft resolution submitted by France, Turkey, the UK, and the US, which, among other things, referred in its preamble to the principle of self-determination as laid down in Article 1(2) of the UN Charter, was not adopted because of a negative vote cast by the USSR.[43] The Indian annexation of the three Portuguese enclaves, although briefly challenged in the Security Council, was thus endorsed *de facto* by the world community, without the slightest regard being paid to the wishes of the population concerned.

---

[39] SCOR, 987th Meeting, para. 46; 988th Meeting, para. 77. As for the position of Liberia, see SCOR, 987th Meeting, paras. 93–5.

[40] The US stated among other things: 'The U.S. stand on the colonial question is that we wholeheartedly believe in progress, in self-government and in self-determination for colonial peoples' (SCOR, 988th Meeting, para. 90).

[41] SCOR, 988th Meeting, para. 30.

[42] SCOR, 987th Meeting, para. 125.   [43] See UN Ybk, 1961, 131.

Let us now turn to the question of West Irian (West New Guinea).[44]

In 1954 Indonesia, which had achieved independence in 1949, asked the UN General Assembly to discuss the question of the status of the territory. According to Indonesia, West Irian had always been an integral part of Indonesia, and must therefore be returned to this State. The Netherlands, supported by other Western countries (Australia, Belgium, Colombia, France, and New Zealand) contended that the Dutch administration of West Irian constituted a peaceful attempt to create conditions for the self-determination of the population; in its view, the interests of the non-self-governing people concerned should prevail above all else.[45] Other States, including Brazil, El Salvador, Pakistan, Peru, and Uruguay, after voicing their opposition to colonialism in all its forms, considered that the General Assembly should adopt a resolution stressing the importance, not of bilateral negotiations between the two States concerned but rather of the attainment of self-determination by the people of West Irian.[46] However, by reason of the lack of agreement no resolution was adopted. In subsequent years the parties reiterated their positions, The Netherlands insisting that the question of sovereignty over the territory was to be ultimately resolved by the inhabitants themselves and Indonesia seeking instead a negotiated settlement between the two States.[47]

---

[44] On this question, see in particular Emerson, *Self-Determination Revisited*, 53–62; H. von Mangoldt, 'Die West-Irian Frage und das Selbstbestimmungsrecht der Völker', 313 *Zeit.*, 1971, 197–245; Rigo Sureda, *The Evolution of the Right of Self-Determination*, 143–51; Blay, 'Self-Determination versus Territorial Integrity', 450–2, as well as the writings by T.M. Franck and M. Pomerance quoted below (notes 58 and 59).

[45] UN Ybk, 1954, 57–8.

[46] *Ibid.*, 58.

[47] See UN Ybk, 1955, 61–2; UN Ybk, 1956, 125–7; UN Ybk, 1957, 76–9. The position of the two parties was clearly restated in 1957. As is recorded in the UN Ybk, 1957 (at 77), the Indonesian stand was as follows: 'Instead of the United Nations being allowed to serve as an instrument for reconciling the differences between the two States, numerous pretexts were being invoked to prevent a peaceful settlement, notably the principle of "self-determination". The Indonesian representative found it curious that certain powers which had proclaimed their adherence to the principle of reunification of divided States were conducting a movement exactly in reverse of that principle with respect to West Irian. Indonesia was fighting against the amputation of West Irian from the rest of Indonesia and for the principle of reunification and national unity. Any thought of splitting Indonesia into several smaller States was illusory. If Indonesia were to disintegrate and if the present democratic character of the State were to come to an end and be replaced by a different political system, it would not be a development designed to increase the stability or ensure the peace and security of South-East Asia.'
The Dutch stand was as follows (*ibid.*, 77–8): 'The representative of the Netherlands summed up the basic position of his Government as follows: (1) The Netherlands, in

The situation remained as stated until 1961, when the question was once again brought before the General Assembly. In this forum the parties underlined their positions: The Netherlands insisted on the principle of self-determination and Indonesia on the principle of negotiation between the two States. It should be noted, in this respect, that the Dutch proposal to consult the population concerned offered a wide range of options: independence, integration into Indonesia, association with the other part of New Guinea or other islands in the Pacific region.[48] Western States sided with The Netherlands while Indonesia mustered the support of socialist and developing countries. However, the basic disagreement existing among States once again made it impossible for a resolution to be adopted.[49]

Subsequently, an agreement was reached by the two States on 15 August 1962; under this agreement The Netherlands would transfer the administration of the territory to a United Nations Temporary Executive Authority (UNTEA), established by, and under the jurisdiction of, the Secretary-General, who would appoint a UN Administrator to lead it. The Administrator would have the discretion to transfer all or part of the administration of the territory to Indonesia at any time after 1 May 1963. The inhabitants of West Irian were to exercise their right of self-

accordance with Chapter XI of the United Nations Charter, was responsible for the administration of Netherlands New Guinea and was fulfilling its obligations under Article 73. (2) If the Netherlands were to agree to transfer the territory to Indonesia without first ascertaining the wishes of the inhabitants, it would be forsaking its duty to them and to the United Nations. (3) The Netherlands had solemnly promised the territory's inhabitants that they would be granted the opportunity to decide their own political future as soon as they were able to express their will on this. (4) In the absence of such a decision, the Netherlands could not and would not comply with any Indonesian demands for the annexation of the territory. Nor would it enter into any negotiations about its future status.... The Netherlands representative further stated that Indonesia was not really advocating negotiations with the Netherlands so as to reach a solution by common consent which would take the wishes of the territory's inhabitants into account. On the contrary, it was urging the General Assembly to advocate negotiations on the basis of two assumptions: (1) that Netherlands New Guinea was legally part of Indonesia and illegally occupied by the Netherlands, and (2) that the territory should be transferred to Indonesia without its population being previously consulted.

The Netherlands, he added, was willing to have the first assumption tested by the International Court of Justice. The second assumption, he thought, was a denial of the right of self-determination and thus contrary to the Charter.'

[48] See UN Doc. A/4954, of 4 November 1961 (letter from the Dutch representative to the President of the UN General Assembly).

[49] UN Ybk, 1961, 51–7.

determination before the end of 1969 and to decide whether they wished to remain with Indonesia or to sever their ties with it.[50] As far as the procedure for establishing the wishes of the inhabitants was concerned, the agreement provided that the act of self-determination was to be held 'in accordance with international practice' and with the participation of 'all adults, male and female, not foreign nationals'. The agreement also referred to the Indonesian system of *musjawarah*, a traditional method of consultation consisting in reaching 'a decision based on discussion, under-standing and knowledge of a problem';[51] however, resort to this system was only provided for with respect to the preliminary issue of the 'procedures and appropriate methods' to be followed in the 'act of self-determination'. The General Assembly approved the treaty by virtue of Resolution 1752(XVII) of 21 September 1962. Control of the territory was eventually handed over to Indonesia after 1 May 1963. In 1969 an 'act of free choice' was held, in accordance with GA Resolution 1752(XVII); the population opted for Indonesia and the General Assembly took note of this choice in its Resolution 2504(XXIV) of 19 November 1969.

In spite of this 'act of free choice', the integration of West Irian into Indonesia amounted to a substantial denial of self-determination. First, the choice provided for in the bilateral agreement of 1962 was limited to 'whether they wished to remain with Indonesia' and 'whether they wished to sever their ties with Indonesia'. No reference was made to the possible alternatives in case the vote was in favour of leaving Indonesia.[52] Second, the criteria for establishing whether a territory ceased to be non-self-governing, listed in GA Resolutions 742(VIII) and 1541(XV) were not met by the bilateral agreement of 1962, as was pointed out by Rigo Sureda;[53] consequently, 'the attitude taken by the General Assembly can be assumed to mean that West Irian was regarded as an "integral part" of Indonesia and, therefore, that there was no need for it to go through the process indicated by the General Assembly to achieve self-determination'.[54] Third, the method of consultation was that of the *musjawarah* system, which undoubtedly did not meet the requirements set forth by the General Assembly. Fourth, no real and direct consultation of the population was made; the 'consultation' was indirect, in that Regional Councils (enlarged by three classes of representatives: regional, organizational, and tribal)

---

[50] UN Ybk, 1962, 124–7.
[51] See below, note 55.
[52] Cf. Rigo Sureda, *The Evolution of the Right of Self-Determination*, 232.
[53] *Ibid.*, 151.   [54] *Ibid.*, 151.

were called upon to decide which of the options to accept.[55] Fifth, by reason of the reduction of UN personnel (due to budget cuts by The Netherlands and Indonesia and to the inability of the Indonesian authorities to provide the UN mission with adequate housing in the capital city of West Irian), the UN staff were unable properly to supervise the elections for the consultative assemblies.[56] Sixth, the Indonesian authorities put strong pressure on the population of West Irian in order to secure support for integration into Indonesia.[57]

---

[55] The Indonesian authorities refused to accept the suggestions for consultation made by the UN Representative. According to his report, in November 1968, at a meeting with Indonesian authorities, 'I pointed out that, in my capacity as United Nations Representative, I could suggest no other method for this delicate political exercise than the democratic, orthodox and universally accepted method of "one man, one vote". However, while maintaining firmly my conviction that the people of West Irian might be given as ample and as complete an opportunity as possible to express their opinion, I recognized that the geographical and human realities in the territory required the application of a realistic criterion. I therefore suggested that the system of "one man, one vote"' should be used in the urban areas, where the communications and transportation, the comparatively advanced cultural level of the population and the availability of adequate administrative facilities made it possible, and that this might be complemented by collective consultations in the less accessible and less advanced areas of the interior. A mixed system of that type would have the merit of being the best possible in the circumstances and would enable the Indonesian Government and the United Nations to state that the orthodox and perfect method of 'one man, one vote' had been used in the act of free choice to the maximum extent compatible with reality. I added that the staff of my mission would be ready to co-operate in the preparations for the exercise and in the registration of the voters and the tabulation of the results. The modalities of the collective consultations in the areas where that system would be applied would have to be the subject of future discussions' (*Report of the [UN] Secretary-General Concerning the Act of Self-Determination in West Irian*, 24 General Assembly, Agenda Item 98, UN Doc. A/7723, 6 November 1969, 29 (para. 82).

The response of the Indonesian government, given in February 1969, was that its 'intention was to consult the representative councils in order to obtain their approval for implementing the act of free choice through the eight representative councils, which would be enlarged to form consultative assemblies where each member would represent approximately 750 inhabitants. The consultative assemblies would not reach a decision through voting but through *musjawarah* which, as explained at that meeting, consisted in reaching a "decision based on discussion, understanding and knowledge of a problem".

This meant that the Government still intended to apply the consultation (*musjawarah*) method of decision through representatives of the people but, in contradistinction to the ideas expressed on 1 October . . . it planned to carry out the act of free choice not through one body of 200 representatives but consecutively through eight consultative assemblies, comprising some 1,025 representatives' (*ibid.*, 30, paras 84–5).

[56] *Ibid.*, 312.

[57] Cf. *Report of the [UN] Secretary-General Regarding the Act of Self-Determination in West Irian*, 54–6, 70. As the UN Representatives pointed out: 'I regret to have to express my reservation regarding the implementation of article XXII of the Agreement, relating to "the rights, including the rights of free speech, freedom of movement and of assembly,

The critical comments that have been made concerning this pseudo-choice – which, as shown above, actually proved to be a charade and a substantive betrayal of the principle of self-determination – by such authors as Pomerance[58] and Franck[59] are fully justified, as are the views put forth by the Dutch delegate to the General Assembly in 1962,[60] which were rightly referred to by Franck as 'an eloquent epitaph to self-determination'.[61]

Three outstanding situations

Three situations still await a proper solution based on respect for the will of the population concerned: Western Sahara, Gibraltar, and the Falklands/Malvinas. Since the first two will be discussed at some length in Chapter 9, only the third case will be briefly dealt with here. Nevertheless, in so doing, reference will be made, if somewhat briefly, to the Gibraltar question, with which that of the Falklands/Malvinas has some common elements.[62]

It is indeed interesting at the outset to note these common features. Both the Falklands/Malvinas and Gibraltar have been under British control for more than 150 years, the former since 1833, as a result of military occupation, and the latter since 1713, as a result of a treaty of cession with Spain subsequent to its occupation in 1704 by the United Kingdom. Both

of the inhabitants of the area". In spite of my constant efforts, this important provision was not fully implemented and the Administration exercised at all times a tight political control over the population' (ibid., 70, para. 251).

58 M. Pomerance, 'Methods of Self-Determination and the Argument of "Primitiveness"', 12 CYIL, 1974, 65; Pomerance, Self-Determination in Law and Practice, 26, 32–5.

59 T. M. Franck, Nation against Nation, New York and Oxford 1985, 76–81.

60 He stated the following: 'Of what happened . . . I will say only this: that the Netherlands Government regrets that in this instance no effective remedy was to be found against the use of force, contrary to the obligations of the States under the Charter of the United Nations. As a result, the Netherlands was faced with the choice between fighting in self-defense or resigning itself to transfer of the territory to Indonesia without a previous expression of the will of the population. War would have meant exposing the Papuans and their country to death and destruction and many Dutchmen and Indonesians to the horrors of combat – without even providing a sensible solution to the problem. And so, with a heavy heart, the Netherlands Government decided to agree to the transfer of the territory to Indonesia on the best conditions obtainable for the Papuan population' (GAOR, XVII, 1127th Pl. Mtg., 21 September 1961, 51).

61 Ibid., 81.

62 On the question of Gibraltar and Falklands/Malvinas, see in particular Blay, 'Self-Determination v. Territorial Integrity', 463–5 and the bibliography quoted there. See also M. Iovane, 'Le Falkland/Malvinas: autodeterminazione o colonizzazione?', in N. Ronzitti (ed.), La questione delle Falkland/Malvinas nel diritto internazionale, Milan 1984, 85–122; R. Dolzer, 'Falkland Islands (Malvinas)', 12 Encyclopedia, 1990, 103–8.

are a considerable geographical distance from the administering country. Furthermore, the inhabitants of both the Falklands/Malvinas and Gibraltar are essentially of 'colonial' (i.e. British) stock (although the present inhabitants of Gibraltar are of a less homogeneous origin, since many of them are also descended from Spaniards or other groups who have moved to Gibraltar over the years). Finally, in both cases the 'contiguous' country – Argentina in the case of the Falklands/Malvinas, Spain in the case of Gibraltar – claims a reversionary title to sovereignty over the territory in question.

As is well known, an armed conflict broke out in the Falklands/Malvinas in 1982, when Argentina attempted to take the islands by force. At the end of the war, Britain, having won a decisive victory, reaffirmed her right to the islands. The self-determination issue, however, remains unresolved. Argentina's claims – based on the reversion of territorial sovereignty, contiguity, and anti-colonialism – remain in fundamental opposition to Britain's claim to title resulting from conquest, the continuing display of territorial sovereignty, and self-determination.[63]

In general, the UN's failures in the Falklands/Malvinas, Gibraltar, and the Western Sahara, and in the other situations still pending, are rooted more in the intricacies of each situation than in the principle of self-determination itself. In some cases the composition of the population and the existence of conflicting claims of sovereign States make the actual implementation of self-determination impracticable. However, the existence of the right demands that those in power take into account the wishes or the interests of the territory's population when a solution is finally worked out. Therefore, despite the present impracticability of the principle in question, it retains a potential role. In other cases, the intractability of the problem is rooted in overriding economic and strategic interests.

However, regardless of the UN's failures – stemming, to some extent, from the non-existence of a UN enforcement mechanism – one point

---

[63] For a reasoned statement on the official British stand on the question of the Falklands/Malvinas and the role of self-determination, see 53 BYIL, 1982, 367 ff. See also 61 BYIL, 1990, 507. It should be noted that in 1991, when discussing in the UN Human Rights Committee the 3rd British Periodic Report on the implementation of the UN Covenant on Civil and Political Rights, the British delegate pointed out the following: '[T]he people of the Falkland Islands expressed their views in regular elections and . . . there was no doubt that their wish was to remain under British sovereignty. Since the 1990 agreement between the United Kingdom and Argentina, the two Governments had been able to agree on a number of issues relating to activities in the Islands and in the South Atlantic region in general' (*Report of the Human Rights Committee to the G.A.*, 1991, UN Doc. A/46/40, para. 366).

needs to be emphasized: in each case the UN has pursued the most logical and realistic course of action. The UN must be credited with promoting *negotiations* between the States claiming title to the Falklands/Malvinas and Gibraltar. Its insistence that all negotiations fully recognize the wishes and interests of the populations concerned is to be welcomed. In addition, it seems difficult to criticize the UN's hesitancy to resolve outstanding differences by merely resorting to the traditional means of implementing self-determination (referendums and plebiscites) in the cases of the Falklands/Malvinas and Gibraltar. Since the British – rightly or wrongly – have for a long time maintained policies designed to keep the two territories in the hands of British people and to exclude Argentinians and Spaniards respectively, perhaps one should not reject out of hand the argument that in the Falklands/Malvinas and Gibraltar cases one ought in principle to take account of the interests and concerns of the 'contiguous' State as well.

Be that as it may, by reaffirming the principle of self-determination as the *basic standard of conduct* while at the same time calling for *direct negotiations* between all parties concerned, the UN has assumed an active and important role in the field of self-determination (see, on this matter, my comments in Chapter 8).

THE PRONOUNCEMENTS OF THE INTERNATIONAL COURT OF JUSTICE

The legal regulation of the self-determination of colonial peoples was authoritatively stated by the ICJ, first in its Advisory Opinion on *Namibia*,[64] of 1971 and then in the Advisory Opinion on *Western Sahara*, of 1975. In the latter Opinion the Court actually placed an interpretation on the existing standards that broadened the purport and impact of self-determination. After mentioning the GA Resolution 1514(XV), the Court pointed out that:

The above provisions, in particular paragraph 2 [defining self-determination], thus confirm and emphasize that the application of the right of self-determination requires a free and genuine expression of the will of the peoples concerned.[65]

The Court then went on to quote two other resolutions of the General Assembly, namely Resolution 1541 (XV), that has been discussed above and the 1970 Declaration on Friendly Relations (Resolution 2625(XXV)). It then concluded as follows:

[64] See above, p. 72 note 12.   [65] ICJ, Reports 1975, 32, para. 55.

The validity of the principle of self-determination, defined as the need to pay regard to the freely expressed will of the peoples, is not affected by the fact that in certain cases the General Assembly has dispensed with the requirement of consulting the inhabitants of a given territory. Those instances were based either on the consideration that a certain population did not constitute a 'people' entitled to self-determination or on the conviction that a consultation was totally unnecessary, in view of special circumstances.[66]

By this pronouncement the Court has significantly and definitively clarified this matter. It is apparent from the GA resolutions in question and from the statements and behaviour of States that at least in the case of the achievement of political independence by a colonial country, it was not formally required by the standards evolved in the 1960s that the relevant people should freely express its will. This requirement is instead set out in Resolution 1541 with regard to peoples that choose association or integration with an independent State. The Court held, instead, that self-determination always entails 'the need to pay regard to the freely expressed will of peoples' but that *exceptionally* this requirement can be and has been dispensed with in two instances (when one is not faced with a 'people' proper, and when 'special circumstances' make a plebiscite or referendum unnecessary). Aside from the fact that the Court does not specify what it means by 'people' or by 'special circumstances', the fact remains that its view of the way self-determination should be applied with regard to colonial peoples favours a liberal interpretation of the legal regulation of the matter, as it evolved in the 1960s and was to a large extent borne out by UN practice.

Having made this point, it is necessary to add that the Court's interpretation is more in keeping with the general spirit and thrust of the principle of self-determination than the standards on the self-determination of colonial peoples that evolved in the 1960s. Although colonialism has now almost disappeared and the question may therefore seem to have become to a large extent immaterial, it can be said that the ICJ's pronouncements set out the correct view of the existing legal regulation of the right of colonial peoples to self-determination.[67]

---

[66] *Ibid.*, 33, para. 59.

[67] A less clear stand was taken by the Chamber of the ICJ in the *Frontier Dispute*. After emphasizing the role of *uti possidetis* as a general rule of international law, the Chamber went on to state the following: 'At first sight this principle conflicts outright with another one, the right of peoples to self-determination. In fact, however, the maintenance of the territorial status quo in Africa is often seen as the wisest course to preserve what has been achieved by peoples who have struggled for their independence, and to avoid a

The self-determination of peoples subjected to foreign domination or occupation

State practice and United Nations resolutions make it clear that external self-determination is a right belonging not only to colonial peoples but also to peoples subject to foreign occupation. This notion, which had already been put forward, albeit in rather vague and ambiguous terms, in the 1960 UN Declaration on the Independence of Colonial Peoples, and then implicitly upheld in Article 1 common to the two UN Covenants on Human Rights of 1966 (see above, Chapter 3), was spelled out in 1970, in the UN Declaration on Friendly Relations. This Declaration refers to two situations which give rise to the right to self-determination: colonialism and the 'subjection of peoples to alien subjugation, domination and exploitation'. Rather than presenting colonialism as an umbrella concept embracing all situations giving rise to the right of self-determination – as argued by many developing and socialist States – the Declaration makes it clear that 'alien subjugation, domination and exploitation', may exist outside a colonial system.[68] The broader ambit of the concept has now

disruption which would deprive the continent of the gains achieved by much sacrifice. The essential requirement of stability in order to survive, to develop and gradually to consolidate their independence in all fields, has induced African States judiciously to consent to the respecting of colonial frontiers, and to take account of it in the interpretation of the principle of self-determination of peoples' (ICJ, Reports 1986, 567, para. 25). It is submitted that it is difficult to see how, in the opinion of the Court, the principle of territorial integrity can be *reconciled* with that of self-determination. The Chamber has made a bold statement that is supported only by compelling political reasons.

68 Proposals submitted to the drafting Committee by the United States and the United Kingdom in 1966 and 1967 respectively, advanced the Western viewpoint (for the US proposal, see UN Doc. A/AC.125/L.32; for the British proposal, see A/AC.125/L.44, 8–9). Specifically, both proposals suggested that, as far as peoples not living in sovereign States were concerned, three classes of peoples ought to have a right to external self-determination: peoples living in colonies or other non-self-governing territories; peoples living in trust territories; and peoples living in 'a zone of occupation ensuing upon the termination of military hostilities'. Not surprisingly, a number of countries took exception to the third category.

For example, Poland attacked the reference to zones of military occupation on the ground that it 'appeared to be aimed at directing the Committee's attention away from the main elements involved in the formulation of the principle under discussion' (see A/AC.125/SR.68, 14). Yugoslavia, sharing the Polish view, added that 'it was strange to see . . . a reference to zones of military occupation, a question which had nothing to do with the subject under discussion' (see A/AC.125/SR.69, 6). In response to these criticisms, the British delegate stated that he was prepared to modify his proposal (see A/AC.125/SR.105, 55). He did not insist upon the inclusion of the third category of peoples, even though the Dutch delegate took up the cause, eloquently pointing out that people living in occupied zones after the end of hostilities 'must certainly be regarded as

been widely accepted not only by individual groupings of States, but by the world community at large; in this connection, it may suffice to quote statements by individual countries such as the US[69] and Brazil,[70] as well as the recent, authoritative pronouncement of the UN International Law Commission.[71]

having a territory and characteristics distinct from those of the occupying Power, just as a colony is distinct from the State administering it' (see A/AC.125/SR.107, 84). The Dutch delegate further noted that external self-determination might also apply where 'a Territory which had freely associated with the former administering Power had exercised its right of self-determination, although that right had not necessarily been used for the last time. As Principle VII of General Assembly Resolution 1541(XV) stated, peoples of a Territory associated with an independent State retained the freedom to modify the status of that Territory by democratic means and constitutional processes' (*ibid.*).

By and large, the Western States did not press their point, their primary goal being to restrict the scope of the proposals put forth by the developing and socialist countries. Undoubtedly troublesome for the Western States was a proposal advanced by a group of non-aligned countries (Algeria, Burma, the Cameroons, Ghana, India, Kenya, Nigeria, Syria, United Arab Republic, and Yugoslavia) which suggested that colonialism was an umbrella concept embracing all forms of the denial of self-determination. Specifically, the proposal stated that 'the subjection of peoples to alien subjugation, domination and exploitation, *as well as any other forms of colonialism*, constitutes a violation of the equal rights and self-determination of peoples' (see A/AC.125/L.31). A subsequent draft submitted by some of the members of the non-aligned group (see A/AC.125/L.48, 4), and a proposal submitted by Czechoslovakia, Poland, Romania (see A/AC.125/L.48, 4), and the USSR (see A/AC.125/L.74) adopted this approach, invoking the phrase 'any other forms of colonialism'.

[69] In 1974 the US delegate to the UN Commission on Human Rights stated that 'the United Nations resolutions directed against colonialism and alien domination were not intended to apply only to overseas colonies and South Africa. Indeed, alien domination was no more acceptable, no more commensurate with the principle of self-determination and no less a violation of the United Nations Charter when it was not based on difference in the colour of the dominator and the dominated' (US Digest 1974, 53).

[70] Brazil has been chosen because this is one of the few developing countries where a digest of national practice in international law is available. It is apparent from this digest that Brazilian delegates have stated on a number of occasions, since 1952, that self-determination does not *only* cover colonial countries, but has a much broader purport. See *Repertório (Período 1941–1960)*, 49, 54–5 and *Repertório (Período 1961–1981)*, 90 ('O exercício do direito de autodeterminaço é, em nosso entender, um conceito amplo que transcende as questes do colonialismo. É um direito que todos os povos deveriam ser capazes de exercer'), 92–3.

[71] Interestingly, when in 1988 the International Law Commission discussed the provision on colonialism of the 'Draft Code of Crimes against the Peace and Security of Mankind', all members of the Commission agreed that self-determination did not only apply to colonial peoples but also to 'peoples under alien subjugation. According to the Report of the ILC to the General Assembly, 'The principle of self-determination, proclaimed in the Charter of the United Nations as a universal principle, had been

The problem, however, arises of ascertaining what is meant by 'alien subjugation, domination and exploitation'. The complexity of this issue is highlighted by reference to the body of State practice and international documents on the subject.[72]

The definition of 'alien domination' cannot be ascertained without first taking into account the practice of the United Nations and its Member States in the years following the adoption of the Declaration. This leads to two preliminary points.

First, there is a striking divergence between the statements made by Third World and socialist States in connection with resolutions advocating a broad definition of self-determination and the actual behaviour of these States. In actual practice, these States adopted a much narrower view of self-determination, one motivated by *Realpolitik* and a concern for territorial integrity.

The second point, which follows from the first, is that the Third World and socialist countries – the States that as a rule espouse an expansive right to self-determination in the General Assembly – in fact advocated a limited right to self-determination at two important junctures in the evolution of the right of self-determination from political principle into legal rules: firstly, and most notably, in 1955–6, during the drafting of Article 1 of the 1966 UN Covenants on Human Rights and secondly, in 1974–7, during the drafting of Article 1(4) of the first 1977 Geneva Additional Protocol to the four 1949 Geneva Conventions on War Victims. As the UN Covenants have already been dealt with (see above, Chapter 3) the discussion will now primarily focus on the Geneva Protocol.

Article 1 of the First 1977 Geneva Protocol supports the thesis that the right to external self-determination is considered to arise when a State dominates the people of a foreign territory using military means. Although the language employed is certainly broad enough to encompass 'foreign domination,' the Article does not contain an express reference to that form of the denial of self-determination. Perhaps even more illuminating is an exchange that took place in the course of the drafting of the 1977 Geneva

applied mainly in eradicating colonialism, but there were other cases in which it had been and could and should be used. By not tying it exclusively to colonial contexts, it would be applied much more widely. In that connection, all members of the Commission believed that the principle of self-determination was of universal application' (*Yearbook* ILC, 1988, vol. II, Part II, 64 (para. 266)).

72 On this issue, see, among others, L. Rohr, 'El principio de la auto-determinación de los pueblos en el derecho internacional', 1 *Anuario de derecho internacional publico*, 1981 (Buenos Aires), 61–2.

Protocol. The inclusion of the phrase 'alien domination' in Article 1(4) (on wars of national liberation as international armed conflicts) was replaced, at the instigation of the Latin American States, by the more restrictive 'alien occupation'.[73]

It should be added that in the United Nations a minority of States – Mexico, Afghanistan, Iraq, and Pakistan – considered economic exploitation of a foreign State (chiefly in the form of 'neo-colonialism') a breach of self-determination.[74] However, the vast majority of States rejected all attempts to broaden the class of peoples entitled to external self-determination to include those suffering from economic exploitation. A number of important General Assembly resolutions on economic matters which fail to equate neo-colonialism with the denial of the right to self-determination bear this out. For example, neither Article 32 of the Charter of Economic Rights and Duties of States[75] nor Resolution 38/197[76] on the economic measures used as a means of political and economic coercion against developing countries, incorporates the right of self-determination into its condemnation of economic interference. Recent General Assembly resolutions on self-determination which characterize 'acts or threats of foreign military intervention and occupation' and 'foreign military intervention, aggression and occupation' as egregious infringements of the right of self-determination also suggest that, in practice, States have agreed to limit the concept of 'foreign domination' to *intervention by use of force* and *military occupation*.[77]

Let us now move to specific situations which the United Nations, as well as individual States, treated as cases falling within the purview of self-determination.

It is fitting to start with State practice proper. In this connection, some caveats must be entered. Firstly, it is often difficult to investigate such practice because only in a few Western countries can one find legal journals or digests that record national practice in international relations. It follows that any analysis of this practice is perforce highly selective.

---

[73] See G. Abi-Saab, 'Wars of National Liberation in the Geneva Conventions and Protocols', 165 HR, 1979-IV, 395.

[74] H. Gros Espiell, *The Right to Self-Determination – Implementation of U.N. Resolutions*, UN Doc. E/CN.4/Sub.2/405/Rev.1, 1980, 6 ff., notes 18, 19, 20, 21.

[75] 'No State may use or encourage the use of economic, political or any other type of measures to coerce another State in order to obtain from it the subordination of the exercise of its sovereign rights' UN GA Res. 3281(XXIX), UN Ybk, 1974, 402.

[76] For the text of this resolution, see UN Ybk, 1983, 412 ff.

[77] See, e.g., UN GA Res. 38/16, of 22 November 1983, UN Ybk, 1983, 828 ff. and GA Res. 41/100, of 4 December 1986, UN Ybk, 1986, 694.

Secondly, even when evidence of State practice can be found, it primarily consists of declarations and statements made by national delegates in United Nations fora. In other words, this practice normally does not consist of actual State behaviour in international dealings, but rather of declarations setting out the State's views on the matter.

To the extent that this practice is available, it appears that it has covered such situations as Afghanistan,[78] Kampuchea (Cambodia),[79] the Arab territories occupied by Israel,[80] the Baltic States,[81] Grenada,[82] East Timor,[83] and Kuwait;[84] to them one should add Namibia,[85] although the

[78] For British practice, see BYIL, 1981, 387; 1983, 402; 1984, 431 ff.; 1985, 401; 1986, 514; 1987, 522; 1988, 443, 444. For Dutch practice, see NYIL, 1984, 274. For French practice, see AFDI, 1982, 1086; 1983, 106; 1988, 962. For the practice of the Federal Republic of Germany, see *Zeit.*, 1982, 512 ff.; 1983, 347; 1984, 501; 1985, 721; 1988, 280. See also the statements made in the General Assembly's Third Committee by the representatives of the US in 1983 (A/C.3/38/SR.16, 21, para. 82) of Ireland in 1984 (speaking on behalf of the EEC Member States, A/C.3/39//SR.34, 12 para. 50), and, in 1988, of Australia (A/C.3/43/SR.7, 7, para. 24), China (*ibid.*, 9, para. 24), FRG (*ibid.*, 17, para. 77), Ireland (*ibid.*, SR.10, 7, para. 23), Turkey (*ibid.*, SR.13, 5, para. 12).

[79] For British practice, see BYIL, 1980, 375; 1981, 388; 1984, 432 ff.; 1988, 443. For the practice of the Federal Republic of Germany, see *Zeit.*, 1981, 595; 1983, 346; 1984, 505; 1988, 281. For Australian practice, see 8 AYIL, 1983, 274–6. See also the statements referred to in the last paragraph of note 95 on p. 97 below.

[80] See the practice mentioned below, pp. 235–42.

[81] For British practice, see BYIL, 1980, 376; 1983, 405; 1988, 444, 447; 1990, 507, 508. For the practice of the Federal Republic of Germany, see *Zeit.*, 1982, 514; 1985, 722. For Australian practice, see 7 AYIL, 1981, 432; 8 AYIL, 1983, 282. For statements of the US in the United Nations, see A/C.3/37/SR.13, 21-2, paras. 89–92 (1982); A/C.3/38/SR.16, 20, para. 80 (1983); A/C.3/43/SR.23, 23, para. 109 (1988). It should also be mentioned that in 1989 President Mitterand and Chancellor Kohl issued a joint statement reaffirming the right of the Baltic states to self-determination but suggesting that this right should be implemented gradually and by means of diplomatic negotiations (see below, p. 264).

[82] For Dutch practice, see NYIL, 1985, 337 ('The people of Grenada must be able to exercise their fundamental right of self-determination free from outside interference. We express the hope that this day will come soon.'). For the practice of the Federal Republic of Germany, see *Zeit.*, 1985, 720 ff. (at 721 there is an important statement pointing to the differences existing, in the opinion of the FRG, between the situation in Afghanistan and that in Grenada).

[83] For British practice, see BYIL, 1980, 375 ff.; 1983, 405; 1984, 431. For Dutch practice, see NYIL, 1978, 195. For Belgian practice, see RBDI, 1977, 575. For French practice, see AFDI, 1987, 994 ff.

[84] See, *inter alia*, the statement made on 8 October 1990 by the Italian Presidency of the Twelve Member States of the European Community, in the IIIrd Committee of the UN General Assembly (Doc. 90/335, 6 *EPC Bul.* 1990, 369–70).

[85] As is well known, Namibia (former South West Africa) was awarded to South Africa as a mandated territory after the First World War. In 1946, following the dissolution of the League of Nations, the United Nations decided to place Namibia under the trusteeship

illegal occupation of that territory by South Africa after 1967 did not result from an armed invasion.

As for United Nations practice, it should be recalled that the major instances of military occupation of foreign territories that occurred in recent years, and on which the UN General Assembly has adopted resolutions, include the following: the Soviet invasion of Hungary in 1956, the Chinese occupation of Tibet in 1959,[86] the Israeli occupation of the

system and rejected South Africa's proposals to incorporate the territory into South Africa. In the face of South Africa's refusal to comply, various pronouncements of the International Court of Justice were requested (see R. Zacklin, 'The Problem of Namibia in International Law', 171 HR, 1981-II, 248–307). Then, on 27 October 1966, by Res. 2145(XXI), the UN General Assembly after declaring that Res. 1514(XV) was 'fully applicable' to the people of Namibia, which had therefore 'the inalienable right to self-determination, freedom and independence in accordance with the Charter of the United Nations', decided that the South African mandate was terminated and Namibia came 'under the direct responsibility of the United Nations' (UN Ybk, 1966, 606). South Africa, however, did not comply with this decision, and continued to exercise its authority in Namibia. Thus, the United Nations, after setting up a 'UN Council for Namibia' (Res. 2248/S-V, of 19 May 1967), started adopting a string of resolutions declaring that 'the *continued illegal occupation of Namibia* by South Africa [constituted] an act of aggression' and that 'the Namibian people must be enabled to attain *self-determination and independence* within a united Namibia' (see, e.g., GA Res. 32/9D, of 4 November 1977). The UN also decided to 'ensure the early independence of Namibia through free elections under the supervision and control of the United Nations' (SC Res. 435/1978 of 29 September 1978). Namibia's independence was declared on 21 March 1990.

See generally L. Ferrari Bravo, 'La questione dell'Africa Sud-occidentale', 14 *Diritto internazionale*, 1960, 34 ff.; J. Dugard, *The South West Africa/Namibia Dispute*, Berkeley and London 1974; L. Lucchini, 'La Namibie, une construction de l'ONU', 15 AF, 1969, 355–74; R. Barsotti, 'In tema di amministrazione diretta di territori non autonomi da parte dell'ONU: il caso della Namibia', 16 *Comunicazione e Studi*, 1980 (Milan), 53 ff.; R. Zacklin, 'The Problem of Namibia', 233 ff.; Shaw, *Title to Territory in Africa*, 105–10, 137–40; E. Schmidt-Jortzig, 'The Constitution of Namibia: an Example of a State Emerging under Close Supervision and World Scrutiny', 34 GYIL, 1991, 413–28.

[86] The question of Tibet was raised in 1959 as an issue of respect for human rights, and the GA adopted Res. 1353(XIV) along these lines (UN Ybk, 1959, 67–9). The item was not considered in 1960 because of the extreme pressure of work. On 20 December 1961 the GA adopted Res. 1723(XVI). In the preamble of this resolution, the GA stated that the 'events in Tibet [i.e. the Chinese occupation] violate the fundamental human rights and freedoms set out in the Charter of the UN and the Universal Declaration of Human Rights, including the principle of self-determination of peoples and nations'. In operative paragraph 2, the GA 'solemnly renewed . . . its call for the cessation of practices which deprive the Tibetan people of their fundamental rights and freedoms, including their right to self-determination'.

One may well doubt whether what happened in 1959 can be regarded as an instance of invasion and occupation of a foreign country. Indeed, it would seem that prior to 1959 Tibet had never been a State entity independent of China. In 1961, in the UN GA socialist countries asserted that Tibet had always been an integral part of China (UN

Arab territories in 1967, the Turkish occupation of Northern Cyprus – which began in 1974 and led firstly to a 1979 proclamation of a Turkish-Cypriot federated State and then to the proclamation of the Turkish Republic of Northern Cyprus in 1983, the Indonesian occupation of East Timor, followed by its annexation in 1975,[87] the 1979 Vietnamese invasion of Kampuchea, the 1979 Soviet invasion of Afghanistan, and the 1990 Iraqi invasion of Kuwait.[88] To these cases one can add that of Namibia, although, as stated above, this case presents unique features.[89]

In most of these cases, UN action was limited to the adoption of resolutions demanding that the right to self-determination be respected.[90] Most of the time the occupying States in question did not heed the UN appeals.[91] It should, however, be added that in some of these cases the UN called upon Member States to *refrain from recognizing*, that is *legitimizing*, the situation brought about by the denial of self-determination. This, in particular, holds true for the Arab territories occupied by Israel,

Ybk, 1961, 139), while the UK representative stated that 'his Government had in the past recognized Chinese suzerainty over Tibet only on condition that Tibet retained its autonomy' (*ibid.*). On the question of Tibet, see in particular P.K. Menon, 'The Right to Self-Determination – A Historical Appraisal', 53 *Revue de droit international et des sciences diplomatiques et politiques*, 1975, 274–9; Driessen, *A Concept of Nation in International Law*, 90–1. See also A. D. Hughes, 'Tibet', 12 *Encyclopedia*, 1990, 375–7. Possibly, the case at issue was more a case of the violation of human rights than a case of self-determination.

[87] I shall return to the matter in Chapter 9, where I shall deal with some particularly problematic issues.

[88] To these cases one might add the United States invasion of Grenada in 1983, followed by a short military occupation (after the US troops had withdrawn, in December 1983, elections were held and a pro-American government was elected to power). On the various facets of the case see J. H. H. Weiler, 'Armed Intervention in a Dichotomized World: The Case of Grenada', in A. Cassese (ed.), *The Current Legal Regulation of the Use of Force*, Dordrecht 1986, 241 ff. Self-determination was invoked in the Security Council, to attack the US intervention, by Mexico (SCOR, S/PV/2487, 6), Guyana (*ibid.*, 41), Bolivia (S/PV/2489, 29–39), Algeria (*ibid.*, 41), Syria (*ibid.*, 56), Cuba (*ibid.*, 61), and Venezuela (S/PV/2491, 58–60).

[89] See p. 94, note 85.

[90] On Afghanistan see, e.g., Res. 6/2 of 14 January 1980; 35/37 of 20 November 1980; 36/34 of 18 November 1981; and 37/37 of 29 November 1982. On Cambodia see, e.g., 34/22 of 14 November 1979; 33/6 of 21 October 1980; 37/6 of 28 October 1982; 45/3 of 15 October 1991; 46/18 of 20 November 1991. On the Arab Territories occupied by Israel, see 2649(XXV) of 30 November 1970; 2949(XXVII) of 8 December 1972; 33/28 of 7 November 1978; 34/44 of 23 November 1979; 34/70 of 6 December 1979; 37/123 F of 20 December 1982; 38/180 A to D of 19 December 1983; 41/162 A to C of 4 December 1986; 43/54 A to C of 6 December 1988; 45/83 of 13 December 1990.

[91] The Soviet Union did finally withdraw from Afghanistan in 1989. However, UN action was not the motivating force behind its decision. See generally D. Ross, 'Beyond the Soviet Invasion: Afghanistan and the Concept of Self-Determination', 48 *University of Toronto Faculty of Law Review*, 1990, 92–116. As for Kampuchea, see p. 94, note 79.

Kampuchea, and the Turkish-Cypriot State. As regards Israel, mention can be made of the various resolutions adopted by the Security Council or the General Assembly to the effect that all measures adopted by Israel for annexing Jerusalem[92] or establishing settlements in the Arab Territories[93] were null and void. In the case of Kampuchea, the United Nations refused to accept the credentials of the Government that had been established after the Vietnamese invasion,[94] whereas some States went so far as to 'derecognize' any Cambodian regime.[95] As for the case of the Turkish-Cypriot State, the Security Council called upon all States 'not to recognize

[92] See, e.g., SC Resolution 252 of 21 May 1968 and Resolution 478 of 20 August 1980.
[93] See e.g., SC Resolution 446 of 22 March 1979.
[94] See GAOR 34th Session, 1979, Pl. Mtg., 3rd and 4th. See also UN Doc. A/37/P2, 43; A/38/PV.34; A/39/PV.32.
[95] In 1981 the Australian representative to the UN Commission on Human Rights stated the following: 'As members of this Commission may be aware, on 14 February 1981 the Australian Government announced its decision to derecognize the Government of Democratic Kampuchea (the Pol Pot regime), with effect from that day. This means that Australia now does not recognize any regime in Kampuchea, including the Heng Samrin regime.

Mr. Chairman, Australia remains committed to a comprehensive political settlement in Kampuchea. We fully support the provisions of ASEAN sponsored General Assembly resolutions on Kampuchea, which aim for a complete withdrawal of foreign troops from Kampuchea and an act of genuine self-determination by the Khmer people. We have very recently spoken to the Secretary-General of the United Nations in support of efforts by the ASEAN and other friendly countries to have an international conference convened on the Kampuchean situation.

Mr. Chairman, my Delegation considers it appropriate that Kampuchea is being considered this year under the item of self-determination. Australia regarded the policies of Pol Pot and other leaders of his regime as abhorrent, and has condemned them repeatedly. The time has now arrived, however, to concentrate attention on the need to create the conditions necessary to see the emergence in Kampuchea of a government truly representative of the Khmer people. Australia very much hopes that its action on derecognizing the Pol Pot regime will contribute to that end.

These recent examples of foreign military intervention and occupation in Kampuchea and Afghanistan which result in the suppression of the right of self-determination, have added a new dimension to the debates on this subject. This dimension was apparent at the Commission on Human Rights last year but it was of particular importance in the consideration of the subject at the General Assembly. Resolution 35/35B – which was foreshadowed in the Sub-Commission's Resolution 26(XXXIII) – requested this Commission to give special attention to the violation of the right to self-determination and other human rights resulting from foreign military aggression, intervention or occupation. The General Assembly's resolution reaffirmed that the universal realization of the people to self-determination was a most fundamental condition for the preservation and promotion of human rights' (10 AYIL, 1987, 263–4).

See also 8 AYIL, 1983, 274–6, where various statements made in 1979 by Australian Ministers are reported.

any Cypriot State other than the Republic of Cyprus';[96] in the case of the Iraqi occupation of Kuwait, the Security Council 'decided that the annexation of Kuwait by Iraq under any form and whatever pretext [had] no legal validity, and [was] considered null and void' (Res. 662 of 9 August 1990).

Despite the importance of these 'sanctions', the fact remains that often the UN was unable to enforce self-determination (the case of Kampuchea is a notable exception).[97] The reasons behind the UN's failure are twofold. First, in all these cases, at least one of the permanent members of the Security Council was either directly involved in, or had a strong interest in the outcome of the conflict; this destroyed all hopes of effective multilateral action. Second, for practical reasons it proved difficult to enforce the resolutions that had been passed.

The successful UN response to Iraq's invasion of Kuwait, which was made possible because of the convergence of the positions of the US and the (then) Soviet Union, bears witness to the need for the full agreement of the 'Big Powers' so that the UN can make headway in this, as in many other areas. The same holds true for Kampuchea.

In sum, although the United Nations has failed to implement the right at issue in quite a few instances, this failure, being motivated by passing political circumstances, does not seem to be such as to call in question the very existence of the right of occupied peoples to self-determination.

It should be added that the rationale behind the view that alien occupation is not only contrary to the basic prohibition of the use of force, but is also in breach of the right to self-determination of the people living in the occupied territory, was clearly set out by the British delegate in 1983,

---

[96] See SC Resolutions 541 of 18 November 1983 (UN Ybk, 1983, 254) and 550 of 11 May 1984 (UN Ybk, 1984, 243–4). It should, however, be stressed that the SC did not make any express reference to self-determination.

[97] In Res. 34/22 of 14 November 1979, the UN General Assembly confined itself to calling for the withdrawal of all foreign troops from Kampuchea and proclaimed that 'the people of Kampuchea should be enabled to choose democratically their own government without any outside interference, subversion or coercion'. Subsequently, the General Assembly increasingly insisted on the implementation of self-determination through the holding of 'élections libres loyales et démocratiques, tenues sous sourveillance internationale': Res. 44/22 of 16 November 1989, Res. 45/3 of 15 October 1990, Res. 46/18 of 20 November 1991. See also the Security Council decision of 28 August 1990, Res. 668(1990) of 20 September 1990, Res. 717(1991) of 16 October 1991, Res. 718(1991) of 31 October 1991, Res. 745(1992) of 28 February 1992, Res. 66(1992) of 21 July 1992, Res. 783(1992) of 13 October 1992, Res. 792(1992) of 30 November 1992, Res. 810(1993) of 8 March 1993. It is well known that, in 1993 on the strength of these resolutions and the Paris Agreement of 23 October 1991, elections were held in Kampuchea under UN scrutiny.

in a statement he made in the 'Committee of the 24'. He pointed out that:

The right to self-determination, as propounded by the international community, offers many small and powerless peoples a moral and legal safeguard against being overwhelmed, assimilated or conquered by ambitious and unscrupulous neighbours.[98]

It is thus reasonable to conclude that the term 'alien domination' or 'subjugation' does not contemplate economic exploitation or ideological domination. Rather, 'alien subjugation, domination and exploitation' covers those situations in which any one Power *dominates* the people of *a foreign territory* by recourse to *force*. If this is correct, self-determination is violated whenever there is a military invasion or belligerent occupation of a foreign territory, except where the occupation – although unlawful – is of a minimal duration or is solely intended as a means of repelling, under Article 51 of the UN Charter, an armed attack initiated by the vanquished Power and consequently is not protracted. The right to external self-determination is thus, in a sense, the counterpart of the prohibition on the use of force in international relations. In many cases, the breach of external self-determination is simply an unlawful use of force looked at from the perspective of the victimized *people* rather than from that of the besieged sovereign State or territory.

Economic self-determination[99]

As the achievement of political independence by colonial countries soon turned out to be only one step towards real independence, the problem arose within the United Nations of the claimed right of newly independent States freely to dispose of their natural resources. Given the historical setting, the problem was chiefly raised as a question affecting *sovereign States* rather than peoples as such. Indeed, the debate that ensued within the

---

[98] See BYIL, 1983, 404–5.
[99] On this matter, see in particular K. N. Gess, 'Permanent Sovereignty over Natural Resources – An Analytical Review of the UN Declaration and its Genesis', 13 ICLQ, 1964, 398–449; J.F. Guilhaudis, *Le droit des peuples à disposer d'eux-mêmes*, 126–36; M. Benchikh, 'Impact de la dépendance économique sur les violations des Droits des peuples', in *Droits de l'homme et droits des peuples, Textes du Séminaire de Saint-Marin*, San Marino 1983, 91–8; H. Reinhard, *Rechtsgleichheit und Selbstbestimmung in wirtschaftlicher Hinsicht*, Cologne 1980; Gayim, *The Principle of Self-Determination*, 62–4; P. Cahier, 'Changement et continuité du droit international – Cours général de droit international public', 195 HR, 1985-VI, 50 ff.; R. Dolzer, 'Permanent Sovereignty over Natural Resources and Economic Decolonization', 7 *Human Rights Law Journal*, 1986, 217–30.

United Nations revolved around the possibility of achieving a formula capable of safeguarding and reconciling two essential principles: respect for the national sovereignty of Third World countries needing to develop their natural resources, and the provision of adequate guarantees for potential foreign investors. The resolution the General Assembly eventually adopted on 14 December 1962 (Res. 1803(XVII), containing the Declaration on Permanent Sovereignty over Natural Resources), was passed by 87 votes to 2 (France, South Africa), with 12 abstentions (socialist countries, plus Burma and Ghana). This resolution,[100] it should be stressed, cannot be regarded *per se* as declaratory of customary international law, nor can it be argued that it has gradually turned into a corpus of customary rules.[101] The better view seems to be that only some of the general principles laid down in the Declaration have gradually led to the formation of corresponding legal rules or principles. Without entering into a subject that to a large extent is extraneous to our inquiry, it can be said that to the extent that it concerns the rights of peoples, the Declaration can now be regarded as sanctioning general international law. On this level, it entails that a people subjected to colonial rule or to foreign domination has the right freely to dispose of its natural wealth and resources. Clearly, this individual right is but a specification and corollary of the general right to self-determination belonging to the peoples at issue.

Since the specific right under discussion is to be exercised 'in the interest of the national development and of the well-being of the people' (ex operative paragraph 1 of the Declaration), any use or exploitation of natural resources of a territory under colonial or foreign domination, carried out by the colonial or foreign Power without acting in the exclusive interest of the people at issue, amounts to a gross infringement of the right of peoples to self-determination.[102]

---

[100] See text in UN Ybk, 1962, 503 ff.

[101] R.-J. Dupuy, as Arbitrator in *Texaco and Calasiatic v. Libya* took a different view. He stated that 'on the basis of the circumstances of adoption . . . and by expressing an *opinio juris communis*, Res. 1803(XVII) seems to this Tribunal to reflect the state of customary law existing in this field . . . The consensus by a majority of States belonging to various representative groups indicates without the slightest doubt universal recognition of the rules therein incorporated' (17 ILM, 1978, 1 at para. 87).

[102] See H. Awartani, 'Israel's Economic Policies in the Occupied Territories: a Case for International Supervision', in E. Playfair (ed.), *International Law and the Administration of Occupied Territories*, Oxford 1992, 399–417; A. Cassese, 'Powers and Duties of an Occupant in Relation to Land and Natural Resources', *ibid.*, 419–42; I. Matar, 'Exploitation of Land and Water Resources by Jewish Colonies in the Occupied Territories', *ibid.*, 443–57.

5

The emergence of customary rules: internal self-determination

Introductory remarks

Internal self-determination means the right to authentic self-government, that is, the right for a people really and freely to choose its own political and economic regime – which is much more than choosing among what is on offer perhaps from one political or economic position only. It is an ongoing right. Unlike external self-determination for colonial peoples – which ceases to exist under customary international law once it is implemented – the right to internal self-determination is neither destroyed nor diminished by its having already once been invoked and put into effect.

Who exactly holds this right? Are all peoples entitled to the right? These are the crucial problems in the customary international law on self-determination.[1]

Of course, the answer to this query can only be found in international practice. If, however, one analyses this practice, one quickly realizes

---

[1] See generally, T. Veiter, 'Le droit des peuples à disposer d'eux-mêmes et à leur foyer natal', *Studi in onore di M. Udina*, vol. I, Milan 1975, 827 ff.; C. Gusy, 'Von der Selbstbestimmung durch den Staat zur Selbstbestimmung im Staat', 405–9; T. Veiter, 'Das Selbstbestimmungsrecht als Menschenrecht', *Fest. für H. R. Klecatsky*, vol. II, Vienna 1980, 984–91; Pomerance, *Self-Determination in Law and Practice*, 37 ff.; S. Oeter, 'Ueberlegungen zur Debatte um Selbstbestimmung, Sezessionsrecht und "vorzeitige" Anerkenung', 52 *Zeit.*, 1992, 760 ff.; A. Rosas, 'Internal Self-Determination', in C. Tomuschat (ed.), *Modern Law of Self-Determination*, Dordrecht, Boston and London 1993, 232–52; J. Salmon, 'Internal Aspects of the Right to Self-Determination: Towards a Democratic Legitimacy Principle?', *ibid.*, 266 ff. See also F. Ermacora, 'Ueber die Innere Selbstbestimmung', in *Menschenrechte, Volksgruppen, Regionalismus – Festgabe für T. Veiter*, 31–7.

that very seldom have States taken a stand on this issue in 'unilateral' statements, declarations or actual behaviour. 'State practice' in this matter takes place primarily within the UN, that is to say, it chiefly manifests itself in statements made, positions taken, and resolutions voted by States in one or other of the UN bodies. This should not be surprising: as I have already pointed out above, in the early 1960s the UN started a process of recasting certain old international principles governing international relations and formulating new ones. One of the principles belonging to the latter category was that on self-determination. This obviously stimulated States to take a stand on the issue, and they did so on many occasions, always however in UN fora, where they contributed to the passing of resolutions or instead barred UN bodies from making pronouncements on some delicate matters.

A right of self-determination for the populations of sovereign States? The UN practice

A discussion of UN action – or States' action in the UN, which amounts to the same thing – with regard to the self-determination of 'populations of sovereign States' necessarily touches upon several diverse situations, including: the internal self-determination of the *whole people* of sovereign States, that is, the right to have a representative and democratic government; the rights of *racial* or *religious* groups living in States which grossly discriminate against them; the rights of *ethnic groups, linguistic minorities, indigenous populations*, and *national peoples living in federated States*.

The issue of the right to internal self-determination afforded to the *entire population of a sovereign State* will be considered first. This right, it should be recalled, exists under treaty law by virtue of article 1 of the 1966 Covenants. United Nations practice and the practice of the UN Committee on Human Rights show that for a long time there has been some resistance to a move towards expanding customary law in order to uphold the rights conferred by treaty law. Indeed, it is difficult to discern any consistent action taken in the international arena to protect the rights of peoples subjected to authoritarian or despotic governments, and based on the principle that such governments are in violation of their people's right to self-determination.

One of the reasons for customary law's resilience in the face of treaty law in this area is the fear on the part of States that any action in the field would lead to undue interference in the domestic affairs of sovereign States. This sentiment is reflected in the early policy papers of the Committee on

Human Rights. The Committee's 'general comments' on Article 1 of the Covenants, made in 1984, assert that:

All States parties to the Covenant should take positive action to facilitate realization of and respect for the right of peoples to self-determination. Such positive action must be consistent with the States' obligation under the Charter of the United Nations and under international law: in particular, *States must refrain from interfering in the internal affairs of other States and thereby adversely affecting the exercise of the right to self-determination.*[2]

Regardless of their political or ideological leanings, many States have for long favoured an extremely cautious and moderate attitude towards conferring the right of self-determination on entire populations, by virtue of a *de facto* application of the Covenants to non-Contracting States. The need to champion democratic values has all too often been subordinated to the desire to preserve intact the principle of State sovereignty.

Having said this, it is however necessary to add that recent practice, as we shall see (below, pp. 302–12), shows that a customary rule on the matter is in the process of formation, although there still exist many hurdles in its way.

The next issue to be dealt with is that of UN action, or more precisely inaction, on behalf of *ethnic groups*, such as the Kurds, Armenians, and Basques; *indigenous populations*, such as the native peoples of Latin America, North America, Australia, and New Zealand; *linguistic minorities* such as the Québecois; and *religious groups* such as the Catholics in Northern Ireland. Here, once again, the UN has remained silent in response to claims asserting the right of self-determination.[3]

---

[2] See *Report of the Human Rights Committee*, UN Doc. A/39/40, 1984, 143 (my italics). This interpretation by the Human Rights Committee – which to a large extent reflected the view historically advanced by the Eastern bloc countries, in particular the German Democratic Republic – in essence equated a State's duty to respect a people's right to self-determination with its right to non-interference in domestic matters. For this to be true, the right to self-determination, at least as far as sovereign countries are concerned, must be considered as a right held by the government of the State, not by its people.

Some Western States have in fact adopted this position. For instance, in a 1981 debate in the House of Lords, the Parliamentary Under-Secretary of State, Foreign and Commonwealth Office stated: 'Although we do not agree with Libyan policies we must accept that Libya is a sovereign State, *and we respect her right to self-determination*', 52 BYIL, 1981, 389 (my italics). It should be added that recently, as noted above (see Chapter 3), the Human Rights Committee has taken a more favourable and open approach to self-determination.

[3] Various authors, among them Y. Dinstein, 'Self-Determination and the Middle East Conflict', in Alexander and Friedlander (eds.), *Self-Determination*, 249–53; Y. Alexander and R. A. Friedlander, 'Collective Human Rights of Peoples vis-à-vis Minorities', in

This view ought, however, to be somewhat qualified. Indeed, there seems to be a tendency towards broadening the concept of internal self-determination in such a way as to cover, at least in some respects, minority groups. In this connection, one can find instances where UN bodies have dealt with minorities for which either in the past, or both in the past and at present, self-determination has been invoked and these UN bodies have approached the question in terms of granting full autonomy to the minority group – that is, from the viewpoint of *internal* self-determination. A case in point is that of South Tyrol/Alto Adige, on which it is worth dwelling at some length.[4]

As I emphasized in Chapter 2, at the end of the First World War South Tyrol/Alto Adige, until then a southern province of Austria mainly inhabited by German-speaking persons, was awarded to Italy without the holding of any plebiscite. At the end of the Second World War, Italy and Austria entered into an agreement on the matter (the so-called De Gasperi–Gruber Agreement of 5 September 1946). Under this treaty the German-speaking inhabitants of the area were entitled to 'complete equality of rights' with the Italian-speaking inhabitants, within the framework of the special provisions designed to safeguard 'the ethnic character and the cultural and economic development of the German-speaking element' (Article 1 paragraph 1). Under Article 2 the 'populations' of the

---

S. Chandra (ed.), *Minorities in National and International Laws*, New Delhi 1985, 77–81, and K. Doehring ('Das Selbstbestimmungsrecht der Völker als Grundsatz des Völkerrechts', 14 *Berichte der Deutschen Gesellschaft für Völkerrecht*, 1974, 21–7, 48–9) hold that not only colonial peoples, but any people or ethnic group or minority are entitled to self-determination under international law. This view, however, is not supported by UN or State practice.

[4] For the historical background of the South Tyrol/Alto Adige question and the relevant bibliography, see Chapter 1, note 40. See also A. E. Alcock, 'The South Tyrol Package Agreement of 1969 and its Effect on Ethnic Relations in the Province of Bolzano', 3 *Irish Studies in International Affairs*, 1982, 47–54; G. Conetti, 'La controversia italo-austriaca relativa alla minoranza di lingua tedesca in Alto Adige e la sua soluzione', in A. De Guttry and N. Ronzitti (eds.), *I rapporti di vicinato fra Italia e Austria*, Milan 1987, 17 ff.; F. Ermacora, 'The Minorities Problem in South Tyrol', 7 *World Justice* 1965, 34–47; A. Fenet, *La question du Tyrol du Sud. Un problème de droit international*, Paris 1968; R. Gaja, 'In margine ai più recenti sviluppi in Alto Adige', *Rivista di studi politici internazionali* 1988, 587–97; A. Gattini, 'Prospettive dell'"accordino' italo-austriaco nel quadro della normativa comunitaria', 74 RDI, 1991, 301 ff.; A. Gattini, 'La chiusura della controversia italo-austriaca sull'Alto Adige', 75 RDI, 1992, 348 ff.; D. Türk, 'National Minorities in Austria, Italy and in the successor States of the former Yugoslavia', in Ermacora, Tretter, and Pelzl, *Volksgruppen im Spannungsfeld von Recht und Souveränität in Mittel- und Osteuropa*, 44–8; A. Benedikter, 'Die Autonomie als Mittel des Minderheitenschutzes am Beispiel Südtirol', *ibid.*, 303–12.

areas were to be granted 'the exercise of autonomous legislative and executive regional powers, within the framework of the areas in question'.[5] Plainly, this Agreement, by tackling the issue from the viewpoint of the protection of linguistic minorities and by implicitly confirming the existing border between Austria and Italy, did not uphold the idea of self-determination *qua* the right of an ethnic or linguistic group freely to determine its *international* status.

A few years later, Austria complained that Italy had reneged on the Agreement's terms and in 1960 brought the issue before the UN General Assembly. It is interesting to note that on that occasion Austria did not raise the question of South Tyrol/Alto Adige as an issue of self-determination, but as 'the problem of the Austrian minority in Italy' and requested that the German-speaking Province of Bozen be granted full autonomy.[6] In 1961 Austria, in asking again that the question be discussed by the General Assembly, once more insisted on 'complete autonomy' for the Province of Bozen. This time, however, it stressed that the application of the principle of self-determination would have been the best solution; nevertheless, Austria would not press for this, lest it be accused of pursuing revisionist aims. It is worth citing the relevant passages of the statement made in the GA Special Political Committee by the Austrian Foreign Minister:

At the outset of the negotiations [between Austria and Italy], in [27–28] January 1961, the Austrian Minister of Foreign Affairs had declared that a truly satisfactory solution of the South Tyrol problem would be achieved only by application of the principles of the right of self-determination. He had added, however, that such a solution was not realizable, since any attempt to settle the problem on that basis would seriously disturb democratic Europe and be harmful to the interests of all concerned. The Austrian Government had accordingly come

[5] For the English text of the Paris Agreement, see the Austrian *Memorandum* annexed to UN Doc. 4/4530, 5 October 1960 (Annex 5, p. 2).

[6] In the Explanatory Memorandum accompanying the Austrian request, it was stated that Italy, instead of granting the Province of Bozen full autonomy, had merged it with the Italian Province of Trento and it was this new region (Trentino–Alto Adige) – inhabited by half a million Italians as compared to 250,000 South Tyroleans – on which autonomous rights had been conferred by Italy. The Memorandum ended with the following: 'In virtue of Art.10 and Art.14 of the U.N. Charter, Austria, therefore, requests the GA to consider the Austrian-Italian dispute that has arisen from Italy's refusal to grant autonomy to the province of Bozen and, in the spirit of the Charter, to bring about a just settlement based on democratic principles, by which the Austrian minority in Italy is conceded a true autonomy so as to enjoy the self-administration and self-government it has asked for and, indeed, it needs for the protection of its existence as a minority' (A/4395 6 July 1960, at 5).

to the conclusion that a permanent settlement satisfactory for both parties should be sought through the implementation of Article 2 of the Paris Agreement, in other words by granting full regional autonomy to the existing Province of Bozen. Thus, the Austrian Government could not be accused of pursuing revisionist aims or seeking frontier changes. But while it had shown moderation by not calling for the application of the right to self-determination, it must demand that the people of the South Tyrol should be granted the right to autonomy. Moreover, autonomy could be carried into effect without modifying the Italian frontier.[7]

The Italian Foreign Minister Segni replied, among other things, that GA Resolution 1497(XV) had

eliminated such Austrian claims as had not been based on the Paris Agreement and, in particular, had rejected the Austrian thesis that self-determination was the most satisfactory solution.[8]

The Austrian attitude shows that – for political and psychological reasons – it propounded self-determination as a means for a minority group to determine its *international* status, but then fell back on full autonomy – that is to say, *internal* self-determination, although it did not go so far as expressly to frame autonomy as a means of realizing internal self-determination.[9]

The General Assembly upheld the position of the two States concerned and itself approached the issue as a question of the protection of minorities through the granting of full autonomy. By two resolutions 1497(XV) and 1661(XVI) of 31 October 1960 and 28 November 1961 respectively, it called upon the parties to settle the dispute peacefully through direct negotiations.[10]

---

[7] GA, VIIth Session, SPC, 289th Mtg, 15 November 1961, para. 3.

[8] *Ibid.*, 290th Mtg., 16 November 1961, para. 2. The Italian Foreign Minister went on to note the following: '[After the January 1961 bilateral negotiations in Milan] the Austrian Minister of Foreign Affairs had made an even more surprising announcement at Milan, which he had repeated at the 289th meeting of the Special Political Committee, that recourse to the principle of self-determination was the truly satisfactory solution of the Alto Adige affair. He had admitted, however, that that solution was not practicable, though only for reasons of political expediency. But in the opinion of the Italian delegation, any revisionist attitude was inconsistent with the treaties in force' (*ibid.*, para. 3).

[9] For the Austrian renunciation, in the UN General Assembly, of external self-determination, see also Ermacora, *Die Selbstbestimmungsidee*, 42–4.

[10] Later on, by two parallel declarations of 3 and 15 December 1969 respectively, Italy and Austria agreed that the former would adopt a 'package' of measures making bilingualism a precondition for public services, guaranteeing German schools and apportioning public jobs, housing and housing benefits to reflect the population mix.

What conclusions can be drawn from the discussion of the South Tyrol/Alto Adige issue in the United Nations?

Admittedly, the existence of the De Gasperi–Gruber Agreement, in a way, conditioned the approach of both the States concerned and the UN. Presumably, had an international treaty been lacking, the General Assembly would have concluded that, since the matter belonged to the domestic jurisdiction of Italy (Italy was not being accused of gross, large-scale, and systematic breaches of human rights), it had no authority to discuss it. The 1946 Agreement thus enabled the UN to consider and pass resolutions upon the matter. The debates that took place in New York and the GA resolutions mentioned above are significant in that: (a) they are indicative of the position of the UN in the area of minorities (for the UN ethnic, religious or linguistic groups have no right to external self-determination); (b) by the same token they point to the fact that in 1960–1 the UN believed – or at any rate did not challenge the view – that those groups (i) are entitled to internal self-determination and (ii) internal self-determination may or should be implemented by the granting of 'complete autonomy' to those groups.

Emphasis should also be laid on the fact that recently many Contracting States of the UN Covenant on Civil and Political Rights have agreed to discuss, under the heading of self-determination, issues relating to regions or minorities. Thus, for example, the UK has been disposed to answer questions relating to Northern Ireland[11] – whereas Iraq has objected to

This package was eventually adopted by Italy in 1992 and consequently both parties declared that the dispute was terminated. See the letters from Austria and Italy to the UN Secretary-General of 17 June 1992 (UN Doc. A/46/939 and 940). By the same token, the two parties agreed to amend *inter se* Art. 27a of the European Convention for the Peaceful Settlement of Disputes so as to make it applicable to any dispute concerning the De Gasperi–Gruber Agreement, which can therefore be unilaterally submitted to the International Court of Justice.

It should be emphasized that Italy considers that the set of measures it adopted between 1969 and 1992 goes beyond the De Gasperi–Gruber Agreement, in that they constitute unilateral concessions. By contrast, according to Austria those measures are simply designed to implement the 1946 Agreement. It follows that for Austria the way Italy applies (or the failure to apply) those measures is an internationally relevant matter and can be submitted to the International Court of Justice.

11 In 1985, the British delegate before the Human Rights Committee pointed out the following: 'Responding to the request for information concerning the political and constitutional process that would enable the people of Northern Ireland to determine their future, the representative explained that two basic elements were involved. Currently, the applicable principle was that of continued direct rule and continued association with Great Britain as part of the United Kingdom. However, there were

questions relating to the Kurds by noting that since this group makes up a minority, it should be treated under that heading.[12]

Subject to these and similar exceptions, the fact remains, however, that it is in the various instances where, rightly or wrongly, self-determination has been invoked by ethnic groups living within sovereign States, that UN practice has been at its most ineffectual.

The right to self-determination of racial groups denied equal access to government

While the practice of States, as it has developed in the United Nations, shows that no right to self-determination accrues under current international law to peoples of sovereign States or to minority groups living in sovereign States, the contention can be made that such a right is granted to racial groups, subject to certain conditions.

This right, not surprisingly, has emerged as a result of a fundamental UN Document: the 1970 Declaration on Friendly Relations, which eventually crystallized and amalgamated the previously conflicting views of States. The debates in the UN that led to the adoption of the Declaration, the text of the Declaration itself, and the subsequent practice of States and the UN, all contributed to the formation of a customary rule on the matter.

---

statutory provisions for testing the wishes of the Northern Ireland electorate on the question of direct rule by means of a poll at periodic intervals of not more than 10 years. In addition, there was also the Northern Ireland Assembly, which had been set up in 1982 to make proposals for devolution and to scrutinize the process of direct rule. Unfortunately, owing to various difficulties not much progress had been made thus far on formulating new constitutional arrangements, although the Assembly had provided a valuable local and democratic contribution to direct rule' (*Report of the Human Rights Committee to the G.A.*, 1985, UN Doc. A/40/40, para 539).

In 1991 the British delegate made the following remarks: 'The Anglo-Irish Agreement of 1986 was a binding treaty which stipulated that the status of Northern Ireland was to be determined by the democratic choice of the people of Northern Ireland. After 14 months of preliminary exchanges between the Secretary of State, the Irish Government and the four main constitutional parties in Northern Ireland, the Secretary of State had, on 26 March 1991, announced the establishment of a basis for formal political talks. It had, nevertheless, been recognized that the announcement marked only the beginning of a very long and difficult process' (*Report of the Human Rights Committee to the G.A.*, 1991, UN Doc. A/46/40, para. 365).

[12] See *Report of the Human Rights Committee to the G.A.*, 1987, UN Doc. A/42/40, paras. 352–3.

The 1970 Declaration on Friendly Relations: its saving clause[13]

During the drafting of the 1970 Declaration, a conflict emerged between the Western States and their socialist counterparts, the latter to some extent being backed by developing countries. The Western States were in favour of extending the right of internal self-determination to all peoples of sovereign States. This was in keeping with the prevalent Western ideology and, at the same time, was a potential political weapon to be wielded against socialist States and authoritarian governments in the developing world. In contrast, the socialist States were eager to restrict the right of internal self-determination as much as possible. In the end, the view of the socialist States prevailed. The majority did not agree with the Western view that internal self-determination ought to be considered a universal right to which the people of independent and sovereign States were entitled.[14] The main thrust of the section of the Declaration on Friendly

---

[13] On self-determination in the 1970 UN Declaration on Friendly Relations, see chiefly: A. Linares, *Los principios y normas internacionales que rigen las relaciones amistosas y de cooperación entre los estados*, Caracas 1969; B. Graefrath, 'Deklaration über die Grundlegenden Völkerrechtsprinzipien, 3 *Deutsche Aussenpolitik*, 1971, 496 ff.; B. Graf zu Dohna, *Die Grundprinzipien des Völkerrechts über die Freundschaftlichen Beziehungen und die Zusammenarbeit zwischen den Staaten* (PhD thesis, Kiel University), Berlin 1973; C.D. Johnson, 'Toward Self-Determination – A Reappraisal as Reflected in the Declaration on Friendly Relations', 3 *Georgia Journal of International and Comparative Law*, 1973, 149 ff.; Thürer, *Das Selbstbestimmungsrecht der Völker – Mit einem Exkurs zur Jurafrage*, 176 ff. See also the works cited in the next two notes.

[14] At first sight, the literal purport of para. 1 of the Declaration's section on self-determination could lead one to believe that the principle *also refers to internal self-determination* ('By virtue of the principle of equal rights and self-determination of peoples enshrined in the Charter of the United Nations, *all peoples* have the right freely to determine, without external interference, their political status and to pursue their economic, social and cultural development, and every State has the duty to respect this right in accordance with the provisions of the Charter'; my italics). Indeed some authors have strongly argued that the Declaration's principle of self-determination has a *universal* scope, hence that it also applies to the whole people of every sovereign State (among the most authoritative of these commentators, see G. Arangio-Ruiz, 'The Normative Role of the General Assembly of the United Nations and the Declaration of Principles of Friendly Relations' 137 HR, 1972-III, 565 and 571; G. Arangio-Ruiz, 'Human Rights and Non-Intervention in the Helsinki Final Act', 157 HR, 1977-IV, 226–7; Arangio-Ruiz, 'Autodeterminazione (diritto dei popoli alla)', 4). The textual elements to which reference is made by those who argue against the *restrictive* view (in particular by G. Arangio-Ruiz) are three: (i) the wording of the para cited above; (ii) the wording of para. 3 ('Every State has the duty to promote through joint and separate action *universal* respect for and observance of human rights and fundamental freedoms in accordance with the Charter'; my italics); (iii) the 'saving clause'

109

Relations devoted to self-determination is the right of *external* self-determination.[15] Internal self-determination was considered of secondary importance. It was only in the saving clause that a right of internal self-determination was envisaged, albeit indirectly. It states:

(para. 7), on which I shall soon dwell, in the text, and which clearly covers internal self-determination.

It can be objected that (i) the wording of para. 1, seemingly cast in the same mould as Art. 1 of the UN Covenants on Human Rights, does not provide compelling evidence of the 'universal view'. Indeed, the expression 'without external interference', included in that paragraph, entails that peoples of sovereign States should not be interfered with in the determination of their political, economic, social, and cultural status: this amounts to stating that, with regard to peoples of sovereign States, self-determination means *the right of States to non-interference* (this interpretation is indeed consonant with the view of self-determination held by the then socialist States and a number of developing countries); (ii) the wording of para. 3 actually disproves the 'universal view': that paragraph, modelled on Art. 55(c) of the UN Charter, only refers to individuals' human rights and freedoms; the fact that the word 'universal' has been used for these rights and freedoms and *not* for self-determination constitutes a strong *argumentum a contrario* corroborating the view that the Declaration does not take a universal approach to self-determination; (iii) it is true that the 'saving clause' refers to internal self-determination; however, this clause does not constitute a specific application of a universal principle to peoples of sovereign States; quite to the contrary, it constitutes an *exception* to the scope of the principle: while the principle only refers to *external* self-determination, the clause exclusively refers to its *internal* dimension.

In any case, other paragraphs of the Declaration's section on self-determination confirm our view because only these paragraphs refer to external self-determination: they are paras. 2, 4, 5, and 6. All of them relate to the *mode of implementation* of self-determination. Now, it would be absurd to lay down in para. 1 a universal principle and then, in the following paras, only refer to the modes of implementation of this principle in its *external* dimension. A *systematic construction* of the Declaration bears out the restrictive interpretation, which in addition is more consonant with the *drafting history* of the text of the 'saving clause' (see my comments on pp. 104, 115–18). In sum, the *literal* and *systematic* interpretation, as well as some *preparatory work*, all converge and lead to the same, compelling conclusion. See also the next footnote.

[15] The only interpretative element that could be adduced against the 'non-universalistic view' can be found in the preparatory work of the Declaration's text, other than the saving clause. Indeed, in the Report to the GA of the 'Special Committee' charged with drafting the Declaration it was stated that 'it was agreed [in the Drafting Committee] that the first paragraph . . . should contain a general statement of the principle [of self-determination], stressing its universality' (GAOR, 24th Session, Suppl. no. 19 (A/7619), 1969, at 63; see also GAOR, 25th Session, Suppl. no. 18 (A/8018), 1970, at 41). However, even in the Special Committee, some States emphasized that self-determination only referred to colonial or military-occupied peoples (see, e.g., France, A/AC.125/SR.113, at 23).

Furthermore, the debates in the GA were not conclusive. Some States argued explicitly or implicitly that the principle only applied to *colonial peoples* (see, e.g., Australia, A/C.6/SR.1178, para. 39; France, *ibid.*, SR.1179, para. 10 ('The principle of equal rights and self-determination implied that States should fully respect the clearly expressed determination of a people to lead an independent life. *That was a universal*

Nothing in the foregoing paragraph [proclaiming the principle of self-determination] shall be construed as authorizing or encouraging any action which would dismember or impair, totally or in part, the territorial integrity or political unity of sovereign and independent States conducting themselves in compliance with the principle of equal rights and self-determination of peoples as described above *and thus possessed of a government representing the whole people belonging to the territory without distinction as to race, creed or colour* ('sans distinction de race, croyance ou couleur'; 'sin distincion por motivos de raza, credo o color').[16]

This clause, which some commentators[17] have overlooked or played down is nevertheless of great importance.[18]

principle of special application to the colonial situation'; my italics); Libya (*ibid.*, SR.1182, paras. 46–7 (referring to both colonial peoples and those under 'foreign occupation'); the Philippines (*ibid.*, para. 55: it took the same view as Libya); Indonesia (*ibid.*, para. 75); Trinidad and Tobago (*ibid.*, SR.1183, para. 5); Ecuador (*ibid.*, para. 39).

A contrary view was taken by the US (*ibid.*, SR.1180, para. 25: the right to self-determination 'was recognized as belonging to "all peoples", not only to dependent peoples'), Portugal (*ibid.*, SR.1182, para. 4) and Spain (*ibid.*, para. 28).

16 My italics.

17 See, e.g., O. Sukovic, 'Principle of Equal Rights and Self-Determination of Peoples', in M. Sahovic (ed.), *Principles of International Law Concerning Friendly Relations and Cooperation*, Belgrade 1972, 323 ff.; J. Crawford, *The Creation of States in International Law*, cit., 89 ff.

Some commentators, although mentioning the clause, do not devote any special attention to it. See, for example, C. D. Johnson, 'Toward Self-Determination – A Reappraisal as Reflected in the Declaration on Friendly Relations', 3 *Georgia Journal International Comparative Law* 1973, 145–63, especially 152–3; Guilhaudis, *Le droit des peuples à disposer d'eux-mêmes*, 56–7; I. M. Sinclair, 'Principles of International Law Concerning Friendly Relations and Cooperation among States', in M.K. Nawaz (ed.), *Essays on International Law in Honour of K. Rao*, Leiden 1976, 130 ff.; Pomerance, *Self-Determination in Law and Practice*, 38 ff. See also, F. Ermacora, 'Die Selbstbestimmung im Lichte der UN-Deklaration', *Internationales Recht und Diplomatie*, 1972, 64 ff.; Thürer, 'Das Selbstbestimmungsrecht der Völker – Ein Ueberblick', 129; Thürer, 'Self-Determination', 474; Oeter, 'Ueberlegungen zur Debatte um Selbstbestimmung, Sezessionsrecht und 'vorzeitige' Anerkennung', 757.

See, in addition, Arangio-Ruiz, 'The Normative Role of the General Assembly of the United Nations and the Declaration of Principles of Friendly Relations', 570 ff.; Arangio-Ruiz, 'Human Rights and Non-Intervention in the Helsinki Final Act', 226–7 and note 40; Arangio-Ruiz, 'Autodeterminazione', at 4; the interpretation offered by Arangio-Ruiz, which eventually plays down or even ignores the words 'race, creed or colour', is all the more surprising because this distinguished author was the delegate to the United Nations who put forward the compromise text that led to agreement.

18 Some authors, although only dealing briefly with the clause, put forward significant views on the matter. See, e.g., E. Jiménez de Arechaga, 'International Law in the Past Third of a Century', 159 HR, 1978-I, 110; G. Abi-Saab, 'Wars of National Liberation in the Geneva Conventions and Protocols', 165 HR, 1979-IV, 396–7; D. Turp, *Le droit de sécession en droit international public et son application au cas du Québec*, Montréal 1979 (Mémoire de Maîtrise en Droit), 261–78 (Turp must, among other things, be credited with having emphasized the legal importance of the statement made by the South African delegate in the UN GA after the adoption of the Declaration).

THE LITERAL AND LOGICAL CONSTRUCTION OF THE CLAUSE

Before embarking on a discussion of the language employed, it must be emphasized that the overwhelming majority of States participating in the drafting of the Declaration took strong exception to the notion that peoples might have a right of secession. The principle of territorial integrity of sovereign States was, and still is, considered sacred, so sacred that the draft provision initially proposed had to be recast. The initial Western proposal commenced with the principle of self-determination; the final text starts with the principle of territorial integrity and the political unity of sovereign States. The rights of racial and religious groups subjected to discrimination are subordinate to the principle of territorial integrity. From this, one thing is made very clear: any licence to secede must be interpreted very strictly.

Turning to the language of the text, one is immediately struck by its convoluted structure. To grasp the provision's true meaning and import one must turn it around – in other words, frame in positive terms what is couched in a negative manner.[19] If so 'translated' the clause provides as follows: if in a sovereign State the government is 'representative' of the whole population, in that it grants equal access to the political decision-making process and political institutions to any group and in particular does not deny access to government to groups on the grounds of race, creed or colour, then that government respects the principle of self-determination; consequently, groups are entitled to claim a right to self-determination only where the government of a sovereign State denies access on such grounds.

Assuming this reasoning is correct, what is meant by 'race, creed or colour'? The first thing to note is that 'race' and 'colour' express an identical concept: race. This pleonasm has its roots in the redundant language of Article 2(1) of the Universal Declaration on Human Rights, which bans any distinction based, among other things, on 'race, colour, sex'.[20] Turning next to the word 'creed': does 'creed' refer to a 'system of

---

19 On this point, see R. Rosenstock, 'The Declaration of Principles of International Law Concerning Friendly Relations: A Survey', 65 AJIL, 1971, 732.

20 It should be noted that neither the Declaration on Human Rights nor any other international instrument contains a definition of 'race'. However, this is not surprising, given that legal texts are often loosely worded, particularly in difficult and controversial areas such as the concept of 'race'. What is meant by 'race' is an issue left for the implementing bodies to decide. 'Self-identification' by groups can also be instructive. In this respect mention should be made of Article 1(2) of the ILO Convention on Indigenous Populations no.169 of 27 June 1989, which stipulates that 'self-identification as indigenous or tribal shall be regarded as a fundamental criterion for determining the

religious beliefs' or is it a broader concept, extending, as the *Oxford English Dictionary* suggests, to any 'set of principles or opinions on any subject'? The ambiguities associated with the Declaration's use of 'creed' are particularly striking when one considers the terminology employed in other international instruments. For example, how do we define 'creed' in the light of Article 2(1) of the Universal Declaration of Human Rights, which states that no distinction should be made on the basis of, among other things, 'race, colour, sex, language, *religion, political or other opinion*'?

It is suggested that 'creed' ought to be interpreted strictly, as covering only 'religious beliefs'. This reasoning rests on a double *argumentum a contrario*. If 'creed' encompassed political opinions as well as religious beliefs, it would then follow that, under the Declaration, any government 'not representing' the opinions of those averse to the government's platform would be at variance with the principles enshrined in the document. Since a government discriminating against a political group would not be 'representative', it would be in breach of the principle of self-determination. It is hardly likely that most of the developing and socialist States would have accepted such a sweeping concept of political democracy – even if dictators generally claim to represent the entire nation and to reflect the will of all groups comprising the population. Although States are aware of the immense advantages afforded by rhetorical and verbal smoke-screens, they tend to oppose any normative developments likely to be used as a political weapon against them. This, it is submitted, supports a strict interpretation of 'creed', one which encompasses religious discrimination but excludes discrimination based on political ideology.

There is, however, an even stronger argument – very closely linked to the first one – that supports the narrow construction of 'creed'. This is because if 'creed' were interpreted to mean 'political opinions' as well as 'religious beliefs', any political group not 'represented' by the government would have the right to self-determination, hence also – at least in

groups to which the provisions of this Convention apply'. (On this Convention, see, in particular, C. M. Brölmann and M. Y. A. Zieck, 'Indigenous Peoples', in C. Brölmann, R. Lefeber, and M. Zieck (eds.), *Peoples and Minorities in International Law*, Dordrecht, Boston and London 1993, 203–12).

It is worth remembering that scholarly literature takes a different approach to the concept of race. For instance, for D. L. Horowitz an ethnic group is a group based on birth and blood, on 'a myth of collective ancestry' and on some form of 'ascription'. 'So conceived, ethnicity easily embraces groups differentiated by colour, language, and religion; it covers 'tribes', 'races', 'nationalities' and castes' (D. L. Horowitz, *Ethnic Groups in Conflict*, Berkeley 1985, 41 ff. and 53). On the concept of race, see also the fundamental remarks of C. Lévi-Strauss, *Race et histoire*, Paris 1961, especially 9–26.

exceptional cases – the right to secession. Surely this is an extreme consequence which the drafters of the Declaration could not possibly have
intended.

Assuming that the foregoing considerations are correct, the right of
internal self-determination embodied in the 1970 Declaration is a right
conferred only on *racial* or *religious* groups living in a sovereign State which
are denied access to the political decision-making process; *linguistic* or
national groups *do not* have a concomitant right. This leads to yet another
question: why did the drafters of the Declaration privilege racial and
religious groups while ignoring other collectivities?

Unfortunately, the debates surrounding the drafting and adoption of the
Declaration cast little light on this problem. One can merely speculate that
the strong anti-racist sentiments voiced by the developing countries
resulted in a consensus that racism was a contemptible ill justifying the
adoption of extreme measures – even, exceptionally, the disruption of
the political unity or territorial integrity of sovereign States. As for the
provision addressing religious discrimination, there were undoubtedly two
contributing factors. First, the feelings voiced by some countries keen to
protect religious groups. Second, and by far the more important, the
widely shared belief that religious persecution is a relatively isolated
phenomenon. Granting a right of self-determination to groups suffering on
religious grounds was unlikely to disturb the political unity and territorial
integrity of sovereign States. Therefore, including a provision pertaining to
religious groups was not controversial. Groups defined in terms of national
origin, culture, or language, however, involved different considerations. In
the opinion of most States, affording a right of self-determination to ethnic,
linguistic or cultural groups would be the 'kiss of death' as far as territorial
integrity was concerned.

By limiting self-determination to racial and religious groups, the draftsmen made it clear that self-determination was not considered a right held
by *the entire people* of an authoritarian State. The existence of a government
which tramples upon its citizens' basic rights and fundamental freedoms
does not give rise to a right of internal self-determination. However, even
those groups that *are* afforded rights under the Declaration are not as well
off as one might expect, for it is *equal access to government* to which they are
entitled, not *equal rights*. The Declaration does not require States to grant
racial and religious groups a menu of rights, nor does it prohibit the
imposition of invidious measures. It simply demands that States allow
racial and religious groups to have access to government institutions. The
draftsmen undoubtedly assumed that once these groups were granted

equal access to government, they would be in a position to ensure that all attempts to pass discriminatory legislation would be defeated – an assumption that is only partially correct.

THE PREPARATORY WORK BEARS OUT THE ABOVE INTERPRETATION

The preparatory work of the 1970 UN Declaration confirms the limitations on self-determination that are noted above.[21] The Western view that self-determination ought to be a *universal* right – a view supported by Yugoslavia, Argentina, and Venezuela – was advanced in two proposals, one put forward by the US in 1966 and one tabled by the UK the following year.[22] The US proposal, designed to further the concept of political democracy,[23] stated:

The existence of a sovereign and independent State possessing a representative Government, effectively functioning as such to all distinct peoples within its territory, is presumed to satisfy the principle of equal rights and self-determination as regards these peoples.

In addition to this clause, both proposals included a provision relating to peoples distinct from the remainder of the population. To quote the British proposal, the right to self-determination also belonged to the people of 'a territory . . . geographically distinct and ethnically or culturally diverse from the remainder of the territory of the State administering it', if the central Government was not representative of the people located in that territory.[24] The US and UK proposals, which were supported by Canada, France, Australia, Japan, and The Netherlands and, at one point, the Soviet Union,[25] raised the ire of many developing and socialist countries. Among the most vocal opponents of the Western proposals were Burma,

---

[21] On the preparatory work of the Declaration's section on self-determination, see in particular Ermacora, 'Die Selbstbestimmung im Lichte der UN-Deklaration', 62–7.

[22] For the US proposal, see UN Doc. A/AC.125/L.32, 2 (para. B); for the UK proposal, see UN Doc. A/AC.125/SR.69, 18 ff.

[23] The US delegate emphasized that the US proposal 'reflected the important link which existed between the principle [of self-determination] and representative government . . . . [the proposal] was designed to reflect the element of representative government in the spirit of article 21 of the Universal Declaration of Human Rights', UN Doc. A/AC.125/SR.68, 4 and 21.

[24] On the UK's attempt to improve upon the US proposal, see UN Doc. A/AC.125/ SR.69, 18.

[25] See UN Doc. A/AC.125/SR.69, 11 ff., 14; A/AC.125/SR.106, 64 and 74; A/AC. 125/SR.70, 6; A/AC.125/SR.105, 53; A/AC.125/SR.107, 82–5; A/AC.125/ SR.106, 62.

India, Poland, Ghana, Kenya, Cameroon, and Romania.[26] The crux of their arguments was that the language of the texts could be invoked to legitimatize secessionist movements and the disruption of sovereign countries. Particularly vociferous was the representative of Kenya, who asserted:

Although the principle applie[s] to all peoples, even in independent countries, it would be an interference in the domestic affairs of sovereign States if the Commission drew up rules for the secession of, to use the words of the 1967 United Kingdom proposal, 'a territory which is geographically distinct and ethnically or culturally diverse from the remainder of the territory of the State administering it'. Kenya is a country of many different tribal, racial, ethnic and religious groups, all of which are treated as equals, and to enunciate the principle that each group is entitled to self-determination would be carrying that principle to an absurd extreme. Although para 4 of the United Kingdom proposal attempts to exclude such a possibility, the inevitability of complaints of unequal treatment wherever ethnically different people coexist in one nation makes the attempt impractical.[27]

In response to the Third World and socialist countries' criticisms, the British delegation announced that it was prepared to revise its proposal. In the meantime, the Italian delegation tabled a draft which it considered a compromise solution. The proposal reproduced *in toto* the US and British general proposal, but it added a saving clause that explicitly stated what was implicit in the American and British drafts and had been clarified during discussion. Specifically, the Italian text stipulated:

States enjoying full sovereignty and independence, and possessed of a government representing the whole of their population, shall be considered to be conducting themselves in conformity with the principle of equal rights and self-determination of peoples as regards that population. Nothing in the foregoing paragraphs shall be construed as authorizing any action which would impair, totally or in part, the territorial integrity, or political unity, of such States.[28]

---

[26] A/AC.125/SR.68, 8 ff., 10, 14, 18; A/AC.125/SR.69, 22 ff.; A/AC.125/SR.105, 49; A/AC.125/SR.70, 15.

[27] UN Doc. A/AC.125/SR.107, 88, 4 September 1969. The Kenyan representative continued: 'Of course, if there was genuine discrimination against any ethnic group in an independent State, that group would have to rebel against the central Government and exercise its right of self-determination, but that would be a domestic matter outside the jurisdiction of the United Nations.' Only racial and religious discrimination were considered *internationally relevant*. It is also worth noting that the final text of the saving clause, which does not include ethnic groups among the holders of the right to self-determination, defeats the Kenyan representative's assertion that ethnic groups have rights to self-determination, albeit rights that do not grant recourse to international institutions.

[28] UN Doc. A/AC.125/L.80.

Although attacked by the Romanian representative, other States, most notably Czechoslovakia, welcomed the draft as a compromise text.[29]

However, the discussion did not end there. After the submission of the Italian text, Lebanon proposed the amendment that is responsible for the inclusion of the phrase at the heart of this discussion: 'race, creed or colour'. Specifically, Lebanon suggested that the phrase 'including the indigenous population and without distinction as to race, creed or colour' ought to be inserted after the word 'population'.[30] Unfortunately, the reasoning behind this amendment is lost to us, the Lebanese text having been referred, along with the Italian proposal, to the Drafting Committee, which agreed upon the final text and for which no records are available. Despite the dearth of background information on the Lebanese amendment, one thing is clear: the Drafting Committee's partial acceptance of the Lebanese suggestion was intended to, and had the effect of, narrowing the scope of the Western proposals.

Bearing this in mind, it is worth noting that the phrase 'without distinction as to race, creed or colour' employed by Lebanon, initially appeared in a 1969 amendment focusing on colonial countries tabled by Czechoslovakia, Poland, Romania, and the USSR which, in turn, was taken from operative paragraph 5 of Resolution 1514(XV) of 14 December 1960 on the granting of independence to colonial countries and peoples.[31] In other words, a clause designed to qualify the right to self-determination of peoples living in *sovereign* States was lifted from texts focusing on a completely different issue: the need to ensure that colonial peoples would be able freely to express their desire to be independent. The consequence of this was that a clause used in 1960 to safeguard against the imposition of State restrictions and to bolster the rights of colonial peoples was reincarnated in 1970 to limit group rights. The insertion of the phrase 'race, creed or colour' was intended to *qualify*, that is, to *restrict*, the general thrust of the Italian compromise text. Indeed, without those words, the scope of the clause would have been very sweeping: any

---

[29] UN Doc. A/AC.125/SR.113, 19 ff.

[30] UN Doc. A/AC.125/L.81.

[31] For the 1969 amendment submitted by Czechoslovakia, Poland, Romania and the USSR, see UN Doc. A/AC.125/L.74. Resolution 1514 reads, in the pertinent section: 'Immediate steps shall be taken, in Trust and Non-Self-Governing Territories or other territories which have not yet attained independence to transfer all powers to the peoples of those territories, without any conditions or reservations, in accordance with their freely expressed will and desire, without any distinction as to race, creed or colour, in order to enable them to enjoy complete independence and freedom.'

national, linguistic, ethnic, racial, or religious group not 'represented' in the government would have had a right to self-determination. In addition, the populations of States with authoritarian and despotic governments would probably also have been entitled to claim the right.

DOES THE DECLARATION ENSHRINE A RIGHT TO SECESSION FOR RACIAL AND RELIGIOUS GROUPS?

The socialist and developing countries scored several victories in the drafting of the 1970 Declaration. They managed to defeat the references to governments *representative of the whole people* that were included in initial drafts of the Declaration. They thereby rid the document of the proposition that governments of sovereign States ought to be democratic, that is, based on the free choice of the people. In addition, by inserting the phrase 'race, creed or colour', they successfully qualified the notion of 'representative governments'. Finally, those favouring a restrictive application of the right to self-determination succeeded in their quest to safeguard as much as possible the territorial integrity and political unity of sovereign States. By moving the clause relating to territorial integrity from the end of the paragraph to the beginning, the socialist and developing States insured that group rights would not unduly disrupt the unity of a sovereign State.

This latter point gives rise to an important question. Under the 1970 Declaration, are racial and religious groups entitled, under the conditions spelled out above, to *internal* self-determination only, or can they go so far as to claim *external* self-determination as well, that is the right to secede from the 'oppressive' State? To put the matter differently, when under the Declaration does the right of self-determination encompass the right to impair the territorial integrity and political unity of the State?[32]

Close analysis of both the text of the Declaration and the preparatory work warrants the contention that secession is not ruled out but may be permitted only when very stringent requirements have been met. The basis for this conclusion is that in the 'saving clause' under discussion, the reference to the requirement of not disrupting the territorial integrity of

---

[32] Jiménez de Arechaga, 'International Law in the Last Third of a Century', at 110, confines himself to stating that under the Declaration 'a State possessed of a government which does not represent the whole people of the territory and which introduces distinctions as to race, creed or colour, is not protected by the safeguard clause and is exposed to actions which, in the name of the principle of self-determination may dismember or impair, totally or in part, its territorial integrity or political unity'.

States was placed at the beginning, in order to underscore that territorial integrity should be the paramount value for States to respect. However, since the possibility of impairment of territorial integrity *is not totally excluded*, it is logically admitted. Some elements of the preparatory work seem to bear out this conclusion. Speaking in the Sixth Committee of the General Assembly after the adoption of the Declaration, the representative of South Africa expressed strong reservations about the section concerning self-determination; in particular, he set forth misgivings about the saving clause because it legitimized the disruption of the territorial integrity of States. Although this statement focused on one particular implication of the saving clause,[33] it went unchallenged. One can perhaps infer from this that the other States did not contest either the specific contention of South Africa, nor its general thrust, namely that the saving clause made allowance for secession.

Although secession is implicitly authorized by the Declaration, it must however be strictly construed, as with all exceptions. It can therefore be suggested that the following conditions might warrant secession: when the central authorities of a sovereign State persistently refuse to grant participatory rights to a religious or racial group, grossly and systematically trample upon their fundamental rights, and deny the possibility of reaching a peaceful settlement within the framework of the State structure. Thus, denial of the basic right of representation does not give rise *per se*

---

[33] The South African delegate stated the following: 'His delegation . . . wished to express its reservation regarding the seventh paragraph of the same principle [the saving clause], which implied that the rule that a State might not violate the territorial integrity of other States would not apply when that State maintained that the other States did not possess governments representing the whole people. His delegation was unable to accept such qualifications of the rule of the inviolability of territorial integrity. In fact, they rendered that principle nugatory, giving every State discriminatory powers to take action against another State to which it was hostile on the pretext that the peoples of the latter State were entitled to its support or that the Government of that State was not representative of the whole people. That could only encourage subversive activities and create situations incompatible with the concept of friendly relations' (GAOR, XXVth Session, Sixth Committee, 1184th Mtg, para. 15). Plainly, the South African delegate focused on the words of the Declaration about '*any action* which would dismember or impair, totally or in part, the territorial integrity or political unity of sovereign and independent States', and took them to also refer to *action by third States*. He thus neglected the most obvious meaning of those words: they primarily refer to possible action (that is, secession) by a discriminated group or people. The reason why the South African delegate only emphasized one possible implication of the words at issue is clearly political: in 1970, what South Africa feared was not so much internal rebellion by the African National Congress or other groups; it mostly feared armed action by third States.

to the right of secession. In addition, there must be gross breaches of fundamental human rights, and, what is more, the exclusion of any likelihood for a possible peaceful solution within the existing State structure.

If this reasoning is correct, the contention could be made that the Declaration on Friendly Relations *links external self-determination to internal self-determination in exceptional circumstances.* A racial or religious group may attempt secession, a form of external self-determination, when it is apparent that internal self-determination is absolutely beyond reach. Extreme and unremitting persecution and the lack of any reasonable prospect for peaceful challenge may make secession legitimate. A racial or religious group may secede – thus exercising the most radical form of external self-determination – once it is clear that all attempts to achieve internal self-determination have failed or are destined to fail.

The saving clause of the 1970 Declaration: is it customary law?

GENERAL

At the time of its drafting and adoption, the Declaration on Friendly Relations did not, as far as internal self-determination is concerned, *reflect* existing customary law. Nor did it crystallize any nascent rule of customary law on the matter. An examination of State practice prior to 1970 bears this out: the record does not reflect any adherence to the principle enshrined in the saving clause. Moreover, the contentious nature of the lengthy debates leading to the adoption of the clause and the compromises reached at the last minute prove that, at the time of the drafting, there was no existing consensus on the legal right to internal self-determination.

Today, however, some provisions of the Declaration rank at the level of customary law. State practice in the UN from the 1970s to the present evidences that the provision granting *internal* self-determination to *racial groups* persecuted by central government has become part of customary international law. In this respect it suffices to recall the string of General Assembly resolutions on Southern Rhodesia[34] and South Africa,[35] as well

---

[34] See, e.g., GA Resolution 31/154 A of 20 December 1976 (UN Ybk, 1976, 158–9), and SC Resolution 460 of 21 December 1979 (UN Ybk,. 1979). For a list of resolutions on Southern Rhodesia, see in particular Guarino, *Autodeterminazione dei popoli*, 341 ff.

[35] See, e.g., SC Resolution 417 of 31 October 1977 (in UN Ybk, 1977, 161–2), and GA Resolution 41/101 of 4 December 1986 (UN Ybk, 1986, 695–7).

as a number of significant statements made along the same lines by Western countries. The weight of these statements, as far as proof of the emergence of a customary rule on the matter is concerned, is greater than that of the declarations of developing and socialist countries. With regard to these two classes of States one might contend that their stand was primarily motivated by merely political or ideological considerations. By contrast, Western States were politically less unfavourable to Southern Rhodesia and South Africa; consequently their upholding of the right of racial groups to self-determination carries greater weight for the formation of a customary rule on the matter.[36]

In contrast, the Declaration's clause relating to *religious* groups has not matured into a customary rule, for no State practice since 1970 has supported such a legal evolution (the reason behind this development lies primarily in the fact that so far there have not been any major cases of religious groups claiming self-determination, as opposed to a radical transformation of the whole society, as is currently advocated by funda-mentalist groups).

By the same token, the possibility of racial groups to *secede* under the extreme circumstances set out above has *not* become customary law. This is an important topic, to which I shall now turn.

---

[36] As for Southern Rhodesia, it suffices to mention here a few statements by US delegates. In 1975, the US delegate to the Third Committee of the General Assembly stated that '[I]n Rhodesia, the U.S. opposes the illegal regime based on white supremacy, and is doing its part through the United Nations to work toward the goal of self-determination. We are hopeful that the courageous efforts of African leaders to bring the parties together will bear fruit' (US Mission to the UN, *Press Release* USUN-114(75), 10 October 1975, 2).

In 1976, the US delegate stated in the Security Council that 'The United States remains firm both in support of United Nations resolutions which have condemned the illegal Smith regime and in our commitment to the implementation of the principles of self-determination and majority rule in Rhodesia' (US Digest 1976, 573).

As for South Africa, reference can be made to the following statement on 9 February 1988 by the UK delegate to the UN Commission on Human Rights: 'A vivid example – perhaps the example *par excellence* – of a people which is today denied the right to be in charge of its own destiny – that is to say, the right to self-determination – is the non-white population of South Africa, the vast majority of the population of that unhappy country. The system of Apartheid, which denies them any role in deciding how they should be governed or what sort of society they should live in, is the very negation of the right to self-determination . . . [T]here should be no doubt that the UK Government joins wholeheartedly in condemning Apartheid as a flagrant violation of the right to self-determination' (59 BYIL, 1988, 442).

IN PARTICULAR: THE REFUSAL OF ANY RIGHT TO SECESSION

Ever since the emergence of the political principle of self-determination on the international scene, States have been adamant in rejecting even the possibility that nations, groups and minorities be granted a right to secede from the territory in which they live. Territorial integrity and sovereign rights have consistently been regarded as of paramount importance; indeed, they have been considered as concluding debate on the subject.[37]

[37] On secession and self-determination see: V. Berny, 'La sécession du Katanga', *Revue juridique et politique 'indépendance et coopération'*, 1965, 563–73; F. Wodie, 'La sécession du Biafra et le droit international public', RGDIP, 1969, 1018–60; J. Salmon, *La reconnaissance d'Etat*, Paris 1971, 198; V. P. Nanda, 'Self-Determination in International Law: The Tragic Tale of Two Cities – Islamabad (West Pakistan) and Dacca (East Pakistan)', 66 AJIL, 1972, 321–36; C. R. Nixon, 'Self-Determination: The Nigeria/Biafra Case', 24 *World Politics*, 1972, 479–97; Calogeropoulos-Stratis, *Le droit des peuples à disposer d'eux-mêmes*, 186–4, 296–300, 342–8; J. Salmon, 'Naissance et reconnaissance du Bangla Desh', *Multitudo Legum, Jus Unum – Festschrift für W. Wengler*, Berlin 1973, vol. I, 447–90; O. S. Kamanu, 'Secession and the Right of Self-Determination: An OAV Dilemma', 12 *The Journal of Modern African Studies*, 1974, 355–76; S. Tiewul, 'Relations between the U.N. Organization and the OAV in the Settlement of Secessionist Conflicts', 16 HILJ, 1975, 259 ff.; Guilhaudis, *Le droit des peuples à disposer d'eux-mêmes*, 163–200; L. C. Buchheit, *Secession. The Legitimacy of Self-Determination*, New Haven and London 1978, especially 43 ff.; Turp, *Le droit de sécession en droit international public*, 79–201; J. N. Saxena, *Self-Determination: From Biafra to Bangladesh*, Delhi 1978; J. Crawford, *The Creation of States in International Law*, cit., 247–70; R. C. A. White, 'Self-Determination: Time for a Re-Assessment?', 28 NILR, 1981, 161–6; V. P. Nanda, 'Self-Determination under International Law: Validity of Claims to Secede', 13 Case WRJIL, 1981, 263–80; D. Turp, 'Le droit de sécession en droit international public', 20 CYIL, 1982, 24–77; M. R. Islam, 'Secessionist Self-Determination: Some Lessons from Katanga, Biafra and Bangladesh', 22 *Journal of Peace Research*, 1985, 211–21; D. Thürer, 'Das Selbstbestimmungsrecht der Völker – Ein Ueberblick', 22 AVR, 1989, 129–30; A. Heraclides, 'Secessionist Minorities and External Involvement', 44 *International Organization*, 1990, 341–78; A. Buchanan, *Secession: The Morality of Political Divorce from Fort Sumtr to Lithuania and Quebec*, Boulder, Col. 1991; L. Brilmayer, 'Secession and Self-Determination: A Territorial Interpretation', 16 *Yale Journal of International Law*, 1991, 177 ff.; M. Eisner, 'A Procedural Model for the Resolution of Secessionist Disputes', 33 *Harvard International Law Journal*, 1992, especially 415–23; J. E. Stromseth, 'Self-Determination, Secession and Humanitarian Intervention by the United Nations', 86 Proceedings ASIL, 1992, 370–4; S. Oeter, 'Selbstbestimmungsrecht im Wandel – Ueberlegungen zur Debatte um Selbstbestimmung, Sezessionsrecht und 'vorzeitige' Anerkennung', 52 *Zeit.*, 1992, especially 749–63; R. W. McGee, 'The Theory of Secession and Emerging Democracies: A Constitutional Solution', 28 *Stanford Journal of International Law*, 1992, 451–76; L. M. Frankel, 'International Law of Secession: New Rules for a New Era', 14 *Houston Journal of International Law*, 1992, 521–64; T. M. Franck, 'Postmodern Tribalism and the Right to Secession', in Brölmann, Lefeber, and Zieck, *Peoples and Minorities in International Law*, 3–21; R. Higgins, 'Postmodern Tribalism and

This concept was enunciated in the international community even before the principle of self-determination had taken on the status of an international legal standard. When the question of the Aaland Islands was being discussed before the League of Nations, after an International Committee of Jurists had concluded that no legal principle on self-determination yet existed in the international community (see above, pp. 28–31), the Rapporteurs subsequently appointed did not hesitate to rule out any right of secession:

> To concede to minorities, either of language or religion, or to any fraction of a population the right of withdrawing from the community to which they belong, because it is their wish or their good pleasure, would be to destroy order and stability within States and to inaugurate anarchy in international life; it would be to uphold a theory incompatible with the very idea of the State as a territorial and political unity.[38]

This position has been restated time and again, both within and outside the United Nations, by States belonging to all of the political groupings (for instance, on the occasion of the attempted secession of Katanga in 1961 and Biafra in 1967–70 and the successful secession of Bangladesh in 1971). The clause of the UN Declaration on Friendly Relations referred to above, to the extent to which it may be logically interpreted as making allowance for secession under certain very strict circumstances, constitutes a notable deviation from this trend. This deviation can perhaps be explained by reference to the drafting history of the clause. The need to reach a compromise between the Western position that favoured both the universal recognition of self-determination and an emphasis on self-determination as democratic rule and the contrary position of the other groupings of States, probably led the draftsmen to devise a convoluted formula, which is open to a literal and logical interpretation that upholds secession. Whatever the intentions of the draftsmen and the result of their negotiations, and whatever the proper interpretation of the clause under discussion, it cannot be denied that State practice and the overwhelming view of States remain opposed to secession. Indeed, it seems that this is one

---

the Right to Secession – Comments', *ibid.*, 31–5; H. Hannum, 'Synthesis of Discussions', *ibid.*, 334–9; D. Murswiek, 'The Issue of a Right of Secession Reconsidered', in C. Tomuschat (ed.), *Modern Law of Self-Determination*, Dordrecht, Boston, and London 1993, 21–39; A. Eide, 'In Search of Constructive Alternatives to Secession', *ibid.*, 139–76.

[38] Report of the Commission of Rapporteurs, 16 April 1921, League of Nations Council, 28.

of the few areas on which full agreement exists among all States. To quote but one fairly recent statement made outside the United Nations, mention can be made of the written reply given in 1983 by the British Foreign Minister to a parliamentary question about the problem of self-determination for Somalis in Ethiopia:

It has been widely accepted at the United Nations that the right of self-determination does not give every distinct group or territorial sub-division within a State the right to secede from it and thereby dismember the territorial integrity or political unity of sovereign independent States.[39]

Similar statements have been made by other Western countries.[40]

The modes of exercising internal self-determination

The customary rules on the right of self-determination of racial groups do not specify how this right should be implemented. A few indications can be gleaned from State practice: (i) racial groups have the right to take part in the national decision-making process; (ii) they do not possess any right of secession. International law does not specify what other ways of implementing self-determination are open to racial groups, if one such group intends to exercise its right to self-determination in a manner other than that suggested by current rules (which envisage the attainment of a full measure of regional self-government, extensive autonomy, etc.). The limitations of present legal regulation are accounted for by the fact that this regulation has evolved with regard to two specific situations (those of Southern Rhodesia and South Africa), where the black (majority) group was denied access to government. It was therefore felt that it was sufficient to demand such access for the racially discriminated group, in order that self-determination be attained.

At least one further element can, however, be deduced from UN and State practice: the setting up by the racially discriminating State of 'independent' entities within the State, which are made up of the racially discriminated group, can in no way be regarded as a proper way of realizing self-determination, if these 'independent' entities in fact perpetuate racial discrimination. This conclusion is based on the fact that although South Africa insisted that it stood by the principle of self-

---

[39] BYIL, 1983, 409.
[40] See, e.g., the practice of The Netherlands, NYIL, 1979, 324 ff.; and Canadian practice, CYIL, 1978, 369 ff.

determination,[41] in particular by creating the so-called *Bantustans*, the UN has repeatedly proclaimed that these entities were in fact designed to perpetuate apartheid, and therefore called upon all States to refrain from recognizing them.[42] This appeal has been heeded by the overwhelming majority of the world community. UN resolutions have been echoed by the declarations of a number of States, including Western countries.[43]

---

[41] In 1975 the Prime Minister of South Africa P. W. Botha stated: 'We stand by the principle of the right to self-determination and that we want to give the peoples in Southern Africa the opportunity, without interference in the domestic affairs of one another, to come to live in a spirit of détente, each exercising its own right of self-determination.' *Hansard*, 6 February 1975, col. 293. In 1976 the Foreign Minister H. Muller stated the following in the House of Assembly: 'Mr Schaufele stated that the policy of the USA in respect of Southern Africa is based on four fundamental tenets. Two of those four tenets deal with the principle of majority rule, and are the following:

(a) Unequivocal support for majority rule, and (b) a strong preference for a peaceful realization of self-determination and majority rule.

One wonders for what States in Southern Africa Mr Schaufele is advocating majority rule? Is he not aware of what is happening in Africa? Is he not aware that majority rule in Africa is the rare exception to the rule? One of the few Black States that approximates most closely to majority rule in the sense in which the West understands it, will be the Transkei when it becomes independent in October, an event which is the direct outcome of South Africa's policy of separate development. I do not know whether Mr Schaufele and his State Department realize this. If Mr Schaufele had South Africa in mind when he insisted on majority rule – quite possibly this is not the case – it would be my duty to point out that he does not understand the policy of our Government at all. Let us examine his statement again.

"A strong preference for peaceful realization of self-determination and majority rule." Surely we are also striving for the peaceful realization of self-determination and majority rule. But we are going further and we are acting in the spirit of the UNO Charter which refers so pointedly to "self-determination of peoples". Our objective is self-determination for all the peoples in Southern Africa. The majority of every nation or population group should be enabled to elect their own Government, as is the case in Transkei and in other homelands which are on their way to independence' (2 SAJIL, 1976, 303).

[42] See, e.g., GA Resolution 31/6A, of 26 October 1976 (UN Ybk, 1976, 134) and Resolution 32/105N, of 14 December 1977 (UN Ybk, 1977, 176).

[43] See, e.g., the stand taken by Australia. In 1976 Senator Withers, the Minister representing the Minister for Foreign Affairs, was asked the following questions in the Senate 'I refer to the South African Government's proposal to make the area known as Transkei independent on 26 October, next week. Will the Government recognise the independence of the proposed state of Transkei? Will the Minister indicate the reasons for the Government's position on the matter?'

Senator Withers replied as follows: 'The answer to the first question is simple. It is no. The answer as to the Government's general attitude is also quite simple. I will read it because it is a statement of some importance. The Australian Government's basic opposition to the philosophy of apartheid embraces also opposition to the policy of creating Bantustans, which constitutes an extension and consolidation of the apartheid philosophy. The Bantustans policy will lead not only to the fragmentation of the South

Conclusion: the general principle and the customary rules on self-determination

The different role of the principle and the rules

Close scrutiny of the views of Governments, State practice and pronouncements of international bodies such as the UN General Assembly and the International Court of Justice warrants the conclusion that the UN Charter provisions on self-determination have been the starting point of a gradual law-making process generating two sets of legal standards: the treaty provisions of the UN Covenants of 1966 and a cluster of general norms. At the level of general international law[44] one

African State and to the perpetuation of privilege for a minority but also to the dispossession of the majority of the people of South Africa. As such, the Bantustans policy has been condemned by the majority of the international community.

Without wishing ill to the people of Transkei, the Australian Government does not find the arguments put forward in favour of the existence of an independent Transkei convincing and has serious misgivings about the process by which it is to acquire the status of independence.

Furthermore, the recent rejection by homeland leaders of the Bantustans policy strengthens our view that the granting of independence to homelands is not the answer to the political aspirations of black people in South Africa' (7 AYIL, 1981, 430).

On 19 August 1980 the Minister for Foreign Affairs, Mr Peacock, in answer to a written question relating to the South African 'homelands' wrote: 'Australia, along with the rest of the international community, has not recognised the "homelands" created by the South African Government (to date, those declared "independent" are Transkei, Venda and Bophuthatswana). The Government believes that to grant recognition to the "homelands" would be to condone the apartheid system and to accord it an unjustified respectability. The rejection by the majority of the homeland leaders themselves of the policy strengthens our view that the grant of nominal independence to the homelands will not meet the political aspirations of the black people of South Africa' (8 AYIL, 1983, 276).

[44] The view that at present self-determination constitutes a principle of international law is taken by a number of authors, among whom the following can be mentioned: G. Scelle, 'Quelques réflexions sur le droit des peuples à disposer d'eux-mêmes', *Mélanges Spiropoulos*, Bonn 1957, 385–91; C. Economides, 'Le droit des peuples à disposer d'eux-mêmes', 9 *Revue hellénique de droit international*, 1957, 298–300; W. Wengler, 'Le droit de libre disposition des peuples comme principe du droit international', 10 *Revue hellénique de droit international*, 1958, 26–39; Q. Wright, 'The Strengthening of International Law', 98 HR, 1959-III, 193; R. Higgins, *The Development of International Law through the Political Organs of the United Nations*, London 1963, 101–6; J. Crawford, *The Creation of States in International Law*, Oxford 1979, 95; I. Brownlie, 'The Rights of Peoples in Modern International Law', in J. Crawford (ed.), *The Rights of Peoples*, Oxford 1988, 4–6; H. Thierry, 'Le Droit des peuples à disposer d'eux-mêmes', in H. Thierry, S. Sur, J. Combacau, and C. Vallée, *Droit international public*, 4th edn, Paris 1984, 477 ff.; Y. Dinstein, 'Self-Determination and the Middle East Conflict', in Alexander and

may discern the formation of a general *principle* and a number of customary *rules*.[45]

Friedlander (eds.), *Self-Determination: National, Regional and Global Dimensions*, 244–5; Y. Dinstein, 'Collective Human Rights of Peoples vis-à-vis Minorities', in S. Chandra (ed.), *Minorities in National and International Law*, New Delhi 1985, 76–8; D. Thürer, 'Self-Determination', 473; Thürer, 'Selbstbestimmungsrecht der Völker – Ein Ueberblick', 125–32; U. O. Umozurike, *Self-Determination in International Law*, Hamden, Conn., 1972; W. Ofuatey-Kodjoe, *The Principle of Self-Determination in International Law*, New York 1977; M. Shaw, *Title to Territory in Africa*, Oxford 1986, 73–91; I. Brownlie , *Principles of Public International Law*, 4th edn, Oxford 1990, 595–8; H. Thierry, 'L'évolution du droit international', 159; P. Thornberry, *International Law and the Rights of Minorities*, Oxford 1991, 14; I. Brownlie, *Treaties and Indigenous Peoples*, Oxford 1992, 47; Driessen, *A Concept of Nation in International Law*, 55–61.

It should however be pointed out that many authors take the view that self-determination only applies in the case of decolonization. See, e.g., Guilhaudis, *Le droit des peuples à disposer d'eux-mêmes*, 175–220; Guilhaudis, 'Le droit positif à l'auto-détermination', in *Le droit à l'autodétermination (Actes du Colloque international de Saint-Vincent, 2–5 déc. 1979)*, Paris and Nice 1980, 22–39; D. Nguyen Quoc, P. Daillier, and A. Pellet, *Droit international public*, 4th edn, Paris 1992, 488 ff.; Shaw, *Title to Territory in Africa*, cit., p. 90 ('Self-determination applies virtually exclusively within the colonial sphere (although with some potential for development)'); L. M. Demetriadou, 'To What Extent is the Principle of Self-Determination a Right under International Law? How Strictly its Framework has been or should be Defined?', 21 *Cyprus Law Review*, 1988, 3332.

Other authors deny that self-determination has acquired the status of a customary rule of international law, as distinct from Art. 1 common to the two UN Covenants. See, e.g., L.C. Green, 'Self-determination and Settlement of the Arab-Israel Conflict', 65 Proceedings ASIL, 1971, 46; G. Arangio-Ruiz, 'Human Rights and Non-Intervention in the Helsinki Final Act', 157 HR, 1977-IV, 231 and 'L'autodétermination dans l'Acte Final de Helsinki – Droit des puissances et droits des peuples', in *Droits de l'Homme et droits des peuples*, Textes du Séminaire de S. Marino, S. Marino 1983, 48–9; 'Auto-determinazione', 2 (Arangio-Ruiz argues that there is no general principle or rule as distinct from the UN Charter or the provisions of other treaties).

[45] A number of commentators hold the view that self-determination has not acquired the status of a legal principle: R. Y. Jennings, *The Acquisition of Territory in International Law*, Manchester 1963, 78 (however, R. Y. Jennings and A. Watts (eds.), *Oppenheim's International Law*, 9th edn, vol. I, London 1992, at 290, state that the principle of self-determination applies to 'the normal colonial situation'); R. Emerson, *Self-determination Revisited in the Era of Decolonization*, Cambridge, Mass. 1964, 63–4; J. L. Kunz, 'The Principle of Self-Determination of Peoples, Particularly in the Practice of the United Nations', in K. Rabl (ed.), *Studien und Gespräche über Selbstbestimmung und Selbstbestimmungs-recht*, vol. I, Munich 1964, 129–33; J. H. W. Verzijl, *International Law in Historical Perspective*, vol. I (1968), 321–9, 557–8; C. de Visscher, *Théories et réalités en droit international public*, 4th edn, Paris 1970, 161; S. Kaur, 'Self-Determination in International Law', 10 IJIL, 1970, 479; R. Emerson, 'Self-Determination', 65 AJIL, 1971, 464–5; L. Green, 'Self-Determination and Settlement of the Arab–Israeli Conflict', 65 Proceedings ASIL, 1971, 40–8; G. Fitzmaurice, 'The Future of Public International Law and of the International Legal System in the Circumstances of Today: Special Report', in *Institut de Droit International, Livre du Centenaire*, 1973, 232–5; G. Schwarzenberger, 'The Purposes

The principle enshrines the quintessence of self-determination, namely the 'need to pay regard to the freely expressed will of peoples' (as it was put by the International Court of Justice in *Western Sahara*)[46] each time the fate of peoples is at issue. In other words, the principle sets out a general and fundamental standard of behaviour: governments must not decide the life and future of peoples at their discretion. Peoples must be enabled freely to express their wishes in matters concerning their condition.

Clearly, this principle poses a very loose standard; it does not define either the *units of self-determination* or *areas or matters* to which it applies, or the *means or methods* of its implementation. In particular, it does not specify whether self-determination should have an *internal* or *external* dimension, nor does it point to the *objective* of self-determination (independent statehood, integration or association with another State, self-government, secession from an existing State, etc.). The principle simply sets out general guidelines for State behaviour and therefore acts as a sort of overarching standard for international relations.

The role and purport of this principle can only be grasped if one moves from a correct analysis of the significance that legal principles currently have in the world community. Principles do not differ from treaty or customary rules simply in that they are more general and less precise – as has been held by a number of commentators,[47] as well as the International Court of Justice in the *Gulf of Maine* case.[48] Rather, principles differ from legal rules in that they are the expression and result of conflicting views of States on matters of crucial importance. When States cannot agree upon definite and specific standards of behaviour because of their principled, opposing attitudes, but need, however, some sort of basic guideline for their conduct, their actions and discussions eventually lead to the formulation of principles. In this respect principles are a typical expression of the present world community, whereas in the old community – relatively homogenous and less conflictual – specific and precise rules prevailed. Principles, being general, loose and multifaceted, lend themselves to various and even contradictory applications, and in addition are

---

of the United Nations: International Judicial Practice', 4 IYHR, 1974, 247, 42–3; Y. Z. Blum, 'Reflections on the Changing Concept of Self-Determination', 10 *Israel Law Review*, 1975, 509–14. Pomerance, *Self-Determination in Law and Practice*, 70–2, also seems to take a negative stand on the issue (in her view, self-determination 'is not really *jus* – or only questionably so').

[46] ICJ, Reports 1975, 33 (paras. 58 and 59).
[47] See, for example, Thierry, *L'évolution du droit international*, 123.
[48] ICJ, Reports 1984, 288–90 (para. 79).

susceptible to being manipulated and used for conflicting purposes. On the other hand, principles have great normative potential and dynamic force: among other things, one can deduce from them specific rules, to the extent that these rules are not at variance with State practice.[49]

Clearly, self-determination is one of the typical legal principles of the present world community. With the other fundamental principles[50] it shares a high degree of generality and abstraction. It primarily points to the course of action to be taken when one is confronted with problems concerning the destiny of a people. The existing ideological and political conflicts among States have however prevented the principle from acquiring specificity, as mentioned above.

The task of specifying the issues that the principle does not address is fulfilled – to some extent, as we shall soon see – by individual customary rules. These rules cover specific areas where a broader measure of agreement has emerged among States as to the proper conduct to be taken by States. We saw above that there have evolved in the international community rules on the external self-determination of (i) colonial peoples and (ii) peoples under foreign military occupation. These rules set out their field of application, the units of self-determination, as well as – at least in one case – the various alternatives that may be pursued. Furthermore, a customary rule (or, more exactly, a set of rules) on internal self-determination for racial groups has crystallized; once again, these rules indicate at least the beneficiary of self-determination.[51] The purport and content of these rules call for some additional remarks.

---

[49] For a masterful treatment of principles in international law, see M. Virally, 'Panorama du droit international contemporain', 183 HR, 1983-V, 174–5. On international principles, see also the important writings of B. Graefrath, *Zur Stellung der Prinzipien im Gegenwärtigen Völkerrecht*, Berlin 1968, particularly 3–15 and G. Herczegh, *General Principles of Law and the International Legal Order*, Budapest 1969. See also H. Kröger (ed.), *Völkerrecht*, vol. I, Berlin 1981, 103–9.

[50] See Cassese, *International Law in a Divided World*, 126–65.

[51] On the concept of peoples, see below, Chapter 12, pp. 326–7. See also A. Kiss, 'The Peoples' Right to Self-Determination', 7 *Human Rights Law Journal*, 1986, 72–3. It is interesting to note that in 1952, in the UN General Assembly, the delegate of Lebanon while stressing that self-determination must be applied 'immediately' to non-self-governing peoples, for this was the most urgent task of the UN (GAOR, 7th session, 3rd Committee, 454th Mtg, paras. 15–16), stated however that self-determination was a universal principle (*ibid.*, paras. 16 and 19) and then went on to point out that 'for the sake of argument' *six categories* of peoples deprived of self-determination, and therefore entitled to enjoy it, could be distinguished: 'The first comprised peoples which constituted independent and sovereign States, whose independence and sovereignty had to be respected. The second comprised the peoples of States which had lost their independence and sovereignty and wished to regain it; their independence should be

Of the three sets of rules just referred to, no doubt the most elaborate is that concerning colonial peoples. International rules on this matter not only point to the units of selfdetermination (colonial peoples) but also specify the techniques for ascertaining the wishes of the populations concerned (plebiscites or referendums) and the various possible objectives to be attained (independent statehood, integration, or association with an existing State). The reasons why it is in this area that international legal regulation – in spite of the ambiguities and loopholes with which it is marred – is more elaborate become evident if recent history is recalled: after the Second World War decolonization was by far the most pressing problem and the one most in need of a prompt solution; States therefore felt it necessary to agree upon detailed rules on the matter. In contrast, the rules on self-determination of peoples under foreign military occupation only point to the units of self-determination. Nothing can be directly deduced from those rules as regards the *means* of exercising self-determination or the *options* available to the 'oppressed' population. The latter is probably so because normally foreign military occupation also amounts to a breach of the fundamental ban on the use of force; States therefore felt that, the right to self-determination of the 'occupied' people being merely one 'side' of the obligation of the occupying Power to pull out of the territory, it was only natural that this should be the normal 'objective' of self-determination. For the same reason, it was not deemed necessary to lay down procedures for the exercise of the right: the withdrawal of the foreign Power from the territory would *ipso facto* realize that right. Or, in some cases such as those of Afghanistan and Kampuchea,[52] to which that of Namibia could be assimilated,[53] it was felt that it was also necessary to rely upon the general *principle* of self-determination, and to this end carry out free and genuine elections under international scrutiny, so

given back to them. The third category comprised peoples which, although constituted in independent and sovereign States, were prevented by their own dictatorial governments from exercising their right of self-determination; their internal liberation should be achieved. The fourth category comprised peoples who formed an integral part of an independent and sovereign State, but considered themselves to be absolutely different from the other elements in that country and wished to set up a separate State; that was the case of some minorities, and the question was one of granting them the right of self-determination as peoples. The fifth category comprised peoples constituting States which were formally or nominally independent and sovereign, but whose independence and sovereignty were forcibly controlled by another State; such control had to be removed. The sixth category comprised non-self-governing peoples whose territories were administered by the so-called colonial Powers; they should be granted the right of self-determination, either immediately or gradually' (*ibid.*, para. 13).

[52] See above, pp. 94 and 148.   [53] See above, pp. 94–5, 149.

that the relevant people could exercise its right to (internal and external) self-determination. Given that this is a plausible explanation, it however remains true that there may be circumstances in which the present legal regulation proves unsatisfactory. A case in point is the Israeli occupation of Arab territories following the six-day war of 1967. As is well known and will also be specified below (see Chapter 10), Israel did not breach Article 2 paragraph 4 of the Charter when it started armed hostilities, for it acted under Article 51, that is, in self-defence. Furthermore, there is legal uncertainty about who is the holder of sovereign rights over the territories. These are all complicating factors that render the situation all the more complex. The rules under discussion do not offer any proper guidelines for this situation.

No less unsatisfactory is the body of rules on the internal self-determination of racial groups. They only define the units of self-determination; in contrast they do not specify the procedures for attaining self-determination. As for the *goal* of self-determination, they confine themselves to contemplating the participation of representatives of racial groups in the decision-making process of government. They do not provide for other possible options. To understand this state of affairs, it should be emphasized again that States had two specific instances in mind when these rules crystallized: Southern Rhodesia and South Africa. In both instances the racial minority prevented the majority from having access to government. As a consequence, when contributing to the gradual formation of the customary rules on this matter, States contented themselves with the request that a racial group be given free access to government. How this access should be achieved was not specified (although it would probably be by the dismantling of racist structures of power), nor whether such access should go beyond the right to elect representatives of the racial group to the national assembly or other representative bodies.

After emphasizing some of the failings of existing rules, let us turn to the general principle on self-determination referred to above, to see what sort of relationship exists between it and the customary rules. I submit that the principle plays a threefold role.

Firstly, it indicates the *method* of exercising self-determination (the free and genuine expression of the will and wishes of the people concerned). This method, it should be emphasized, applies to any form of self-determination, whether external or internal. In this respect, the principle fulfils the crucial role of pointing to the procedures through which the right of self-determination provided for in customary law should be implemented[54] – to the extent, of course, that this is rendered possible by the specific factual circumstances.[55]

Secondly, the principle can serve as a basic *standard of interpretation* in cases when a customary rule is either unclear or ambiguous. For instance, the principle can prove helpful if it is disputed whether a people under foreign domination can exercise its right by simply demanding the withdrawal of the occupying Power, or should instead be enabled freely to choose its international status by referendum. Similarly, the principle could help clarify the content of the customary rule on internal self-determination (racial groups denied equal access to government are entitled freely to decide how to realize this access), as well as the purport of the treaty provisions on the subject (Article 1 common to the two UN Covenants on Human Rights should be so construed as to enable peoples of the Contracting States to express their will in a truly free and genuine way, hence to be able freely to choose their rulers without any hindrance whatsoever).

Thirdly, the principle can be of use *in cases not covered by specific rules*. This can be said to have been so as far as territorial cessions are concerned. It

---

[54] The procedures are normally the holding of plebiscites or referendums. On the practice of plebiscites, see in particular Johnson, *Self-Determination within the Community of Nations*, 59–98. More generally, see K. Doehring, 'Formen und Methoden der Anwendung des Selbstbestimmungsrechts', in Blumenwitz and Meissner, *Das Selbstbestimmungsrecht der Völker und die Deutsche Frage*, 61 ff.

[55] The principle, of course, does not specify what is meant by the 'genuine' expression of the free will of a people. Some light, however, is shed on this notion by the discussion that took place in the UN on the occasion of the elaboration of Art. 25 of the Covenant on Civil and Political Rights. The relevant debate was concisely summarized by K. J. Partsch ('Freedom of Conscience and Expression, and Political Freedoms', in Henkin, *The International Bill of Rights*, 240) as follows: 'The principal question is whether one can interpret the term 'genuine' as covering an election in which not more than one candidate or one list is presented to the voters and no opposition to the ruling party is allowed. When the Universal Declaration was drafted, there were strong expressions that genuine elections required a genuine choice among parties and candidates and the right to vote against the government, free of any pressure. Discussions during the drafting of the Covenant were less candid. In the final discussions of the draft Covenant in the Third Committee in 1961 the delegate of Chile reported that the adjective "genuine" in subparagraph (b) had been used to guarantee "that all elections of every kind faithfully reflected the opinion of the population and to protect the electors against governmental pressure and fraud".

This very diplomatic formulation avoided any allusion to a choice between at least two parties or to opposition against the government; perhaps it was sought to make it possible for single-party states to adhere to the Covenant. But it is difficult to avoid the conclusion that an election in which voters have no meaningful choice between parties or candidates and cannot express that choice without compulsion or fear is not "genuine" but a violation of Article 25'.

does not seem that the pronouncements of States and the international practice in this matter have hardened into a specific customary rule to the effect that the population concerned must always be enabled to express its free and genuine will as to whether or not to be transferred to another country (to use the language of the Atlantic Charter, this would be a rule providing that no 'territorial changes' are permissible 'that do not accord with the freely expressed wishes of the people concerned').[56] Nor, on the other hand, does a rule exist stating that the people's views are irrelevant or should not be sought. Here the principle at hand comes into play and requires that no cession or transfer should be carried out if the population concerned is not in agreement (see below, pp. 189–90).[57]

Self-determination as imposing obligations towards the whole international community and as part of jus cogens

Two distinguishing features of the law on self-determination should now be emphasized, which are indicative, at the legal level, of the overriding importance self-determination has now acquired in the world community.

---

[56] However, some national Constitutions lay down the principle. Mention can be made, for example, of the French Constitution of 1958, Art. 53(3) which provides that 'Nulle cession, nul échange, nulle adjonction de territoire n'est valable sans le consentement des populations intéressées' (this provision takes up Art. 27(2) of the 1946 French Constitution). Art. 53(3) was applied by the 'Conseil Constitutionnel' with regard to the Comoros Islands in 1975 (see J.C. Mestre, 'L'indivisibilité de la République française et l'exercise du droit à l'autodétermination', RDP, 1976, 431–62; L. Favoreu, 'La décision du 30 décembre 1975 dans l'affaire des Comores', *ibid.*, 537–81).

[57] In spite of the joint working and interplay of the principle and the rules on self-determination, the fact remains that the international regulation of this matter is far from satisfactory. In this connection, it is fitting to recall the wise remarks set out in 1958 by W. Wengler: 'Plus on étudie donc le principe de la libre disposition des peuples jusque dans les détails de son application pratique, plus il paraît nécessaire de le compléter par d'autres règles du droit international. Il faut des garanties internationales pour la liberté des plébiscites. Si la population du territoire, qui est choisie comme base d'un plébiscite, n'est pas d'opinion unanime et si une majorité l'emporte sur une minorité, le droit de disposer d'elle-même exercé par la collectivité doit être complété par le droit d'option et par une protection efficace internationale de la minorité. La libre disposition des peuples exige aussi une réglementation internationale des migrations, basée sur la liberté de mouvements de l'individu, l'interdiction de priver un homme de son foyer, et l'interdiction des manipulations gouvernementales destinées à changer la composition de la population d'un territoire. Il faut surtout réprimer l'abus du droit de la libre disposition par la population habitant un territoire contenant des richesses naturelles nécessaires à l'humanité entière' ('Le droit de libre disposition des peuples', 38–9).

First, the obligations flowing from the principle and rules on self-determination are *erga omnes*, that is, they belong to that class of international legal obligations which are not 'bilateral' or reciprocal, but arise in favour of all members of the international community. As is well known, following the celebrated dictum of the ICJ in the *Barcelona Traction* case,[58] there is now a firm distinction between two sets of international legal obligations: (a) those which (i) only arise as between pairs of States and (ii) are reciprocal or 'synallagmatic' in kind, in that their fulfilment by each State is conditioned by that of the other State, and (b) the obligations which (i) are incumbent on a State towards all the other members of the international community, (ii) must be fulfilled regardless of the behaviour of other States in the same field, and (iii) give rise to a claim for their execution that accrues to any other member of the international community.[59]

There can be no gainsaying that the set of norms on self-determination, to which attention has been drawn above, imposes obligations *erga omnes*. This proposition is supported by the fact that both within and outside the United Nations States have consistently taken the view that (a) self-determination must be respected by any State (be it a colonial State or a Power occupying a foreign territory or a State denying a racial group equal access to government), (b) it must be respected regardless of whether or not third States, finding themselves in the same situation, comply with the norms on self-determination and (c) any other international subject is entitled to demand respect for self-determination. However, we shall see below (pp. 147–58) that in actual practice States have only seldom made use of their right to demand compliance with international standards on self-determination by a given State.

Let us now turn to the question of *jus cogens*. According to a number of commentators,[60] self-determination has now become a peremptory norm

---

58 ICJ, Reports 1970, 32.
59 On obligations *erga omnes*, see: J. Juste Ruiz, 'Las obligaciones *erga omnes* en Derecho internacional público', *Estudios de derecho internacional – Homenaje al Profesor Miaja de La Muela*, vol. I, Madrid 1979, 219 ff.; P. Weil, 'Towards Relative Normativity in International Law?' 77 AJIL, 1983, 413 ff.; J. Frowein, 'Die Verpflichtungen erga omnes in Völkerrecht und ihre Durchsetzung', *Fest. H. Mosler*, Berlin, Heidelberg, and New York 1983, 241 ff.; P. Picone, 'Obblighi reciproci e obbligazioni *erga omnes* degli Stati nel campo della protezione internazionale dell'ambiente marino dall'inquinamento', in V. Starace (ed.), *Diritto internazionale e protezione dell'ambiente marino*, 1983, 15 ff.
60 See Brownlie, *Principles of Public International Law*, 513, 515; H. Bokor-Szegö, 'The International Legal Content of the Right of Self-Determination as Reflected by the

of international law from which no derogation is admissible by means of a treaty or any similar international transaction. These authors, however, do not provide any element of State practice or *opinio juris* in support of their view.

Two issues should be discussed in this respect. Firstly, on what basis can it be contended that self-determination belongs to the body of international peremptory norms? Secondly, given the distinction outlined above between a principle proper of self-determination and a set of specific customary rules, which of them can be said to be part of *jus cogens*?

As far as the first issue is concerned, the legal basis for the transformation of self-determination into *jus cogens* cannot of course be found in views – however authoritative – put forward by persons acting in their individual capacity. I am referring to the well-known separate opinion of Judge Ammoun in the *Barcelona Traction* case,[61] to the opinion of some members of the International Law Commission,[62] as well as the views expressed in the UN Sub-Commission on the Prevention of Discrimination and Protection of Minorities,[63] and, more recently, in the UN International

Disintegration of the Colonial System', in *Questions of International Law*, Budapest 1966, 39–41; H. Gross-Espiell, 'Self-Determination and Jus Cogens', in A. Cassese (ed.), *United Nations. Fundamental Rights*, Alphen aan den Rijn1979, 167; Ermacora, 'The Protection of Minorities before the United Nations', 325; E. Klein, 'Vereinte Nationen und Selbstbestimmungsrecht', in D. Blumenwitz and B. Meissner (eds.), *Das Selbstbestimmungsrecht der Völker und die deutsche Frage*, Cologne 1984, 121; Shaw, *Title to Territory in Africa*, 91; A. Kiss, 'The Peoples' Right to Self-determination', at 174; N. Quoc Dinh, P. Daillier, and A. Pellet, *Droit international public*, 4th edn, Paris 1992, 490; A. Pellet, 'The Destruction of Troy Will Not Take Place', in Playfair, *International Law and the Administration of Occupied Territories*, 184; J. A. Frowein, 'Self-Determination as a Limit to Obligations under International Law', in Tomuschat, *Modern Law of Self-Determination*, 218–21. Cf. also Cassese, *International Law in a Divided World*, 136.

By far the most extensive treatment of this issue can be found in L. Hannikainen, *Peremptory Norms (jus cogens) in International Law*, Helsinki 1988, 357–424. This author concludes that 'all States are *under the peremptory obligation*: (1) not to forcibly subject alien peoples to a colonial-type domination; (2) not to keep alien peoples by forcible or deceitful means under a colonial-type domination; and (3) not to exploit the natural resources of those alien territories, which are under their colonial-type domination, to the serious detriment of the people of those territories' (at 421).

That self-determination has become part of *jus cogens* is *denied* by Calogeropoulos-Stratis, *Le droit des peuples à disposer d'eux-mêmes*, 269–71; Crawford, *The Creation of States in International Law*, at 81; Pomerance, *Self-Determination in Law and Practice*, 70–2; and B. Driessen, *A Concept of Nation in International Law*, 60–1, at note 57.

[61] ICJ, Reports 1970, 304, 312.

[62] See, e.g., *Yearbook of the ILC*, 1963, vol. II, 199.

[63] In 1978, in reporting to the UN Human Rights Commission on the work of the Sub-Commission (a body consisting of experts acting in a personal capacity), T. van Boven, Director of the UN Division of Human Rights, stated that: 'The view had been

Law Commission by the Special Rapporteur on State Responsibility, G. Arangio-Ruiz.[64] These views cannot be held to reflect State practice, although they are highly indicative of the new trends emerging in the international community and may contribute, and have indeed contributed, to the evolution of State practice. More weight should of course be attributed to statements made by State organs (it should be noted, in passing, that in the absence of State practice proper, for the purpose of classifying an international rule as belonging to *jus cogens*, the *opinio juris* of States as to the legal standing of that rule may prove sufficient).[65]

In this respect, reference can be made to the pronouncements of various States in the UN General Assembly on the occasion of a discussion on the Draft Articles on the Law of Treaties in 1963,[66] at the Vienna Conference on the Law of Treaties in 1968–9,[67] as well as in the General Assembly in 1970, on the occasion of the discussion on the Declaration on Friendly

widely expressed in the Sub-Commission that the principle of self-determination had the character of *jus cogens* – a peremptory norm of international law' (UN Doc. E/CN.4/SR 1431, at 3, para. 6). The same view was expressed in the Human Rights Commission by the representative of the PLO (*ibid.*, 1437, at 8, para. 26), but it is doubtful whether it can be equated to that of a State, for the purpose of the formation of international practice.

[64] G. Arangio-Ruiz, *Fourth Report on State Responsibility*, UN Doc. A/CN.4/444/Add. 1 (25 May 1992), at 31 (para. 91).

[65] Recently, it has been authoritatively held by C. Dominicé ('Le grand retour du droit naturel en droit des gens', *Mélanges J.-M. Grossen*, Basle and Frankfurt am Main 1992, especially 401–9; cf. also J. Verhoeven, 'Le droit, le juge et la violence', RGDIP 1987, 1205) that some general precepts based upon *ethical* values, and in particular those precepts which belong to *jus cogens*, can acquire the status of legally binding rules or even peremptory norms of international law without the confirmation by any State practice proper, provided the element of *opinio juris* is present.

[66] See GAOR, XXIst Session, VIth Committee, 905th Meeting.

[67] See the statements of the delegates of the USSR (United Nations Conference on the Law of Treaties, First Session, 1968, *Official Records*, 294, para. 3), Sierra Leone (*ibid.*, 300, para. 9), Ghana (*ibid.*, 301, para. 16), Cyprus (*ibid.*, 306, para. 69), Poland (United Nations Conference on the Law of Treaties, Second Session, 1969, *Official Records* 99, para. 71), Byelorussia (*ibid.*, 105, para. 48). See also the statements of those delegates who affirmed that all the principles laid down in Art. 1 (or Arts. 1 and 2) of the UN Charter belong to *jus cogens*: Poland (United Nations Conference on the Law of Treaties, First Session, *Official Records*, 302, para. 35; see also Second Session, *Official Records*, 99, para 70), Romania (First Session, *Official Records*, 312, para. 55), Czechoslovakia (*ibid.*, 318, para. 25), Ecuador (Second Session, *Official Records*, 96, para. 35), Cuba (*ibid.*, 97, para. 42), Ukraine (*ibid.*, 100, para. 75), the USSR (*ibid.*, 104, para. 41).

Relations.[68] Reference can also be made to the submissions made in 1975 before the ICJ both by a Western State (Spain) and by Algeria and Morocco (this last State asserted, however, that only the 'principle of decolonization' – of which self-determination is only one of the possible methods of implementation – has the status of *jus cogens*).[69]

The problem with these pronouncements is that they mostly emanate from two groups of States: that is, the developing and 'socialist' States (as they were then called) but not from Western countries. Thus, in the UN General Assembly a view favourable to regarding self-determination as *jus cogens* was taken by Ukraine, Czechoslovakia, the USSR, Peru and Pakistan, Iraq, Ethiopia, and Trinidad and Tobago while at the Vienna Conference a similar view was expressed by the USSR, Sierra Leone, Ghana, Cyprus, Byelorussia, and Poland. As for Western countries, it would seem that only Greece in 1970,[70] Spain,[71] and Italy in 1975[72] are on record as upholding the view at issue. However, an important statement by the US should also be mentioned. It was made in 1979 by the Legal Adviser to the US State Department in a memorandum submitted to the then Acting Secretary of State Warren Christopher. In this document the Legal Adviser stated that the Soviet invasion of Afghanistan was contrary to Article 2(4) of the UN Charter as well as to the principle of self-determination of peoples, to which that provision referred. As Article 2(4)

---

68 See the statements of Iraq (GAOR, 25th Session, Sixth Committee, A/C.6/SR.1180, para. 6), Ethiopia (*ibid.*, 1182, para. 49) and Trinidad and Tobago (*ibid.*, 1183, para. 5). A contrary view was taken by Hungary (*ibid.*, 1179, para. 35: 'The Declaration would not have the status of a treaty and could not be considered *jus cogens*').

69 See, e.g., the Memorial of the Spanish Government to the ICJ in the *Western Sahara* case, ICJ, *Pleadings. Oral Arguments. Documents*, Western Sahara, vol. I, 206–8; the oral statement of Mr Bedjaoui, counsel for Algeria, *ibid.*, vol. IV, 497–500 and vol. V, 319–20; and the oral statement of Mr Vedel, counsel for Morocco, *ibid.*, vol. V, 179–80.

70 In 1970, in the UN General Assembly, on the occasion of the debate on the Declaration on Friendly Relations, the Greek delegate stated that 'The Declaration would constitute an important contribution to the safeguarding of international peace and security, and the consensus reached on the text of the seven principles furnished greatly needed clarification of the content of the related *jus cogens* provisions of the Charter' (GAOR, 25th Session, VIth Committee, A/C.6/SR.1181, para. 31).

71 See above, note 69.

72 In 1975, Prof. G. Sperduti, in his capacity as Italian delegate to the UN Human Rights Committee stated that 'The right of peoples to self-determination was not just one of the fundamental principles of the new world order. It could also be classified in a new category of international legal rules recently stated and still in the course of codification. The principle might be reckoned among those which came under the head of *jus cogens*. If it was thus classified, it would have very important repercussions and the two Special Rapporteurs appointed by the Sub-Commission should try to study the problem from that standpoint too' (UN Doc. E/CN.4/SR.1300, 91).

was to be regarded as a peremptory norm of international law, the Treaty of 1978 between Afghanistan and the USSR, to the extent that it would support the Soviet intervention, was to be regarded as null and void as being in conflict with *jus cogens*.[73] No doubt this was a very skilful and subtle way of elevating self-determination – albeit in an indirect and roundabout way – to the rank of *jus cogens*. It can be contended that a more straightforward way of relying on self-determination would consist in arguing that any invasion of a foreign territory such as that of Afghanistan amounts to the breach of two distinct and closely intertwined peremptory norms: the one prohibiting any unauthorized use of force and the norm on the right of peoples to self-determination. The US adverted instead to self-determination only insofar as it is referred to in Article 2(4). Nevertheless, whichever of these two views is regarded as the more correct, the fact remains that the US statement constitutes an important contribution to the consolidation of self-determination as a norm of *jus cogens*.

One should also mention that in its Opinion no. 1, of 11 January 1992, the 'Arbitration Committee' set up by the EC 'Conference on Yugoslavia' held that 'the peremptory norms of general international law and, in particular, respect for the fundamental rights of the individuals and the rights of peoples and minorities, are binding on all the parties to the

[73] It is worth quoting the relevant passages of this important pronouncement by the US authorities: '1. By the terms of Article 2(4) of the UN Charter, the USSR is bound "to refrain in its international relations from the threat or use of force against the territorial integrity or political independence of any State, or in any other manner inconsistent with the Purposes of the United Nations". Among those Purposes are "respect for the principle of equal rights and self-determination of peoples" (Article 1(2)). The use of Soviet troops forcibly to depose one ruler and substitute another clearly is a use of force against the political independence of Afghanistan; and it just as clearly contravenes the principle of Afghanistan's equal international rights and the self-determination of the Afghan people . . . 3. No treaty between the USSR and Afghanistan can overcome these Charter obligations of the USSR. Article 103 of the Charter provides: "In the event of conflict between the obligations of the Members of the United Nations under the present Charter and their obligations under any other international agreement, their obligations under the present Charter shall prevail." 4. Nor is it clear that the treaty between the USSR and Afghanistan, concluded in 1978 between the revolutionary Taraki Government and the USSR, is valid. If it actually does lend itself to support of Soviet intervention of the type in question in Afghanistan, it would be void under contemporary principles of international law, since it would conflict with what the Vienna Convention on the Law of Treaties describes as a "peremptory norm of general international law" (Article 53), namely, that contained in Article 2(4) of the Charter. While agreement on precisely what are the peremptory norms of international law is not broad, there is universal agreement that the exemplary illustration of a peremptory norm is Article 2(4)' (in 74 AJIL, 1980, 418 ff.).

succession [to Yugoslavia]'.[74] Although this ruling, restated in Opinion no. 9, of 4 July 1992,[75] may be regarded as too sweeping and in addition emanates from a body consisting of individuals and not of States, it is nevertheless indicative of the increasingly strong movement among Western countries towards *jus cogens*.[76]

The criticism may, however, be made that these elements of Western State practice are too few and far between to signal a consistent and generalized attitude. If this view is accepted, one could adopt the following line of reasoning. It is well known that for a norm of *jus cogens* to have developed the 'acceptance and recognition' of 'the international community of States as a whole' is required (ex Article 53 of the Vienna Convention on the Law of Treaties, which in this respect can be regarded as part of customary law).[77] The lack of support by an important segment of the world community might therefore lead to the conclusion that self-determination has not acquired the rank and force of *jus cogens*. Arguably, however, for a norm of *jus cogens* to evolve, it is not always necessary for all States to say in so many words that they consider that norm as existing. Although such formal 'labelling' proves important and in some cases indispensable, there may be instances where the upgrading of a rule to *jus cogens* may result *implicitly* from the attitude taken by States in their international dealings and in collective fora. Self-determination is a case in point. Undisputedly *Western* countries have stated time and again that self-determination is one of the fundamental principles of the world community; they have consequently agreed to such international instruments as the 1970 UN Declaration on Friendly Relations and the 1975 Helsinki Final Act; they have also insisted on the universality of self-determination, thereby showing that they intend to assign to self-determination a scope and impact extending far beyond the meaning advocated by the developing and the then socialist countries. By the same token, Western countries, except for France, have eventually accepted the formation of *jus cogens* as a class of 'special' international norms.[78] It would

---

[74] For the text of the Opinion, see 3 EJIL, 1992, 182–3.

[75] For the text, see 4 EJIL, 1993, at 89.

[76] In addition and *generally speaking*, one should not underevaluate, as an element of international practice, the arbitral award in the *Guinea-Bissau* v. *Senegal* case (*Détermination de la frontière maritime*) of 31 July 1989; the Tribunal *implicitly* regarded self-determination as a peremptory norm of international law (see 94 RGDIP 1990, 234–5).

[77] See Cassese, *International Law in a Divided World*, 175–9.

[78] See also the dictum of the International Court of Justice in the *Nicaragua* case (ICJ, Reports 1986, 100–1, para. 190).

therefore seem appropriate, in this case, to rely upon a syllogism: (i) Western countries have accepted *jus cogens*; (ii) they regard the principle of self-determination as fundamental and universal in international relations; (iii) they consequently may be assumed to consider self-determination as non-derogable on the part of States. It is submitted that resort to this 'syllogistic reasoning' is warranted in this case (but possibly not in others) because of the exceptional wealth of pronouncements by Western States on the fundamental importance of self-determination in its various versions that have become accepted at the normative level.

The aforementioned reasoning can therefore make up for the lack, among Western countries, of widespread explicit support for considering self-determination as a part of *jus cogens*. Consequently, the conclusion is justified that self-determination constitutes a peremptory norm of international law. This view, it should be added, is warranted even though so far no case has been raised in the appropriate fora of the world community of a possible conflict of a treaty with *jus cogens* (the case of East Timor, as we shall see, has been brought by Portugal before the ICJ as an instance of State responsibility because the lack of the necessary procedural requirements has prevented Portugal from raising the question of the possible nullity of the treaty in question).

Let us now turn to the second issue raised above, namely the question of whether the peremptory nature of self-determination is a quality attaching to the aforementioned general principle or to the various customary rules specifying and elaborating this principle. Given the close link and indeed complementarity of the principle and the rules, it would be artificial and improper to attribute a different legal force to each of the two classes of standards. Furthermore, it is no coincidence that whenever States have referred to self-determination as belonging to *jus cogens*, they have not specified either the areas of application of self-determination, the means or methods of its implementation, or the permissible outcome of self-determination. States have generically adverted to the 'principle' (*lato sensu*) or, more simply, to self-determination. It follows that the whole cluster of legal standards (the general principle and the customary rules) on self-determination should be regarded as belonging to the body of peremptory norms.

6

The holders of the right to self-determination and the means of ensuring observance of the right

Introductory remarks

In the inter-war period, John Maynard Keynes, among others, criticized Wilson for having launched his grand concept of self-determination without proper regard to specifics. The vision was there but not the means of implementing it or of establishing a nexus between the ideal and the complex reality of the modern age:

> [Wilson] had no plan, no scheme, no constructive ideas whatever for clothing with the flesh of life the commandments which he had thundered from the White House. He could have preached a sermon on any of them or have addressed a stately prayer to the Almighty for their fulfilment; but he could not frame their concrete application to the actual state of Europe.[1]

This problem is still with us today, despite the fact that the 'Wilsonian principle' has to a large extent evolved into a set of international norms. Although one can speak of the right to self-determination, the methods of asserting the right and the means of insuring that the people's will is respected are still somewhat embryonic.

The recipients of the right to self-determination under the UN Covenants: two possible views

Under the UN Covenants, the attendant *obligations* for the realization of self-determination no doubt fall on the Contracting States. Each of them is duty-bound to grant self-determination to those peoples entitled to it and

---

[1] J. M. Keynes, *The Economic Consequences of the Peace*, London 1919, 39.

to respect their expressed choice. Each Contracting State also has a *legal right* to demand that all other Contracting States in violation of Article 1 rectify their behaviour.

Whilst the rights and obligations of the States can be identified with relative ease, ascertaining those of the peoples is quite difficult in comparison. In fact, it is questionable whether the Covenants grant '*peoples*' an international *right* proper to self-determination. As we shall see, two differing views are possible.

The view according to which peoples are only beneficiaries of Article 1

Arguably, it makes little sense to assert that an aggregate of individuals has a substantive legal right if the group has no means of enforcing that right and no legal redress when the right is violated. 'Peoples' cannot set in motion the various implementation measures provided for in the Covenants, in particular in the Covenant on Civil and Political Rights. The Optional Protocol to this Covenant only provides for the right of *individuals* to lodge 'communications' with the UN Human Rights Committee (Article 1 of the Protocol provides for the 'competence of the Committee to receive and consider communications from individuals, subject to its [i.e. of the State Party to the Covenant which has ratified the Protocol] jurisdiction, claiming to be victims of a violation by that State Party of any of the rights set forth in the Covenant'). In addition – as pointed out above (see Chapter 2) – the Human Rights Committee has taken the view that it can only consider 'communications' emanating from individuals alleging that they are victims of breaches of their *individual rights* by the State complained of. Consequently, according to the Committee, no complaint can be lodged by individuals concerning alleged contraventions of Article 1 on self-determination. The reasons for this state of affairs and, in particular, for the case-law of the Human Rights Committee just referred to are not difficult to discern. Both the draftsmen of the Covenants and the Protocol, and the Human Rights Committee, have shied away from admitting that individuals having some sort of status as representatives of a whole people could complain about alleged breaches of Article 1 or, alternatively, of consistent violations of other provisions of the Covenant that amount to a blatant violation of the right to self-determination. To be sure, it would have proved difficult to identify the elements that would secure the standing of a complainant in order to lodge a communication concerning Article 1; in particular, it would have proved difficult to establish whether he should act as a 'representative' of the people and, if so, on what conditions, or if he could bring a class action (on this issue see below, Chapter 12). The Human Rights Committee has chosen a strict interpretation whereby the '*collective right*' set out in Article 1 cannot be indicated by individuals. Under this interpretation only '*individual* rights' can be invoked before the Committee.

It follows from this that ultimately, under the Covenants, peoples do not actually possess a veritable right to self-determination. To assert that peoples possess a legal right would be tantamount to asserting the existence of a right that exists in theory only. It is the Contracting States which hold the rights conferred by the Covenants. Peoples are simply 'beneficiaries' of these State rights and of the corresponding duties incumbent upon each Contracting State.[2]

The view according to which peoples are holders of legal rights proper

A different and, I submit, better view can, however, be advanced, to the effect that under the Covenants peoples are more than beneficiaries of rights and duties accruing to Contracting States, and indeed are among the direct addressees of Article 1. Three arguments can be put forward to support this view.

First, to contend that ultimately peoples do not hold any right under Article 1 would be contrary to the actual wording of that provision ('All peoples *have the right* to self-determination. *By virtue of the right* they freely determine their political status . . . The States Parties to the present Covenant . . . *shall promote* the realization of *the right* of self-determination, and *shall respect that right*'). This wording was carefully chosen and no doubt is meant to convey the idea that on the strength of Article 1 peoples become 'partners' with the Contracting States, in that they are put on the same footing as those States. It would indeed be contradictory or even illogical to refer, in an international treaty, to a 'right' of peoples and then

---

[2] A number of authors have either argued that the international rules on self-determination do not confer any rights at all, or that they grant rights to, and impose duties, only on States: in the latter case, peoples are mere beneficiaries of those rules. For the former, more radical view, see in particular those authors who deny the existence of any rule of international law on the matter (see above, Chapter 5). For the latter view, see in particular Arangio-Ruiz, 'The Normative Role of the General Assembly of the United Nations and the Declaration of Principles of Friendly Relations', 562–5; Arangio-Ruiz, *Autodeterminazione*, at 2; Guarino, *Autodeterminazione dei popoli*, 6–14, 189–91.

actually to mean that what is granted is not a legal entitlement proper but simply an indirect benefit accruing to peoples because of the interplay of rights and obligations between Contracting States. To hold that peoples as such are not entitled to any legal claim proper means to gloss over the significance of the step taken in 1966 by Member States of the UN when adopting Article 1 – a step designed to *upgrade* peoples to the status of *co-actors* in the world community, of participants in at least some international dealings.

My second argument is that it would be unsound to object that the Covenants also provide for 'rights' of individuals and that this however does not imply that individuals are granted *international* rights. Admittedly, all the rights and freedoms enshrined in the Covenants are enjoyed by individuals within the municipal system of each Contracting State. At the international level individuals have only the right to file 'communications' with the Human Rights Committee (provided of course the State complained of has ratified the Optional Protocol). The condition of peoples is, however, different. The Covenants do not grant only a right to internal self-determination. As I emphasized in Chapter 2, they also provide for *external* self-determination, at least in two ways. First of all, they confer on the people of each Contracting State the right to be free from external interference (i.e. from foreign military occupation); furthermore, they grant dependent – that is, colonial or non-self-governing – peoples the right to freely choose their international status. Plainly, these rights cannot be taken advantage of and exercised within the domestic legal system of a Contracting State but only at the international level. It would be artificial and illogical to argue that in the case of external self-determination the Covenants grant an international right, whilst in the case of internal self-determination this right would only exist and manifest its effects within the municipal system of each Contracting State. The better view is that Article 1 common to the Covenants addresses itself directly to peoples, whatever the 'dimension' (internal or external) of the legal entitlement it provides for. Peoples are thus holders of international rights to which correspond obligations incumbent upon Contracting States *vis-à-vis* both peoples and other Contracting States.

I shall now turn to my third argument. Admittedly, it is correct to contend that substantive legal rights usually go hand in hand with the possibility, for the holder of the right, to set in motion some form of mechanism or procedure for the observance or even enforcement of the right: substantive rights are usually accompanied by legal remedies.

However, in the case at issue there is room for believing that the restrictive line of thought chosen in this matter by the UN Human Rights Committee is not necessarily the right one. The contention is warranted that Articles 1 and 2 of the Optional Protocol do not rule out the right of the legal representatives of a people to complain about breaches of Article 1 of the Covenant on Civil and Political Rights. It can be legitimately argued that an individual or a group of individuals acting on behalf of a people could file a 'communication' complaining about a violation of some basic rights (e.g. the right of peaceful assembly, Article 21; freedom of association, Article 22; the right to take part in the conduct of public affairs, Article 25) and *at the same time* of Article 1. In other words the complainant could claim that the breach of some basic political rights amounts to a violation of the right of the whole people to 'freely determine' its internal 'political status'. Similarly, possible infringements upon some basic provisions of the Covenant could be taken to amount to a breach of the right of the whole people 'freely to pursue' its 'economic, social and cultural development'. Furthermore, an individual or a group of individuals representative of a people oppressed by a foreign Power militarily occupying their country could complain about this gross breach of Article 1 (if that Power is a Contracting Party to the Optional Protocol). By the same token, a 'communication' could be filed with the Human Rights Committee by one or more individuals who act as representatives of the people of a 'dependent territory' claiming that the administering authority is not complying with Article 1.

To sum up, if a liberal interpretation is placed on Articles 1 and 2 of the Optional Protocol, peoples would be enabled to profit from the 'communications procedure', through persons appropriately legitimized to act and speak on their behalf.

The conclusion is thus warranted that in addition to States (other than those wielding authority over a particular people) peoples also hold the right to demand respect for self-determination by Contracting States.

Means of ensuring respect for the right to self-determination under the Covenants

Article 1(3), which governs the administration of non-self-governing and trust territories, is the relevant provision as far as external self-determination is concerned. It stresses the need to realize or respect the right of self-determination 'in conformity with the provisions of the

Charter of the United Nations'.[3] Where the Charter is silent, customary international law governs and, in the case at hand, can usefully supplement the Covenants.

The Covenant on Civil and Political Rights is more specific with regard to the implementation of internal self-determination. Internal self-determination, the primary focus of the Covenants, is implemented by adherence to, and the safeguarding of, the freedoms granted in the Covenant. Articles 18, 19, and 21, which guarantee freedom of thought, expression, and peaceful assembly, Article 25, which grants the right to take part in the conduct of public affairs, to vote, and to be elected at periodic elections, and Article 26, which prohibits discrimination, set basic guidelines for the exercise of democracy.

Once again the question is raised as to how adherence to the freedoms expressed is to be enforced. The Covenant provides for several supervisory procedures, including a reporting system, inter-State complaints and 'communications' by individuals. However, the second procedure is only valid *vis-à-vis* the accused Contracting State if, pursuant to Article 41 of the Covenant, that State has filed a special acceptance of the Human Rights Committee's competence. As for the 'communications' of individuals, they can only be submitted pursuant to the Optional Protocol to the Covenant. This means that the accused State must be a contracting party to the Protocol and that the individual complainant acting on behalf of a people must be subject to the jurisdiction of the State against which he is filing grievances.

The recipients of the right to self-determination under customary international law[4]

Who are the holders of the rights and duties conferred on peoples under customary international law? This body of law, which grants international rights to, and imposes international obligations on, organized entities demands that the right to self-determination be claimed and exercised by an organization that is representative of the entire people. Thus, as far as external self-determination is concerned, there must be a liberation

---

[3] Having dealt with this clause elsewhere, I do not think it necessary to cover it in depth here. For a detailed discussion of the matter, see A. Cassese, 'The Self-Determination of Peoples,' in Henkin, *The International Bill of Rights*, 98 ff.

[4] See generally, S. R. Chowdhury, 'The Status and Norms of Self-Determination in Contemporary International Law', 24 NILR, 1977, 74–6; Gusy, 'Von der Selbstbestimmung durch den Staat zur Selbstbestimmung im Staat', 389–97.

movement or another type of body representative of the whole people. As regards internal self-determination, arguably racial groups are entitled to claim self-determination and vindicate their rights only if there is a representative organization capable of acting on behalf of the entire group.

The manner of exercising self-determination under customary law

The actual modes of implementing the external right to self-determination are clearly set forth in the 1970 UN Declaration on Friendly Relations. The relevant paragraph of the Declaration, which can be regarded as declaratory of customary international law, provides for 'the establishment of a sovereign and independent State, the free association or integration with an independent State or the emergence into any other political status freely determined by a people'.

However, these three alternatives mainly apply to colonial peoples. What choices are instead offered to peoples under alien military occupation?[5] We saw above (Chapter 4) that no explicit regulation of this matter can be currently found in the body of international law. Nevertheless, close scrutiny of State practice and the general principle on self-determination can lead to the conclusion that one ought to distinguish between four situations.

First, one can envisage the case of a sovereign country endowed with a democratic regime, militarily occupied by a foreign Power. In this case the right to self-determination is realized through the withdrawal of foreign troops (which at the same time will put an end to the act of aggression).

A second, more frequent situation is that of a country in which, before foreign invasion, various political factions are fighting each other without the incumbent government being able to impose its authority due to the fact that the government itself is one of the factions. Normally, the foreign Power that sends in its troops sides with one of the warring factions, be it that supporting the government or the faction opposing it. Plainly, one of the salient features of the situation before the foreign occupation is the lack of a democratic regime capable of channelling the will of the people in a peaceful way. For a vivid image of this kind of situation, it may be sufficient to think of Afghanistan and Kampuchea. Whenever one is confronted with this type of situation, the inescapable conclusion is that the implementation

[5] See generally, Ross, 'Beyond the Soviet Invasion: Afghanistan and the Concept of Self-Determination', especially 105 ff.

of the right of the invaded people to self-determination cannot simply lie in the withdrawal of foreign troops: in this case external self-determination is inextricably bound up with internal self-determination. Accordingly, along with the liberation of the country from the invading army, a process proves necessary that enables the whole people freely to choose its institutions and its rulers and also to decide upon the international status of the country. That in the situation just described the evacuation of foreign troops is not sufficient for the realization of the right to self-determination, but must be accompanied by an internal democratic process of free choice, is borne out by State practice concerning Afghanistan[6] and Kampuchea.[7]

[6] It is interesting to note that on many occasions the Twelve Member States of the European Community have stressed that the Afghan problem could only be solved through both the withdrawal of Soviet troops and 'the establishment of a representative government formed in a process of self-determination'. See, e.g., the answer given by the Italian Presidency to written questions in the European Parliament, on 2 July 1985 (doc. 85/117, 1 *EPC Bul.*, 1985 no. 1, 105) the statement made by Luxemburg, on behalf of the Ten members, plus Spain and Portugal, in the UN General Assembly, on 11 November 1985 (doc. 85/251, *ibid.*, 1, no. 1, 148–9), the general declaration by the Belgian Presidency, on 16 March 1987 (doc. 87/143, *ibid.*, 3, 1987, no. 1, 126–7), the statement by the Danish Presidency, of 5 December 1987 (the Twelve called upon the Soviet Union 'to (i) withdraw all its troops by a date in 1988 according to a fixed timetable; (ii) agree to the establishment of a transitional government, whose independence could not be contested, to make preparations for a new Constitution and a genuine act of self-determination; (iii) recognize that the participation of the Afghan resistance is essential to a comprehensive political settlement' (doc. 87/511, *ibid.*, 3, 1987, no. 2, 296–7), the statement by the German Presidency, on 14 April 1988 (doc. 88/094, *ibid.*, 4, 1988, no. 1, 120) and on 28 June 1988 (doc. 88/182, *ibid.*, 4, 1988, no. 1, 186), the statement by the Greek Presidency, in the UN General Assembly, on 27 September 1988 ('An over-all political settlement of the Afghan problem involves the withdrawal of all Soviet troops in accordance with the agreed timetable, the unimpeded return of refugees in safety and honour, the establishment of a fully representative government through a genuine act of self-determination, re-establishment of a genuinely independent and non-aligned Afghanistan': *ibid.*, 4, 1988, no. 2, 124), the statement made by the Spanish Presidency, on 14 February 1989, after the withdrawal of Soviet troops ('The Twelve urge all the parties concerned, including the resistance, to exercise moderation and realism in order to achieve the establishment of a fully representative government formed through a genuine act of self-determination. The Twelve reiterate their continued support for the efforts of the United Nations Secretary-General to assist the formation of such a government, while accepting that it is the exclusive responsibility of the Afghan people to decide upon its composition': doc. 89/053, *ibid.*, 5, 1989, no. 1, 70–1). As for UN General Assembly resolutions, see Chapter 3, note 90. See also Ross, 'Beyond the Soviet Invasion: Afghanistan and the Concept of Self-Determination', 92 ff.

[7] See, e.g., the statement made in the UN General Assembly on 4 November 1985, by the Luxemburg Presidency, on behalf of the Ten (doc. 85/237, 1 *EPC Bul.*, 1985, no. 1, 133–5), the declaration made on behalf of the Twelve by the German Presidency on 21 June 1988 (doc. 88/170, *ibid.*, 4, 1988, no. 1, 181), the declaration made on

A third possible situation is slightly different from the one just discussed and is essentially exemplified by Namibia. In this case there is neither a foreign military occupation of a sovereign State, nor is there civil strife before the invasion. More simply, a territory and a population living on it, are under the authority of an alien State that illegally exercises its powers there (in the case of Namibia, South Africa wielded authority on the strength of its former title as Mandatory Power, in spite of the decision of the United Nations that South Africa's continued presence in Namibia was illegal and that the only legitimate authority was the world organization). In this class of situation, as in the previous one, the simple withdrawal of alien authority is not sufficient for the realization of the right of the occupied people to self-determination. It is also necessary for the people of the territory to be put in a position freely to choose its internal institutions and its rulers, as well as its international status (before the initiation of this process of internal and external self-determination, the people has never been given the opportunity of freely expressing wishes). That this is the right way of implementing the principle of self-determination in this kind of case is borne out by the international practice concerning Namibia.[8]

16–17 February 1990 by the Irish Presidency (stressing, *inter alia*, not only 'the total withdrawal of foreign forces verified by the UN', but also 'the fundamental right of Kampucheans to choose their own government in free, fair and UN-supervised elections, in which all Kampuchean parties should commit themselves to honouring the results of these elections': doc. 90/093, *ibid.*, 6, 1990, 107–9). As for UN General Assembly resolutions on this matter, see above, p. 98, note 97.

[8] By way of illustration, mention can be made of a number of statements by the Member States of the European Community emphasizing the need for the 'illegal occupation' of Namibia to be put to an end, while at the same time providing for the Namibian people freely to exercise its right to self-determination by choosing its rulers. See, e.g., the declaration made on 18 November 1985 in the UN General Assembly by the Luxemburg Presidency, on behalf of the Ten as well as Spain and Portugal (doc. 85/279, 1 *EPC Bul.* 1985, no. 2, 180–1), as well as that of 26 November 1985 (doc. 85/300, *ibid.*, 206–7) and 13 December 1985 (doc. 85/327, *ibid.*, 240–1), the statement of 3 February 1986 by the Dutch Presidency ('The Namibian people have a right to self-determination and independence, which they should be able to exercise as soon as possible through free elections, conducted according to the plan laid down in Security Council resolution 435 and supervised by the United Nations': doc. 86/067, *ibid.*, 2, 1986, no. 1, 92), the statement by the British Presidency of 8 July 1986 ('The Twelve have consistently reiterated their view that the illegal occupation of Namibia by South Africa must be brought to an end. The right of the people of Namibia to self-determination and independence must be exercised through free and fair elections under the supervision and control of the United Nations in keeping with the provisions of the Settlement Plan set forth in Security Council Resolution 435 (1979)': doc. 86/199, *ibid.*, no. 2, 1986, to 2, 34–5), the 'Circular concerning Namibia Day', by the British Presidency, of 19 August 1986 (doc. 86/247, *ibid.*, 66–7), the statement by the same Presidency in the UN General Assembly, of 18 September 1986 (doc. 86/273,

Finally, one can envisage a fourth situation, which shares some traits with the two previous ones (the second and the third). This is the case of a people living in a territory that is occupied by a foreign country without this occupation being contrary to the international ban on the use of force. As in the third situation referred to above, for historical reasons the people at issue has not been able freely to choose internal institutions and to elect rulers, nor has it been in a position to decide upon its international status. It goes without saying that Palestine is a case in point. Clearly, in this situation as well the mere departure of foreign troops and the end of the military occupation are not sufficient for the realization of self-determination. Along with the end of foreign occupation, the initiation of a democratic process of internal self-determination is also necessary, with a view also to pronouncing upon the international status of the territory (the constitution of an independent State? The integration into an existing State? The setting up of a confederation with a sovereign State? And so on). What distinguishes and indeed characterizes this fourth situation is the involvement in a host of complicated political and military problems, with the consequence that no easy, ready-made solution can be envisaged for the implementation of self-determination (see below, pp. 230–48).

So much for external self-determination. If we move on to internal self-determination, it is immediately apparent that no provision similar to that of the 1970 Declaration on Friendly Relations, referred to above, exists. However, one may infer *a contrario* from the 'saving clause' and State practice that the primary means of implementing internal self-determination requires the co-operation of the sovereign State in which the 'oppressed' people live. The oppressive State must grant the group exercising its right a means of taking part in the political decision-making process or, failing this, of choosing some sort of 'autonomous' internal status (see on this ambiguity and, indeed, lacuna of existing law below, pp. 330–2).

Enforcement of self-determination by the peoples concerned

A crucial question is whether an oppressed people is legally permitted to take some sort of action to enforce its right to self-determination. In the

ibid., 84–5) and 12 November 1986 (doc. 86/354, *ibid.*, 184–5), as well as the statement made on 4 November 1987 by the Danish Presidency in the UN General Assembly (doc. 87/448, *ibid.*, 3, 1987, no. 2, 226–8). For the UN resolutions on Namibia, see pp. 94–5 and note 85.

past, many Third World countries and the socialist bloc in the United Nations took the view that peoples entitled to external self-determination were authorized to use *force* to secure self-determination. To render this view consistent with the Charter system, those countries argued that the use of force by colonial peoples was warranted as a form of self-defence against the armed aggression constituted by colonial domination. Sometimes they also relied upon another justification: they claimed that the ban on resort to force enshrined in Article 2(4) of the Charter only concerns States and therefore leaves 'peoples' unaffected, notwithstanding the fact that these are endowed with a distinct legal personality in international relations.[9] The Western States have always rejected these propositions, as do a number of Latin American States.[10] This ongoing debate as to whether a liberation movement may legally resort to violence has given rise to an awkward legal situation in which liberation movements do not possess a right to use force but they cannot be held responsible for a breach of international law when they use violence in response to the 'forcible denial of the right of self-determination'.[11] The Declaration on Principles

[9] Several UN General Assembly resolutions affirm that liberation movements may resort to force. See, e.g., General Assembly Resolutions 32/14, 7 November 1977 (Rights of Palestinians), UN Ybk, 1977, 705; 39/50A, 12 December 1984 (Question of Namibia), UN Ybk, 1984, 1033; 39/72A, 13 December 1984 (Policies of Apartheid of the Government of Namibia), *ibid.*, 128.

[10] For a discussion on this point, see A. Cassese, 'Return to Westphalia? Considerations on the Gradual Erosion of the Charter System,' in A. Cassese (ed.), *The Current Legal Regulation of the Use of Force*, Dordrecht 1986, 514. See also below, pp. 197–8. The view that the use of force by oppressed peoples was justified by the right to self-defence was still maintained in the early 1980s by H. Kröger (ed.), *Völkerrecht* vol. II, Berlin 1982, 188.

[11] Various statements by US representatives in the United Nations would seem to make allowance, albeit in an implicit and oblique way, for some sort of limited licence for national liberation movements to use force. For instance, in 1973 a US delegate pointed out the following: 'The United States is opposed to the use of force to deny the right of self-determination and would not be party to any action adversely affecting that right.' The US statement went on to point out that self-determination did not however justify resort to terrorism (US Digest 1973, 125). The contention could thus be made that eventually the US delegate did not regard resort to force (other than terrorism) by liberation movements as unlawful. In the General Assembly's Third Committee, in 1976, the US delegate voted against a resolution on self-determination (Res. 31/34), *inter alia*, because 'operative paragraph one seems to give *blanket unqualified endorsement* to armed struggle' (US Digest 1976, 13; my italics). Again, the inference is perhaps warranted that a 'limited' use of armed force was regarded as lawful. In other instances the US has however refused to endorse any use of force. See US Digest 1977, 218–19 (concerning the armed struggle in South Africa, the US representative said the following in the General Assembly: 'We cannot . . . accept that Member States should endorse, or provide assistance to, the violent seizure of power within another State . . . We believe that it is inappropriate for the United Nations, a body dedicated to the

of International Law concerning Friendly Relations and Co-operation among States and the 1974 Definition of Aggression[12] reflect this state of affairs.[13]

What is the position as far as third parties are concerned? Although it is clear that third States must refrain from doing anything likely to encourage or induce the State to use repressive measures against peoples, it is unclear to what extent third States are entitled to aid liberation movements and exercise force on their behalf. All States have the right to demand that a State depriving a people of the right to self-determination comply with the relevant international rules; after all, the duty to grant self-determination is a duty *erga omnes*. The accused State must fulfil this duty. It cannot claim that the matter falls within its domestic jurisdiction and is not of international relevance. Nevertheless, is a State permitted to do more than enter protests and make diplomatic representations? There seems to be agreement to the effect that while States may give military equipment and financial or technical assistance to a liberation movement, they are prohibited from sending armed troops.[14] Even if one characterizes the forcible denial of self-determination as a 'crime of State' falling within

---

peaceful settlement of disputes, to advocate the use of armed force to solve political problems').

Other Western States also seem to take a stand whereby, whilst not endorsing a right to wage war, they sympathize with the position and attitude of liberation movements. Thus, for example, in 1982 an Australian Minister said the following to the Australian Senate: 'Australia is also unable to endorse armed struggle as a means for achieving independence for Namibia. Nonetheless, we understand the frustrations which have led many countries and people to conclude that armed struggle may inevitably occur as a last resort to end institutionalised racial discrimination in southern Africa. Australia continues to make modest contributions to the United Nations Fund for Namibia and the Commonwealth Special Fund for Namibia. Honourable members will know that the Jackson Committee is currently reviewing the Australia aid program, including the question of aid to southern Africa' (10 AYIL, 1987, 272).

[12] GA Res. 3314(XXIX), 14 December 1974, UN Ybk, 1974, 846.

[13] Some authors hold the view that liberation movements have a *right* proper to resort to force against the oppressive Power, i.e., possess a *jus ad bellum*. See, e.g., G. Abi-Saab, 'Wars of National Liberation and the Laws of War', 3 *Annales d'Etudes internationales* 1972, 100; A. Eide, 'Sovereign Equality Versus Global Military Structure: Two Competing Approaches to World Order', in A. Cassese (ed.), *The New Humanitarian Law of Armed Conflict*, vol. I, Naples 1979, 25; Verdross and Simma, *Universelles Völkerrecht*, 245.

[14] A more restrictive view has been taken by Judge Schwebel in his dissenting opinion in the *Nicaragua* case (merits). He stated that 'it is lawful for a foreign State or movement to give to a people struggling for self-determination moral, political and humanitarian assistance; but it is not lawful for a foreign State or movement to intervene in that struggle with force or to provide arms, supplies or other logistical support in the prosecution of armed rebellion' (ICJ, Reports 1986, 351, para. 180).

the scope of Article 19 of the ILC Draft Convention on State Responsibility – as has been argued[15] – the conclusion remains the same: State practice and the spirit of the UN Charter's basic provisions on the use of force do not allow third States to go so far as to send troops to assist peoples invoking the right to self-determination.[16] The rationale for this conclusion is the need (a) to avoid abuses in a community lacking central organs entrusted with the task of establishing the facts and pronouncing on the law and (b) to contain force as far as possible, by preventing possible escalations of violence as a result of the involvement of third States in conflicts where one or more peoples are pitted against the State. The same is true if one considers the numerous pronouncements issued by both States and international organizations supporting the view that States may oppose a State that grossly infringes a people's right to exercise self-determination by recourse to actions short of force that are otherwise prohibited by international law. Thus, as far as third States are concerned, the actions permitted in the case of civil wars (lawfulness of military and other aid to the incumbent government, unlawfulness of any assistance to rebels) *have been narrowed down and reversed*. In the case of wars for self-determination, third States must refrain from helping the State but are authorized to provide assistance (short of sending military troops) to national liberation movements.

This general picture of the international law in force in this area – which is plainly the result of the conflicting views of groups of States and represents a *via media* or compromise between these views – can be summed up by stating that liberation movements have been given a *legal entitlement* that is less than a *right* proper but more than the *absence of any authorization whatsoever*. This position can be best expressed by holding that liberation movements, although they do not possess a *legal right* to enforce their substantive right to self-determination by resort to war, nevertheless have a *legal licence* to do so. This notion is intended to encapsulate the idea that wars for self-determination are not ignored by international law, or left in a legal vacuum as being outside the realm of law *qua* mere factual occurrences. Rather, legal rules take these wars into account, without however upgrading them to the status of manifestations of *jus ad bellum*

---

[15] See A. Cassese, 'Remarks on the Present Legal Regulation of Crimes of States,' in *International Law at the Time of its Codification, Essays in Honour of R. Ago*, Milan 1987, vol. III, 51 ff.

[16] See the apposite remarks of E. Jiménez de Aréchaga, 'International Law in the Past Third of a Century', 159 HR, 1978-I, 98–9.

proper. The practical aspects or consequences of this middle-of-the-road legal position are as follows: (a) liberation movements do not breach international law if they engage in armed action against a State that forcibly denies their right to self-determination, and cannot therefore be held responsible for an international wrongdoing; (b) neither the State against which they fight, nor third States, are legally authorized to take any forcible measures to repress the action undertaken by liberation movements to realize self-determination; (c) third States are legally authorized to grant assistance to liberation movements, within the limits set out above; (d) third States are strictly forbidden from granting any military or economic assistance to the oppressive State, let alone to send troops to its aid; (e) liberation movements are authorized to pursue their political and diplomatic aims within the international bodies willing to grant them observer status.[17]

Turning to internal self-determination, one cannot speak of an oppressed racial group's *right* to use arms against the central authorities. Nor, however, can the group's resort to violence be better thought of as a mere fact of life, a reality. Here, again, the contention can be made that the group has been granted a *legal licence* to resort to armed force, subject to the strict conditions set out above. As for third parties, international law allows them to behave *vis-à-vis* the conflicting parties (the oppressive State and the oppressed racial group) in a manner different from that *vis-à-vis* battling factions during civil strife. They may not assist the State but are allowed to lend economic, financial or political assistance to the rebellious

---

[17] The legal and practical value of the above-mentioned *licence* to use force can be better understood by comparing the *resort to armed force* by liberation movements with *secession* generally. In both cases international law issues neither an *authorization* nor a *prohibition*. However, secession is normally looked upon *negatively* by international rules (and indeed the 1970 Declaration on Friendly Relations includes the famous saving clause stipulating that 'nothing in the foregoing paragraphs shall be construed as *authorizing* or *encouraging any action* which would dismember or impair, totally or in part, the territorial integrity or political unity of sovereign or independent States'). Secession is a fact of life, outside the realm of law, that States however disfavour and repudiate. It follows, among other things, that no military, economic or political assistance to rebellious groups or peoples seeking secession is authorized by international rules.

By contrast, the 1970 Declaration on Friendly Relations makes explicit provision for resort to force by liberation movements ('In their actions against, and resistance to, such forcible action [by a State, seeking to deprive a people of its right to self-determination] in pursuit of the exercise of their right to self-determination', etc.). In addition, the Declaration authorizes third States to 'support' these peoples. In short, the use of force by liberation movements is a fact of life towards which international rules, far from being in condemnation, or even neutral, take a *favourable stand*.

racial group (on the whole matter of the use of military violence to enforce self-determination, see also below, pp. 185, 193–200).

Enforcement of self-determination by third states

Third States, besides possessing the right to provide assistance (short of troops) to liberation movements, have other means available to exercise their right to enforce respect for self-determination by States that allegedly infringe it. As the customary rules on self-determination impose obligations *erga omnes* (see above, Chapter 5) and breaches of these obligations may amount to international crimes of States (see below, pp. 177–85), third States are entitled to resort to all those 'countermeasures' currently authorized by international law.[18]

In this connection, it seems appropriate to briefly dwell on two issues: first, the conditions that the taking of countermeasures must generally meet in order for them to be lawful; secondly, and more specifically, the extent to which States have resorted in actual practice to countermeasures for the purpose of exacting the implementation, by other States, of the right to self-determination.

As far as the first issue is concerned, arguably members of the international community must always be guided by the general ban on the use of force and the attendant obligation to refrain from disrupting friendly relations among States, as well as the obligation incumbent upon all States to settle their disputes, as far as possible, peacefully. It follows from these principles that a State is not authorized unilaterally to characterize the behaviour of another State as a breach of the principle of self-determination and consequently to decide to carry out peaceful reprisals. If international subjects were allowed to do so, abuses and misbehaviour by States claiming to resort to lawful countermeasures would be difficult to avert; this would run counter to the objectives of peace and justice that States are currently enjoined to pursue and, by the same token, would be

---

[18] On countermeasures in international law, see C. Leben, 'Les contre-mesures inter-étatiques et les réactions à l'illicite dans la société internationale', 28 AFDI, 1982, 9–77; E. Zoller, *Peacetime Unilateral Remedies: an Analysis of Countermeasures*, Dobbs Ferry, NY 1984; L.-A. Sicilianos, *Les réactions décentralisées à l'illicite – Des contre-mesures à la légitime défense*, Paris 1990, 247 ff.; more generally, see B. Conforti, 'Cours général de droit international public', 212 HR, 1988-V, 185 ff.; O. Schachter, *International Law in Theory and Practice*, Dordrecht, Boston, and London 1991, 184–201. See also the Reports for the ILC drawn up by G. Arangio-Ruiz, *Fourth Report on State Responsibility*, UN Doc. A/CN.4/444 (12 May 1992) and Add. 1 (25 May 1992) and 3 (17 June 1992).

highly detrimental to international relations. In order to take counter-measures lawfully, States must therefore refrain from resort to any unilateral action unless a multilateral forum (e.g. the UN General Assembly) has declared that a certain State has grossly infringed the principle or a rule on self-determination and has possibly called upon the Member States of the international community to take action against the delinquent State. Alternatively, the State that nevertheless wishes to take unilateral countermeasures should be prepared to submit the issue to international conciliation or arbitration or any other means for the peaceful settlement of disputes, *prior* to the actual resort to sanctions.

In sum, countermeasures must meet all the substantive criteria (in particular, necessity, proportionality and conformity with humanitarian standards) required for their lawfulness. Furthermore, it seems quite reasonable, as well as consonant with the general principles of modern international law, to require, as suggested by G. Arangio-Ruiz in the ILC, that (i) prior to the taking of countermeasures all amicable settlement procedures available to the parties must be exhausted and that appropriate and timely communication of the intention to employ countermeasures must be given;[19] and in any event (ii) the State taking the counter-measures must accept the recourse to international conciliatory arbitration or other peaceful means of third-party legal appraisal, if the target State should complain that the sanctions were contrary to international legal standards.[20]

Let us now move to the second issue raised above, namely the extent to which States have in actual fact resorted to countermeasures in order to demand compliance with self-determination. In this connection, it should be noted that on quite a few occasions States have asserted their right to intervene whenever self-determination was infringed. By way of illustration, it can be mentioned that in the general debate on self-determination in the UN General Assembly, the Danish delegate, speaking on behalf of the twelve Member States of the European Community, stated on 5 October 1987 that:

The United Nations has a very important role to play in this regard [i.e. with regard to the implementation of self-determination]. Wherever the exercise of the right to self-determination is violated, it is only natural that the matter be dealt

---

[19] See Arangio-Ruiz, *Fourth Report on State Responsibility*, A/CN.4/444, 6–19 and 40.
[20] See G. Arangio-Ruiz, *Fifth Report on State Responsibility*, A/CN.4/453 (12 May 1993), and Add. 1 (28 May 1993).

with in the world organization. *The denial of this right anywhere is a concern of peoples everywhere.*[21]

However, this statement, repeated word for word by the Italian Presidency of the European Community on 8 October 1990, again in the UN General Assembly,[22] does not seem to be corroborated by the actual behaviour of the Member States of the European Community, as is borne out by their extremely cautious attitude on the question of East Timor (see below, p. 228), and Eritrea,[23] as well as in the early stages of the evolution of the situation in the Baltic States[24] and Yugoslavia.[25] The crux of the matter is that issues of self-determination have more political and military overtones than any other question concerning human rights and States therefore show a strong propensity to take into account a whole gamut of extra-legal considerations before deciding to intervene in this area. Indicative of this position is a statement on 'The Principle of Self-Determination in International Relations' made on 12 November 1955 by the US Deputy Under-Secretary Murphy, in Washington, DC. He pointed out the following:

In considering the more abstract difficulties in applying the principle of self-determination, it must not be forgotten that the US position must also be based on practical considerations. In many instances self-determination is not the only issue involved. Frequently there are security and constitutional considerations, domestic jurisdiction, and other matters which must be taken into account.[26]

---

[21] Doc. 87/349, in 3 *EPC Bul.*, 1987, no. 2, at 130 (my italics).

[22] See Doc. 90/355, in 6 *EPC Bul.*, at 371.

[23] On 15 February 1991, the Twelve called upon Ethiopia and Eritrea 'to demonstrate their sincerity, facing up to the heavy responsibilities which lie upon them, by addressing substantive issues in a constructive spirit. In this context, the Community and its Member States recall their conviction that a just solution can only be achieved through a negotiated settlement, based on the respect for the territorial integrity and unity of Ethiopia and the need to take into account the distinct identity and aspirations of Eritrea' (quoted in R. Dehousse, 'The International Practice of the European Communities: Current Survey, European Political Cooperation in 1991', 4 EJIL, 1993, at 153).

[24] See *ibid.*, at 141.

[25] On 26 March 1991, the Twelve expressed their conviction that 'the process of moving Yugoslav society in the direction of democratic reforms satisfactory to all Yugoslavs should be based on the results of a political dialogue between all parties concerned. Such a process will enable the full development of the cooperation which already exists between the Community and the Federal authorities. *In the view of the Twelve, a united and democratic Yugoslavia stands the best chance to integrate itself in the new Europe*' (*ibid.*, at 153).

[26] In US *Dep. St. Bul.*, 1955, 892. Subsequently, speaking in particular with regard to the right of self-determination of colonial peoples, he went on to state the following: 'I have tried to consider with perfect frankness the objectives and aims of the United States on

This view, restated years later by the then US Deputy Legal Adviser to the State Department, George H. Aldrich, with regard to East Timor (see below, pp. 227–8), is in practice largely shared by most other countries – which however, unlike the United States, shy away from frankly setting out in so many words their policy with regard to self-determination.

The above remarks are by no means intended to imply that until now no State has ever taken any countermeasure to react to blatant breaches of self-determination by other States. Indeed, careful scrutiny of State practice shows that thus far the countermeasure most widely resorted to is the *refusal of legal recognition* of a situation which breaches the right to self-determination.[27] It has been exercised in the case of Namibia, Southern Rhodesia, the South African *Bantustans*, the Arab territories occupied by Israel, Kampuchea, and the Turkish-Cypriot State.[28] Other countermeasures have included UN sanctions against Southern Rhodesia[29] and South Africa,[30] as well as UN enforcement measures against Iraq.[31]

the question of self-determination. Before closing I should like to make it clear that we believe it to be our duty to approach colonial questions in terms of the enlightened self-interest of the United States' (*ibid.*, 894).

[27] See in general G. Ziccardi-Capaldo, *Le situazioni territoriali illegittime nel diritto internazionale*, Naples 1977.

[28] See S. K. N. Blay, 'Self-determination in Cyprus: The New Dimensions of an Old Conflict', 10 AYIL, 1987, 67–100.

[29] On sanctions against Southern Rhodesia, see P. M. Eisemann, *Les sanctions contre la Rhodésia*, Paris 1972; G. Ziccardi-Capaldo, *Le situazioni territoriali illegittime nel diritto internazionale*, 67–77; B. Conforti, *Le Nazioni Unite*, 4th edn, Padua 1986, 186–93, 266–70.

[30] On sanctions against South Africa, see G. Ziccardi-Capaldo, 'Il disconoscimento delle credenziali del Sud Africa come sanzione contro l'apartheid', 68 RDI, 1985, 299 ff.

[31] See M. Weller, 'The Kuwait Crisis: A Survey of Some Legal Issues', 3 AJICL, 1991, 1 ff.; O. Schachter, 'United Nations Law in the Gulf Conflict', 85 AJIL, 199, 452 ff.; D. L. Bethlehem (ed.), *The Kuwait Crisis: Sanctions and their Consequences*, Dordrecht, Boston, and London 1991; B. Graefrath and M. Mohr, 'Legal Consequences of an Act of Aggression: The Case of the Iraqi Invasion and Occupation of Kuwait', 43 *Austrian Journal of Public and International Law*, 1992, 109 ff.; S. Bohr, 'Sanctions by the United Nations Security Council and the European Community', 4 EJIL, 1993, 256 ff.

7

Comparing customary law and treaty law

When customary and treaty law are compared in the area of self-determination, it is immediately apparent that neither customary rules nor the Covenants confine self-determination to its anti-colonial dimension. Both embrace a broader concept. The assertion that self-determination will become obsolete the moment the last remaining colony achieves independence is thus wrong.

An analysis of how these two bodies of law have come into being immediately brings out one fundamental element: customary rules, as well as the general principle on self-determination, have evolved under the impetus of treaty law; indeed, treaty law has been one of the major contributing factors to the gradual formation of general legal standards. In particular, the UN Charter (Article 1(2)) has constituted the major driving force behind the emergence of a growing *opinion* about the importance of self-determination. Article 1 common to the Covenants in its turn has had a twofold role. On the one hand, it has for the first time crystallized one of the goals laid down in the UN Charter; on the other hand it has formed a sort of stepping-stone towards the evolution of general legal standards: the discussions its elaboration elicited among States and its subsequent, gradual implementation within the UN context gave a substantial boost to the widening of self-determination's scope and in particular to a broadening awareness of the legal *necessitas* of self-determination. The actual conduct of States and the UN practice added the needed element of *usus*.

Which of these two bodies of law affords greater protection to peoples and what are the relationships between the two? Except for one issue (which is, however, a major one: the internal self-determination of the peoples of sovereign countries), customary law affords greater protection to

159

self-determination. For one thing, customary law includes the general principle to which I referred above (see Chapter 5). This principle is an overarching standard. In spite of its general content and relative lack of precision, it encompasses a broad range of situations and contributes to its regulation, either indirectly (by supplementing customary or treaty rules) or directly, when specific legal regulation is lacking and the factual situation at issue lends itself to being governed by a general standard of behaviour (see the instances I mentioned above, in Chapter 5).

Turning now to specifics, it can be said that customary law in the area of *external* self-determination is similar in scope and content to the right provided in the Covenants. Customary rules confer a substantive legal right to external self-determination both on peoples suffering due to colonial rule and on those under foreign military occupation. This is also the case with the Covenants, although these are somewhat less clear and specific than customary law. However, only general international law grants peoples a licence (but clearly not a right) to vindicate their substantive rights by recourse to force in extreme cases of the forcible denial of their right to self-determination.

The differences between customary law and treaty law as regards *internal* self-determination are slightly more complex. First, the situations covered by the two bodies of law are not identical. Customary law confers a right to internal self-determination on racial groups which are denied equal access to government. The Covenants provide for the self-determination of the whole population of each Contracting State but not of racial groups (nor, for that matter, of ethnic, religious or linguistic minorities). Second, under customary law, racial groups have a licence (but not a right) to achieve self-determination through the use of force in response to a forcible denial and where peaceful measures prove ineffective. The Covenants do not provide for the employment of force. Nor do they lay down any effective means of enforcement of the right.

It may be asked what the causes of the differences between customary law and treaty law are. To answer this question, it should be noted that at the time the Covenants were drafted, internal self-determination – that is, the right of the whole population of a Contracting State freely to choose its rulers – gradually became an issue of primary importance. The major emphasis was on the human rights and basic freedoms of *individuals* and self-determination was to constitute but the propylaeum, as it were, to the imposing Temple of Human Rights. Although all socialist countries and many developing States were satisfied with the significant references to dependent or colonial territories, Western States insisted that self-determination was a concept having a universal application, that is, applied to the people of any Contracting State. However, the draftsmen of the two Covenants, keenly aware, from the outset, that they were preparing international instruments destined to acquire legally binding force upon ratification or accession, chose a cautious route. They avoided radical language and any provisions which might threaten the delicate balance reached in the drafting process, or excessively jeopardize State sovereignty.

No similar precautions were needed for the Declaration on Friendly Relations drafted a few years after the Covenants, although the Declaration, by definition, was not legally binding *per se*. This is not to suggest, however, that the drafters of the Declaration proceeded in a haphazard fashion, with no regard for the concepts used. Quite the opposite is true. The purpose of the Declaration was twofold: to update certain traditional international legal principles and to clarify and better define certain political principles within a legal framework. Accordingly, perceiving the Declaration as a document likely to have at least a knock-on effect in the realm of law, the developing and socialist States insisted with great vehemence that the Declaration reflect their views and aspirations, thus laying emphasis only on colonial peoples and peoples subjected to foreign domination. The West went on the defensive in response and was unable to score a victory on the internal self-determination of all peoples. The conflict resulted, as we have seen, in a set of provisions which reflects the view of the developing countries and the pre-1989 Eastern Bloc. Although even this part of the Declaration is imprecise and riddled with ambiguities it is apparent that it does not provide for any right to internal self-determination accruing to the whole people of sovereign States. In this respect, the Declaration fully and faithfully reflects the State practice of that period as well as the *opinio juris seu necessitatis* shared in that period by the overwhelming majority of Member States of the world community.

Be that as it may, it is striking to note that although treaty law in an important respect is more generous in that it bestows a legal right proper upon peoples, customary international law is more liberal in other respects. As was stated above, customary law, besides granting peoples under colonial rule or foreign domination a right to external self-determination and racial groups (denied equal access to government) a right to internal self-determination, gives legal licence to these classes of peoples or groups to resort to armed violence in extreme cases in order to enforce their right.

The reasons behind this difference are twofold. First, the range of peoples envisaged in Article 1 of the UN Covenants is much broader than the three categories contemplated by customary law; hence the reluctance of States to confer enforcement rights on such a far-reaching class of peoples. Second, the whole legal regime of self-determination has undoubtedly been influenced by the attitude of developing and pre-1989 socialist countries, and these have always been *selective* about self-determination: over-cautious about the possible repercussions and ramifications of a "generous" approach to internal self-determination and, by contrast, exceedingly liberal as regards the external self-determination of at least two classes of peoples (those under colonial or foreign domination).

Thus, the resulting legal picture can appear to lack balance and indeed seem substantially biased. International legal rules are, however, a simple reflection of the constellation of power in the world community, as well as the prevailing ideologies and political concerns. The scholar, however dissatisfied he may be with this state of affairs, cannot but take note of the present legal condition; all he can do is to delineate the existing legal regime with all its flaws and lacunae, and pinpoint the emerging trends of the international community.

Returning to the enumerated differences between customary law and treaty law on self-determination, one final point ought to be mentioned, namely, the joint jurisdiction of the Covenants and customary international law. When a State Party to the Covenants is confronted with a situation which is also regulated by customary law, that State must give effect to both bodies of law. The reason for this is that the two sets of legal rules, being mutually supplementary, do not give rise to a conflict which must be resolved by recourse to one body of law at the expense of the other. When a State party to the Covenants is faced with a problem concerning internal self-determination, it is required to grant the right to the whole population as well as to any racial group being denied equal access to Government. In short, treaty law and customary law in the field of self-determination are cumulative. Neither set of rules trumps the other.

PART III

The right to self-determination in operation

8

The impact of self-determination on traditional international law

Introductory remarks

The principle of self-determination has had a very extensive impact on traditional international law. It has undermined its *statist* outlook. The international community is no longer comprised solely of sovereign governments. Today, some classes of peoples (as well as individuals) are international legal subjects – although their participation in international dealings is still very limited. The political ideal of the French Revolution has thus yielded fruit.

Self-determination's impact on international law has not been so decisive as to change the structure of international law. It has, however, had an enormous influence on the *content* of some fundamental international norms and, more generally, on the *outlook* of States towards the present world community.

International legal subjects

Traditionally sovereign States were the only entities in the world community that possessed legal rights and duties under international law. Each State was deemed to have absolute control over its peoples and was free to do as it pleased within its own territorial jurisdiction. There were no exceptions to the principle of non-intervention in the domestic affairs of a sovereign State.

Although some jurists and diplomats disagree, it is submitted that this is no longer true today. The ascendancy of international norms governing human rights has forced the traditionally rigid, pure-statist regime to recognize individuals as legal subjects: under present-day international law, individuals have legal rights, albeit only of a most fundamental and limited nature. Similarly, the crystallization of the principle of self-determination has given rise to a new class of subjects: liberation movements representing peoples oppressed by a colonial power, foreign occupier, or racist regime. Inasmuch as the international norms governing self-determination confer rights and impose duties on peoples, peoples or, to be more precise, the liberation movements and other bodies which represent peoples entitled to self-determination, are legal subjects of international law.[1]

This conclusion generates an important question: on what basis does the international community elevate a liberation movement to the rank of international subject? The response is twofold. Firstly, reference is made to the movement's political goals. Do the movement's goals fall within the scope of the principle of self-determination; is the movement fighting a colonial power, foreign occupier, or racist regime? In addition, is the aim to acquire effective control over a population living in a given territory? Secondly, the representative factor is called into account. Is the movement

---

[1] See Kröger, *Völkerrecht*, vol. I, 150–5; M. Bedjaoui, *La révolution algérienne et le droit*, Brussels 1961; C. Tomuschat, 'Die Befreiungsbewegungen in den Vereinten Nationen' 22 *Vereinte Nationen*, 1974, 65 ff.; M. Bennouna, *Le consentement à l'ingérence militaire dans les conflits internes*, Paris 1974, 159–70; C. Lazarus, 'Le statut des mouvements de libération nationale à l'Organisation des Nations Unies', 20 AFDI, 1974, 173 ff.; J. Verhoeven, *La reconnaissance internationale dans la pratique contemporaine*, Paris 1975, 140–67; G. Petit, 'Les mouvements de libération nationale' et le droit', *Annuaire du Tiers Monde*, 1976, 57–75; E. Klein, 'Nationale Befreiungsbewegungen und Dekolonisierungspolitik der Vereinten Nationen: Zu einigen Völkerrechtlichen Tendenzen', 36 *Zeit.*, 1976, 618 ff.; Lombardi, *Bürgerkrieg und Völkerrecht*, 311–42, 354–7; S. Tyner, 'Wars of National Liberation in Africa and Palestine: Self-Determination for Peoples or for Territories?', 5 *Yale Studies in World Public Order*, 1978, 234 ff.; A. Hasbi, *Les mouvements de libération nationale et le droit international*, Rabat 1981; K. Ginther, Die Völkerrechtliche Stellung nationaler Befreiungsbewegungen im südlichen Afrika', 32 *Österreichische Zeitschrift für öffentliches Recht und Völkerrecht*, 1981, 131 ff.; H. Freudenschuss, 'Legal and Political Aspects of the Recognition of National Liberation Movements', 11 *Millennium: Journal of International Studies*, 1982, 115 ff.; K. Ginther, 'Liberation Movements', 3 *Encyclopedia*, 1982, 245 ff.; J. A. Barberis, 'Nouvelles questions concernant la personnalité juridique internationale', 179 HR, 1983-I, 259 ff.; Cassese, *International Law in a Divided World*, 90–9; M. Shaw, The International Status of National Liberation Movements', 5 *Liverpool Law Review*, 1983, 19 ff.; Shaw, *Title to Territory in Africa*, 173–9; Verdross and Simma, *Universelles Völkerrecht*, 3rd edn, 243–7 (who speak of 'partielle Völkerrechtsfähigkeit'); P. Cahier, 'Changement et continuité du droit international', 195 HR, 1985-VI, 148–54; R. Ranjeva, 'Peoples and National Liberation Movements', in M. Bedjaoui (ed.), *International Law: Achievements and Prospects*, Paris 1991, 101–12; D. Nguyen Quoc, P. Daillier, and A. Pellet, *Droit international public*, 4th edn, Paris 1992, 494–6.

a legitimate representative of the oppressed people? Does it have broad-based support among those it claims to represent?

Since the international status of national liberation movements flows from the principle of self-determination, liberation movements which cannot be classified among those fighting for freedom from colonialism, foreign occupation, or racism – the three situations covered by the principle – are not entitled to international status. This is clearly borne out by State practice and by the statements of States in the UN, as well as the pronouncements of UN bodies. For example, movements fighting on behalf of peoples living in a sovereign state controlled by an authoritarian government are not afforded international status under general international law (although, as I pointed out in Chapter 2, they may hold a right to internal self-determination under the UN Covenants). The same holds true for bodies representing populations of sovereign States dominated by despotic elites which wield control with the economic and military support of a foreign Power. Although this may be judged a serious deficiency in the current international legal regime, one must not allow political or ideological aspirations to obscure reality. The truth is that most members of the world community are reluctant to accept a form of international legislation which has the potential to undermine State sovereignty. The same considerations which militate against granting international status to insurgents – who, unlike liberation movements, primarily derive their claim to international legitimacy from the control of territory – also militate against granting international status to a broader range of bodies or agencies that are representative of peoples.

However, even if a liberation movement claims legitimacy within the context of colonialism, military occupation, or racism, there is still the issue of whether it is representative of a people. Due to the lack of international guidelines or standards clarifying what constitutes 'representativeness', the issue tends to be handled on a case-by-case basis. UN General Assembly Resolution 2918(XXVII), adopted in 1972, entrusts the task of weighing the 'representativeness' of African movements to the OAU. Resolution 3102(XXVIII), passed in 1973, delegates responsibility *vis-à-vis* movements in the Middle East to the Arab League. The General Assembly judges the 'representativeness' of liberation movements existing in other areas of the world.

A liberation movement may, however, acquire the status of international legal subject even though it lacks a regional organization's or the United Nations' seal of approval. Although recognition by international organizations is of great importance, it is by no means a *sine qua non* condition; recognition by States is, on the contrary, usually sufficient.[2] For both pragmatic and political reasons, regional organizations generally only recognize those liberation movements whose adversaries lie outside the membership of the organization.[3] To compensate for this situation, a liberation movement not recognized as an international subject by the governing regional organization may claim international status by reference to recognition by other States. For example, before Eritrea's independence, the two Eritrean liberation fronts were considered to be international legal subjects even though the OAU had refused to grant them international status on account of Ethiopia's strong opposition.

Arguably, recognition – be it granted by regional organizations, the UN or single States – is ultimately 'constitutive' of the liberation movement's international legal personality.[4] The truth of the matter is that, like all other international subjects, liberation movements can claim international status as soon as they have satisfied all the requisite conditions. Nevertheless, the views and attitudes of States and organizations are particularly crucial where the issue is the status to be afforded to a liberation movement. In actual practice, a liberation movement recognized by only a very limited number of States cannot be considered eligible for membership in the international community.

The fact that we are now at the point where one could reasonably argue that some classes of peoples are subjects of international law is a step forward. However, that there is still a long way to go should not be overlooked. Peoples can be said to have wedged open the door to the sovereign States' sacred domain but they have not advanced beyond the threshold. They enjoy a very limited set of rights. In addition, their international legal status is by definition *provisional*, like that of insurgents: if self-determination

---

[2] Turkey submitted a proposal at the Geneva Diplomatic Conference of 1974–7 designed to entrust regional intergovernmental organizations with the task of selecting the liberation movements entitled to invoke Protocol I. Had the proposal been accepted, one might have argued that an intergovernmental 'screening' was a prerequisite for acceptance into the international community. However, since it was not adopted, the absence of a Geneva Protocol provision mandating 'screenings' suggests that the approval of a regional intergovernmental organization is only one means of acquiring international legal status.

[3] Cf. G. Abi-Saab, 'Wars of National Liberation in the Geneva Conventions and Protocols', 165 HR-IV, 1979, 408.

[4] See, e.g., Lazarus, 'Le statut des mouvements de libération nationale à l'organisation des Nations Unies', 173 ff.; Freudenschuss, 'Legal and Political Aspects of the Recognition of National Liberation Movements', 115 ff.

is eventually realized, they are destined to become the governmental authority of the people on whose behalf they fight; or they will disappear if the 'oppressive' or 'parent' State succeeds in driving them out and the other members of the world community acquiesce in this state of affairs. If a people is represented by a liberation movement which has been granted international status, it may enter into *agreements* with States and international organizations. Indeed, the making of international agreements is the most conspicuous manifestation of their international legal personality.[5] Of course, it is not because they possess this personality that they can enter into these agreements. The contrary is true. It is because these agreements are regarded by the contracting parties (national liberation movements and States or international organizations) as *international treaties proper*, that the inference can be drawn that the national liberation movements entering into such agreements are endowed with international legal personality (albeit of a limited kind). In addition, it has the right to demand respect for and protection of the persons representing them in a 'diplomatic capacity'. Otherwise, peoples are afforded little else than the 'right to live'.

Moreover, even if a people has a substantive right to invoke, it still has no means of legal redress other than resort to armed violence. This is true even where a people's survival is at issue. This consequence is particularly disturbing in light of the international community's reticence to take the initiative even to combat genocide. In essence, therefore, it can be said that those peoples which hold international legal entitlements are no more than spectators having the right to protest. Considering each development in the field of group rights as a grave threat to State sovereignty, most States refuse to grant peoples substantive rights and effective means of legal redress. This will be true as long as they continue to believe that any new group right necessarily translates into the partial usurpation of the rights held by sovereign States.

Sources of law: the rise of *jus cogens*

In the 1960s, the international community decided to attribute a heightened status to a select group of principles considered more fundamental than other general principles of international law. These were referred to as *jus cogens*, the set of principles from which no State may

---

[5] For a careful analysis of such treaties, see Barberis, 'Nouvelles questions', at 259–64.

derogate for any reason.[6] For the first time the international community agreed that certain values – peace, the dignity of the human person (hence respect for fundamental human rights, and the ban on slavery and genocide), the right of self-determination – had to be championed, even at the expense of competing national interests. The doctrine of self-determination, combined with the new emphasis on individual human rights and the international prohibition of aggression, was largely responsible for this new outlook. In fact, when the creation of the new set of principles was being discussed, the representatives of the various States participating in the discussions often referred to the need to safeguard the self-determination of peoples.[7]

In 1966 the International Law Commission proposed the adoption of a provision of the Draft Convention on the Law of Treaties embodying *jus cogens*.[8] However, on this occasion only a few States took a public stand on the inclusion of self-determination within this category. Portugal was strongly against, probably on account of its still being a colonial Power,[9] whereas the US supported the concept[10] but clearly limited its scope to the instances mentioned by the ILC, which did not include self-determination.[11] Only the Philippine delegation warmly welcomed the

---

[6] See above, pp. 133–40. Article 53 of the Vienna Convention on the Law of Treaties provides that: 'A treaty is void if, at the time of its conclusion, it conflicts with a peremptory norm of general international law. For the purposes of the present Convention, a peremptory norm of general international law is a norm accepted and recognized by the international community of States as a whole as a norm from which no derogation is permitted and which can be modified only by a subsequent norm of general international law having the same character'. See also Art. 64, on the emergence of a new peremptory norm of general international law. On these provisions, see the authoritative view of R. Ago, 'Droit des traités à la lumière de la Convention de Vienne', 134 HR-III, 1971, 297.

It is claimed that in the 1960s, alongside these provisions, there evolved in the international community a *customary* rule on *jus cogens*; a rule whose content is slightly different from that of the provisions of the Vienna Convention. See Cassese, *International Law in a Divided World*, 176 ff.

[7] See above, pp. 136–7.

[8] See *Yearbook of the ILC*, 1966, vol. II, 20 ff.

[9] Portugal, although favourable to the concept of *jus cogens*, stated that: 'the inclusion [in the relevant norm] of acts constituting crimes against international law or other offences constituting violations of human rights or of the principle of self-determination would [not] be helpful; for it considers that these notions have become corrupt in reality and that any reference to them would not assist in removing the confusion which surrounds them', *ibid.*, 21.

[10] *Ibid.*, 21.

[11] The Commentary of the ILC on Article 37 (*jus cogens*) stated, *inter alia*: 'Examples suggested of treaties conflicting with such rules [of *jus cogens*] included: (*a*) a treaty

reference, in the Commentary of the ILC on *jus cogens*, to 'human rights and self-determination as of the essence of *jus cogens*'.[12]

This very cautious and reserved attitude in the General Assembly was however abandoned by States at the Vienna Diplomatic Conference on the Law of Treaties. There (as stated above, pp. 135–40), various States explicitly referred to the principle of self-determination as a typical instance of a norm of *jus cogens*: the Soviet Union,[13] Sierra Leone,[14] Ghana,[15] Cyprus,[16] Poland,[17] and Byelorussia.[18] In addition, the same countries, as well as others also participating in the Vienna Conference, explicitly stated that all the principles laid down in Articles 1 and 2 of the UN Charter, hence also self-determination, were to be regarded as part and parcel of *jus cogens*.[19]

Admittedly, it was primarily the socialist and Third World countries that explicitly stated that the principle of self-determination came within the purview of the body of peremptory rules of international law. However, it

contemplating an unlawful use of force contrary to the principle of the Charter; (*b*) a treaty contemplating the performance of any other act criminal under international law; and (*c*) a treaty contemplating or conniving at the commission of acts, such as trade in slaves, piracy or genocide, in the suppression of which every State is called upon to co-operate. Other members expressed the view that, if examples were given, it would be undesirable to appear to limit the scope of the article to cases involving acts which constitute crimes under international law; treaties violating human rights or the principle of self-determination were mentioned as other possible examples', *Yearbook of the ILC*, 1963, vol. II, 199.

12 *Ibid.*, 22.
13 'There could be disagreement as to the nature of these norms, though everyone would admit that they included such principles as non-aggression and non-interference in the internal affairs of States, sovereign equality, national self-determination and other basic principles of contemporary international law and Articles 1 and 2 of the United Nations Charter.' See United Nations Conference on the Laws of Treaties, *First Session*, Vienna, 26 March–24 May 1968, *Official Records*, Summary Records of the plenary meetings and the meetings of the Committee of the Whole, 52nd Meeting, 294, para. 3.
14 *Ibid.*, 53rd Meeting, 300, para. 9.
15 *Ibid.*, 53rd Meeting, 301, para. 16.
16 *Ibid.*, 53rd Meeting, 306, para. 69.
17 See United Nations Conference on the Law of Treaties, *Second Session*, Vienna, 9 April–22 May 1969, *Official Records*, Summary Records of the plenary meetings and of the meetings of the Committee of the Whole, 19th Meeting, 99, para. 71.
18 *Ibid.*, 20th Meeting, 105, para. 48.
19 Soviet Union: *Official Records*, First Session, 52nd Meeting, para. 3, 294; Lebanon: *ibid.*, para. 43, 297; Sierra Leone: *ibid.*, 53rd Meeting, para. 9, 300; Poland: *ibid.*, para. 35, 302, as well as Second Session, 19th Meeting, para. 70, 99; Romania: First Session, 54th Meeting, para. 55, 312; Czechoslovakia: *ibid.*, 55th Meeting, para. 25, 318; Ecuador: Second Session, 19th Meeting, para. 35, 96; Cuba: *ibid.*, para. 42, 97; Ukraine: *ibid.*, para. 75, 100.

would seem that other factors warrant the conclusion that at present the whole world community regards the principle as of such paramount importance as to rank among the norms of *jus cogens*: the proclamation of self-determination in the most important contemporary international instruments (the UN Charter; the 1960 General Assembly Declaration on Colonial territories; the 1970 UN Declaration on Friendly Relations), as well as in many resolutions of the General Assembly. The pronouncements of a few Western States on the fundamental importance of self-determination[20] also seem to indicate that alongside the socialist (now ex-socialist) States and developing countries, Western States are no longer opposed to the view that the principle in question properly belongs within the body of peremptory norms of international law.

It is necessary to add that one should be aware of the inherent *limits of the concept of jus cogens*. First, it is generally stressed that under the Vienna Convention on the Law of Treaties only the contracting parties to a treaty that is alleged to be contrary to a peremptory rule of international law are entitled to challenge the validity of that treaty by initiating the procedures laid down for declaring the treaty void (recourse to the ICJ, under Article 66 of the Vienna Convention).[21] For example, if it were the case that an international treaty was drafted which was contrary to *jus cogens* (think of a treaty providing for the subjugation of a people, or for the suppression of the fundamental freedoms of a whole population), that treaty would undisputedly offend not only the people against whom it operates but the international community as a whole. Nevertheless, in actual fact, only those parties that are directly involved are entitled to react against the treaty and claim it to be declared null and void. In particular, in the case of bilateral treaties falling foul of *jus cogens* (for example, a treaty by which two States agree to act contrary to the right of a people to self-determination), no third State can ask that the treaty be declared null and void. This power is still in the hands of the two contracting parties, which alone can request the ICJ to declare the treaty null (this might happen at the initiative of one of the two States after a change of government).

---

[20] See above, pp. 137, 139.

[21] For this view, see F. Capotorti, *Convenzione di Vienna sul diritto dei trattati*, Padua 1969, 66–71; F. Capotorti, 'L'extinction et la suspension des traités', 134 HR, 1971-III, 567–81; A. Verdross and B. Simma, *Universelles Völkerrecht*, 534–5; B. Conforti, *Diritto internazionale*, 4th edn, Naples 1992, at 181; Quoc Dinh, Daillier, and Pellet, *Droit international public*, 206–7. See also G. Gaja, '*Jus cogens* beyond the Vienna Convention', 172 HR, 1981-III, note 17. For the contrary view, see Jiménez de Arechaga, 'International Law in the Past Third of a Century', 68–9.

This is the prevailing view of commentators, based on the Vienna Convention. There is however room for believing that under general international law third States have some sort of possibility to challenge the treaty at issue. For one thing, under customary law third States can challenge the treaty by using such legal means as diplomatic *démarches* or public protests. Indeed, since peremptory norms generally impose obligations *erga omnes*, the making of a treaty inconsistent with *jus cogens* infringes upon a *legal right* of all the member States of the world community. Furthermore, if on the strength of the 'optional clause' (Article 36 of the Statute of the ICJ) a third State has the right to institute proceedings against one of the contracting Parties, arguably judicial action can be taken with a view to asking the Court to declare that the respondent State has entered into a treaty contrary to an obligation *erga omnes* (hence, as a rule, to *jus cogens* as well) and is therefore bound to denounce it or at any rate to refrain from complying with it. More generally, any State entitled – under a general jurisdictional clause – to bring a claim against one or more contracting Parties before an international court, would have the right to so act. Admittedly, the court would not be authorized to declare the treaty null and void; however, it would have jurisdiction to pronounce upon both the compatibility of the treaty with an *erga omnes* obligation (normally laid down in the peremptory norm) and upon whether or not the respondent State (or States) are consequently under an obligation to denounce (or withhold implementation) of the treaty.

The second and more substantial limitation of *jus cogens* is that generally speaking it is highly implausible for two or more States that intend to violate an essential rule protecting peoples to conclude a treaty in which their illegal behaviour is recorded for all to see. It would be even less plausible for several States to agree to form a customary rule permitting the oppression of a whole people. States that intend to behave in an 'immoral' fashion do so in fact; they do not firstly formulate a set of rules and standards to effect such a purpose. This, however, does not exclude that there are more subtle, consequential or indirect ways in which a treaty can come into conflict with *jus cogens*, as is proved by the Australia–Indonesia Timor Gap Treaty of 1989.[22] (Cf. below, pp. 223–30).

Admittedly, to date no treaty bearing upon self-determination has been declared null and void by the International Court of Justice as being in

---

[22] Text in 29 ILM, 1990, 469 ff.

conflict with a peremptory norm of international law.[23] The fact remains that the whole concept of *jus cogens* is of revolutionary import. Even if it does not have an immediately ascertainable legal impact, it is influential in the moral and psychological sphere; it fosters a new ethos in the international community. States, individuals, and peoples all have a higher set of expectations. Today, as a result, no one would question the idea that an international treaty can be considered void on grounds of 'immorality', as did a French delegate to the League of Nations less than sixty years ago.[24]

The principle of non-interference in domestic affairs

In 1859, United States President James Buchanan summed up one of the major international legal principles of his day, that of non-interference. Called upon to deal with questions concerning the alleged abduction from his parents, by the authorities of the Papal States, of Mr E. Mortara, a Jewish national of those States, Buchanan asserted, in a note of 4 January 1859:

I have long been convinced that it is neither the right nor the duty of this government to exercise a moral censorship over the conduct of other independent governments and to rebuke them for acts which we may deem arbitrary and unjust towards their own citizens or subjects. Such a practice would tend to embroil us with all nations. We ourselves would not permit any foreign power thus to interfere with our domestic concerns and enter protests against the legislation or

---

23 Some jurists have claimed that the 1960 Zurich Agreement permitting armed intervention in Cyprus and the 1978 Camp David Agreements allegedly infringing the right of the Palestinian people to self-determination are contrary to the 'peremptory rules' of international law (see references in Gaja, '*Jus cogens* beyond the Vienna Convention', notes 26 and 41). Mention can also be made of the *Guinea Bissau–Senegal Maritime Boundary Arbitration* (83 ILR, 1989, 1, paras. 37 ff.). Guinea Bissau argued that the 1960 Delimitation Agreement between France and Portugal, on which Senegal intended to rely, was void for inconsistency with *jus cogens*. The Tribunal did not in the event accept that the norm on which Guinea relied (that a colonial Power may not conclude treaties on behalf of its colony once the process of decolonisation has been initiated) had the status of a peremptory norm. But it seemed to accept (see *ibid.*, para. 45) that had this norm had that status, Guinea Bissau would have been entitled to have the treaty declared null and void.

24 In 1933, when the Peruvian delegate to the League of Nations stated that a treaty between Peru and Colombia was 'immoral', the French delegate took him to task, arguing that a treaty could not be considered void on grounds of 'immorality'. For a discussion of the debates regarding the Leticia case (Peru violated its 1922 treaty with Colombia providing for the cession of Leticia to Colombia), see A. Cassese, *Human Rights in a Changing World*, Cambridge, Mass. 1990, 169 ff., n.5.

the action of our government towards our own citizens. If such an attempt were made we should promptly advise such a government in return to confine themselves to their own affairs and not intermeddle with our concerns.[25]

However, despite Buchanan's oratory, and despite numerous statements issued by other States along the same lines, the international legal setting before the First World War offered few guarantees that a State could be secure in its boundaries. States vociferously claimed, as they continue to claim today, the right to be free from foreign influences. Nevertheless, few governments actually adhered to the legal principle advanced by Buchanan and their own foreign offices. The right to non-interference always fell by the wayside when a State resorted to force against another State in order to further its aims. The absence of an international legal principle restricting the use of force rendered the right to non-interference a hollow right. Since there was no international norm prohibiting the use of force, States were entitled to use military and economic coercion to further national interests, whether or not the protection of those interests entailed forcibly meddling in the domestic affairs of other States.

With time, however, new rules gradually evolved. On the one hand, the emergence of legal rules banning or at any rate extensively restricting the resort to force resulted in the enhancement of the norms on non-interference: these norms came to acquire the effectiveness of which they had previously been devoid.[26] On the other hand, and by the same token, new international rules crystallized and eventually placed significant legal limitations on the scope of the principle of non-intervention. Chief among these rules rank those governing individual human rights[27] and the self-determination of peoples.

As the foregoing chapters have shown, under present international law peoples living under foreign occupation or colonial domination have the right to external self-determination. By the same token, a racist State which is oppressing a racial group, in particular, by denying it equal access to government, is duty-bound to grant this group internal self-determination. Most importantly, with reference to the changing parameters of the principle of non-interference, is the third prong of the principle of

---

[25] In J. B. Moore, *A Digest of International Law*, vol. VI, Washington 1906, 350.

[26] Cf. Cassese, *International Law in a Divided World*, 143–8.

[27] On the impact of human rights on the principle of non-interference in domestic affairs, see in particular the resolution proposed by G. Sperduti to the 'Institut de Droit International' and adopted, in an amended version, by the Institut at its 1989 Session at Santiago de Compostella (for the text of the resolution see 72 RDI, 1989, 725–7; see *ibid.*, at 719–23, the introductory statement by Sperduti).

self-determination: each State is entitled to help oppressed peoples living in other States to achieve self-determination.

This last point renders the principle of non-interference inapplicable where the right of a people to self-determination is at stake. States are no longer bound to remain silent, regardless of how a government behaves towards the people within its jurisdiction. They can denounce the government's repressive measures and publicly expose how it treats those subjected to its authority. In addition, as we have seen above (see also below, pp. 155–8), States can directly interfere in the authorities' relationship with the people entitled to external self-determination by aiding and assisting those people. In short, it is well settled that, under international law, the principle of non-interference must yield to the right of States to concern themselves with a peoples' legitimate quest for self-determination.[28]

State responsibility

The changing paradigm of state responsibility

In classical international law, State responsibility was governed by a few primitive rules. When a State failed to comply with an international obligation and caused harm to another State – by invading its territory, refusing to grant privileges and immunities to its diplomats, detaining its citizens illegally, or sinking its ships – it was obliged to make reparations. If it refused to make good the damage or give full satisfaction, the injured State had a legal right to impose military or economic sanctions. Obviously, the actual chain of events in each situation was dependent on the relative power of the two States involved. If the State in breach was less powerful than the State injured by its unlawful act, the payment of reparations or the 'punishment' by military coercion was a basic assumption. However, if the perpetrator was the more powerful of the two, the injured State was *de facto* unable to resort to sanctions and the duty to compensate incumbent upon the delinquent party was often ignored.

---

[28] For the impact of self-determination on the restriction of the 'domestic jurisdiction' provided for in Art. 15(8) of the League of Nations Covenant and Art.2(7) of the UN Charter, see G. Arangio-Ruiz, 'Le domain réservé – L'organisation internationale et le rapport entre le droit international et le droit interne', 225 HR, 1990-VI, 185–203, 320–7, 335–6.

A second feature of the traditional system of State responsibility was that the consequences of an internationally wrongful act, including any payment of reparations, remained a 'private' matter. The State in breach and the injured party were to settle the matter as between themselves. No other legal subject was entitled to intervene unless a previously concluded bilateral treaty provided for such intervention or the two States jointly agreed to refer the matter to a third party. The perpetrator and the victim would decide what was a just settlement whilst the rest of the international community looked on, indifferent, detached or perhaps anxious, if concerned about the possible repercussions of the settlement.

The natural consequence of the bilateral nature of this system of State responsibility was that many unlawful acts went unchecked. In addition, *volenti non fit injuria* (no damage is caused to somebody who expresses his will to tolerate it) was one of the basic precepts. Thus, if an injured party 'consented' to the unlawful act, either before it was carried out or *ex post facto*, the situation was treated as if no wrong had been committed. 'Consent' was deemed to annul the wrongful nature of international delinquencies. Obviously, this system played into the hands of the Great Powers, which had both the will and the might to secure the consent of their weaker counterparts.

Today, things are a good deal different, thanks in part to the principle of self-determination, which – together with other dynamic concepts – played an important role in reshaping the rules governing State responsibility. State practice and international treaties now recognize that there is a class of State actions which constitutes a gross breach of fundamental legal standards, and is so grave as to authorize *all States* – not exclusively the injured party – to take appropriate remedial action. Furthermore, this particularly serious category of wrongdoings cannot be justified by 'consent': a victim's 'consent' does not validate the criminal conduct of his attacker.

'Crimes of States' in the International Law Commission's Draft Convention on State Responsibility

The UN International Law Commission has divided international wrongs into two distinct classes: 'international delicts' and 'international crimes of States'. The division, as Article 19 of the ILC Draft Convention on State Responsibility and the attendant ILC Commentary make clear, is based on the premise that the international norms specifically designed to protect fundamental values by their very nature impose obligations *erga omnes*, the breach of which is the concern of every State.[29] The corollary to this special body of rules which imposes obligations *erga omnes* is the 'special regime of responsibility' envisaged in the commentary on Article 19. This provides that a 'crime' may give rise not only to a demand for reparations by the victim State but to 'sanctions' and 'remedies' by other States as well.[30]

Although Article 19 of the ILC draft does not specify what type of sanctions may be employed, it is logical to conclude that the stringency of the sanctions should be commensurate with the gravity of the breach.

The wording of Article 19 of the Draft Convention and the attendant Commentary, drafted by the then Special Rapporteur on State Responsibility, Roberto Ago, and approved by the International Law Commission, further evinces that values such as the right to self-determination and respect for human dignity were influential in the move to a two-tiered system of State responsibility. Article 19, which enumerates international wrongdoings that are classified as international crimes of States, lists among them grave breaches of the right of peoples to self-determination.[31] The Commentary is no less explicit. Cited as one of the factors that contributed to the gradual formation of an international category of wrongs more serious than ordinary 'delicts' is the famous *obiter dictum* of the *Barcelona Traction* case, whereby the International Court of Justice took

---

[29] On this matter, see in particular M. Spinedi, 'International Crimes of States: The Legislative History', in J. H. H. Weiler, A. Cassese, and M. Spinedi (eds.), *International Crimes of States: A Critical Analysis of the ILC's Draft Article 19 on State Responsibility*, Berlin and New York 1989, 7–138; G. Carella, *La responsabilità dello Stato per crimini internazionali*, Naples 1985; M. Mohr, 'The ILC's Distinction between "International Crimes" and "International Delicts" and its Implications', in M. Spinedi and B. Simma (eds.), *United Nations Codification of State Responsibility*, New York, London, and Rome 1987, 115 ff.; A. J. J. de Hoog, 'The Relationship between *Jus Cogens*, Obligations *erga omnes* and International Crimes: Peremptory Norms in Perspective', 42 *Austrian Journal of Public International Law*, 1991, 201 ff.

[30] Art. 19 was proposed by R. Ago in his *Fifth Report on State Responsibility* (*Yearbook ILC*, 1976, vol. II, Part 1, paras. 79–154). The ILC's commentary on the Article is in *Yearbook ILC*, 1976, vol. II, Part 2, 95–122). Professor W. Riphagen took up the matter in his *Preliminary Report* (*Yearbook ILC*, 1980, vol. II, Part 1, para. 98), his *Third Report* (*Yearbook ILC*, 1982, vol. II, Part 1 and his *Fourth Report* (*Yearbook ILC*, 1983, II, Part 1). Recently G. Arangio-Ruiz has undertaken a masterful survey of both the debates on the notion at issue and the 'problematic aspects' of a possible special regime of responsibility for crimes (*Fifth Report on State Responsibility* A/CN.4/Add. 2 and 3).

[31] See generally, E. Gayim, 'Reflections on the Draft Article of the ILC on State Responsibility: Articles 14, 15 and 19 in the Context of the Contemporary Law of Self-Determination', 54 NTIR, 1985, 85–110; H. Atlam, 'International Liberation Movements and International Responsibility', in Spinedi and Simma, *United Nations Codification on State Responsibility*, 35 ff.

the view that there was a class of international obligations which was of greater importance than others and which granted to *all* other States a claim to their fulfilment.

In the opinion of the ILC, the existence of legal obligations *erga omnes* – among the most prominent of which are the norms governing peace, self-determination and human rights – contributed to signalling an acceptance, by the international community, that there exists a body of legal rules, the breach of which entails consequences far more serious than those following from ordinary wrongs, such as the violation of trade agreements. In the ILC's view, this was true even though nothing in State practice indicated that a fully fledged category of 'crimes of States' had emerged. It is claimed that such a conclusion was a natural deduction from international standards and State practice in the fields of self-determination and human rights and the growing weight placed on the ban on war.

The heightened standards developed in the fields of self-determination and human rights, referred to in the ILC Report and evidenced by State practice in those areas, support the notion of a special class of particularly serious international wrongs. Moreover, the work of the Commission and the generally, albeit not universally, favourable reaction to its conclusions concerning Article 19 are contributing to the *gradual crystallization* of a general rule providing that some international delinquencies ought to be classified as 'crimes of States'.

It should be added that another provision of the Draft Treaty on State Responsibility adopted by the ILC, namely Article 29, strengthens the possible reactions of the world community to international crimes of States, by providing that 'consent' does not legitimate an act running counter to a rule of *jus cogens* (hence also to the rule on self-determination). Article 29(2) of the Draft Convention explicitly states that paragraph 1, which provides for the general principle of consent, does not apply if the obligation arises from a peremptory norm of general international law. Since consent to an otherwise wrongful act is deemed to amount to the conclusion of an agreement between the delinquent State and the State waiving its right to reparation, the agreement must necessarily be held to be void whenever a rule of *jus cogens* is involved (a rule of *jus cogens* is by definition a rule from which no State may derogate, even by the conclusion of a treaty with another State).[32] Consequently, any serious

---

[32] In its commentary the ILC illustrates the point made in Article 29 by reference to the right of peoples to self-determination: 'Some Governments have at times expressed doubts as to the exculpatory effect of consent given by a Government to action by a

breach of the right to self-determination cannot be validated by the consent of the State concerned; it remains a 'crime of State'.

State responses to gross breaches of the principle of self-determination

Let us now briefly examine State practice with regard to one of the 'crimes' listed in Article 19(3) of the ILC draft: the violation of obligations concerning self-determination.

In this connection, three questions deserve to be considered: first, can the standards classifying the serious denial of self-determination as an international crime be already considered as a well-established rule of international customary law? Second, under what circumstances can (or could) gross breaches of self-determination be regarded as tantamount to an international crime? Third, what actions are third States and international organizations legally entitled to take in order to react to the commission of such a crime?

As regards the first question, it seems difficult to contend that a fully fledged legal rule on the matter in question has already crystallized. Indeed, one can find little support for the existence of such a rule in State practice. To be sure, there are cases where States and the UN have reacted to very serious breaches of self-determination in a manner different from the usual reaction to an ordinary wrongdoing. It suffices to recall the reactions to the strongly authoritarian racist regime in South Africa, the Soviet invasion of Afghanistan, and the actions of the Israeli authorities in the Arab territories that were occupied in 1967. However, the attitude of third-party States in these circumstances has seldom gone so far as to characterize the actions of the wrongdoer as a 'crime of State'. The better interpretation seems to be that the ILC has tried to

foreign Government that would constitute "interference with the fundamental right of every people to choose the kind of Government under which it wants to live" or to intervention "to support and maintain [unpopular Governments] in power against the wish of a majority of their people and thus deny to the people the elementary right . . . of self-determination". Would it, for example, be an acceptable proposition today that the consent of the Government of a sovereign State to the establishment *ex novo* of a protectorate over that State, or of some other system making it dependent on another State, could have the effect of precluding the wrongfulness of the act of establishing such a system? The generally recognized peremptory nature of the prohibition of encroachment on the independence of other States and on the right of self-determination of peoples would clearly rule out any such acceptance', *Yearbook of the ILC*, vol. II, Part 2, 115. Cf. G. Gaja, 'Obligations *Erga Omnes*, International Crimes and *Jus Cogens*: A Tentative Analysis of Three Related Concepts', in Weiler, Cassese, and Spinedi, *International Crimes of States*, 151–60.

conceptualize and form a theoretical legal framework for the trends emerging in State practice – trends which have not included, however, an awareness by States that in reacting to some breaches of international principles they were treating these breaches as international 'crimes'. All in all, the present condition of international law in this area can perhaps be best explained by stating that at present the classification of grave breaches of self-determination is the subject of a rule *in statu nascendi*, that is, a rule which is in the process of formation.

The answer to the second question (under what circumstances could denial of self-determination be regarded as tantamount to an 'international crime'?) seems, on the face of it, clear; it would appear to be sufficient merely to refer to international general rules concerning self-determination. Since these general rules only grant self-determination to peoples under colonial or alien domination or to those oppressed by a racist regime (denying racial groups equal access to government), any occasion in which self-determination is refused in these contexts could amount to an international crime. However, it should be pointed out that the emerging international rules on international crimes require that a wrongdoing be particularly grave for it to be classified as an international crime. It follows that one could not regard simply any denial of self-determination as an international crime: only those of a particularly serious nature could be so labelled. This view is the result of the serious consequences flowing from the commission of an international crime: were one to place a broad interpretation on this class of breaches, peaceful international relations might easily be jeopardized by excessive resort to these categories. In short, very strict requirements should be met before an international wrong is classified as a 'crime of State'.

Should one therefore hold the view that only the denial of self-determination carried out by means of *military force* can amount to an international crime? This view has actually been put forward by a distinguished Italian jurist, Professor Vincenzo Starace. In his opinion,[33] infringements of the right to self-determination amount to international crimes only because international rules assimilate them to violations of the ban on the use of force. Consequently, the forcible denial of self-determination is but one category of the unlawful use of force.

This view, it is submitted, is unsound. In laying down the obligation on States to respect the right to self-determination and in granting to

---

[33] V. Starace, 'La responsabilité résultant de la violation des obligations à l'égard de la communauté internationale', 153 HR, 1976, 299.

organized peoples (i.e. to liberation movements) the 'right' to use force, the 1970 Declaration on Friendly Relations, the 1974 Definition of Aggression,[34] and other international documents do not make the latter 'right' conditional on the use of *military force* by the oppressing State. They merely provide that liberation movements may respond to any *forcible action* of the oppressive State designed to deprive them of their right to self-determination. 'Forcible action' ('toute mesure de coercition', in French) means the establishment of a repressive regime which does not allow the oppressed people to determine its future status by free means. That expression does not necessarily entail that the State should continuously use military violence against the oppressed people: the existence of institutionalized violence (such as that long obtaining in South Africa) is sufficient to grant the people a licence to resort to force, and to third States the right to take individual or collective 'sanctions'.

It should be added that the proposition that a resort to force by liberation movements does not necessarily and exclusively follow from the use of military force by the colonial, foreign or racist Power, is borne out by the fact that the relevant international instruments do not grant liberation movements a right to 'individual self-defence'.

Finally, it should be remembered that in commenting upon Article 19(3), the ILC pointed out that in the provision describing crimes of States as serious breaches of 'an international obligation of essential importance for safeguarding the right of self-determination of peoples, such as that prohibiting the establishment or maintenance by force of a colonial domination', the expression 'by force' 'should be understood as meaning *against the will of the subject population,* even if that will is not manifested, or has not yet been manifested, by armed opposition'.[35]

---

[34] UN GA Res. 3314(XXIX), 14 December 1974.

[35] *Yearbook ILC,* 1976, vol. II, Part 2, 121 (my italics). Various members of the ILC dwelt on this matter: see Castañeda, *Yearbook ILC,* 1976, vol. I, 243, para. 33; Sette Camara, *ibid.,* 246, para. 72; Njenga, *ibid.,* 246, para. 78; Ramangasoavina, *ibid.,* 247, para. 5; Quentin-Baxter, *ibid.,* 249, para. 23. In his reply, R. Ago noted that 'It was the act of opposing by force the desire for liberation of a people under colonial domination which was today considered criminal. There could, however, be cases where such a people might feel no need to separate from the mother country, so care should be taken not to make the notion of an international crime too broad', *ibid.,* 252, para. 44. It can be noted that important consequences follow from the above-mentioned statement of the ILC: whilst *State's* consent can never legitimate a breach of a peremptory norm of international law, in a way the *population* subjected to colonial domination is entitled to determine whether or not force has been illegally used against it, that is, to establish whether or not there has been a breach of a peremptory norm. Thus, the will of a 'subjected population' is granted greater legal weight than State's consent.

What has been set out thus far chiefly concerns the denial of self-determination in *colonial* situations. This is no doubt the typical instance of a 'crime of State' against self-determination on which agreement has emerged, at least within the ILC. Indeed it is striking that both the Commentary by the Special Rapporteur, R. Ago, on his own proposed Article 19[36] and his Commentary on the draft provision (Article 18) eventually adopted by the ILC[37] only refer to *colonial* situations when dealing with self-determination. However, the loose wording of Article 18(3b) and the clear indication that it does not purport to be exhaustive[38] warrant the conclusion that situations other than colonial can come within the purview of international crimes of States. In view of the need to set out the strict conditions that need to be met before such situations can amount to crimes of States, the contention can be made that not each and every 'alien domination' or 'racist regime' can be classed as an international crime. Since this latter class of international violations must be strictly construed, the following view seems appropriate: in addition to (a) the *forcible denial of self-determination to colonial peoples*, two other classes of actions can be classified as crimes of States, (b) the *military occupation of foreign territory* in contravention of Article 2(4) of the UN Charter, and (c) the *systematic* and *forcible imposition of a racist system of government* denying the racial community discriminated against not only equal access to government but also the most elementary human rights. It stands to reason that in category (b) the wrongful action at the same time infringes the ban on the resort to military force laid down as a general principle of international law (as well as Article 2(4) of the UN Charter) and the principle on self-determination.

Turning now turn to the third question, namely the kind of 'countermeasures' which could be authorized by international law against a State forcibly and gravely violating self-determination, since the ILC has not yet agreed upon specific rules on the matter,[39] the following are only tentative

---

[36] See *Yearbook ILC*, 1976, vol. II, Part 1, 31, para. 97; 35, para. 108; 52, para. 148.

[37] See *Yearbook ILC*, 1976, vol. II, Part 2, 95.

[38] See on this point the remarks made by R. Ago on 6 July 1976, in *Yearbook ILC*, 1976, vol. I, 252, para. 42.

[39] Generally on countermeasures, see the excellent Reports by G. Arangio-Ruiz for the ILC (Third and Fourth Report, A/CN.4/440 and Add. 1 and A/CN.4/444 and Corr. 1 and Add. 1–3). See also the summary of the debates on countermeasures in the ILC and the GA's Sixth Committee in G. Arangio-Ruiz's Fifth Report, A/CN.4/453, 23–9. In the legal literature, see in particular: C. Leben, 'Les contre-mesures étatiques et les réactions à l'illicite dans la société internationale', 28 AFDI, 1982, 9–77; P. M. Dupuy, 'Observations sur la pratique récente des sanctions de l'illicite', 87 RGDIP, 1983, 505–48; E. Zoller, *Peacetime Unilateral Remedies: an Analysis of Countermeasures*, Dobbs

remarks, which are mostly based on some elements of existing State practice.

It cannot be denied that the enforcement measures permitted by international law in the cases at issue are less far-reaching than those authorized in the case of violations by States of the ban on force. First, third States are duty-bound not to take any military action: the attempt made by certain States to transfer the concept of collective self-defence to this area has not been endorsed by the world community at large. Only the oppressed people may use armed violence without breaking the international prohibition on the resort to force.

Secondly, the possibly grave repercussions of unilateral countermeasures for friendly relations in the international community suggest that they should restrict, as much as possible, the right to resort to them. It seems that a third State should only be allowed unilaterally to *demand the cessation of the wrongdoing from the delinquent State* (this is an action that would otherwise be contrary to the general principle banning interference in domestic and international matters of other States). Other countermeasures should only be admissible on *two alternative conditions*.

The first condition is that these countermeasures should be recommended by an international body such as the UN General Assembly or the Security Council, or the competent organs of a regional Organization (for example, the OAS or the OAU) or of other fora such as the EC or the CSCE. One might even go so far as to regard as sufficient a decision by one of these bodies that it is satisfied that a serious breach of international law amounting to a crime of State has been perpetrated. Be that as it may, what is evidently needed is a pronouncement by an international body on the commission of a crime: this pronouncement ensures that the unilateral action by a State in response to an international crime is not arbitrary or abusive.

An alternative condition, where no international body has passed judgment on the matter, or has yet taken a stand on it, is that the third State that is willing to take countermeasures should be prepared to submit its decision to visit sanctions upon the wrongdoer to the impartial assessment of a conciliation or arbitral body. Submission to third-party

Ferry, NY 1984; K. Doehring, 'Die Selbstdurchsetzung völkerrechtlichen Verpflichtungen' 47 *Zeit.*, 1987, 50 ff.; O.Y. Elagab, *The Legality of Non-Forcible Counter-Measures in International Law*, Oxford 1988; A.L. Sicilianos, *Les réactions décentralisées à l'illicite: des contre-mesures à la légitime défense*, Paris 1990, especially 247 ff.; E. Klein, 'Sanctions by International Organizations and Economic Communities', 30 AVR, 1992, 102 ff.; J. Delbrück, 'International Economic Sanctions and Third States', 30 AVR, 1992, 92 ff.

appraisal should take place both prior to the taking of sanctions and afterwards.[40] The reasons supporting this proposition are self-evident. It stands to reason that in a legal order lacking centralized enforcement agencies and where in addition the risks to peace and security are so high, readiness to submit to an impartial evaluation is the only safeguard against the possible escalation of violence. Furthermore, the principle of the peaceful settlement of disputes is one of the seven basic principles governing international relations:[41] in spite of its pitfalls and lacunae, it does enjoin that all member States of the world community must first try peaceful means of settling disputes before resorting to any coercive action or procedure.

Thirdly, we should ask ourselves what countermeasures are allowed once *unilateral* actions can be regarded as admissible under one of the two criteria just set out. It would seem that in case of crimes of states involving self-determination, third States can (i) provide economic, political and military assistance (short of sending armed troops) to the liberation movement fighting against the Power denying the right to self-determination (if it were not legitimized as a countermeasure, such assistance would run counter to the ban on non-interference in internal affairs); (ii) refrain from complying with commercial, military and other treaties previously made with the delinquent State; (iii) withhold recognition of situations that are illegally established by the wrongdoer.

Moving now to my fourth and final remark, I shall point out that States are also clearly entitled (and even duty-bound, depending on the statute of each relevant international Organization) to participate in all *collective* sanctions against the delinquent State, recommended or decided upon by the competent body of that Organization.

Territorial sovereignty

Introductory remarks

The principle and the rules on self-determination have extended their influence and sway to a traditional part of international law: that

---

[40] A forceful and persuasive plea for the introduction of dispute settlement procedures, in the area of the resort to countermeasures, has been recently made by G. Arangio-Ruiz in his *Fifth Report on State Responsibility* (A/CN.4/ 453, 5 ff.) See also the Fourth Report (on prior resort, etc.).

[41] See thereon Cassese, *International Law in a Divided World*, 126-65, Cahier, 'Changements et continuité du droit international – Cours général de droit international public', 31-92, as well as the works cited below, pp. 333-7, and notes 17 and 18.

governing modes of acquisition, transfer, and loss of legal title over territory.

This cluster of problems has already been dealt with, although somewhat tangentially, in the discussion on the ambiguities inherent in the rules concerning the external self-determination of colonial peoples (Chapter 4). There, it was emphasized that the famous General Assembly Resolution 1514(XX), while providing for the right of colonial peoples to self-determination, also insisted on respect for the territorial integrity of States.

The focus here will now be on the impact of self-determination on the international legal regime concerning the following issues: (1) the validity of existing title over territory; (2) the acquisition of title; (3) the transfer of title; and (4) the determination of boundaries.

The validity of existing title over territory

It is well known that under classical international law the legal modes of acquisition of territory included *colonial conquest* (if the two cumulative conditions of intent to appropriate the territory and actual display of sovereign authority were met) and the *transfer* of sovereign title over a colonial territory by way of a treaty of cession between two States (one of which being of course the holder of title over the territory).[42]

The new law of self-determination has not resulted in the *invalidation* of these legal bases of title *ipso facto*.[43] However, a legal process, starting with the League of Nations mandate system, followed by the United Nations trusteeship system and compounded by the gradual emergence of legal rules on self-determination, has led to the emergence of a set of *legal obligations* for those countries still enjoying sovereignty over colonial territories. These obligations make it incumbent on those States to enable the people of colonial territories freely to choose whether to opt for independent statehood, or association or integration with an existing State. Thus, those obligations do not produce the immediate legal effect of rendering the legal title over colonial territories null and void. Rather,

---

[42] Sometimes the transfer of authority was made by local potentates holding authority over the area. The legal literature often spoke of 'colonial protectorates' to denote this form of relationship (see, e.g., D. Anzilotti, *Corso di diritto internazionale*, 117–18; L. Oppenheim and H. Lauterpacht, *International Law*, vol. I, 6th edn, London, New York, and Toronto 1947, 178; R. Quadri, *Diritto internazionale pubblico*, 5th edn, Naples 1968, 431; Crawford, *The Creation of States in International Law*, 198–201).

[43] As is instead held by some authors: see, e.g., Calogeropoulos-Stratis, *Le droit des peuples à disposer d'eux-mêmes*, 113; Rigo-Sureda, *The Evolution of the Right of Self-Determination*, 353.

besides setting out a series of limitations and qualifications intended greatly to restrict sovereignty, they envisage a temporary legal regime that must of necessity lead to the eventual *extinction* of legal title.[44] In a way, these obligations act as a sort of time-bomb: the holder of the sovereign title has to fulfil them knowing that by this action it will eventually have to relinquish its title.

The above remarks apply to colonial territories proper. Self-determination, however, also has a bearing on the legal status of some 'special' territories. These territories are unique in that they exhibit two features. First, they do not fall neatly into the category of colonial territories, either because it was not as a result of colonial conquest that they were subjected to the sovereignty of the State currently wielding authority over them (for example, Gibraltar, which was ceded by Spain to Great Britain by the Treaty of 1713) or because for historical reasons they are not inhabited by an indigenous population but exclusively by settlers (for example, the Falklands/Malvinas). The second feature is that these territories, although they cannot be regarded as 'colonial' in the classical sense, are nevertheless situated far away from the State holding the sovereign rights and have consequently been regarded by this State itself as different from its territory proper, so much so that they have been included, in the UN, in the list of 'non-self-governing territories'.

With regard to these territories the principle of self-determination entails a set of obligations for the holder of sovereign title. First, this Power must enable the relevant people freely to express their choice as to their external and internal status; such a choice must be genuine, in that the people must be offered a wide range of options (independence; association with a sovereign State; maintenance of the existing links with the Power that holds sovereignty; participation in an international union; etc.). Second, this choice must not be offered once and for all, but on a regular basis, that is at intervals to be agreed upon with the population. Third, the sovereign State must allow international scrutiny and monitoring of the way it ascertains the population's wishes. Fourth, the sovereign State must enable any other State directly concerned (in practice, the contiguous State) to participate, in some way, in the consideration of the interests and concerns of the relevant population (for example, by entering into consultations and negotiations with the sovereign State).

---

[44] See on this matter Jennings, *The Acquisition of Territory in International Law*, 79–87; Crawford, *The Creation of States in International Law*, 363–4; Shaw, *Title to Territory in Africa*, 149 ff.

It is thus apparent that the impact of the principle of self-determination on the legal status of these territories entails that the sovereign Power does not enjoy unfettered rights. Indeed, it can only exercise its rights and powers subject to a set of limitations which may also result in its eventual relinquishment of the legal title over the territory.

Acquisition of legal title to territorial sovereignty

One of the consequences of the body of international law on self-determination is that at present no legal title over territory can be acquired in breach of self-determination. A good illustration of this concept is the case of East Timor. As we shall see (pp. 223–4), in 1975 Indonesia annexed East Timor without meeting the requirement of having secured the 'free and genuine expression of the will of the people concerned' set out by the ICJ in the *Western Sahara* case. The extension of Indonesia's sovereignty over East Timor was therefore unlawful and hence incapable of conferring on Indonesia a legal title over the territory.

The same principle also governs cases where sovereignty over a territory is uncertain. Thus, for instance, assuming that the legal regime of the Arab territories occupied by Israel in 1967 is uncertain because Jordan never acquired a sovereign title, or, alternatively that the recent renunciation by Jordan of any legal claims to those territories has brought about the extinction of the Jordanian sovereign title, it follows that Israel cannot acquire such title on the strength of customary rules relating to acquisition of territory. Apart from the fact that international norms on belligerent occupation rule out any transfer of sovereignty over occupied territories, a major stumbling-block is constituted by the principle of self-determination and its requirement that the relevant population freely express its wishes on the status of the territory.

It should, however, be added that in some exceptional instances the acquisition of authority over a territory in breach of the principle of self-determination can be subsequently validated by the recognition or acquiescence of other member States of the international community. This, it is submitted, holds true in such cases as Goa (1961) and West Irian (1969). The subsequent attitude of third States and the United Nations made it possible for the violation of self-determination gradually to lose its initial vitiating effect and for the title over territory gradually to be consolidated in favour of India and Indonesia respectively.

A further aspect of the legal bearing of self-determination on territorial title can be inferred from the ICJ's Advisory Opinion on *Western Sahara*.

It relates to territories inhabited by indigenous populations that are collectively organized, although not in such a manner as to constitute a State proper. If the State wielding sovereign authority over one of these territories decides to withdraw from it, it does not follow that the territory automatically becomes *terra nullius*, hence open to appropriation by any State. Even if the indigenous populations may not come to be regarded as international legal subjects proper, they must be enabled freely to express their will as to the international status of the territory, that is, whether they wish to associate or integrate into an existing sovereign State, or acquire some sort of international status gradually leading to independent statehood.[45]

Cession

Neither State practice nor resolutions adopted by the United Nations or other intergovernmental organizations has recently laid special emphasis on the principle that in the case of a transfer of territorial sovereignty by one State to another, the wishes of the people concerned should always be taken into account. This however does not mean that this has been discarded or neglected by States or international organizations. The truth of the matter is that the concept was simply regarded as obvious, that is as logically following from the whole thrust and basic content of the principle of self-determination. As Judge Dillard put it in his separate opinion in the *Western Sahara* case, 'it is for the people to determine the destiny of the territory and not the territory the destiny of the people'.[46]

To mention but one illustration, reference can be made to a statement in 1986 by the British Prime Minister who, in answering a parliamentary question concerning Northern Ireland, pointed to the agreement between the UK and the Republic of Ireland of 15 November 1985 and emphasized that this agreement and 'in particular the joint affirmation that any change in the status of Northern Ireland would come about only with the consent of the majority of the people of Northern Ireland' were fully consistent with the principles (laid down, *inter alia*, in the 'Helsinki accords')

---

[45] See ICJ, Reports 1975, 37–40 (paras. 75–83). It should, however, be noted that the question asked of the Court, and which the Court answered in the affirmative, was whether Western Sahara was *terra nullius* at the time of *Spanish colonization, not* at the time of *decolonization*. Nevertheless, there is room for believing that the above inference from the Court's Opinion is well-founded. Cf. also Brownlie, *Principles of International Law*, 598.

[46] ICJ, Reports 1975, 122.

of the inviolability of frontiers, the territorial integrity of States, and the right to self-determination of peoples.[47]

It can therefore be concluded that one of the consequences of the general principle of self-determination relates precisely to changes of territory, that is, to cases where sovereignty over a particular territory is transferred by one State to another by mutual agreement (obviously, acquisition of territory by force is no longer admissible in current international law). In the case of such transfers, the States involved are duty-bound to ascertain the wishes of the population concerned, by means of a referendum or plebiscite, or by any other appropriate means that ensure a free and genuine expression of will.[48] It follows, of course, that any inter-state agreement that is contrary to the will of the population concerned would fall foul of the principle of self-determination. On account of the legal status that the principle has now acquired in international law, the agreement would be in conflict with *jus cogens*.

However, the import of the sweeping principle just referred to carries an exception for special historical and political reasons, as will presently be seen.

Boundaries (uti possidetis v. self-determination)

As is well known, towards the beginning of the nineteenth century a practice developed in Spanish America whereby, on the accession of the various former colonies of Spain to independence, their boundaries followed the former colonial boundaries. This practice manifested itself in a host of bilateral treaties, as well as a number of national constitutions of newly independent Latin American countries. It is not clear whether this practice turned into a customary rule of international law endowed with a

[47] See BYIL, 1986, 515.
[48] A contrary view is held by Brownlie, *Principles of International Law*, 170 ('[A]t present, there is insufficient practice to warrant the view that a transfer is invalid simply because there is no sufficient provision for the expression of opinion by the inhabitants.'). The same view was taken by L. Oppenheim and H. Lauterpacht, *International Law*, vol. I, 8th edn, 1955, 551–2 ('[I]t is doubtful whether the Law of Nations will ever make it a condition of every cession that it must be ratified by a plebiscite. The necessities of international policy may on occasions allow or even demand such a plebiscite, but in some cases they will not allow it') and Wengler, *Völkerrecht*, vol. II, 982–3 and 1031–2 ('Die Berücksichtigung des Willens der Wohnbevölkerung bei der einsitigen oder verträglichen Bestimmung des Staatsgebiets kann derzeit nur als eine von den meisten Staaten anerkannte rechtspolitische Richtlinie verstanden werden, ohne dass jedoch ihre Verletzung allein einen Gebietsstand als völkerrechtswidrig erscheinen lässt', at 982–3), and seems to be shared by Jennings, *The Acquisition of Territory in International Law*, 78.

regional scope, or remained a simple practice devoid of any binding force, or rather crystallized into a general principle of law as was held by the two Latin American judges of the ICJ (Armand-Ugon and Moreno Quintana) in the *Sovereignty over Certain Frontier Land* case.[49] Since this practice developed and was upheld at a time when self-determination had not yet reached the status of a legal principle in the international community, for our purposes the specific question of the legal status of the practice is largely immaterial.

In contrast, the subject becomes relevant to our enquiry with regard to recent times. The wave of decolonization in Africa, which started in the 1950s and continued until 1963, posed a crucial problem as to the borders of the newly independent countries. Except for a few cases where the boundaries were agreed upon within the framework of the United Nations (see above, Chapter 4), the general trend was to accept the colonial boundaries that existed at the time of independence. This practice was sanctioned, although in a rather oblique way, in one of the clauses of the 1960 UN Declaration on the Independence of Colonial Peoples (see above, Chapter 3). It was then upheld (although indirectly) in Article III(3) of the Charter of the Organisation of African Unity of 1963, and subsequently spelled out in a resolution adopted in 1964 by the Assembly of Heads of State and Government of the Member States of the Organization, in Cairo.[50] This resolution is important because it emanates from the highest authorities of the countries concerned (only Morocco and Somalia refused to accept it). It is also important because it forcefully specified (in operative paragraph 2) that all Member States of the OAU pledged themselves 'to respect the borders existing on their achievement of national independence', and in addition it set forth the rationale behind this pledge: the fact that 'border problems constitute a grave and permanent factor of dissension', 'the existence of extra-African manoeuvres aimed at dividing African States', as well as the fact that 'the borders of African States, on the day of their independence, constitute a tangible reality' (preambular paragraphs of the resolution).

There is some controversy over both the status of the Cairo resolution and that of the principle it embodies. According to a distinguished commentator, I. Brownlie, the resolution was not binding as such but contributed to the crystallization of a generally accepted view; the

[49] ICJ, Reports 1959, 240 and 255.
[50] For the text of the resolution, see I. Brownlie, *African Boundaries – A Legal and Diplomatic Encyclopaedia*, London 1979, 10–11.

subsequent State practice based on the resolution gradually gave rise to a 'rule of regional customary international law binding those States which have unilaterally declared their acceptance of the principle of the *status quo* as at the time of independence'.[51] A different view was taken by a Chamber of the International Court of Justice in the *Case Concerning the Frontier Dispute*. The Chamber held that the Cairo resolution simply 'defined and stressed' the principle of *uti possidetis*; the principle itself – according to the Chamber – constitutes 'a rule of general scope', that is to say a customary rule of international law having a universal, that is, non-regional, purport. After noting that the principle had first been applied in Spanish America, the Chamber pointed out the following:

> Nevertheless the principle is not a special rule which pertains solely to one specific system of law. It is a general principle, which is logically connected with the phenomenon of the obtaining of independence, wherever it occurs. Its obvious purpose is to prevent the independence and stability of new States being endangered by fratricidal struggles provoked by the challenging of frontiers following the withdrawal of the administering power.[52]

Whatever view is taken, it is beyond dispute that at present *uti possidetis* constitutes a general rule of international law.[53] It is plain that this rule, in that it is designed to 'freeze the territorial title' and to 'stop the clock' at the time of a colonial country becoming independent or at the time of the secession of a region from a unitary State (or of a member State from a federated State),[54] is in sharp contrast with that of self-determination. This

---

[51] Brownlie, *African Boundaries*, 11. On this matter, see F. Wooldridge, 'Uti possidetis Doctrine', in 10 *Encyclopedia*, 1987, 519 ff. Cf. also J. A. Frowein, 'Self-Determination as a Limit to Obligations under International Law', in Tomuschat (ed.), *Modern Law of Self-Determination*, 216–18.

[52] ICJ, Reports 1986, 565, para. 20. See also at 566 para. 23. The words quoted in the text, concerning the Cairo resolution, can be found at 566, para. 22.

[53] On this principle, see, among others, T. M. Franck, 'Postmodern Tribalism and the Right to Secession', in C. Brölmann, R. Lefeber, and M. Y. A. Zieck (eds.), *Peoples and Minorities in International Law*, Dordrecht, Boston, and London 1993, 5–10, 18–20; J. Klabbers and R. Lefeber, 'Africa: Lost between Self-Determination and *Uti possidetis*', ibid., 54–76; R.Y. Jennings, 'Closing Address', ibid., 345–6.

[54] Recently *uti possidetis* has been upheld by the Arbitration Committee established by the 'Conference on Yugoslavia'. In its 'Opinion' no. 2 the Committee, called upon to pronounce on whether 'the Serbian population in Croatia and Bosnia-Herzegovina, as one of the constituent peoples of Yugoslavia, have the right to self-determination', stated that 'it is well-established that, whatever the circumstances, the right to self-determination must not involve changes to existing frontiers at the time of independence (*uti possidetis juris*) except where the States concerned agree otherwise' (text in 3 EJIL, 1992, 183–4). See also the comment by A. Pellet, ibid., 178–81.

is because the population living on or around the borders of the newly independent State may wish to choose a different sovereign or even opt for independent status or some sort of autonomy. We are here confronted with an area in which historical and political considerations were regarded by States as of such paramount importance as to make it necessary to set aside the right of peoples to self-determination. In this area, the principle of self-determination, instead of influencing the content of international legal rules, has been 'trumped' by other, overriding requirements.

This, however, is not the end of the story. For, the principle of self-determination might still have an impact after the attainment of independence, when two former colonial countries or secessionist States decide to modify their borders by mutual agreement. If this happens, the agreement must be consonant with the wishes of the population concerned (see my general comments above, pp. 189–90). In other words, the two States cannot decide on possible transfers of territory without duly consulting the population affected. In addition, this consultation should aim at enabling that population freely to express its genuine will; for example, it must take the form of a plebiscite or a referendum properly monitored by an international and independent authority. If these conditions are not fulfilled, the treaty providing for the transfer of territory would be contrary to *jus cogens* and could therefore be declared null and void (if, of course, one of the contracting parties raises the issue before the International Court of Justice, under Article 66(a) of the Vienna Convention on the Law of Treaties).

The use of force

It is well known that the UN Charter laid down a general ban on the threat or use of force (Article 2(4)) and exceptionally authorized resort to force either in individual or collective self-defence (Article 51) or in the form of collective action (Chapter VII). We should now ascertain if and to what extent the principle of self-determination has brought about any change in this legal regulation.[55]

---

[55] See above, Chapter 7, pp. 147–58. Generally, on the question of self-determination and the use of force, see Bowett, 'Self-Determination and Political Rights in the Developing Countries', 132–3; C. Dugard, 'The OAU and Colonialism: An Inquiry into the Plea of Self-Defence as a Justification of the Use of Force in the Eradication of Colonialism', 46 ICLQ, 1967, 172 ff.; S.K. Panter-Brick, 'The Right to Self-Determination: Its Application to Nigeria', 44 *International Affairs*, 1968, 254–66; G. Abi-Saab, 'Wars of National Liberation and the Laws of War' 3 *Annals of International Studies*, 1972, 93 ff.;

The use of force by the oppressive state

As I pointed out above, in this chapter (pp. 180–5), it now seems well established that international law bans not only the use of *military force* by States for the purpose of denying self-determination to a colonial or foreign people or a racial group, but also *other forms of forcible action* designed to pursue the same goal.

The first case occurs when a State uses armed violence to maintain or enforce its denial of self-determination. The second case is when a State wielding authority over a colonial people, besides failing to take all the

T. M. Franck and N. S. Rodley, 'After Bangladesh: The Law of Humanitarian Intervention by Military Force', 67 AJIL, 1973, 275 ff.; Rigo Sureda, *The Evolution of the Right of Self-Determination*, 324–51; N. Ronzitti, *Le guerre di liberazione nazionale e il diritto internazionale*, Pisa 1974; N. Ronzitti, 'Resort to Force in Wars of National Liberation', in A. Cassese (ed.), *Current Problems of International Law*, Milan 1975, 327 ff.; M. R. Rwelamira, 'Contemporary Self-Determination and the U.N. Charter: an Appraisal of the Use of Force against Colonialism and Racial Discrimination in Southern Africa', 6 *The African Review*, 1976, 375–402; G. Arangio-Ruiz, 'Human Rights and Non-Intervention in the Helsinki Final Act', 157 HR, 1977-IV, 266–74; R. Gorelick, 'Wars of National Liberation: Jus ad Bellum', 11 Case WRJIL 1979, 71 ff.; V. P. Nanda, 'Self-Determination Outside the Colonial Context: The Birth of Bangladesh in Retrospect', in Alexander and Friedlander, *Self-Determination: National, Regional and Global Dimensions*, 193–220; N. Feinberg, 'The Legality of the Use of Force to Recover Occupied Territory', 15 Israel L. Rev. 1980, 160–79; Pomerance, *Self-Determination in Law and Practice*, 48–62; W. M. Reisman, 'Coercion and Self-Determination: Construing Charter Article 2(4)', 78 AJIL, 1984, 642 ff.; O. Schachter, 'The Legality of Pro-Democratic Invasion', 78 AJIL, 1984, 645 ff.; Guarino, *Autodeterminazione dei popoli*, 298 ff.; M. R. Islam, 'Use of Force in Self-Determination Claims', 25 IJIL, 1985, 424–47; Kimminich, 'Die Renaissance des Selbstbestimmungsrechts nach dem Ende des Kolonialismus', 607–15; M. J. Levitin, 'The Law of Force and the Force of Law: Grenada, the Falklands and Humanitarian Intervention' 27 HILJ, 1986, 621–57; Lattanzi, 'Autodeterminazione dei popoli', 23–6; Arangio-Ruiz, 'Autodeterminazione (diritto dei popoli alla)', 7–9; H. A. Wilson, *International Law and the Use of Force by National Liberation Movements*, Oxford 1988, 91 ff.; Sicilianos, *Les réactions décentralisées à l'illicite*, 429–55; A. D. Sofaer, 'Remarks on the Panamian Revolution: Diplomacy, War and Self-Determination in Panama', 84 *Proceedings* ASIL, 1990, 182–4; O. Schachter, *International Law in Theory and Practice*, Dordrecht, Boston, and London, 1991, 119–20, 128; A. Randelzhofer, 'Art. 2(4)', in Simma, *Charta der Vereinten Nationen*, 72 ff.; K. Ryan, 'Rights, Intervention and Self-Determination' 20 *Denver Journal of International Law and Policy*, 1991, 55–71; D. J. Scheffer, 'Toward a Modern Doctrine of Humanitarian Intervention', 23 *The University of Toledo Law Review*, 1992, 253–93; I. O. Bokatola, *L'Organisation des Nations Unies et la protection des minorités*, Brussels 1992, 134–60; O. Corten and P. Klein, *Droit d'ingérence ou obligation de réaction?*, Brussels 1992, 251–68; M. Bothe, 'The Legitimacy of the Use of Force to Protect Peoples and Minorities', in Brölmann, Lefeber, and Zieck (eds.), *Peoples and Minorities in International Law*, 289–99; J. A. Frowein, 'Self-Determination as a Limit to Obligations under International Law', in Tomuschat, *Modern Law of Self-Determination*, 213–15.

necessary measures for enabling the people to exercise its rights to self-determination, also sets up institutional, coercive mechanisms designed to prevent the implementation of self-determination (or in the course of its military occupation of a foreign country establishes procedures and takes measures designed to thwart any attempt by the occupied people to exercise its right to self-determination; or alternatively sets up in its domestic legal system institutions which deny a racially discriminated group equal access to government).[56] In both classes of cases the denial of self-determination has a twofold legal relevance under international law: firstly, it constitutes a violation of international legal rules; secondly, as we shall shortly see, it legitimizes the resort to military force by the organization representing the oppressed people or group.

Let us now dwell on the substantive rules governing these two classes of cases. The general legal prescriptions are laid down in the section on the use of force in the 1970 Declaration on Friendly Relations.[57] This provides that:

Every State has the duty to refrain from any forcible action which deprives peoples referred to in the elaboration of the principle of equal rights and self-determination of their right to self-determination and freedom and independence.[58]

---

[56] It should be noted that before the adoption of the 1970 Declaration on Friendly Relations, some States put on record their view of the circumstances in which an administering Power was allowed to use force. Thus, Australia pointed out that the Declaration 'prohibited the use of force to deprive a people of its right to self-determination – that and nothing more. It did not diminish the responsibility of an administering Power to maintain order in a Non-Self-Governing Territory, nor did it diminish the limitations imposed elsewhere on the use of force' (UN Doc. A/C.6/SR.1178, para. 40). Similarly, the US stated that the Declaration 'did not limit the right of an Administering Authority to use appropriate police measures in the territories for which it was responsible' (ibid., SR.1180, para. 25). The Indonesian delegate replied as follows: '[S]ome Governments had expressed the view that the principle of equal rights and self-determination did not preclude police action limited to the maintenance of law and order. These words awoke bitter memories of Indonesia's struggle against colonialism and racism. Police action with regular military troops armed with tanks, bombers and guns, against colonized peoples were actually full-scale military operations. Imposing "law and order" in such situations meant imposing "colonial law and order", that is the law of the jungle and the order of prisons' (ibid., SR.1182, para. 75).

[57] On this section of the Declaration, see, in particular K. Obradovich, 'Prohibition of the Threat of Use of Force', in M. Sahovic (ed.), *Principles of International Law Concerning Friendly Relations and Cooperation*, New York 1972, 61 ff.; Arango-Ruiz, 'The Normative Role of the General Assembly of the United Nations', 528 ff.

[58] This clause can also be found, in the same terms, in the Declaration's section relating to self-determination.

This provision is strengthened, at least in some respects, by a clause in the Declaration's section on non-intervention:

The use of force to deprive peoples of their national identity constitutes a violation of their inalienable rights and of the principle of non-intervention.[59]

What is the legal standing of these clauses? I submit that in some respects they *restate* existing law, while in others they *crystallize* or *codify* new developments in the international community. Let us briefly consider these two points.

The provisions at issue restate, with regard to colonial and militarily occupied foreign peoples, the ban on the use of force laid down in Article 2(4) of the UN Charter. As is well known, this provision (and the corresponding general rule) strictly prohibits resort to force by States 'in their international relations'. It now seems uncontested that since the 1950s the relations between a colonial Power and the colonial people have no longer been regarded as internal or municipal, but are seen as coming within the purview of international relations proper. The same of course has for long held true, even before the adoption of the UN Charter, for relations between the occupying Power and the people of the occupied territory. Hence, the use of force by the oppressive Power, in these two classes of cases, comes under the ban laid down in Article 2(4) of the UN Charter (and the corresponding general rule). Indeed, besides the fact that we are here faced with instances of forcible action pertaining to international relations, military force is also being used 'in a manner inconsistent with the purposes of the United Nations', in particular the purpose laid down in Article 1(2), namely the self-determination of peoples.

By contrast, the provisions of the 1970 Declaration referred to above crystallize new developments in State practice in two other respects.

First, they ban the resort to military force by States for the purpose of denying the right to self-determination to racial groups. There is no gainsaying that the relations between the oppressive State and the racial group are internal in nature. Here, the ban on the use of force by States constitutes a novel departure from the general prohibition laid down in Article 2(4) (and the corresponding general rule). In this respect the clauses of the 1970 Declaration crystallize a new State practice with the attendant *opinio juris*: all the UN General Assembly and Security Council resolutions condemning the use of force by Southern Rhodesia

---

[59] On this clause, see in particular Arangio-Ruiz, 'Human Rights and Non-Intervention in the Helsinki Final Act', 270–2.

and South Africa against the black majority, attest to the gradual formation of a rule on the matter, a rule that was eventually codified in the 1970 Declaration.

Second, a codification of new trends in State practice can also be discerned in the 1970 Declaration's provisions in so far as they ban the denial of self-determination (to colonial peoples, to peoples in militarily occupied territories and to racial groups) through institutional coercive measures designed to impede the realization of self-determination. In this respect as well the Declaration innovates. It codifies numerous international pronouncements and a great wealth of State practice: all the UN General Assembly resolutions on self-determination which condemn the existence of repressive mechanisms or the taking of coercive measures for denying self-determination; the corresponding State practice concerning colonialism, Southern Rhodesia and South Africa, as well as the Arab territories occupied by Israel. It should be added that the 'rules' codified in the 1970 Declaration were confirmed by the subsequent practice of States, in particular by other instances of alien military occupation accompanied by the persistent and institutionalized refusal to enable the oppressed people to exercise its right to self-determination (for example, the military occupation of Northern Cyprus by Turkey in 1974 and the Soviet occupation of Afghanistan by the Soviet Union in 1979).

The importance of these normative developments should not be underestimated: the international community has gone so far in its protection of self-determination as to prohibit not only the use of military force by the oppressive State but also what could be termed 'institutionalized violence', namely all those measures, mechanisms, and devices destined to prevent peoples or racial groups from exercising their right to self-determination.

The use of force by the oppressed people

The UN Charter neither authorizes nor bans the use of force by dependent peoples (or rather, by liberation movements representative of those peoples) for the realization of external self-determination – the ban laid down in Article 2(4) is only imposed upon *States*. The reason why this question was held in abeyance by the Charter is self-evident: in 1945 none of the founding fathers anticipated the rapid break up of colonial systems and the emergence of pugnacious and vociferous liberation movements willing to overthrow colonial power violently. In the 1950s and 1960s, quite a few developing countries, supported by socialist States and wishing to enhance and fortify the role of liberation movements, argued that armed force by dependent peoples to free themselves from colonial power was authorized by Article 51 of the UN Charter as a form of self-defence against armed aggression (colonial domination). This political view was however rejected by the majority of the Member States of the United Nations,[60] because, among other things, it entailed a dangerous consequence: third States could have claimed to act in collective self-defence in order to send troops to fight against the colonial Power. This involvement of third States could have produced highly undesirable consequences for world peace.

Although no legal right proper was thus bestowed upon liberation movements to resort to force, gradually the view emerged among States that nevertheless resort to force by these movements was not in violation of the *general* ban on force that had meanwhile emerged in the world community (this ban, generated by and modelled on Article 2(4) of the UN Charter, was however legally distinct in many respects from that provision; among other things, it enjoined that not only States, but any international entity endowed with legal personality, must refrain from force).

However, the attitude of the world community was qualified by a basic condition: that resort to force by liberation movements should only be effected as a response to the forcible denial of self-determination by the oppressive Power, that is by the refusal of the latter State, backed up by armed force or even coercive measures short of military violence, to grant self-determination to colonial peoples (or to peoples subjected to foreign military occupation or to organized racial groups denied equal access to government).

Furthermore, the world community did not go to the lengths of conferring a *legal right* proper on liberation movements, but only granted a *licence* to use force (as was pointed out above, in Chapter 6, pp. 150–8).

---

[60] See on this matter, J. Dugard, 'The OAU and Colonialism', 172 ff.; P. L. Lamberti Zanardi, *La legittima difesa nel diritto internazionale*, Milan 1972, 184 ff. (on the debate on the 1970 Declaration on Friendly Relations); Ronzitti, *Le guerre di liberazione nazionale e il diritto internazionale*, 101 (on the debate concerning the Definition of aggression); F. Lattanzi, *Garanzie dei diritti dell'uomo nel diritto internazionale generale*, Milan 1983, 478 ff. (on the discussion on some provisions of the ILC Draft on State responsibility).

The use of force by third states

RESORT TO FORCE BY THE STATE CLAIMING REVERSIONARY RIGHTS OVER THE TERRITORY OF A DEPENDENT PEOPLE

In a few instances the State contiguous to the territory of the colonial people, or at any rate the State claiming reversionary rights over the colonial territory, has resorted to force for the purpose of establishing (or re-establishing) its rights over the dependent people. In this connection, the armed intervention by India in the case of Goa and by Argentina in the case of the Falklands/Malvinas should be recalled (these cases have already been mentioned above: in Chapter 4, pp. 80–1 and pp. 86–8 respectively). The reaction of the international community to these instances of the use of force shows that they were regarded as being in violation of Article 2(4) of the UN Charter (and the corresponding general principle).

The conclusion is therefore warranted that no derogation from the ban on force has emerged in the international community to the effect that a State can resort to armed violence to enforce its claim over a territory where a people is being denied the right to self-determination.

RESORT TO FORCE BY OTHER THIRD STATES

As was stated above (Chapter 6, pp. 150–5), despite the efforts of many Third World and socialist countries in the early 1960s, no general rule has crystallized in the world community envisaging a derogation from the Charter system to the effect that third States can use force in collective self-defence against a State forcibly denying self-determination. Faced with the dangers stemming from the formation of such a rule, the majority of the world community strongly opposed it. Similarly, the claim has been rejected that a State can use force (outside the right to collective self-defence) for the purpose of helping a liberation movement realize its right to self-determination. The reaction of the international community to the claim by India in the case of Bangladesh in 1971[61] to be using military force to, among other things, 'facilitate self-determination' bears this out.

Consequently, third States can only provide economic, political and logistical support to liberation movements, as well as sending arms

---

[61] See in particular, T. M. Franck and N. S. Rodley, 'After Bangladesh: The Law of Humanitarian intervention by Military Force', 67 AJIL, 1973, 275 ff.

and ammunitions. States are not allowed to overstep this threshold in helping liberation movements: the requirement of peace and security has been regarded as of overriding importance by the international community.

On the other hand, third States must refrain from assisting a State that forcibly opposes self-determination. Any substantial help to the oppressive State, be it military or economic in nature, is regarded as illegal under current international law.

Final remarks

It is apparent from the above that political and military restraints and chiefly the need to pursue peace have greatly circumscribed the attempt at innovation in the area of the use of force, repeatedly made in the early 1960s by a large segment of the international community. As a consequence, the main innovations introduced by recent practice in the UN Charter system (or, more exactly, in the general legal regulation of the use of force) are: (i) the formation of a general rule prohibiting the use of force by States against racial groups in their territory, to which they deny equal access to government; (ii) the crystallization of a general ban on resort to coercive institutional action for the purpose of denying self-determination to colonial (or militarily occupied) peoples or racial groups; (iii) the emergence, in favour of liberation movements, of a legal licence to use armed violence against oppressive States forcibly denying self-determination; and (iv) the formation of a legal ban on third States to provide military or economic assistance to oppressive States. Any further development for the benefit of dependent peoples has been successfully opposed by a number of members of the world community (chiefly Western States and some developing countries) lest peaceful relations should be seriously jeopardized.

Thus, to the question raised by I. Brownlie ('If a State uses force to implement the principle of self-determination, is it possible to assume that one aspect of *jus cogens* is more significant than another?'),[62] it can be answered that under current international law the right to self-determination must substantially yield to the ban on the use of force by States. This ban remains paramount. The only minor restrictions introduced by post-1945 practice and law are the ones I have just endeavoured to highlight. Furthermore, as rightly pointed out by the same

---

[62] Brownlie, *Principles of Public International Law*, 515.

author,[63] 'if force be used to seize territory and the object is the implementation of the principle [of self-determination], then title may accrue by general acquiescence and recognition more readily than in other cases of unlawful seizure of territory'.

The humanitarian law of armed conflict

The principle of self-determination was a major factor leading to the creation of a new category of armed conflict covered by the rules of international warfare: wars of national liberation.

Between 1960 and the mid 1970s, States from the Third World and the socialist bloc sought to convince the United Nations that wars of national liberation ought to be raised to the level of international armed conflicts, with the consequent application of the rules of warfare. Western countries opposed their efforts, arguing that wars of national liberation were internal conflicts and as such ought to continue to be governed by the laws of civil war; it was said to be unwise to treat one particular type of domestic strife differently from other types. Such differentiation, they argued, being based on ideological considerations, would inevitably lead to a revival of the concept of *bellum justum*, or 'just war', which enjoyed great popularity in the Middle Ages and, fortunately for the international community, was thereafter jettisoned. In the end, the view of the Third World and socialist States prevailed. The final vote in the Geneva Conference of 1974 was 84 in favour of upgrading wars of national liberation and 1 against, with 11 abstaining. The only State to reject the measure totally was Israel.[64] Thus Article 1(4) of the First Additional Geneva Protocol of 1977 came into being.[65]

---

[63] *Ibid.*, 597–8.

[64] By 1977, the Western States no longer considered classifying wars of liberation as international armed conflicts the grave threat they had earlier. This is partially due to the fact that Angola and Mozambique had gained independence in the intervening years, lessening the proposed rule's potential political impact. The States which abstained – ten industrialized States plus Guatemala – voiced misgivings about the possibility of applying the provision consistently. They challenged the political and practical wisdom of the rule; but they did not dismiss it out of hand: they merely considered Art. 1(4) *bad law*.

[65] 'The situations referred to in the preceding paragraph include armed conflicts in which peoples are fighting against colonial domination and alien occupation and against racist régimes in the exercise of their right of self-determination, as enshrined in the Charter of the United Nations and the Declaration on Principles of International Law concerning Friendly Relations and Co-operation among States in accordance with the Charter of the United Nations.'

One might argue that the result of the vote and the tenor of the 'reservations' entered by a number of the abstaining States suggest that even those who abstained accepted that the rule represented a new law of the international community. Statements issued by Egypt, Greece, and Australia,[66] emphasizing that the provision embodied a general norm binding on all States because it was a mere codification of prior State practice, could support this position. Arguably, even more indicative of the rule's general character could be the fact that no delegations challenged Egypt, Greece, or Australia on this point. Finally, support could also be secured from the fact that a number of Western States which had voted against the rule in 1974 abstained or voted in favour of it in 1977.

If the adoption of Article 1 is regarded as testifying to the gradual formation of a rule binding on all the States participating in the Conference (irrespective of whether or not they ratified the Protocol, save for Israel, which consistently rejected Article 1(4)), it follows that States covered by Article 1(4) must apply to wars of national liberation the fundamental principles of customary law governing the conduct of hostilities and the protection of war victims in inter-State conflicts.[67] In

---

On wars of national liberation, see chiefly G. Abi-Saab, 'Wars of National Liberation and the Law of War', 3 *Annals d'Etudes Internationales*, 1972, 93-117; R. R. Baxter, 'The Geneva Conventions of 1949 and Wars of National Liberation', 57 RDI, 1974, 193-203; N. Ronzitti, 'Wars of National Liberation: A Legal Definition', 1 *Italian Yearbook of International Law*, 1975, 192-205; C. J. R. Dugard, 'SWAPO: The *Jus ad Bellum* and the *Jus in Bello*', 93 *South African Law Journal*, 1976, 144-58; G. Abi-Saab, 'Wars of National Liberation in the Geneva Conventions and Protocols', 165 HR, 1979-IV, 353-445; D. Schindler, 'The Different Types of Armed Conflicts According to the Geneva Conventions and Protocols', 163 HR, 1979-II, 116-63; B. Graefrath, 'Zum Anwendungsbereich der Ergänzungsprotokolle zu den Genfer Abkommen vom 12.August 1949', 15 *Staat und Recht*, 1980, 133 ff.; Hasbi, *Les mouvements de libération nationale et le Droit international*, 173-85; G. H. Aldrich, 'New Life for the Laws of War', 75 AJIL, 1981, 764-83; P. Benvenuti, 'Développements récents au sujet de l'applicabilité du Droit international humanitaire', in *Droits de l'homme et droits des peuples, Textes du Séminaire de Saint-Marin*, S. Marino 1983, 99-126; H.A. Wilson, *International Law and the Use of Force by National Liberation Movements*, 91 ff.; A. Mangas Martin, 'La Calificacion de la guerras de liberacion nacional como conflictos armados internacionales', 4 *Annuario Argentino de Derecho Internacional*, 1990-1, 11-36.

66 For references, see A. Cassese, 'Wars of National Liberation and Humanitarian Law', in *Etudes et essais en l'honneur de J. Pictet*, Geneva 1984, 321-2.

67 It should be added that those provisions of Protocol I which do not crystallize or reflect general rules, but merely have contractual force, only apply to wars of national liberation if two conditions are met: first, the colonial, racist or occupying Power against which the war is conducted must be a party to the Protocol; second, the national liberation movement fighting for self-determination must make the declaration provided for in Article 96.3, by which it undertakes to apply the four Geneva Conventions of 1949 and the Protocol. Plainly, the first requirement is unlikely to ever

other words, since a war waged by an oppressed people fighting for self-determination against a colonial or occupying power or a racist regime would have the status of an international conflict, wars of liberation would be covered by the laws of inter-State war, as opposed to civil war (the former are far broader in scope, better defined, and more favourable to the oppressed peoples involved).

Contrary to the above view, it has been suggested that Article 1(4) is valuable in theory only. After all, the two major countries against which it was aimed, Israel and the Republic of South Africa, are not even bound by it, the former on account of its explicit decision to opt out, the latter primarily because it did not participate in the final session of the Geneva Conference.

Undoubtedly, Article 1(4) has a significance transcending its immediate value: it has an indisputable 'agitational' or 'rhetorical' value. States and public opinion may point to the provisions of the Article to expose the conduct of other States not living up to the standards it enshrines. However, can it be contended that Article 1(4) has already turned into a generally binding legal standard?

If, to answer this question, one turns to State practice, one is struck by the fact that thus far Article 1(4) has never been applied in recent armed conflicts. States faced with a situation that amounted to a war of national liberation have neither denounced the existence of Article 1(4), nor blatantly and wittingly disregarded its provisions – while admitting, if only implicitly, that they should have been applied. Instead, they have implicitly denied its application, asserting that the situation ought not be categorized as a war of national liberation. For instance, in the case of the Soviet occupation of Afghanistan, the Soviet Union claimed that the lawful Afghanistani authorities had requested that the Soviet Union enter Afghanistan and suppress the insurgents; even more relevant is the Soviet assertion that the Afghanistan conflict was not a war of national liberation but rather a civil war. In the case of East Timor, Indonesia claimed sovereignty over the whole island and asserted that the fighting on the island was merely a case of civil disorder.

The fact however remains that no elements of State practice can be adduced to support the contention that Article 1(4) has acquired the value of customary law. The better view is therefore that in spite of the strong *opinio juris* that emerged in Geneva at the time of the adoption of Article

be met. Thus, the actual scope of the provisions of Protocol I which do not reflect general rules is narrow indeed.

1(4), the basic element of State practice is still lacking – or at any rate is insufficient – to justify the aforementioned contention. Only if and when such practice supports the expansion of Article 1(4) beyond its treaty value can it be argued that a customary rule has emerged.

Leaving aside technical considerations of law, it can be fairly stated that the intrusion of the principle of the self-determination of peoples into at least one category of a common and savage phenomenon, non-inter-State armed conflict, should be hailed as a significant advance in the field of humanitarian law. Jurists, diplomats, and humanitarian organizations have put the rules on paper. Now it is up to national legislative bodies and government officials to see that these legal imperatives are applied in reality.

9

Testing international law – some particularly controversial issues

Introductory remarks

Having traced self-determination's development from a political postulate into a set of international legal norms, I shall now set out to explore the role that self-determination, as it is currently conceived, actually plays in practice in some exceedingly complex cases. To what extent does the existence of a legal right to self-determination shape State behaviour in these instances? Does the body of law on self-determination have a real bearing on the outcome of extremely complex cases? These are the principal questions I shall endeavour to answer. In other words, this chapter is intended to set forth some particularly intricate and difficult contemporary disputes involving claims of self-determination, with a view to ascertaining the ultimate relationship between law and fact in the context of self-determination. Each of these case studies provides a brief history of the dispute in question, a summary of the positions advanced by the principal parties concerned and a discussion as to whether the parties claiming a right to self-determination actually hold such a right under international law. The final sections of each case-study are the focus of this chapter: to what extent the relevant norms of self-determination are or can be applied in practice, or whether they are instead wholly ignored or continually marginalized. It is by identifying the areas in which self-determination is likely to play a constructive role in complex or controversial fact situations – as opposed to those situations in which it is easily implemented – that we are able to determine the potential developments in the law on self-determination which can be most productively pursued.

In selecting the case-studies, I have concentrated on situations where the question of self-determination has arisen as a result of the decolonization process (Gibraltar, Western Sahara, East Timor, Eritrea). In my view it is in these circumstances that the rules of international law, which I have already examined (see Chapter 3), are particularly ambiguous and do not provide clear indications as to the resolution of the crucial conflict between self-determination and the territorial integrity of States (or the territorial claims of contiguous States). The objective is to show that while self-determination is to a large extent taken for granted – or is at least more easily accepted, in the area of decolonization – it is precisely in this area that a number of problems arise when the legal rules are concretely applied.

One of the five above-mentioned cases, namely East Timor, exhibits an important feature; the denial of self-determination at the time of decolonization by virtue of the occupation of the territory by Indonesian troops now poses the problem of the right to self-determination belonging to a people whose territory has been occupied by a foreign Power. We are therefore here confronted with a case in which the claim to self-determination is based on principles other than those applicable to the rights of colonial peoples. Another instance of a possible application of the same rule is that of Palestine; here, again, it would seem that the legal basis for a Palestinian right to self-determination may only be foreign military occupation.

Finally, I shall discuss an intriguing non-colonial case: Quebec. The purpose will be, first, to see whether a linguistic minority is granted a right to external self-determination by either international or constitutional law, as is claimed by some Canadian commentators; second, and more importantly, to ascertain what role the international legal principle of self-determination is playing in the *political process* currently taking place in Canada and how this principle may be implemented; third, to pinpoint the complications that the possible external self-determination of an ethnic group may entail as far as smaller minorities living in the territory of that group are concerned.

Attempts at implementing self-determination: some case studies

Gibraltar

GENERAL

There are cases where self-determination has proved to be unworkable, even in the area where the principle is unquestioned and is universally regarded as being applicable. In particular, there are some cases of 'colonial' occupation which are anomalous inasmuch as (1) the 'colonial' territory is very small, and (2) the inhabitants of the territory are not natives from the region but rather the descendants of settlers. In these cases the unqualified application of self-determination would automatically result in the concerned people opting to join the European Power which exercises jurisdiction over the territory: it goes without saying that traditions and language, as well as economic and social links with that Power, would prompt the vast majority of the people concerned to favour integration with that Power.

Such a step is, however, resented by the State contiguous to the territory at issue as an undue attack on its territorial sovereignty and integrity. This State, feeling that the contiguous territory is but an integral part of its own territory, claims that, whatever the composition of the people in the territory under discussion and its consequent wishes, it would be unacceptable and indeed contradictory to condone past 'colonialism' on the strength of a principle (self-determination) which was primarily designed to dismantle colonialism.

The cases of this type are those of Gibraltar and the Falklands/Malvinas. Since in some respects they are somewhat similar (although the Falklands/Malvinas are not territorially contiguous to Argentina, they are proximate to that country and undoubtedly within its geographical and historical province), only the case of Gibraltar will be dealt with here. In point of fact this is a much simpler situation but one which lends itself to considerations that to some extent can also be applied to the Falklands/Malvinas.

HISTORICAL BACKGROUND

The Rock and the harbour of Gibraltar were ceded by Spain to Great Britain under Article X of the Treaty of Utrecht of 1713, subject to the proviso that should Great Britain decide 'to grant, to sell, or by any means to alienate' the territory, Spain would have a right of pre-emption. For a great many years Gibraltar has remained under British sovereignty, as an overseas territory. In 1946, after the Second World War and the adoption of the UN Charter, the UK requested that Gibraltar be granted in the UN the status of a 'non-self-governing territory' under Article 73 of the UN Charter, with the UK consequently becoming the 'Administering Power'. Shortly after becoming a member of the UN, Spain started in 1957 to record a 'jurisdictional reservation' with respect to the right of the UK to submit information on Gibraltar as a 'non-self-governing territory', since the Spanish government regarded Gibraltar as an integral part of Spain. The issue was considered for the first time in 1963 by the UN Special Committee on Decolonization (the 'Committee of 24'). Since then the Committee and the General Assembly have adopted a number of resolutions, urging the two States to try and reach a negotiated solution.[1] In 1964 the two parties started negotiations but were unable to reach an agreed solution. On 10 September 1967, the British authorities held a referendum inviting Gibraltarians to choose between two alternative solutions: (a) 'to pass under Spanish sovereignty' or (b) 'voluntarily to retain their link with Britain, with democratic local institutions and with Britain retaining its present responsibilities'. A total of 12,762 people were found to be eligible for participating in the vote. The results were as follows: 44 for alternative (a), 12,138 for alternative (b), plus 55 void ballots (some of those who were eligible to vote actually did not participate).

The General Assembly, by Resolution 2353(XXII) of 19 December 1967, declared, however, that the holding of a referendum had been in contravention of one of its previous resolutions, namely Resolution 2231(XXI) of 20 December 1966.[2]

Since then the matter has been discussed many times by the Special Committee on Decolonization and the General Assembly. These two bodies have continued to urge the parties to negotiate but each of the two States has simply reaffirmed its initial position.

THE POSITION OF SPAIN

According to the Spanish authorities, the principle of self-determination does not apply to the population of Gibraltar. British jurisdiction over

---

[1] For an analysis of various UN resolutions, see, *inter alia*, J. E. S. Fawcett, 'Gibraltar: The Legal Issues', 43 *International Affairs*, 1967, 236 ff.; Rigo Sureda, *The Evolution of the Right of Self-Determination*, 183–98, 282–8; D. Mathy, 'L'autodétermination de petits territoires revendiqués par des Etats tiers', 11 RBDI, 1975, 135; Franck and Hoffman, 'The Right of Self-Determination in Very Small Places', 374–5; Blay, 'Self-Determination versus Territorial Integrity in Decolonization', 403 ff.; H.S. Levie, *The Status of Gibraltar*, Boulder, Col. 1983, 102 ff.; J.A. Pastor Ridruejo, *Curso de Derecho Internacional Público y Organizaciones Internacionales*, 3rd edn, Madrid 1989, 263 ff.; J. Diez-Hochleitner, 'Les relations hispano-britanniques au sujet de Gibraltar: état actuel', 35 AFDI, 1989, 167 ff.

[2] In this resolution the General Assembly, among other things, restated that Gibraltar came within the purview of the 1960 Declaration on Colonial Peoples, called for negotiations which should take into account the interests of the inhabitants of the Territory and asked the UK to expedite the decolonization process of the territory in consultation with Spain.

Gibraltar therefore constitutes a violation of Spanish territorial integrity and sovereign rights. Spain consequently advocates the restoration of Spanish sovereignty over the territory, although accepting that the interests of the Gibraltarians must be protected upon termination of the territory's colonial status.

To support this view, the Spanish authorities have put forward the following arguments: (1) the relevant UN resolutions, in particular GA Resolution 2231(XXI), do not necessarily require that for non-self-governing territories, in particular for Gibraltar, independence be the necessary goal; what is required is simply that 'the interests of the people' of Gibraltar be taken into account. (2) Gibraltar has an 'artificial population without any genuine autonomy'; this population is not 'indigenous' and has no origin other than the British settlers and other persons who had come from abroad to work and trade in the British military base; the original population of Gibraltar was expelled from the territory during the occupation by the British navy. On the other hand, various British Orders in Council, dating from 1873, prohibited residence in Gibraltar to Spaniards, with the consequence that the Spanish labour force working in Gibraltar until the sealing off of the border in 1969 could not stay overnight there. (3) Gibraltar is a small foreign, colonial enclave in Spanish territory. (4) Article X of the Treaty of Utrecht provides for a right of pre-emption in favour of Spain; consequently, in the case of a grant of independence by the UK to the people of Gibraltar, Spain would be immediately entitled to exercise this right and thus recover her sovereignty over Gibraltar.[3]

THE POSITION OF THE UK

First of all, the British government strongly insists on the continued validity of its legal title over Gibraltar, derived from a regular treaty of cession that has never been called into question since its making.[4] Furthermore, since Gibraltar has the status of a non-self-governing territory, the interests of the inhabitants are paramount and the UK, as the Administering Power, is bound by Article 73 of the UN Charter to respond to their wishes. On the strength of the right of peoples to self-determination, it is

---

[3] See, in particular *Documentos sobre Gibraltar presentados a las Cortes Generales por el Ministerio de Asuntos Exteriores*, 5th edn, Madrid 1966, 13 ff.
[4] For recent restatements of the British position, see BYIL, 1982, 373; 1984, 437; 1988, 444; 1990, 505, 509–10.

for the Gibraltarians freely to decide on their international status. As was provided in the preamble to the 1969 Constitution of Gibraltar, 'Her Majesty's Government will never enter into arrangements under which the people of Gibraltar would pass under the sovereignty of another State against their freely and democratically expressed wishes.' As for the Spanish argument relying on the Treaty of Utrecht, the UK points out that Article X of that Treaty merely entails that the choices to be offered to Gibraltarians for the exercise of their right to self-determination should be so limited as to include only integration or association with one of the two countries concerned, thus excluding independent statehood.[5]

THE POSITION OF THE UN

As stated above, for many years the UN General Assembly has urged the two States concerned to undertake negotiations with a view to settling the question.

It should, however, be stressed that the General Assembly very soon sided with the Spanish position. In 1965 it first passed a rather 'neutral' Resolution 2070(XX) by which it called upon the two States concerned to begin talks without delay in order to reach a negotiated solution in conformity with the Declaration on the Independence of Colonial Peoples and bearing in mind the interests of the people of the territory.[6] Then, in 1966 the GA adopted Resolution 2231(XXI) in which it restated that Gibraltar fell within the category of territories to which the Declaration referred, reiterated its call for negotiations 'taking into account the interests of the people of the Territory' and asked the UK 'to expedite, without any hindrance and in consultation with the Government of Spain, the decolonization of Gibraltar'.[7] A stronger stand in favour of the Spanish position was taken in 1967, in Resolution 2353(XXII) of 19 December 1967, in which the General Assembly stated in the fifth paragraph of the preamble:

that any colonial situation which partially or completely destroys the national unity and territorial integrity of a country is incompatible with the purposes and principles of the Charter of the United Nations, and specifically with paragraph 6 of General Assembly Resolution 1514(XV).

---

[5] In 1990, the British Minister of State for Foreign and Commonwealth Affairs wrote in a reply to a parliamentary question that 'Under the Treaty of Utrecht independence is not an option, unless Spain is prepared to agree' (BYIL, 1990, 510).

[6] UN Ybk, 1965, 581–3.   [7] UN Ybk, 1966, 584–8.

Clearly, this paragraph was intended to stress that British colonial dominion in Gibraltar was contrary to the principles of the Charter and those of the 1960 Declaration on Colonialism. Furthermore, the General Assembly declared the referendum held by the British authorities 'to be a contravention' of GA Resolution 2231(XXI) but did not go so far as generally to prohibit the holding of a referendum.[8] The General Assembly did not spell out the reasons for this statement. It is submitted that the only criticism to which the British decision was open was that, in organizing the referendum, the UK authorities offered the Gibraltarians only two options: either to join Spain or to remain under British jurisdiction. Arguably, this was too limited a choice – a choice bound to lead to only one result – which may not have been considered to have given much effective choice to the people of Gibraltar in view of the political and economic conditions prevailing in Spain in 1967: a harsh dictatorship and severe economic difficulties which still plagued the country.

Subsequently the General Assembly, by Resolution 2429(XXIII) of 1968, regretted the non-observance of its Resolution 2353(XXII), stated that the 'continuation of the colonial situation' was incompatible with the Charter and Resolution 1514(XV) and called upon the UK to terminate the 'colonial situation' before 1 October 1969 by means of negotiations with Spain.[9] As no settlement was reached, the General Assembly has repeatedly insisted, since then, that the two States concerned should undertake negotiations 'with a view to the final solution of the question, taking into account the relevant resolutions of the General Assembly and the spirit of the UN Charter'.[10]

SOME TENTATIVE REMARKS

As a preliminary to our discussion of this case, emphasis should be laid on the fact that to some extent it is not strictly correct to label British rule over Gibraltar as a 'colonial' situation. After all, the territory was not invaded

---

[8] In operative para. 2 the GA again called upon 'the two parties to continue their negotiations, taking into account the interests of the people of the Territory' and again asked 'the administering Power to expedite, without any hindrance and in consultation with the Government of Spain, the decolonization of Gibraltar' (see UN Ybk, 1967, 668–76).

[9] UN Ybk, 1968, 745–50.

[10] See, e.g., the consensus decision of 14 December 1973 (UN Ybk, 1973, 699), decision 35/406 of 11 November 1980 (UN Ybk, 1980, 1082), decision 39/410 of 5 December 1984 (UN Ybk, 1984, 1075), decision 40/413 of 2 December 1985 (UN Ybk, 1985, 1146–7).

by Great Britain as part of its drive to colonize overseas territories but was regularly ceded by the sovereign State, Spain, by means of the classical institution normally resorted to in such matters: a treaty between two sovereign States. Thus, neither colonial conquest, nor a 'colonial protectorate', was at the origin of British rule over Gibraltar. If one speaks of Gibraltar as a 'colonial' situation, one should therefore be aware that such a categorization must be used subject to some qualifications.

Having made this preliminary point, we may now ask ourselves whether self-determination is unable to lead to a satisfactory settlement of the question under discussion, and similar issues. In other words, do we here come up against an inherent flaw in the principle? Or is the principle instead capable of indicating the path to be taken?

Arguably, it follows from the body of general principles and rules on self-determination that, first, the legal title over the territory held by the UK, although it has not been invalidated *ipso facto* as a result of the emergence of international norms on self-determination, can no longer be accepted. Since Gibraltar is a non-self-governing territory under Article 73 of the UN Charter, the holder of the territorial title is duty-bound to see to it that a decision on the international and internal status of the territory be taken in accordance with the free and genuine wishes of the population concerned.

Second, in view of the reversionary claims put forward by Spain, one can deduce from the body of law on self-determination, as well as from the whole spirit of the UN Charter and the basic international instruments that have implemented its fundamental principles, that any disagreement over the implementation of self-determination should be settled by *peaceful means*: chiefly through bilateral or multilateral negotiations. However, negotiations may not lead to an agreed solution. This holds true for the case under discussion. In spite of repeated appeals by the UN General Assembly, and their sincere efforts to achieve agreement, Spain and the UK have been unable to agree upon any settlement. Can we nevertheless derive from the principle indications for a *substantive* solution?

We thus come to the third point. As was stated above (see Chapter 5), the general thrust of the principle ultimately demands that the *wishes and free choice of the people concerned* constitute the decisive test. This is the crux of the principle and it overrides any other factor, even the 'anti-colonial' element. Consequently, in complex cases where self-determination and 'anti-colonial' claims collide, the former should always prevail – provided, of course, that this does not prove contrary to other principles such as that of friendly settlement of disputes. In other words, one cannot stretch anti-colonialism to such a point as to claim that, for the sake of making good past 'colonial' domination, one should ignore the free will of the population of the territory concerned.

This last proposition is however subject to at least two qualifications.

First, in making self-determination the dominant value in cases such as that of Gibraltar and in consequently using the most suitable device to this effect, that is, a referendum or a plebiscite, one should not artificially predetermine the issue, for example, by offering a limited set of alternatives, as happened in the 1967 referendum. The people concerned should be enabled to choose from among a *number of realistic and viable alternatives*, to be selected through a democratic process (for instance, by means of consultations with the representative organizations of the people, the appropriate international bodies, the States concerned, and so on). Only in this way would one ensure the application of the 'genuine and free expression of will' required by the framers of the UN Charter (see above Chapter 3) and restated by the International Court of Justice in its *Western Sahara* Opinion (see above, Chapter 5). It should be added that the range of choices to be offered to the Gibraltarians might include some sort of autonomous status within the general framework of the European Community, or association with one of the States concerned under EC scrutiny. Clearly, while the Lisbon Declaration of the Spanish and British foreign Ministers of 11 April 1980, followed by the Brussels Declaration agreed upon on 27 November 1984 by the two Foreign Ministers, set up a framework for peaceful and constructive negotiations, Spanish membership of the European Community (as from 1 January 1986) opened up new vistas and fresh prospects for solutions within the general framework of the European Community.[11] Another option for a referendum could be based on the proposal put forward in 1988 by the then Spanish Foreign Minister, Mr F. Moran, whereby a British–Spanish condominium could be established for an interim period of twenty years, after which Gibraltar would pass into Spanish sovereignty but the Gibraltarians would retain their political institutions as well as their British nationality.[12]

Second, any referendum should be honestly organized. In other words, the State exercising jurisdiction over the people at issue should not try to alter the composition of the constituency by moving in persons from other

[11] For recent developments in this area and, in particular, the impact of Spain's joining the EC on the question of Gibraltar, see Diez-Hochleitner, 'Les relations hispano-britanniques', 178 ff.

[12] See F. Moran, 'Las relaciones hispano-britanicas', *Revue de Occidente*, 1988, 17.

territories. We know from history that this occurred in some instances after the First World War, when massive transfers of population were organized with a view to modifying the social unit called upon to express its wishes in a referendum. Such manipulative measures would be totally contrary to the doctrine of the 'free and genuine expression of will' referred to above; they would therefore nullify the value of referendums as a means of ascertaining a people's choice.

Western Sahara

INTRODUCTORY REMARKS

The situation of Western Sahara differs greatly from that in the Falklands/Malvinas or Gibraltar. However, once more we are faced with contiguous States (Morocco and Mauritania) claiming title to land. Once again there is a dilemma: should decolonization lead to the political independence of the colonial territory or can the contiguous States claiming historic title over the territory demand its integration into them (or into one of them)? How should the principle of self-determination be acted upon in such a case?

HISTORICAL BACKGROUND

Western Sahara became a Spanish colonial territory in 1884, following the Spanish occupation of the coast and the conclusion of a number of agreements with the chiefs of local tribes.[13] Since the area was at that time of no great economic or political interest, the Spaniards for a long time confined themselves to holding some coastal outposts, chiefly in order to control fishing. Only in the 1930s did Spain effectively occupy the whole area, primarily with a view to taking military measures in order to withstand the Berber rebellion mounting in neighbouring Morocco. The discovery of rich deposits of phosphates in 1947 meant that the area was now of great

---

[13] For a factual analysis of the case, see in particular Franck, 'The Stealing of the Sahara', 694 ff.; S. Oeter, 'Die Entwicklung der WestSahara-Frage unter besonderer Berücksichtigung der völkerrechtlichen Anerkennung', 46 *Zeit.*, 1986, 48 ff. and bibliography there cited. More generally see Rigo Sureda, *The Evolution of the Right to Self-Determination*, 212–15; M. Shaw, 'The Western Sahara Case', 49 BYIL, 1978, 119 ff.; L. Condorelli, 'Le droit international face à l'autodétermination du Sahara occidental', *Mélanges offerts à L. Basso*, Milan, 1979, 653 ff.; Shaw, *Title to Territory in Africa*, 123–30; Blay, 'Self-Determination v. Territorial Integrity', 460–3.

economic interest and in the 1960s Spain commenced full economic exploitation. Meanwhile, however, the drive towards decolonization had also started in that area and in 1973 various liberation movements joined to set up the 'Polisario' front. Faced with guerilla fighting and pressure from the UN, Spain commenced the process of granting autonomy to the territory and in 1966, in the UN 'Committee of the 24', expressed itself to be in favour of the decolonization of the territory via the exercise by the population of their right to self-determination. This view was upheld by the General Assembly, in paragraph 4 of its Resolution 2229(XXI) of 1966: it invited Spain to hold a referendum under the supervision of a UN mission but left to the Administering Power the task of determining, in consultation with Morocco and Mauritania 'and any other interested party', the procedures for holding the referendum. This position was reiterated in subsequent resolutions adopted during the period until 1974,[14] despite the claims by Morocco and Mauritania that Western Sahara constituted an integral part of their territory.[15]

A change however occurred in 1974, when Morocco and Mauritania mustered sufficient support in the General Assembly to have a resolution passed which on the one hand urged Spain to postpone the referendum that it contemplated holding in Western Sahara and, on the other, requested the International Court of Justice to give an Advisory Opinion on two issues: 'Was Western Sahara at the time of colonization by Spain a territory belonging to no-one'? If the answer to this question was in the negative, the Court was called upon to address a second issue: 'What were the legal ties between this territory and the Kingdom of Morocco and the Mauritanian entity'?

The International Court of Justice issued its Advisory Opinion in 1975. After giving a negative answer to the first question, it held that although Mauritania and Morocco both had historical ties to the Western Sahara, those ties were not 'of such a nature as might affect the application of

---

[14] See Resolutions 2354-II(XXII), 2428(XXIII), 2591(XXIV), and 2711(XXV).

[15] As stated by M. Shaw (*Title to Territory in Africa*, 124), Moroccan and Mauritanian claims were based 'on the proposition that ethnic, historical, and other ties pre-dating colonization could operate to override the wishes of the people within the colonially established territorial framework, in other words, that the "self" in question was not necessarily territorially defined but could be determined in the light of ethnic, historical, and other factors. Morocco, for example, noted that the problem of decolonization in this case was identical to the return of "territories and populations torn away by colonial usurpation" to the Moroccan State. To put it another way, "the decolonization of Western Sahara implied *ipso facto* its reintegration into the Moroccan State"'.

Resolution 1514(XV) [on the granting of independence to colonial peoples] to the decolonization of Western Sahara and, in particular, of the principle of self-determination of peoples through the free and genuine expression of the will of the peoples of the Territory'.[16] In the wake of this opinion, Spain, Morocco, and Mauritania concluded an agreement which provided for an interim tripartite administration, then set 28 February 1976 as the date on which Spanish presence in the territory should come to an end and guaranteed the population a voice in the legislative affairs of the territory. All parties were also to respect the positions advanced by the Jemaa, the local assembly instituted by Spain in 1967. Unfortunately, the agreement did not lead to lasting peace. On 11 December 1975, the day after the UN General Assembly passed two contradictory resolutions calling for the holding of referendums,[17] Mauritanian and Moroccan troops marched into the Western Sahara. Two-and-a-half months later, on 26 February 1976, the Jemaa, asserting that it was the authentic and legitimate spokesman for the Saharan population, praised the tripartite agreement and expressed its satisfaction with Western Sahara's reintegration into Mauritania and Morocco. A day later, Polisario, the liberation movement, commenced armed conflict with Mauritania and Morocco and proclaimed the creation of the Saharan Arab Democratic Republic (SADR). In August 1979, war-weary Mauritania gave up its claims to the Western Sahara and ceased its military operations in the area. Only Morocco remained. In 1980 a majority of the member States of the OAU recognized SADR as the rightful Government of Western Sahara, which took its seat at the 1989 OAU Summit, whereupon Morocco left the OAU in protest.

Since 1979, the General Assembly has passed several resolutions aimed at finding a solution to the dispute. Each time the Assembly has reaffirmed the principle of the self-determination of the Saharan people and called for a lasting solution to be agreed upon by the parties concerned. A long-term peaceful solution now appears to be in the offing. A 1988 bilateral treaty concluded by Algeria (a country which from the outset has strongly supported Polisario) and Morocco has brought relative calm to the region. By virtue of this treaty the parties agreed in principle to a UN peace plan,

---

[16] ICJ, Reports 1975, 68, para. 162.
[17] GA Res. 3458A(XXX), which was strongly advocated by Algeria, required Spain, as the administering power, to conduct a referendum under UN auspices. In contrast, GA Res. 3453B, which was sponsored by Morocco, requested that an interim administration organize a referendum with the presence of a UN observer. See UN Ybk, 1975, 188 ff. and 817 ff.

which called for a cease-fire, an exchange of prisoners, and a referendum designed to give the inhabitants of the territory a choice between independence or integration into Morocco.

On 11 December 1989 the UN General Assembly adopted by consensus a resolution recognizing the joint efforts of the UN and the OAU to achieve a peaceful solution to the Saharan conflict and insisted on the importance of bringing about direct negotiations between Morocco and the Polisario Front. Subsequently the Security Council decided to send a UN Mission to the territory to assess the logistical difficulties of holding a referendum. On 29 April 1991, the Security Council unanimously passed Resolution 690 approving a schedule whereby a referendum was to be held by January 1992. Various practical problems have, however, arisen, which have so far made a postponement of the referendum necessary.

A THUMB-NAIL SKETCH OF THE POSITION OF THE STATES CONCERNED

On the face of it, the question of Western Sahara was easy to settle in the light of the guidelines set out by the UN General Assembly in its Declaration on Colonial Countries (Resolution 1514(XV) of 14 December 1960) and Resolution 1541(XV) of 15 December 1960 (see above, Chapter 3). As will be recalled, the latter resolution provides that in case of 'free association' or 'integration' with an independent State, the people concerned should be given the possibility of freely choosing their international status; the choice should be 'free and voluntary', 'expressed through informed and democratic processes' and 'impartially conducted', possibly under UN supervision.

It would therefore have been logical to allow the inhabitants of Western Sahara to make such a choice, by means of a referendum under UN supervision. This was actually the view advocated by the Spanish colonial power. However, it was strongly opposed by both Morocco and Mauritania. The former claimed that 'decolonization may come about through the reintegration of a province with the mother country from which it was detached in the process of colonization'. It also consistently rejected calls for a referendum, arguing, among other things, that the population concerned had expressed its will through the meeting of the territorial assembly (the Jemaa). The latter, until it abandoned its claims, stressed the principle of territorial integrity, which in its view was to be given pride of place in 'situations where the territory had been created by a colonizing power to the detriment of a State or country to which the territory belonged'.

As T. M. Franck judiciously pointed out in 1976, 'the disposition of the Sahara case by the United Nations has been monumentally mishandled, creating a precedent with a potential for future mischief out of all proportion to the importance of the territory'.[18] Actually, in this case the UN has for many years departed from its fairly consistent policy of ascertaining the will of the population concerned by means of an internationally supervised referendum.

Political and territorial claims, economic considerations (on account of the rich deposits of phosphates existing in Western Sahara), as well as the transfer of large numbers of Moroccans into Sahara, have been a major stumbling-block to the application of international law and a consequent speedy implementation of the right of self-determination. Admittedly, an added complication, which no doubt rendered the holding of a referendum problematic, was constituted by the nature of the area (desert) and the fact that it was inhabited by nomadic tribes. This problem, however, could have been settled by dint of ingenuity and patience.

The case of Western Sahara proves, however, that it is precisely when the conflicting political interests of the various international actors are at stake that the principle of self-determination and the consequent freedom of choice of the population concerned ('let the people decide!') could offer a solution. It is a matter of regret that the States concerned have only come to this conclusion after some sixteen years of fighting and bloodshed in the field and political confrontation in various international fora.

Eritrea

What makes the case of Eritrea unique is that, although it is also concerned with decolonization (Eritrea was an Italian colony), the State that has for a long time claimed territorial rights over it, Ethiopia, had itself been subjected to colonial rule by Italy. Furthermore, Ethiopia's reversionary

---

[18] Franck, 'The Stealing of the Sahara', 694.

claims were not based on mere contiguity but on the fact that in the remote past Eritrea had allegedly been part of Ethiopian territory.[19]

HISTORICAL BACKGROUND

As early as the Kingdom of Axum (first to fifth centuries AD) Eritrea was part of Abyssinia. Between the eleventh and the nineteenth centuries, with the development of the Ethiopian Empire, Eritrea became a peripheral part of Ethiopia, to a large extent subject to the *de facto* control of Muslim rulers on the coast and of Christian rulers in the highlands. It was occupied by Italy in 1885–9. Following the Treaty of Uccialli of 1889, with Ethiopia, Eritrea became an Italian colony in 1890. It remained an Italian distinct colony until 1936, when it became part of 'Italian Eastern Africa' (Libya, Eritrea, Abyssinia, and Somaliland) following the Italian aggression in Abyssinia of 1935–6. When Italian colonial rule came to an end in 1941, Eritrea was administered by Great Britain under a trusteeship, until 1952. By the Peace Treaty of 1947 with the Allies, Italy gave up all rights and titles to her colonial possessions in Africa; the final disposal of these colonies was to be decided upon by the Four Powers (UK, US, France, and the USSR). Since, however, they failed to reach agreement, the matter was submitted to the UN General Assembly, which by Resolution 269(IV) of 21 November 1949, set up a Commission responsible for the submission of proposals by 1950. Pursuant to this resolution, the Commission, in fulfilling its responsibilities, was to 'ascertain all the relevant facts, including written or oral information from the present administering power, from representatives of the population of the territory, including minorities, from Governments and from such organizations and individuals as it may deem necessary'. In making its proposals to the General Assembly, the Commission was to take into account '(a) the wishes and welfare of the inhabitants including the views of the various racial, religious and political groups of the provinces of the territory and the capacity of the people for self-government; (b) the interests of peace and security in East Africa; (c) the rights and claims of Ethiopia based on geographical, historical, ethnic or economic reasons, including in particular Ethiopia's legitimate needs for adequate access to the sea' (paragraph 2).

[19] On Eritrea, see, in particular Rigo Sureda, *The Evolution of the Right of Self-Determination*, 133–9; A. Fenet, 'Erythrée – Le droit pour une indépendance', A. Fenet, L. H. Thuan, and T. van Minh, *La question de l'Erythrée, Droit international et politique des deux grands*, Paris, 1979, 12–50; Shaw, *Title to Territory in Africa*, 117–19; Blay, 'Self-Determination v. Territorial Integrity', 468–9.

It is thus clear that the General Assembly did not envisage the holding of a referendum or a plebiscite to ascertain the wishes of the population. Consequently, the Commission assessed 'the political wishes of the parties and people' by collecting the views of 'the principal political parties and associations' and holding 'hearings of the local population'.[20] As a result, it concluded that the majority of the Eritreans favoured political association with Ethiopia.[21] Nevertheless, the five States composing the Commission failed to reach a consensus in submitting proposals. Thus, different proposals were put forward; Burma and South Africa advocated a federation between Eritrea and Ethiopia, under the sovereignty of the latter; Norway called for the 'complete and immediate reunion' of Eritrea with Ethiopia; Guatemala and Pakistan, on the contrary, suggested that Eritrea should be granted complete independence, after a period of direct trusteeship under the UN of a maximum duration of ten years.[22]

The General Assembly chose the path proposed by Burma and South Africa and in Resolution 390-A(V) of 2 December 1950 decided that 'Eritrea shall constitute an autonomous unit federated with Ethiopia under the sovereignty of the Ethiopian Crown' (paragraph A1); it set out the powers of the Eritrean Government (paragraph A2)[23] as well as the matters falling under the jurisdiction of the Federal Government (paragraphs A3–4).

In 1952 the British administration was terminated and at the same time the Federation was established. In March 1952 an Eritrean Assembly was freely elected and in July of the same year this Assembly adopted a Constitution providing for federation with Ethiopia. In August the Constitution was 'ratified' by the Ethiopian Emperor, who then approved the Ethiopian 'Federal Act'. The Federation was, however, short-lived and on 14 November 1962 the Eritrean Assembly voted for the incorporation of Eritrea into Ethiopia; Eritrea thus became a province of Ethiopia.

In 1961 the Eritreans had set up an Eritrean Liberation Front (ELF), followed in the 1970s by the Eritrean People's Liberation Front (EPLF); these two liberation movements then engaged in an armed struggle with the Ethiopian authorities.

[20] UN Report of the United Nations Commission for Eritrea, 1950, UN Doc. A/1285, 17 ff., paras. 106–31.

[21] Ibid., 21, paras. 132–5.

[22] Ibid., 24 ff.

[23] 'The Eritrean Government shall possess legislative, executive and judicial powers in the field of domestic affairs.'

Recently, following the collapse of the Mengistu government, Eritreans acquired full control over Eritrea and, after a referendum in 1993, proclaimed their independence.

THE VIEWS AND CLAIMS OF ETHIOPIA

Over the years Ethiopia has strongly advocated the absolute legitimacy of Eritrea being an integral part of Ethiopia. This view was based on the following arguments: (1) before the colonial conquest of Eritrea by Italy, Eritrea was part of Ethiopia: as asserted in an official Ethiopian document, 'ever since Ethiopia emerged from the distant horizon of time as a body-politic, its northern part, including the area now called Eritrea, has been at the beginning and at the centre of its development';[24] (2) Eritrea was an artificial creation of Italian colonialism; (3) there was no Eritrean nation, since Eritrea was made up of nine ethnic groups; (4) the Eritrean people exercised self-determination in 1952, when the Eritrean Assembly, consisting of the representatives of the Eritrean people, voted unanimously for reunion 'with the motherland'. Pursuant to the UN Declaration on Friendly Relations, the exercise of the right of self-determination by Eritrea put an end to this right, which therefore could no longer be claimed and was in any case in conflict with Ethiopia's right to territorial integrity.

THE VIEWS AND CLAIMS OF THE ERITREANS

The Eritreans contended that they were entitled to the right to self-determination and that Ethiopia had ignored and actually denied this right. The grounds on which the Eritrean claim rested are as follows: (1) in pre-colonial history there had not been a nation-State with a stable territorial base encompassing both Eritrea and Ethiopia and to which Ethiopia could claim continuity; (2) in 1952 Eritrea was federated with Ethiopia against its will; no plebiscite or referendum was held to establish the will and the wishes of Eritreans, as in accordance with UN practice (e.g. in Togoland and in the Southern and Northern Cameroons in 1961); (3) in actual fact, it was Ethiopia that in 1962 unilaterally repealed the federal

---

[24] Quoted by G. H. Tesfagiorgis, 'Eritrean Self-Determination', 6 *Wisconsin International Law Journal*, 1987, 119, note 227.

arrangement and then forcibly annexed Eritrea; in other words, in 1962 the Eritrean assembly did not express a genuine choice, for it was actually coerced into opting for union with Ethiopia; (4) the forcible annexation of Eritrea by Ethiopia amounted to a grave denial of the right to self-determination.

CONCLUDING REMARKS

Unlike other African countries, Abyssinia has been for centuries a sovereign and independent State. Therefore, when Italy conquered Eritrea by force, in 1885–9, this was an act of colonialism against a sovereign State. Nevertheless, the fact remains that, by the Treaty of Uccialli, Ethiopia agreed to the acquisition of sovereignty by Italy over Eritrea. This region thus became a *colonial unit* and remained as such at least until the Italian aggression against Abyssinia in 1935–6 and the consequent merger of the two territories under Italian colonial domination. The Four Powers, and later the UN, behaved correctly when, in 1945–50, they decided to separate the two issues, that of the future of Eritrea and that of the independent status of Abyssinia/Ethiopia.

Where the UN action can be faulted is in its failure to organize a referendum in 1950 to establish the wishes of Eritreans. Actually, the manner in which the five-member UN Commission ascertained the will of Eritreans is highly questionable. In short, it seems that political and strategic considerations took the upper hand, and self-determination – as the 'genuine and free expression of will' of a people – was set aside.

This being so, it is questionable whether the *federation* decided upon by the UN in 1952 'exhausted' the right of Eritreans to self-determination. This right could only lapse, under the Declaration on Friendly Relations, if it was properly exercised. Since this was not the case in Eritrea, the Eritrean people could still claim the right freely to choose its destiny.

It is well known that the Eritrean People's Liberation Front, after setting up a separate provisional government in May 1991, decided to defer a formal declaration of independence until a referendum was held in two years' time. This decision was in keeping with the principle of self-determination. It seems that the referendum held in April 1993 was organized in an honest and correct way and held under international scrutiny, and it really established the free and genuine will of Eritreans to become independent.

East Timor

INTRODUCTORY REMARKS

This case is particularly interesting for three reasons. First, in spite of the long and bitter debate between, on the one hand, the United Nations and Portugal and, on the other, the UN and Indonesia as to whether or not self-determination had been realized, it is a fact that Indonesia has incorporated East Timor as part of its territory. Thus, on a factual level, the matter has been resolved by the mere use of force. Second, this unfortunate outcome was to some extent made possible by the geo-political concerns of a Superpower, the US, which from the outset was lukewarm in its condemnation of Indonesia and gradually acquiesced in its use of force (the US did not, however, go to the lengths of using its veto power in the UN Security Council, as the USSR had done in 1961 in the case of Goa, in order to prevent a condemnation of India; see above, Chapter 8). Third, in spite of this situation and the fact that after 1982 even the UN General Assembly seemed to believe that it was a *fait accompli* so that it ceased to condemn Indonesia,[25] Portugal decided in 1991 to institute proceedings before the International Court of Justice against Australia *qua* State party to a treaty of 1989 with Indonesia for the exploration and exploitation of the continental shelf of East Timor (an area between East Timor and Australia).[26] This situation therefore represents the first case ever brought before the ICJ – acting in its judicial capacity – with a view to ensuring respect for self-determination.[27]

---

[25] However, even after 1982 East Timor has been continuously included on the UN list of non-self-governing territories, with the agreement of Portugal as the 'Administering Power'. In addition, the UN 'Committee of 24' is still dealing with the question of East Timor. Furthermore, in 1983 the UN Commission on Human Rights adopted a resolution on the right of the East Timorese to self-determination (UN Ybk,. 1983, 833–4).

[26] See 29 ILM, 1990, 469 ff.

[27] On the question of East Timor, see in particular, T. M. Franck and P. Hoffman, 'The Right of Self-Determination in Very Small Places', 8 NYUJILP, 1975–6, 331 ff.; J. F. Guilhaudis, 'La Question de Timor', 23 AFDI, 1977, 307 ff.; P.D. Elliot, 'The East Timor Dispute', 27 ICLQ, 1978, 238 ff.; R.S. Clark, 'The Decolonization of East Timor and the United Nations Norms on Self-Determination and Aggression', 7 *Yale Journal of World Public Order*, 1980, 2 ff.; K. Suter, *East Timor and West Irian*, London, Minority Rights Group, Report no. 42, 1982; Blay, 'Self-Determination v. Territorial Integrity', 455–8; K. Rabl, 'Das Selbstbestimmungsrecht der Völker in der neuester Praxis' in D. Blumenwitz and B. Meissner (eds.), *Das Selbstbestimmungsrecht der Völker und die deutsche Frage*, Cologne 1984, 132 ff.; P. Lawrence, 'East Timor', 12 *Encyclopedia*, 1990,

HISTORICAL BACKGROUND

Timor, an island situated off the north-west coast of Australia, has been politically divided into two parts for centuries. The eastern part (which has a surface of 18,899 square kilometres and about 600,000 inhabitants) has been under Portuguese colonial domination since 1586 (in 1896 it became a Portuguese province). The western part of the Island, after being under Dutch colonial rule, became part of Indonesia in 1946, on Indonesia's accession to independence.

Since 1960 East Timor has been regarded by the UN as a non-self-governing territory. In 1974, when the political regime in Portugal changed, this country recognized the right of the East Timorese people to self-determination and decided that the future political status of East Timor should be decided by an Assembly to be elected by universal, secret, and direct ballot in 1976. Soon two opposing political movements (Fretilin, or the Revolutionary Front for the Independence of East Timor, and MAC, or the Anti-Communist Movement) put forward conflicting claims, the former demanding the independence of East Timor, the latter advocating its integration into Indonesia. On 7 December 1975 Indonesian troops invaded East Timor. Portugal immediately protested in the UN and both the General Assembly and the Security Council upheld Portugal's claims, thus condemning the Indonesian invasion, although they did not state that it amounted to an act of aggression.[28] In spite of these solemn condemnations, on 31 May 1976 an unelected 'Regional Popular Assembly' set up by a provisional government established by pro-Indonesian political parties passed a resolution in favour of East Timor's incorporation into Indonesia. On 17 July 1976 the Indonesian legislature enacted Law 7/76 making East Timor the 27th province of Indonesia.

94–6; R. S. Clark, 'Some International Law Aspects of the East Timor Affair', in 5 *Leiden Journal of International Law*, 1992, 265–71. For the factual background, see also UN Doc. A/AC.109/623 of 11 August 1980.

[28] See UN GA Res. 3485(XXX) of 12 December 1975, UN Ybk, 1975, 865; 3153 of 1 December 1976, UN Ybk, 1976, 754; 32/34 of 28 November 1977, UN Ybk, 1977, 890; 33/39 of 13 December 1978, UN Ybk, 1978, 869; 34/40 of 21 November 1979, UN Ybk, 1979, 1056; 35/27 of 11 November 1980, UN Ybk, 1980, 1094; 36/50 of 24 November 1981, UN Ybk, 1981, 1185; 37/30 of 23 November 1982, UN Ybk, 1982, 1349. As for the Security Council, see Res. 384 (1975), adopted on 22 December 1975, UN Ybk, 1975, 866 and 389 (1976) adopted on 22 April 1976, UN Ybk, 1976.

THE VIEWS OF PORTUGAL

Portugal has always claimed to be the sole entity entitled by the UN Charter, in its capacity as the administering power of a non-self-governing territory, to speak on behalf of East Timor and to ensure the realization of the right of the East Timorese to self-determination.[29] Portugal also contends that the 'Regional Popular Assembly' appointed in 1975 by the provisional government of East Timor, when deciding on the integration of East Timor into Indonesia did not ascertain the free and genuine will of the people in a proper manner. According to Portugal the Indonesian invasion actually prevented the East Timorese population from making a free choice.

THE VIEWS OF INDONESIA

According to Indonesia the inhabitants of East Timor were offered a chance to choose whether or not to integrate with Indonesia, when the 'Regional Popular Assembly' decided on the matter in 1976. Furthermore, before incorporating the territory, Indonesia invited the UN (in particular, the Secretary-General, the Security Council, and the Committee on Decolonization) to send a mission for the purpose of verifying on the spot the wishes of the population, but the UN refused to comply for political reasons (i.e., it did not wish to endorse the invasion of the territory by Indonesian troops). Consequently, according to Indonesia, the people concerned did express their will, thus exercising their right to self-determination. It follows that as from 17 July 1976 (the date of the promulgation by the President of Indonesia of Law 7/76 providing for the establishment of East Timor as the 27th province of Indonesia),

---

[29] In 1990, during the discussion before the UN Human Rights Committee on Portugal's second periodic report on the Covenants, the Portuguese delegate stated that: 'East Timor remained on the United Nations list of Non-Self-Governing Territories, Portugal being recognized as the administering power because of its former responsibilities as the colonial power. Portugal had declared the Covenant to be applicable to East Timor but was unfortunately not in a position to ensure that it was applied and effectively respected since it had no access to the Territory, which was under occupation. Portugal was continuing to co-operate in the Secretary-General's efforts to find a just, comprehensive and internationally acceptable solution to the problem' (*Report of the Human Rights Committee to the G.A.*, 1990, vol. I, UN Doc. A/45/40, para. 133).

whatever had subsequently occurred in East Timor had become an internal affair of Indonesia.[30]

SOME TENTATIVE REMARKS

It seems an undisputable fact that the people of East Timor were not permitted freely to express their will through a plebiscite organized under UN supervision. Actually, the decision in favour of integration with Indonesia, which, according to the latter, amounted to the exercise of the right to self-determination, was marred by two factors; (1) it was not made directly by the people concerned by means of a referendum or a plebiscite but rather indirectly through a decision of the 'Regional Popular Assembly' and (2) it was made under circumstances that were hardly likely to be conducive to a free expression of the political will, that is to say under foreign military occupation.

There are therefore grounds for contending that in this case there was a complete denial of the right of peoples to self-determination.

It is worth pointing out that this denial, when it first occurred, amounted to a breach of the general rule that bestows upon colonial peoples the right freely to choose their international and internal political and legal status. However, the continuation of Indonesian occupation and the incorporation of East Timor into this country entailed *a further violation* of international law; that is to say, an infringement of the customary rule conferring a right to self-determination on those peoples whose territory is occupied by a foreign Power. It follows that at present the continuing occupation by Indonesia is in breach of two distinct rules of customary law

---

[30] This view was supported in the UN by other States. Thus, for example, on 4 December 1978 the representative of Malaysia stated the following in the General Assembly's Fourth Committee: 'The people of East Timor had on previous occasions expressed and even documented their genuine desire to attain independence through integration with Indonesia. In accepting their request the Malaysian Government is satisfied that the Government of Indonesia had gone to the extremes to [*sic*] carefully make sure that the request was in accordance with [the] wishes of the people, for we are convinced that they would not have acceded to it were it against their wishes. It is therefore the firm view of my Government that East Timor is part of the sovereignty and territorial integrity of Indonesia and my delegation supports the view of the Indonesian delegation that the present discussion is an interference in the internal affairs of the Indonesians . . . It remains our position that the people of East Timor have already exercised their right of self-determination through the legitimate People's Assembly in accordance with Resolutions 1514(XV) and 1541(XV)' (*Press release* of the Permanent Mission of Malaysia to the UN, New York 1978, 2–3, 4).

on self-determination: the rule concerning colonial peoples and that relating to foreign military occupation.

Three considerations should be added. First, the UN failed to enforce self-determination in circumstances which, because of their extremity, might instead have rendered easier the task of deciding who was right and who was wrong (here reference is made to the Indonesian armed intervention and the consequent lack of the basic conditions permitting the free exercise of self-determination). This failure is accounted for by political considerations, in particular the strategic importance of Indonesia for the West. Such importance explains not only why the Security Council refrained from calling the Indonesian invasion a breach of Article 2(4) of the UN Charter, but also why the US – the Superpower more directly concerned, for geopolitical reasons – failed, either within or outside the UN, to take steps to ensure the withdrawal of Indonesian troops.

In this connection, it is instructive to mention the statement made on 19 July 1977 by the then US Deputy Legal Adviser, George H. Aldrich, before the Sub-Committee on International Organizations of the US House of Representatives' Committee on International Relations. Although stating that the US was committed under Articles 55 and 56 of the UN Charter to promote respect for the right of peoples to self-determination, Mr Aldrich pointed out that this had to be reconciled with US political concerns:

The US Government did not question the incorporation of East Timor into Indonesia at the time [in 1976]. This did not represent a legal judgment or endorsement of what took place. It was, simply, the judgment of those responsible for our policy in the area that the integration was an accomplished fact, that the realities of the situation would not be changed by our opposition of what had occurred, and that such a policy would not serve our best interests in light of the importance of our relations with Indonesia.[31]

After reiterating the US commitment to the right of peoples to self-determination, Mr Aldrich went on to add the following:

However, the question remains what we are required to do if this right is not observed as we might wish in a situation in which we believe that efforts by us to change the situation would be futile and injurious to other national interests of the United States. We do not believe that we are required in such circumstances to refrain from acting on the basis of the prevailing factual situation.[32]

---

[31] *Dept. St. Bul.*, 5 September 1977, 326.   [32] *Ibid.*

These remarks are no doubt highly significant, for they are indicative of the attitude of third States *vis-à-vis* possible breaches of the right of peoples to self-determination. As long as third States do not see their own interests as being directly affected by such breaches, they tend to lay greater emphasis on other considerations than those relating to respect for international law.

A confirmation of this proposition can be found in the attitude adopted towards the question of East Timor by the Member States of the European Community. Close scrutiny of the stand taken over the years by the Twelve shows that, pressed to declare their position on the right of the East Timorese people to self-determination, the Twelve have confined themselves to vague statements, or have pointed out that the matter was of bilateral concern (Portuguese–Indonesian), or else have preferred to dwell on the question of human rights as regards the treatment of individual East Timorese by the Indonesian authorities.[33]

---

[33] See for instance the extremely loose and vague answer given on 15 July 1985 by the Italian Presidency to a detailed and sweeping written question in the European Parliament (doc. 85/141, in *EPC Bul.*, 1985, no. 1, 118–19), as well as the totally evasive answer given on 18 February 1987 by the Belgian Presidency to a specific oral question in the European Parliament (the question was: 'I should like to hear from the President-in-Office of the [European] Council not so much what was discussed at this Conference [between the Twelve and the ASEAN countries] but whether the Council is really prepared to endorse and support the position adopted in the resolution of 12 July 1986 [of the European Parliament], that East Timor has a right to self-determination. I am not talking about the general declaration of willingness to stand up for human rights but about support for the position adopted in the resolution. Will the Minister do this, and if so, how?' The answer by Mr Tindemans was as follows: 'The problem raised by the Honourable Member is a bilateral problem. No part is played in such matters by the Community or the Twelve': doc. 87/100, *ibid.*, 3, 1987, no. 1, 94–5).

See also the answer given on 15 June 1988 by the German Presidency to an oral question in the European Parliament (the question in part ran as follows: 'How do the Foreign Ministers of the Twelve intend to support the right of the people of East Timor to self-determination and press for the vital withdrawal of Indonesian troops? Will any joint action be taken in connection with the forthcoming session of the UN General Assembly?' In the answer the Presidency stated, among other things, that: 'The Government of Indonesia is aware of the views of the Twelve concerning the question of East Timor. The Twelve support contacts between Portugal and Indonesia under the auspices of the UN Secretary-General, with a view to achieving a comprehensive and internationally acceptable settlement ensuring to the people of East Timor its rights and cultural identity. Speaking at a press conference after the closing of the ministerial meeting, Minister H.-D. Genscher said that the Twelve will make their agreed position known in greater detail in the United Nations, which is the appropriate forum to address this matter': doc. 88/162, *ibid.*, 4, 1988, no. 1, 171).

See also the answers given on 5 July 1988 by the Greek Presidency to some oral questions in the European Parliament (answers that were first vague, and subsequently

My second point is that the Indonesian incorporation of East Timor and its actual control over the territory and its inhabitants (in spite of frequent disturbances triggered by a section of the population which objected to Indonesian rule) gives rise to an important legal question: which of two conflicting principles – effectiveness or non-recognition of illegal situations – should prevail? According to some States, among which can be counted Australia,[34] the international community cannot help but take account

totally evasive: doc. 88/206, *ibid.*, 4, 1988, no. 2, 68–9). In the same vein, the Greek Presidency confined itself to a few generalities in its statement of 27 September 1988 in the UN General Assembly (doc. 88/298, *ibid.*, 4, 1988, no. 2, 124), generalities that were reiterated by the French Presidency in the statement of 18 October 1989 in the same forum (doc. 89/241, *ibid.*, 5, 1989, no. 2, 90), as well as in the general memorandum issued by the Italian Presidency to the UN General Assembly on 25 September 1990 (doc. 90/338, *ibid.*, 6, 1990, 347–8) and in the statement made by the same Presidency on 22 October 1990 in the Fourth Committee of the UN General Assembly ('The Twelve follow closely the developments in East Timor, including the human rights situation. They reiterate their support for the contacts being held between Portugal and Indonesia under the auspices of the Secretary-General. They express the hope that a just, comprehensive and internationally acceptable settlement may soon be achieved, in accordance with the principles of the UN Charter, thus fully respecting the legitimate interests of the East Timorese': doc. 90/394, *ibid.*, 6, 1990, 412).

[34] On 20 January 1978 the Australian Minister for Foreign Affairs, Mr Peacock, stated that the Australian Government had decided to accept East Timor as part of Indonesia although it deplored these developments and above all the use of force by Indonesia: 'The Government had made clear publicly its opposition to the Indonesian intervention and has made this known to the Indonesian Government', Mr Peacock said but 'Since November 1975 the Government has made every effort to seek a peaceful solution of the problem. In this it has espoused neither the ambitions of any particular East Timorese political movement nor the position of the Indonesian Government. Movement for international intervention whether by the United Nations or other countries has never gained the required support. Since November 1975 the Indonesian Government has continued to extend its administrative control over the territory of East Timor. This control is effective and covers all major administrative centres of the territory.'

In conclusion Mr. Peacock noted that the future progress of 'family' reunion and the rehabilitation of Timor were important ingredients in a practical contribution to the peace of the area. He emphasized that in order to pursue these objectives Australia would need to continue to deal directly with the Indonesian Government as the authority in effective control. 'This is a reality with which we must come to terms' and 'Accordingly, the Government has decided that although it remains critical of the means by which integration was brought about it would be unrealistic to continue to refuse to recognize de facto that East Timor is part of Indonesia.' (8 AYIL, 1983, 279).

Following criticisms from the opposition party (the Australian Labour Party), on 23 February the Minister restated his position as follows: 'We recognize the fact that East Timor is part of Indonesia, but not the means by which this was brought about. My statement on 20 January gave the reasons . . . Firstly, that Indonesian control is effective and covers all major administrative centres; secondly, that it is necessary to press on expeditiously with the question of family reunion; thirdly, that it is necessary

of the 'realities' of the situation, and must accordingly recognize the annexation as effective. It is submitted instead that in this, as in any similar case, effectiveness is denied any legal weight by the body of rules on self-determination. Third States are consequently duty-bound to consider the Indonesian annexation as illegal and to refrain from granting any recognition of Indonesian rule over East Timor. This is also the prevailing view in the United Nations, as evidenced by the fact that East Timor is still regarded by the 'Committee of 24' as a non-self-governing territory.

Third, the case of East Timor provides clear evidence of the rich potential of this realm of law. For, although the UN political organs have so far failed to enforce respect for the right of the people of East Timor to self-determination, the recent decision by Portugal to institute proceedings against Australia before the ICJ[35] shows that States have many legal means at their disposal to ensure at least partial compliance with the lofty principles of the international community. It is to be hoped that the Court will eventually come to a decision on the merits of Portugal's application, thereby providing a further elaboration of the law on self-determination.

Palestinian rights

INTRODUCTORY REMARKS

Unlike the cases considered so far, in the case of Palestine the right of self-determination has been based by most members of the world community not on the rule relating to decolonization but on the rule concerning foreign military occupation.

Irrespective of the basis for the application of self-determination, it goes without saying that the question of Palestinian rights is one of the most difficult, controversial, and divisive issues in the present international community. In particular, the discussion revolves around the question of

---

to do the same with the rehabilitation of Timor; and fourthly, that to carry out the last two matters in particular we need to have more extensive direct dealings with the Indonesian Government as the authority in effective control. It was therefore a reality with which we had to come to terms. Any other matters to be negotiated are not, were not, and have never been salient considerations at all . . . ' (*ibid.*, 280; see also 282). The Australian view was reiterated in the following years, see 10 AYIL, 1987, 273. For the attitude previously taken by Australia (in 1975–6), which was strongly in favour of self-determination, see 6 AYIL, 1978, 208–10 and 7 AYIL, 1981, 426–8.

[35] See thereon, C. M. Chinkin, 'East Timor Moves into the World Court', 4 EJIL, 1993, 206–22 and M. C. Maffei, 'The Case of East Timor before the International Court of Justice – Some Tentative Comments', *ibid.*, 223–38.

whether the Palestinians have a right to self-determination (as is claimed by the Palestinians themselves and practically all Member States of the world community as well as the United Nations), or if this right has already been exercised through the establishment of Jordan (as has for long been claimed by Israel). A number of factors contribute to the particularly intractable nature of the issue. Among others, they are: the legacy of the past (the ambiguous attitude of Great Britain, before and at the time of the British Mandate over Palestine); the need for Jews to emigrate to Palestine in order to escape the Nazi genocide; the deep frustration of Arabs over their eviction from a land where, in the early 1900s, they constituted the majority; the religious dimension of a conflict between two peoples which are so radically opposed; the obdurate unwillingness to bow to international appeals and proposals, which in 1947 led the Arabs to reject the UN partition plan and attack Israel and presently results in the Israeli refusal to comply with UN exhortations for a prompt and peaceful settlement.

The task of finding a solution to the problem is rendered even more difficult by the existence of the Holy Places in Jerusalem (so important for the three religions involved), the tiny physical dimension of the territory now in dispute (the West Bank, the Gaza Strip, and Eastern Jerusalem together measure only about 6,500 square kilometres) and the fact that it is so closely intertwined with the territory under Israeli sovereignty, with all the ensuing economic and security problems.[36]

---

[36] On the question of the Palestinian right to self-determination, in addition to the annotated bibliography by D. B. Knight and M. Davies, *Self-Determination. An Interdisciplinary Annotated Bibliography*, New York and London, 1987, 169 ff., see in particular: E. Lauterpacht, *Jerusalem and the Holy Places*, London 1968, 13–53; W. M. Reisman, *The Art of the Possible – Diplomatic Alternatives in the Middle East*, Princeton and New York 1970, 46, 49–50; N. Feinberg, 'The Arab–Israeli Conflict in International Law' (1970), in N. Feinberg, *Studies in International Law*, Jerusalem 1979, 440 ff.; L. C. Green, 'Self-Determination and the Settlement of the Arab-Israeli Conflict', 65 AJIL, 1971, 40 ff.; M. C. Bassiouni, 'Self-Determination and the Palestinians', 65 Proceedings ASIL, 1971, 31 ff.; H. Cattan, *Palestine and International Law*, 2nd edn London and New York 1976, 213–23; M. C. Bassiouni, *The Palestinians' Right to Self-Determination and National Independence*, Association of Arab-American University Graduates, Information Paper no. 22, 1978, especially at 4 ff.; F. L. M. van den Craen, 'The Territorial Title of the State of Israel to "Palestine": An Appraisal in International Law', 14 RBDI, 1978–9, 500 ff.; E. Oeser, 'Das Selbstbestimmungsrecht des Palästinischen Volkes und die Abkommen von Camp David', 11 *Deutsche Aussenpolitik*, 1980, 80 ff.; J. A. Collins, 'Self-Determination in International Law: The Palestinians', 12 Case WRJIL, 1980, 137 ff.; Y. Dinstein, 'Self-Determination and the Middle East Conflict', in Alexander and Friedlander, *Self-Determination*, 243 ff.; M. Mautner, 'West Bank and Gaza Strip: The Case for Associate Statehood', 6 *Yale Journal of World Public Order*, 1980, 297–380;

HISTORICAL BACKGROUND

The origin of the Palestine problem can be traced back to the conflicting commitments undertaken by the British and her allies in the years 1915–18. In 1915–16, in what is known as the Hussain–McMahon correspondence, the British authorities, seeking Arab support in their war against the Ottoman Empire, assured Sherif Hussain, the Emir of Mecca, that Great Britain was willing to 'support the independence of the Arabs in all the regions within the limits demanded by the Sherif of Mecca'.[37] A little more than a year later, in the letter sent by British Foreign Secretary Lord Balfour to Baron Rothschild and known as the 'Balfour Declaration', Great Britain, which was by then administering Palestine as an occupying Power, informed the World Zionist Organization that it favoured the establishment in Palestine of a 'homeland' for the Jewish people which would not 'prejudice the civil and religious rights of existing non-Jewish communities'.[38] These documents, though perhaps reconcilable in terms of the language employed, pitted the Arabs living in Palestine (the Palestinian people), who believed themselves to be entitled to independence, against the Zionists, who saw the Balfour programme

Guilhaudis, 'Le droit positif à l'autodétermination', in *Le Droit à l'autodétermination*, 26–30; I. Rabinovich, 'The Autonomy Plan and Negotiations for the West Bank and the Gaza Strip in their Political Context', in Y. Dinstein (ed.), *Models of Autonomy*, New Brunswick and London, 1981, 261 ff.; Y. Dinstein, 'Autonomy', in Dinstein, *Models of Autonomy*, 291 ff.; Y. Gotlieb, *Self-Determination in the Middle East*, New York 1982; E. Murlakov, *Das Selbstbestimmungsrecht der Völker im israelisch-arabischen Konflikt*, Zurich 1982, especially 35 ff.; S. V. Mallison and W. T. Mallison Jr, 'The Juridical Bases for Palestinian Self-Determination', 1 PYIL, 1984, 36–67; D. H. Ott, 'Autonomy and the Palestinians: A Survey', 1 PYIL, 1984, 68–94; Y. Dinstein, 'Collective Human Rights of Peoples vis-à-vis Minorities', in S. Chandra (ed.), *Minorities in National and International Laws*, New Delhi 1985, 79–80; J. Weiler, *Israel and the Creation of a Palestinian State – A European Perspective*, London, Sydney, and Dover 1985, 42–6, 59–62; A. Cassese, 'Legal Considerations on the International Status of Jerusalem', 3 PYIL, 1986, 13–39; M. Curtis, 'International Law and the Territories', 32 HILJ, 1991, 457 ff.; R. A. Falk and B. H. Weston, 'The Israeli-Occupied Territories, International Law, and the Boundaries of Scholarly Discourse: A Reply to M. Curtis', 33 HILJ, 1992, 191 ff.; P. J. C. M. de Waart, 'Statehood and International Protection of Peoples in Armed Conflict in the "Brave New World": Palestine as a UN Source of Concern', 5 *Leiden Journal of International Law*, 1992, 4–31; B. Driessen, *A Concept of Nation in International Law*, The Hague 1992, 92–5; Pellet, 'The Destruction of Troy will not Take Place', in Playfair, *International Law and the Administration of Occupied Territories*, 180–6.

[37] See below, note 39.
[38] For Jewish–British relations between 1920 and 1939, see, among others, A. Eban, *My People – The Story of the Jews*, New York 1968, 377–84.

(which was incorporated into the League of Nations Mandate for Palestine) as the first step in the creation of a Jewish State in Palestine. A 1919 memorandum by Lord Balfour which discusses an Anglo-French declaration of November 1918 supporting the 'complete and definite emancipation of the [Arab] peoples and the establishment of national governments and administration deriving their authority from the initiative and free choice of the indigenous populations',[39] underscores the contradictions in the British policy and Britain's subordination of the nascent principle of self-determination:

Palestine should be excluded from the terms of reference because the Powers [have] committed themselves to the Zionist programme, which inevitably excluded numerical self-determination. Palestine present[s] a unique situation. We are dealing not with the wishes of an existing community but are consciously seeking to re-constitute a new community and definitely building for a numerical majority in the future.[40]

The legacy of Great Britain's twin obligations in Palestine has been one of permanent strife.[41]

The Arabs' belief that the Balfour Declaration implied a denial of the principle of self-determination and would lead to Jewish control of the region led to major outbreaks of violence in 1920, 1921, 1929, and 1933. By 1936, with the influx of Jewish immigrants fleeing annihilation at the hands of the Nazis greatly exacerbating tensions, there was open rebellion. Recognizing the need to take action, the British Government established the Palestine Royal Commission to investigate the 'disturbances' and to propose a plan for the region. This Commission recommended that Britain abandon its attempt to reconcile the Jews and Arabs and proposed that Palestine be partitioned into an Arab State and a Jewish State; Jerusalem and Bethlehem were to be neutral regions under continued British administration. Zionist leaders expressed reservations. Arab leaders rejected the plan *in toto*. Eventually, after a number of other proposals were also defeated, Britain referred the matter to the United Nations. In

---

39 British Government, Correspondence between Sir Henry McMahon and Sherif Hussain of Mecca, Cmd 5957 (1939), 50, cited in *The Right of Self-Determination of the Palestinian People*, ST/SG/SER.F/3, United Nations, New York 1979.

40 British Government, Public Records Office, Foreign Office no. 371/4183, 1919.

41 As Reisman, *The Art of the Possible*, at 6, rightly states regarding the conflicting promises made by Great Britain: '[W]hatever the political effect within Britain may have been, the result of these chiastic promises in Palestine was to reinforce the complementary expectations of the contending groups.'

response, the General Assembly created the United Nations Special Committee on Palestine (UNSCOP) to examine the controversy.

The Committee members were divided. The majority recommended that Palestine be split into an Arab and a Jewish State with economic union and an internationalized zone in Jerusalem. The minority proposed a federal union between autonomous Arab and Jewish regions. Ultimately, despite the objection of the Palestinians and the Arab States bordering Palestine, the General Assembly adopted Resolution 181(II), of 29 November 1947, partitioning Palestine into an Arab State, a Jewish State, and an internationalized zone in Jerusalem. The Arabs living in Palestine and the Arab States bordering the area refused to accept this resolution. Subsequently, when Britain withdrew from the region and the Zionist leaders (led by David Ben Gourion) declared the birth of the State of Israel on 15 May 1948, Egypt, Syria, Lebanon, and Jordan invaded.

At the end of the war, Transjordan had absorbed the West Bank of the river Jordan, thus forming the Hashamite Kingdom of Jordan; Egypt was in possession of the Gaza Strip; the State of Israel included approximately 3 per cent more of Palestine than had been allocated to the Jewish State by the UN and 750,000 Palestinians were living in exile. The Arab–Israeli war in June 1967 led to a second redrawing of the map. When the fighting ceased, Israel occupied the West Bank, the Gaza Strip, East Jerusalem, the Sinai Desert, and the Golan Heights. The Sinai Desert was later returned to Egypt as part of the Camp David Agreements of 17 September 1978. The other territories remain under Israeli control.

It should be mentioned that the Camp David Agreements, although they do not mention the right to self-determination of the Palestinian people, provide for a general framework for the gradual attainment of 'full autonomy for the inhabitants' of the West Bank and Gaza and the subsequent determination, through negotiations, of the 'final status' of the territories. Article A-1 stipulates that there should be three successive stages, at the end of which a solution should be agreed upon which would 'recognize the legitimate rights of the Palestinian people and their just requirements'. The Agreements also make allowance for the participation of Palestinians in this process, through the election of 'representatives of the inhabitants of the West Bank and Gaza'; these representatives are given the right to take part in the negotiations on the 'final status' of the territories and to decide 'how they shall govern themselves'.[42]

---

[42] For the text of the Agreements, see 17 ILM, 1978, 1466–9. On the Agreements and self-determination, see Murlakov, *Das Selbstbestimmungsrecht der Völker*, 76–7, 143–4; Dinstein,

On 15 November 1988, after twenty-one years of Israeli occupation of the West Bank and Gaza Strip, the Palestine National Council (PNC) proclaimed the establishment of the State of Palestine,[43] invoking, in its Declaration of Independence, the right of the self-determination of peoples.

THE VIEW ADVANCED BY THE GOVERNMENT OF ISRAEL

The Israeli government[44] justifies its continued occupation of the West Bank and Gaza Strip on two grounds: the relative superiority of its claim over the claims of those in control prior to 1967, and its right to self-defence. Israel argues that it cannot be considered an 'occupying Power' within the meaning of the Fourth Geneva Convention of 1949 in any part of the former Palestine Mandate due to the *sui generis* situation in the area. In its view, the Geneva Convention is only applicable where one Power seizes territory under the sovereignty of another Power; since the Arab States which controlled the occupied territories prior to 1967 were not legitimate sovereigns in those areas, Israel is not bound by the Geneva Convention.

As for the right of Palestinians to self-determination, the Israeli position was authoritatively set out by the Israeli delegate, Professor Blum, in his speech of 2 December 1980 to the General Assembly. He made the following points: (1) the Palestinian Arabs have already 'achieved their self-determination' in their own State, namely Jordan; consequently, 'it is patently false to maintain that the Palestinian Arabs do not have a State of their own'.[45] (2) The claim of Palestinians to realize self-determination by

---

Models of Autonomy, 255–87, 291–303. According to M. Chemillier-Gendreau and J. P. Colin ('Le droit du peuple palestinien à l'autodétermination et les accords conclus à Camp David et à Washington', *L'Afrique et l'Asie moderne, Revue Trimestrielle*, 1980, no. 125, 26 ff.), the Agreements' clauses concerning autonomy are incompatible with the principle of self-determination. See also the resolution adopted by the UN General Assembly on 29 November 1979 (Res. 34/65B), in UN Ybk, 1979, 377–8.

43 Palestine National Council, Declaration of Independence, 43 GAOR, Annex 3, Agenda Item 37, 13, UN Doc. A/43/827, S/20278, 1988. The exact parameters of the declared State of Palestine are unclear. See, generally, F. A. Boyle, 'The Creation of the State of Palestine', 1 EJIL, 1990, 301–6 and J. Crawford, 'The Creation of the State of Palestine: Too Much Too Soon?', *ibid.*, 307–13.

44 On the Israeli position, see Murlakov, *Das Selbstbestimmungsrecht der Völker*, 140–56.

45 'The Palestinian Arabs have long enjoyed self-determination in their own State – the Palestinian Arab State of Jordan. As is well known, the Palestine Mandate originally embraced territory on both sides of the River Jordan. It was in that territory that the League of Nations Mandate provided for the establishment of the Jewish National

establishing a Palestinian State on the West Bank and the Gaza Strip, is unfounded. Before the Israeli occupation of these territories, in 1967, 'there was no demand for the establishment of a "Palestinian State" in those areas' and this demand would amount to requesting the creation of 'a second Palestinian Arab State';[46] (3) to provide 'a dignified solution for the needs of the Arab population' of the West Bank and the Gaza Strip, Israel is ready to grant 'full autonomy' to the inhabitants of these areas, in accordance with the 'Camp David Framework' of 1978 which enables those inhabitants to take part in the 'negotiations which will determine the final status of the areas they live in'.[47]

Home. In 1921 Great Britain decided to establish on the area east of the river an emirate under Abdullah ibn Hossein of the Hashemite family of Mecca. That area – Transjordan – comprised about three quarters of the total territory of the Palestine Mandate. In 1922 the "Jewish National Home" articles of the Mandate were declared inapplicable to Transjordan, which nevertheless remained an integral part of Mandated Palestine. With the passage of time, Transjordan became in 1946 an independent State, subsequently renamed "Jordan". Thus there was established an independent Arab State on the territory of Palestine. The independent Jewish State in Palestine – that is, Israel – was established only two years later, in 1948. By virtue of its history, territory, population and culture, Jordan remains the Palestinian Arab State. The Palestinian Arabs have achieved their self-determination there. More than two-thirds of Jordan's citizens are Palestinian Arabs, and, similarly, the vast majority of Palestinian Arabs are Jordanian citizens. Palestinian Arabs are the backbone and mainstay of the country. It is patently false, therefore, to maintain that the Palestinian Arabs do not have a State of their own'. GAOR, XXXVth Session, Plenary Meetings, 77th Meeting, 1318, paras. 108–9.

[46] 'Much has been made in recent years of the need for a so-called Palestinian State in Judea, Samaria and the Gaza District. It will be recalled that before 1967 Israel did not control those territories. Yet there was no demand then for the establishment of a 'Palestinian State' in those areas. The Arab States which now so sanctimoniously preach about the necessity for such a State in those areas did scarcely anything at the time – and this was despite the fact that Judea, Samaria and the Gaza District were under Arab control between 1949 and 1967. The explanation for this is very simple: the entire world knew that the Kingdom of Jordan is the Arab State in Palestine just as the State of Israel is the Jewish State in Palestine. After their defeat in the six-day war of 1967 the Arabs changed their strategy. Recognizing their inability to destroy Israel by force of arms, they explored alternative avenues to reach the same goal. Arab tacticians seized upon slogans and a terminology that would catch on in the political climate which had developed in the world by that time. They estimated that they stood more to gain by promoting the alleged existence of a second Palestinian Arab people, entitled to self-determination in a second Palestinian Arab State, in addition to Jordan' (ibid., paras. 112–13).

[47] 'The Camp David Framework invites the Palestinian Arab residents of Judea, Samaria and the Gaza District to play an active role in shaping their future by calling on them to participate not only in the current negotiations but also in the negotiations which will determine the final status of the areas they live in as well as in the eventual negotiations on a peace treaty between Israel and Jordan, in which the delimitation of boundaries

The same position was reiterated in the following years, although the concepts subsequently propounded by Israel seem to have been couched in somewhat more flexible language.[48]

THE VIEW ADVANCED BY THE PALESTINE LIBERATION ORGANIZATION

For a long time, the Arabs have depicted British policy after the First World War as having fostered the growth of a Jewish homeland in Palestine – which was supported by the United States and the other Western Powers – and as a fundamental denial of the Palestinian people's right to independence and self-determination. In the Arab view, the 1922 Mandate for Palestine, which incorporated the Balfour Declaration, was contrary to international law. In particular, it was inconsistent with the source of the authority of the mandate system: Article 22 of the Covenant of the League of Nations. The Arab view on this point is that the Palestine Mandate was contrary to Article 22 on three grounds: (1) the Mandate was not conceived for the well-being and development of the inhabitants of Palestine; (2) the role of the Mandatory was not restricted to the rendering of administrative advice and assistance to the Palestinian population; instead, the Mandatory was granted 'full powers of legislation and administration', and these powers were not used in the interest of the inhabitants; (3) while Article 22 required that the wishes of the communities concerned must be a principal consideration in the selection of the Mandatory, these wishes were in fact ignored.[49]

The official position of Palestinians is reflected in the speech made on 13 November 1974 by Mr Arafat, Chairman of the Executive Committee

---

between the two countries will be agreed. The programme of autonomy which we have proposed for the Palestinian Arab inhabitants of Judea, Samaria and the Gaza District, as accepted in principle in the Camp David Frameworks, is the first practical proposal to be advanced to provide a dignified solution for the needs of the Arab population of those areas. It comes in place of all the empty declarations with which the Palestinian Arabs concerned have been deluded by States and organizations over the years' (*ibid.*, paras 130–1).

[48] In 1988, the Israeli delegate to the Third Committee of the General Assembly stated that: 'Israel believed that true negotiated peace with all its neighbours was feasible, and that within the framework a solution could be found to the problems and aspirations of the Palestinians. Israel had committed itself, as a signatory to the Camp David Accords, to seek and obtain a resolution to the Palestinian problem in all its aspects and had recognized the legitimate rights of the Palestinians' (UN Doc. A/C.3/43/SR.23, 23). See also S. Peres, 'A Strategy for Peace in the Middle East', 58 FA, 1980, 892 ff.

[49] On these points, see Cattan, *Palestine and International Law*, 65–8.

of the Palestine Liberation Organization (PLO), to the UN General Assembly. His main points were as follows; (1) Zionist immigrants who occupied Palestine in the past 'became the elements of settler colonialism intimately allied to racial discrimination';[50] (2) after the 1967 war, Israel illegally occupied Arab territories, which are now subject to foreign domination;[51] (3) the PLO, 'in its capacity as the sole representative of the Palestinian people', has the right 'to establish an independent national State on all liberated Palestinian territory'.[52]

It is thus apparent that the PLO, first, regards itself as the *legitimate representative* and spokesman of the Palestinian people. Second, in advocating the right to self-determination, it relies on the *three major international 'justifications' for such right*, namely colonialism, racism, and foreign domination. Third, it invokes *external* self-determination and, in particular, asserts that this should be realized by the setting up of a Palestinian State in the Arab territories occupied by Israel[53] (a position that has seemingly been recently moderated in the multinational negotiations on the Middle East sponsored by the United States).

THE POSITION OF THE UNITED NATIONS

After the creation of the State of Israel, international discourse and UN practice relating to Palestinian self-determination was initially limited to consideration of the 'refugee problem' and the attendant 'right of return'.[54] In fact, the famous Security Council Resolution 242 of 22 November 1967, which was intended to establish a framework for peace in the Middle East, did not even address the issue of Palestine, nor recognize a Palestinian right to self-determination. Gradually, talk turned from the right of return of each individual to the Palestinian people's right to self-determination. On 10 December 1969 the UN recognized 'the inalienable rights of the

---

[50] GAOR, XXIXth Session, 2282nd Mtg, A/PV.2282 and Corr. 1 paras. 26–8.

[51] *Ibid.*, paras. 38–40.

[52] *Ibid.*, paras. 63–6.

[53] See on this point the statement made by a PLO representative on 13 November 1973 in UN Doc. A/SPC/SR.884, 8.

[54] The United Nations recognized the right of return as early as 1948. Paragraph 11 of Resolution 194(III), of 11 December 1948, states: '[T]he refugees wishing to return to their homes and live at peace with their neighbours should be permitted to do so at the earliest practicable date ... compensation should be paid for the property of those choosing not to return and for the loss of or damage to property which, under principles of international law or in equity, should be made good by the governments or authorities responsible.'

people of Palestine' (Resolution 2535/B(XXIV)) and then, on 8 December 1970, adopted Resolution 2672/C(XXV) which proclaimed that the people of Palestine were 'entitled to equal rights and self-determination, in accordance with the Charter of the UN'.[55] Four years later, following the October 1973 Arab–Israeli War, Arab heads of state recognized the PLO as 'the sole legitimate representative of the Palestinian people' and the General Assembly invited the PLO to participate in its proceedings. The next month, on 22 November 1974, the General Assembly passed, by 89 votes to 8, with 37 abstentions, Resolution 3236(XXIX), a major instrument that reaffirms the Palestinian right to self-determination. The Assembly also conferred on the PLO observer status in the Assembly and in other international conferences held under UN auspices.

It should be added that the UN position is supported by Western countries,[56] although they normally proclaim the right of the Palestinians to self-determination without specifying how this right should be implemented.[57]

---

[55] See also Resolutions 2649(XXV) of 30 November 1970, 2792D(XXVI) of 6 December 1971, 2963E(XXVII) of 13 December 1972, and 3089D(XXVIII) of 7 December 1973.

[56] See, for instance the position taken by some members of the European Community, either individually, or jointly. For the United Kingdom, see BYIL, 1980, 375; 1981, 386 ff.; 1982, 366; 1984, 434; 1985, 395, 401; 1986, 515 ff.; 1987, 519. For the FRG, see *Zeit.*, 1977, 718 ff.; 1979, 561; 1981, 599; 1982, 517; 1983, 343 ff.; 1984, 502; 1986, 304; 1987, 326. For The Netherlands, see NYIL, 1981, 177; 1983, 262 ff.; 1986, 185. For Belgium, see RBDI, 1976, 220 ff.; 1977, 577 ff. See also the position of Switzerland: ASDI, 1982, 116–17; 1983, 209.

See finally the position taken in the Third Committee of the UN General Assembly by the US in 1983 (A/C.3/38/SR.16, 20), by Portugal in 1987 (plenary, A/42/PV.93, 24 ff.), and by the following countries in the Third Committee, in 1988: Australia (A/C.3/43/SR.7, 7), Japan (*ibid.*, 8), FRG (*ibid.*, 17), Ireland (*ibid.*, SR.10, 7), Turkey (*ibid.*, SR.13, p.4), Australia (*ibid.*, SR.23, 25) and Greece, speaking on behalf of the Twelve Members of the EC (*ibid.*, 25). For a short summary of the positions of various States, see also Murlakov, *Das Selbstbestimmungsrecht der Völker*, 130–40.

[57] Some interesting indications concerning the view of the US can, however, be found in a statement made on 19 October 1977 by Mr A.L. Atherton, Assistant Secretary for Near Eastern and South Asian Affairs, before the Sub-committees on International Organizations, Europe and the Middle East of the Committee on International Relations of the US House of Representatives. He stated the following: 'You have asked me to comment on the relationship between the settlements in occupied territories and the right of self-determination of the people of those territories.

To begin with, it is essential to understand an important difference between the Sinai and the Golan Heights, on the one hand, and the West Bank and Gaza, on the other.

– Territory in the Sinai and the Golan from which Israel withdraws as a result of a negotiated agreement will clearly revert respectively to Egypt and Syria, whose

A FEW GENERAL REMARKS

State practice as well as declarations made by States within the UN and the resolutions adopted by the World Organization seem to warrant the following conclusions: (1) practically all States (and inter-governmental organizations) except Israel, take the view that the Palestinians are entitled to self-determination; (2) as for the legal ground for this right, it seems to be constituted by foreign military occupation; arguably, it follows that only those Palestinians living in the territory occupied by Israel since 1967 are entitled to the exercise of the right; (3) there is general agreement that the objective of granting Palestinians self-determination should go hand in hand with that of safeguarding the existence, security and independence of Israel as a sovereign State; (4) there is widespread agreement that these two objectives should be achieved through peaceful negotiations involving all the parties concerned; recently the convening of an international peace conference has garnered broad support in the world community; (5) by contrast, for a long time, there has been no agreement as to how specifically to implement the Palestinians' right to self-determination (through a plebiscite? Through elections? By providing for intermediate stages of self-government or autonomy, or by immediately offering a choice between independence or integration? And so on);[58] (6) there is no agreement either

---

sovereignty is not disputed. The issue of self-determination is therefore not germane in these two cases.

- In the West Bank and Gaza, however, the situation is different. Both of these territories were part of the British mandate of Palestine. While the legitimate existence of a sovereign Israel in part of Palestine is recognized, the question of sovereignty in the part of Palestine remaining outside of Israel under the 1949 armistice agreements has not been finally resolved. Jordan in May 1950 declared that its annexation of the West Bank was without prejudice to the final settlement of the Palestine issue, and Egypt did not make any sovereign claim to the Gaza Strip during the time it was the administering authority there. Israel similarly notes the undefined nature of sovereignty in the West Bank and Gaza.

The relationship between the settlements and the principle of self-determination cannot be discussed in isolation, because the settlements are but a single factor involved in negotiating peace treaties that will provide, among other things, for the future of the West Bank and the Gaza Strip. In the view of the United States, the important thing concerning the future disposition of the West Bank and Gaza is that the arrangement be acceptable to the parties concerned' (US Digest 1975, 924–5).

[58] It should be pointed out that a few years ago the member States of the European Community expressed their support for the Jordano-Palestinian Agreement of 11 March 1985 that envisaged a confederation of Jordan with the future State of Palestine. See the statement by the Italian Prime Minister, of 17 April 1985 (85/051, in

on the exact territory in which the right to self-determination is to be exercised (for instance, should it include East Jerusalem?). The only indications that can be drawn from the international legal rules and UN resolutions are to the effect that the right must be exercised peacefully, that is, through negotiations between all the parties concerned and on the basis of the freely expressed wishes of the population of the territories.

However, close scrutiny of the international norms makes it possible to use their rich potential. Thus, the undisputed existence of two communities or peoples in Palestine and their aspiration to different structures of government and styles of life should lead to the sensible and elementary conclusion that each of them should conduct its own existence in a different territorial area. One cannot but share the opinion of Y. Dinstein: 'In Palestine there are (and there have been for a very long time) primarily two peoples: Arabs and Jews. Both peoples are entitled to self-determination, but each craves to determine its political fate in the whole of Palestine, and actually denies – completely (in the case of the Arabs) or partly (in that of the Jews) – the other's right to self-determination. In such circumstances, only partition of the disputed area can resolve the conflicting claims'.[59]

Furthermore, one can infer from the indications provided by international law that the proper way of exercising self-determination in Palestine should consist in the holding of a referendum or plebiscite in the contested area, so as to offer to the population a range of fair and realistic choices. Such a referendum or plebiscite, one could contend, would meet

---

1, *EPC Bul.*, 1985 no. 1, at 61), the statement of the Foreign Ministers, of 29 April 1985 (85/069, *ibid.*, at 75), the press release of the Luxemburg Presidency of 19 November 1985 (85/294, 1 *EPC Bul.* no. 1, at 197), the declaration of the Luxemburg Presidency to the UN General Assembly, of 3 December 1985 (85/309, 1 *EPC Bul.*, 1985 no. 1, at 219) the Report of the European Council to the European Parliament, of 3 December 1985 (85/341, 2 *EPC Bul.*, 1986 no. 1, at 38: 'the [Member States of the EC] believe that this initiative, which represents a constructive step forward in the search for a peaceful and comprehensive settlement, has revived the peace progress'), the answer of the Dutch Presidency to questions in the European Parliament, 9 April 1986 (doc. 86/411, unpublished).

However, it should be pointed out that even the Jordano-Palestinian Agreement (text in 2 PYIL, 1985, at 224) did not provide any specification of the way the right of the Palestinian people should be implemented (on the follow-up to the Agreement, see 33 *Keesing's*, 1987, 34898–901).

[59] Dinstein, 'Collective Human Rights of Peoples vis-à-vis Minorities', 79. H. O. Schoenberg, 'Limits of Self-Determination', 6 IYHR, 1976, 103, advocates a solution 'either through population transfer or through self-determination for the Palestinian Arabs, coinciding with boundary recognition by the Arab States of Israel's right to exist within secure and recognized boundaries'.

the requirement set out by the ICJ for 'a free and genuine expression of the peoples concerned'. Two possible objections against this view can be easily dismissed. The first objection could be that the area in question is not under the sovereignty of one particular State (Jordan in 1987 formally renounced all the sovereign rights it had previously claimed over the West Bank) and indeed its international status is uncertain and disputed. The response to this objection is that self-determination is not contingent on sovereignty; it is a concept geared to peoples, not to sovereign legal titles. To put it differently, in the case of controversy over a territory, its legal status, and the status of the population inhabiting it, the law of self-determination focuses on the wishes of the people concerned; by the same token, it subordinates the issue of who is the holder of sovereign title. The crucial matter for the rules on self-determination is that the State that wields effective authority over a territory, whatever its legal entitlement, should grant the population concerned the possibility of freely choosing its international (and internal) status.

The second possible objection could be that as a result of the policy followed by Israel since 1967, the population of the contested area has been modified, in that settlements of Israeli nationals have been established in that area. This objection can be rejected by noting that, as those settlements are illegal as being contrary to the international norms on belligerent occupation,[60] Israeli settlers should not be permitted to take part in a possible referendum or plebiscite.

Whether or not the above legal remarks are convincing, the fact however remains that security, economic, and political reasons are so compelling in the present case as to make the suggested solution unworkable – unless it becomes part of a 'package deal' gradually agreed upon by all the parties concerned.

Admittedly, the 'response' of international law to complex problems such as the one under discussion is unsatisfactory. On the other hand, one cannot demand from legal standards more than they can realistically offer: a set of general guidelines, that must be pragmatically and realistically applied by all the parties concerned, taking into account – in the case at issue – not only the wishes of the population concerned but also the host of non-legal problems that beset Arab–Israeli relations.

---

[60] On this matter, see the cogent arguments of the US Assistant Secretary made in the aforementioned statement of 1977, US Digest 1977, 924.

THE ISRAEL–PLO AGREEMENT OF 13 SEPTEMBER 1993: SOME TENTATIVE OBSERVATIONS

The Agreement and self-determination

It is well known that on 13 September 1993 Israel and the PLO signed a 'Declaration of Principles on Interim Self-Government Arrangements'.[61] A peaceful process was thus initiated that could (or at least should) lead to a final settlement of this age-old question. It is opportune to appraise briefly the Declaration from the viewpoint of self-determination of Palestinians.

It is striking that the Declaration does not mention self-determination, either directly and explicitly, or indirectly; the only two UN texts to which it adverts are the famous Security Council Resolutions 242 (of 22 November 1967) and 338 (of 22 October 1973), and none of them mention self-determination. A vague and non-committal reference to the Palestinian right to self-determination might be distilled from Article III(3), where reference is made to 'the realization of the legitimate rights of the Palestinian people and their just requirements'. However, by itself this clause does not spell out in unambiguous terms the right to self-determination, as is borne out by the fact that the same clause was already in the Camp David Agreement of 17 September 1977 (Section A(c)), and it is well known that at that time the attitude of Israel was enigmatic and indeed baffling – to say the least – with regard to the final granting of self-determination to Palestinians.

Nevertheless, the Declaration has clearly been agreed upon in the perspective of self-determination, as can be easily inferred from both the text and the context (and that is, the statements made by the contracting parties before, or upon, or after the signature of the Declaration). The Declaration provides first of all for *internal* self-determination. Article III(1 and 2) stipulates that:

In order that the Palestinian people in the West Bank and Gaza Strip may govern themselves according to democratic principles, direct, free and general political elections will be held for the Council [the Palestinian Interim Self-Government Authority] under agreed supervision and international observation, while the Palestinian police will ensure public order. These elections will constitute a significant interim preparatory step toward the realization of the legitimate rights of the Palestinian people and their just requirements.

---

[61] Text published in 4 EJIL, 1993, 572–81. See *ibid.* the essays by E. Benvenisti (542–54), R. Shihadeh (555–63) and A. Cassese (564–71).

The Council, once established, will exercise the powers and responsibilities transferred to it both by the Israeli Military Government and its Civil Administration. These powers will encompass the three branches of government, that is, legislation, executive authority and judicial functions (Article VII(2)). After the setting up of the Palestinian Council the Israeli 'Civil Administration will be dissolved' and 'the Israeli military government will be withdrawn' from the West Bank and the Gaza Strip (Article VII (5)); it is therefore clear that in this lapse of time, that should not exceed five years as from 13 April 1994, Palestinians will exercise *full self-government*.

What about *external self-determination*? The Declaration is silent on this point, in particular on whether it is envisaged that the Palestinians will attain independent statehood, or some form of association with one of the existing States (e.g., Jordan or even Israel), or both. However, various provisions stipulate that the primary goal of the Declaration is to lead to the attainment of a 'permanent status' for the West Bank and the Gaza Strip and that this 'permanent status' should be consonant with the afore-mentioned Security Council resolutions. It is well known that those resolutions, and particularly the first, which is more sweeping, hinge upon the following fundamental objectives: (i) the 'establishment of a just and lasting peace in the Middle East'; (ii) the 'withdrawal of Israel armed forces' from occupied territories as a consequence of the 'inadmissibility of the acquisition of territory by war'; (iii) 'respect for and acknowledgment of the sovereignty, territorial integrity and political independence of every State in the area'; (iv) 'a just settlement of the refugee problem'. The attainment of all these objectives logically presupposes not only the estab-lishment of an autonomous Palestinian authority in the occupied territories, but also the acquisition, by this authority and the territories which it shall control, of some sort of independent international status. Hence, it can be safely asserted that, although in an oblique and round-about way, the Declaration is grounded upon, and logically presupposes, the idea of the final attainment by Palestinians of external self-determina-tion. Unsurprisingly, this view is shared by the President of the PLO, Mr Yasser Arafat, who declared upon the signing of the Declaration that the final status of the Arab territories occupied by Israel should be the achieve-ment of independent statehood, and the setting up of a confederation with Jordan.[62]

How will the right to external self-determination be exercised? The Declaration simply states that the 'permanent status' of the West Bank and

[62] See *The International Herald Tribune*, 16 September 1993, at 4.

the Gaza Strip shall be the subject of negotiations between Israel and the 'Palestinian people representatives' (Articles I and V(2)), and that these negotiations must start as soon as possible, at any rate 'not later than the beginning of the third year of the [five year] interim period' (Article V(2)), namely 13 April 1997). This means that the determination of the *international status* of the Palestinian territories currently occupied by Israel will be the subject of negotiations between the democratically elected Palestinians and the Israeli authorities. Thus, the process of exercising external self-determination will constitute the natural outcome both of internal Palestinian self-determination, and of negotiations with the other Party concerned. Everything is left to the agreement of these two Parties. In particular, the Declaration does not spell out the possible final options: independent statehood free from any military or territorial servitudes; independent statehood subject to a set of servitudes or disabilities in favour of Israel (e.g., right of passage for Israeli troops or nationals, Israeli jurisdiction over Israeli settlements, the maintenance of Israeli military bases, the obligation for the Palestinians not to militarize certain areas, etc.); free integration into another State; or free association with another State. Nor does the Declaration specify whether the Palestinians will have to hold a referendum or plebiscite on the matter.

The Agreement and the Camp David Accord
This feature of the Declaration should not, however, lead us to under-estimate the momentous importance of this agreement. To appraise how significant the Declaration is and to what extent it marks a real turning-point in the Middle East negotiations, it may suffice to compare some of its clauses to those of the 1978 Camp David Agreements (apart from the obvious but exceedingly important – indeed *crucial* – difference that the former were concluded by two States, Israel and Egypt, while the latter has been made by Israel with the PLO, the internationally recognized and representative organization of the Palestinians.

The 1978 Agreements were rightly termed a 'misty penumbra of formulational ambiguity'.[63] Actually, they included a host of loose clauses or expressions that lent themselves to conflicting interpretations. Thus, for instance, they provided for 'full autonomy to the inhabitants' of the West Bank and the Gaza Strip, to be achieved by means of the free election of a 'self-governing authority'. They also provided for the withdrawal of the

---

[63] Shapira, 'Reflections on the Autonomy: The Camp David Accords and the Obligation to Negotiate in Good Faith', in Dinstein (ed.), *Models of Autonomy*, 285.

'Israeli military government and its civilian administration' (Section A(1)). However, the vague character of these expressions soon gave rise to radically differing interpretations by Israel and Egypt. Thus, for instance, 'full autonomy for the inhabitants' was interpreted by Israel as meaning 'personal autonomy', whereas for Egypt it meant 'territorial autonomy'; that is the autonomy of the West Bank, the Gaza District, and East Jerusalem.[64] Plainly, the difference between these two interpretations is broad indeed. Similarly, the expression 'self-governing authority' was taken by Israel to denote an authority exercising powers and providing services 'normally associated with the administration of the services and facilities of a particular group of people',[65] whereas Egypt argued that the 'authority' in question should exercise legislative, executive, and judicial powers. Opinions between the two Contracting States differed widely on a third crucial point: what was meant by 'withdrawal' of the Israeli military government and civil administration? For Israel it did not imply the total evacuation of the occupied territories, because the Israeli army and military administration were entitled to remain in certain specific areas in the West Bank and the Gaza Strip. For Egypt the contrary interpretation was valid.[66] Another major bone of contention concerned the 'source' of the powers devolving upon the 'self-governing authority'. According to Egypt, by transferring the various powers to the 'authority', Israel would relinquish them for good. By contrast, Israel contended that it would not divest itself of those powers, for its military administration would continue to be the source of authority for the self-governing bodies in the territories in issue.[67] The truth of the matter is that the Camp David agreements loosely amalgamated two different 'models' that in actual fact were poles apart. They were aptly summarized as follows by a distinguished commentator:

The Israeli concept regards the autonomy regime as a means for preserving the essence of the existing political-strategic state of affairs in the West Bank and Gaza. It tends toward the consolidation, and possible strengthening, of certain elements of self-rule which now already exist in the West Bank and Gaza, while striving to ensure Israeli control over central and sensitive matters of government. The

---

[64] See Gabay, 'Legal Aspects of the Camp David Framework for Peace in Relation to the Autonomy Proposal', *ibid.*, at 256. See also Rabinovich, 'The Autonomy Plan and Negotiations for the West Bank and the Gaza Strip in their Political Context', *ibid.*, at 270.

[65] Gabay, *ibid.*, at 256.

[66] *Ibid.*, at 257; Rabinovich, *ibid.*, at 270.

[67] Gabay, *ibid.*, at 257–8; Rabinovich, *ibid.*, at 270.

Egyptian concept is completely different, aspiring to bring about the establishment of a comprehensive governmental administration which harbours elements of independent – political-territorial – Palestinian sovereignty.[68]

While it would be fallacious to believe that the Israel–PLO Agreement is free from ambiguity – indeed, this Agreement is also marred by quite a few excessively loose formulas, and numerous loopholes and lacunae – nevertheless it does not lend itself to the conflicting interpretations to which I have just referred.[69]

Concluding remarks

To appraise the prospects for the implementation of the PLO–Israel Agreement one should of course take into account various factors: the unique features and content of the Agreement; the fact that – whatever the legal purport and impact of its clauses – the application of the Agreement is *ultimately* contingent upon the persistence of the will of both parties to settle the matter; the looming presence of a host of 'external' elements (psychological, political, economic, military). All this makes it difficult to predict whether or not a settlement will eventually be reached in actual fact. By the same token, it is difficult to forecast the way in which *external* self-determination will be implemented. For the time being, international lawyers must be content with emphasizing two things: firstly, that at long last, the path suggested by international norms, that is, a peaceful process of negotiation between the parties concerned, has been taken; secondly, that as an initial measure, provision has been made for the exercise of *internal* self-determination by the Palestinians, as a

---

[68] Shapira, *ibid.*, at 284.

[69] Thus, for instance, Art. V(2) provides for the principal issues that the negotiations for the 'permanent status' should cover. Art. VI(2) specifies the subjects with regard to which the Palestinians will exercise powers following the withdrawal of Israel from the Gaza Strip and the Jericho Area. Art. VII(2) provides in a fairly detailed way for the powers and responsibilities to be transferred to the 'Council', and in any case specifies that the future agreement on the matter should grant the Council legislative and executive functions, and in addition envisages 'independent Palestinian judicial organs'. Furthermore, Art. XIII is not as vague as the Camp David Accords as regards the 'redeployment of Israeli military forces in the West Bank and Gaza Strip'. Annex II, containing the Protocol on withdrawal of Israeli forces from the Gaza Strip and Jericho Area, provides in para. 3 a detailed list of the issues that the future agreement on the matter should cover. Annex III, containing the Protocol on Israeli-Palestinian co-operation in economic and development programmes, touches upon the extremely delicate and important issue of water resources, and provides for, *inter alia*, 'the equitable utilization of joint water resources for implementation in and beyond the interim period'.

stepping-stone to external self-determination. No one could underestimate the importance of these two elements. Whenever one is confronted with such complicated and intractable situations as that of Palestine, it proves exceedingly difficult to suggest an easy path to solutions that are both rapid and satisfactory to all those concerned. A good start has been made: a long overdue settlement, that for so many years was even unthinkable, may now be in the offing.

Quebec

HISTORICAL BACKGROUND

Quebec, one of the ten provinces and two national territories which comprise the federal parliamentary State of Canada, has a population of about six and a half million people; 80 per cent of the population is French speaking. Settled by the French in 1608, Quebec was conquered by British troops in 1759; by the Treaty of Paris of 1763, which formally ended the Seven Years War in Europe, sovereignty over Quebec was transferred from France to Great Britain. Subsequently, when the British North America Act creating the State of Canada was concluded in 1867, Quebec became part of the federal State.

A century later, when Quebec, leaving behind its agrarian economy, emerged as an industrial power within Canada, the province began its offensive against the English-speaking forces that governed Canada. First came the 'Quiet Revolution' initiated by the emerging French-Canadian middle class. They demanded greater participation in the economic and commercial decisions of Quebec, challenging the dominance by Anglo-Saxon interests of Quebec commercial and economic life. Next, in the late 1960s and early 1970s, came the language programme of the French-Canadian nationalists, whose aim was the increased use of the French language in industry, business, the justice system, the legislature and schools; their efforts resulted in the passage, in 1974, of Bill 22, which made French the official language of the province of Quebec. Soon thereafter came the separatist Parti Québecois, which, headed by René Lévasque, won control of the Quebec legislature in 1976.

While campaigning, René Lévasque promised a public referendum on the issue of the constitutional secession of Quebec from the Canadian federal system. Four years later, a referendum was held. The majority, 1,900,000 persons, voted to remain a part of Canada; 1,300,000 voted in favour of independence. Fear that prosperity might be the price of

independence is considered to have been one of the main factors leading to the vote in favour of continued union.

After several years of intense negotiations and debates on extending special constitutional status to Quebec and increasing the powers of the provincial governments in 1987, the new Quebec government which had come to power in 1985 announced that it would adhere to the Constitution Act of 1982 if five conditions were met: (1) explicit consti-tutional recognition of Quebec as a distinct society; (2) the constitutional guarantee of broader powers in the field of immigration; (3) the limitation of federal spending power with respect to programmes falling under Quebec's exclusive jurisdiction; (4) changes in the constitutional amend-ment procedure enshrined in the 1982 Act; (5) Quebec's participation in appointing judges from Quebec to sit in the Supreme Court of Canada.[70] In June 1988 the Canadian House of Commons ratified a package of amendments to the Canadian constitution known as the Meech Lake Accord: it reflected the aforementioned five points.

The Accord, intended to appease separatist sentiments, proved extremely divisive. Two provinces, Manitoba and New Brunswick, initially withheld ratification on the grounds that it offered insufficient protection to Quebec's English-speaking minority, while a third, Newfoundland, rescinded its original ratification after a change in the provincial government. To justify their position, they pointed to the Quebec provincial government's attempt to counteract a 15 December 1988 Canadian Supreme Court opinion finding Article 58 of Quebec's French Language Charter (which required French-only public and commercial signs) incompatible with the province's Charter of Rights: immediately after the handing down of the opinion, the Premier of Quebec, Robert Bourassa, had announced that new legislation would continue to require commercial premises to display French-only signs outside but would allow bilingual notices inside as long as the French version was predominant.

However, it would seem that the level of protection afforded to Quebec's English-speaking population under the Accord was not the only contro-versial issue and this is not what ultimately brought down the Accord. Allegedly, the decisive factor was not Anglo-Canadian but rather Native-Canadian opposition. After an all-party agreement in the Manitoba legislature to ratify the Accord, the ratification vote was blocked

---

[70] See *Report of the Commission on the Political and Constitutional Future of Quebec*, Quebec, March 1991, 31–2.

by the filibustering of a Cree Indian legislator, Elijah Harper, who opposed the Accord on the grounds that it did not recognize the 350,000 native Canadians as a distinct society. The day after Harper's vehement statement, the Accord broke down, having failed to achieve the necessary ratification by the legislatures of all ten provinces within two years of its passage by the House of Commons.

The Accord's collapse in June 1990 was widely viewed as making it much more likely that Quebec would eventually secede from the 123-year-old Canadian State.

In 1991 a provincial law was passed in Quebec (Bill 150) providing for the holding of a referendum before 26 October 1992, either on sovereignty or on a 'binding offer' from the federal government and the other provinces. However, before the holding of this referendum, on 22 August 1992, Canada's Prime Minister, Mr Brian Mulroney, struck a political and constitutional deal (the so-called Charlottetown Agreement) with the ten provincial premiers and the territorial and native leaders. Under this Agreement a nation-wide referendum would be held to amend the Canadian Constitution in order to introduce the following changes: Quebec would be recognized as a 'distinct society' with enhanced powers, primarily because of its French language and culture; in addition, it would be guaranteed a quarter of seats in the House of Commons in perpetuity, even if its population were to fall below a quarter of Canada's total; native Canadians would have their 'inherent' right to self-government recognized (it is claimed that this would have implied a third order of government along with the national and provincial governments); the appointed Senate (where now Quebec and Ontario possess nearly half the seats) would be replaced by an elected chamber, with equal representation for all provinces.

As is well known, on 26 October 1992 the referendum was held but 54 per cent of the voters cast a negative vote (six of the ten provinces, plus the Yukon territory, voted no; in Quebec there was a 55 per cent No vote). Since the package of changes needed the approval of all provinces, as well as the federal government, its rejection was all too clear.

Thereafter no referendum has been held in Quebec, probably because declared separatists make up only one-third of Quebec's electorate, and the majority is still in the hands of the Liberal Party led by Mr Robert Bourassa who has intermittently been Prime Minister of Quebec since 1970. However, Mr Jacques Parizeau, the leader of the opposition Parti Québecois has vowed to make Quebec sovereign by 1995.

THE POSITIONS ADVANCED BY THE PRINCIPAL POLITICAL PARTIES IN QUEBEC

The separatist Parti Québecois, although not currently the dominant party in the Quebec legislature, has a sizeable influence on the legislature's (and Québecois Premier's) activities. When championing secession, its leaders, who consider independence to have been the destiny of Quebec since its conquest by the British, invoke constitutional law as well as international law in general, and the right to self-determination in particular. They insist that Quebec has a right of secession under national and international law. This view is strongly supported by a number of Québecois international lawyers.

THE VIEW ADVANCED BY THE FEDERAL GOVERNMENT

The ruling Progressive Conservative Party (PCP) appears willing to trade self-determination, in the form of extensive *provincial powers*, for the continued territorial integrity of the State. In contrast, the federal Liberal Party campaigns in favour of '10 equal provinces' without 'distinct society' provisions.

DO THE QUÉBECOIS HAVE A LEGAL RIGHT TO SELF-DETERMINATION?

Although the inhabitants of Quebec – as much as all other inhabitants of Canada – may be deemed to have a continuing right to internal self-determination under the UN Covenants, they do not have a legal right, under international law, to secede from Canada. As stated above (see Chapters 2 and 4), international law does not grant autonomous regions or States within a federal government the right freely to determine their international status, regardless of whether or not they represent ethnic and cultural groups distinctly different from the rest of the population.

The contrary view put forward by a number of authors, mostly of Québecois origin, is not substantiated by any valid legal arguments.[71] It

---

[71] See in particular, Turp, *Le droit de sécession en droit international public et son application au cas du Québec*, 307–22; R. Beaugrand, 'Le Quebec', in *Le droit à l'autodétermination*, Paris and Nice 1980, 125–32; 'Le droit de sécession en droit international public', 20 CYIL, 1982, 24–78; R. Beaugrand, 'Quebec's Democratic Right to Self-Determination', in *Tangled Web: Legal Aspects of Deconfederation*, The Canada Round 15, C. H. Howe Institute, Toronto 1992, 107–15. The view that Quebec has no international right to self-

should be added that, strikingly, these commentators, while they advocate self-determination for Quebec, refuse any similar right for the indigenous populations of the region (about 60,000 Amerinds and Inuit, formerly known as Eskimos), for whom they are prepared to recognize only 'aboriginal self-government'.[72]

Equally unfounded appears to be the view that Quebec has a legal right to choose independent statehood under the Canadian *Constitution*. Given that no provision can be found in this Constitution authorizing secession, those upholding such a right have contended that a 'constitutional convention had evolved in practice regarding Quebec's right to self-determination'.[73] This convention is allegedly based on 'precedents', chiefly consisting of acts of acquiescence by the Canadian government and Parliament in the 1980 referendum in Quebec and consequently in the (alleged) right of that province to decide its own legal and political status. While it seems highly questionable that such a constitutional convention has evolved, it should be admitted that at the political level a kind of tacit acceptance of the possibility for Quebec to secede seems to have emerged in large sections of the Canadian population.[74] This political feeling,

---

determination has been upheld, among others, by C. Campiglio, 'Profili internazionali della questione del Québec', 74 RDI, 1991, 84–6, and the authors (A. Pellet, M. N. Shaw, C. Tomuschat, R. Higgins, and T. M. Franck) of the Memorandum on 'L'integrité territoriale de Québec dans l'hypothèse de l'accession à la souveraineté' annexed to the 'Projet de Rapport' of the 'Commission d'étude des Questions Afférentes à l'accession du Québec à la souveraineté', Assemblée Nationale du Québec, September 1992, paras. 3.05–3.09. More generally, see N. M. Poulantzas, 'Multiculturalism, Affirmative Action Programs under the Canadian Charter of Rights and Freedoms, and the Protection of Minorities', 63 *Revue droit international, sciences diplomatiques et politiques*, 1985, 309–17.

[72] See *Report of the Commission on The Political and Constitutional Future of Quebec*, Quebec, March 1991, 67–9 and Turp, 'Quebec's Democratic Right', 115–21. It should be noted that aboriginal peoples claim a right to land, control over their own schools, child-care programmes, laws regulating marriage and divorce, and other powers that are now out of their hands.

[73] See in particular, Turp, 'Quebec's Democratic Right', 103–7.

[74] This is borne out by, among other things, the reply given on 7 November 1990, in the Canadian House of Commons, by the Prime Minister to a question put by an MP: 'L'hon Jean Lapierre (Shefford): . . . Monsieur le Président, ma question s'addresse au très honorable premier ministre. A plusieurs reprises, le premier ministre a reconnu publiquement la légitimité et la légalité de la Commission Bélanger-Campeau. Je demande donc au premier ministre: Est-ce qu'il est aussi d'accord avec le préambule de la loi établissant cette commission, qui stipule, et je cite: "Considérant que les Québécoises et les Québécois sont libres d'assumer leur propre destin, de déterminer leur statut politique et d'assurer leur développement économique, social et culturel"?

Est-ce que le premier ministre peut nous dire une fois pour toutes s'il est oui or non d'accord avec le droit à l'autodétermination du peuple du Quebec?

however, does not appear to be reflected in any legal change at the constitutional level.

RIGHTS VERSUS REALITY

The situation of Quebec is interesting, but not so much because of the fact that one is confronted here with a political claim to secession that is *totally unsupported by law* (although legal arguments are vociferously employed by the proponents of secession as a means of lending support to their political claims). This is not a unique feature of Quebec because there exist many other cases where minorities, ethnic groups, and nations demand secession without having any legal entitlement to it, and there is also a case where a part of a federated State has peacefully achieved secession *de facto* and outside the realm of law: Singapore's secession from the Greater Malaysian Union in 1965.[75]

What is unique about Quebec is that some major problems that beset minorities are here brought into sharp focus: (i) the tension and indeed the dramatic dilemma between enhanced autonomy and secession; (ii) the problem of how to ensure respect for the rights of minorities living within Quebec (chiefly the indigenous people); (iii) the nature of the political process that will lead either to greater autonomy or to secession.

Plainly, all these problems must be settled at a political level and the law can only intervene at a further stage, when political solutions have already been found and there is a need for their consecration in norms and

---

Le très hon. Brian Mulroney (premier ministre): Monsieur le Président . . . je pense que mon ami sait fort bien que la participation du premier ministre du Canada et des chefs de l'opposition, de la quasi totalité des premiers ministres des autres provinces et de lui-même, d'ailleurs, qui était député fédéral, au référendum de 1980, implique bien sûr l'acceptation par tous les Canadiens d'un vote démocratique et libre selon les circonstances et les critères normaux et acceptables.

Alors, sans entrer dans un domaine que je ne peux pas toucher à cause de la raison que je viens de mentionner, je pense que l'expérience de M. Trudeau, du secrétaire d'Etat aux Affaires extérieures, en 1980, de la quasi totalité des membres de la Chambre et des premiers ministres indique la volonté démocratique de tous les Canadiens' (in 29 CYIL, 1991, 515–16).

[75] This is precisely a case on which Québecois greatly rely. It should however be stressed that, first, Malaysia had been set up as a federal State only in 1963 and, secondly, that 'Malaysia was a contrived constellation whose components had been forced into federation for external and adventitious reasons and upon the assumption that the territories tacked on to Malaya could not exist on their own' (P. Calvocoressi, *World Politics Since 1945*, 4th edn, London and New York 1982, 315). The situation is markedly different in Quebec.

institutions. Nevertheless, it is opportune to stress one point. Although, as I have already emphasized, the legal rules do not grant any right to self-determination, international law has already played (and will be playing) a role as a guiding standard, in that all the parties concerned in Canada agree at least on one issue: any decision as to the future of Quebec must be taken by the people of the province by means of a referendum. Thus, one can see once again that the legal *principle* of self-determination has had a kind of 'trickling-down' effect: it has presented the path to be taken regarding decisions about the destiny of a people, even where no legal entitlement to that people is granted by any specific legal *rule*.[76]

Concluding comments

The extreme diversity, as well as the inherent intricacies of each of the six cases examined above, makes it difficult to draw general conclusions on the role that international law can or should play in these complex situations. Our analysis can therefore only warrant some tentative remarks.

First, in some instances (Western Sahara and Eritrea), the conflicting political and economic interests at stake have impeded the prompt realization of self-determination. However, the armed struggle engaged by representatives of the peoples concerned and (in the case of Western Sahara) the concerted action of the world community and some of its political or judicial agencies, may eventually lead to the realization of self-determination. It appears that in both cases the holding of a referendum is the only way of allowing the population to make a free and genuine choice (a choice already made in Eritrea, under UN supervision, resulting in the achievement of independence in 1993).

Also in the case of Gibraltar, the holding of a referendum could meet the test of self-determination, provided the options offered to the population concerned are not as rigid and 'one-sided' as occurred in 1967 but instead offer various realistic alternatives. It would seem that, in addition, the two States concerned (Spain and the UK) should further negotiate as to possible solutions and choices for the population before a referendum is organized. The fact that both States belong to the European Community

---

[76] It may be mentioned that recently D. Conacher ('Power to the People: Initiative, Referendum, Recall and the Possibility of Popular Sovereignty in Canada', 49 *University of Toronto Faculty of Law Review*, 1991, 174–232) has made a plea for the institutionalization of the 'right of initiative, referendum and recall' at all levels of government in Canada.

and both seem interested in, or open to, the implementation of constitutional mechanisms that would grant Gibraltarians wide autonomy within an internationally agreed framework other than integration into one of the two States, indicates that this might be one of the possible options upon which Gibraltarians should be called upon to decide.

In the case of East Timor, the use of force by Indonesia has been exposed to the condemnation of the international community. Although force has eventually gained the upper hand and the aspirations of the East Timorese have been suppressed, international law has shown that its rich potential may be drawn upon to vindicate rights collateral to or stemming from that of self-determination. For example, the fact that Portugal, *qua* the former colonial Power in the instant case, has instituted proceedings against Australia before the International Court of Justice might lead to a partial resurrection of self-determination or, at least, more realistically, to an indirect challenge to the legality of Indonesian occupation. Whatever the result of the proceedings before the ICJ, Portugal's application shows that an illegal act that one might have regarded as a *fait accompli* may subsequently be put into question – provided of course the necessary procedural preconditions are fulfilled.

The case of Palestine stands by itself, on account of its extreme difficulty and because it is indicative of the inherent limitations of law. In this case legal rules do indicate the path to be followed; the solution must perforce be political, that is based on patient negotiations between all the parties concerned. Law cannot do more than suggest the need for a *peaceful* solution based both on negotiations involving all the parties concerned and the free expression of the will of the populations concerned. More than that one cannot demand from law. It is for politicians and diplomats not only to work out imaginative formulas capable of mustering a substantial measure of agreement (as they did by drawing up the 1993 Agreement), but also to endeavour in good faith to implement them, with a view to reaching a final settlement.

The same holds true for Quebec. There, again, it is for politicians to agree upon solutions capable of peacefully resolving the dilemma: enhanced autonomy (i.e., internal self-determination) versus secession (i.e., external self-determination). Although in this case international rules do not grant any legal entitlement to the people concerned, in actual fact the general principle on self-determination has been heeded and acted upon by all the parties concerned because they all seem to agree that no solution should be found that is contrary to the wishes of the relevant population, to be ascertained by means of a referendum. This conclusively shows that the international principle on self-determination has such a broad scope that it can reach out to areas that seem, at first sight, to be totally unsubjected to any international legal regulation. The combination of the useful effects of the legal principle with political wisdom on the part of the statesmen involved will hopefully prove conducive to viable and peaceful solutions.

10

The role of self-determination in the recent break up of the Soviet Union and Yugoslavia

Introductory remarks

In recent years the United Nations' role in promoting the self-determination of colonial countries has become less and less significant. There remain only a few territories whose status is still controversial and in regard to which States have not yet reached agreement on how to resolve the outstanding problems. However, as we have seen in Chapter 9, some of the 'foreign domination' situations, such as that of Palestine, are still awaiting satisfactory settlement.

While the momentum gained by self-determination within the United Nations is thus slowing, dramatic events in two countries, the USSR and Yugoslavia, have recently brought the whole 'problématique' of self-determination back into focus. Self-determination has been continually invoked by most of the political actors involved in the collapse of the central State structures of these two countries, as a basic tenet that legitimates the actions of the break-away republics.

It is therefore appropriate to investigate whether the body of principles and rules of international law governing self-determination has had a bearing on the secessionist trends witnessed in the USSR and Yugoslavia. It will also be of interest to ascertain whether the rules on self-determination laid down in the national constitutions of the two countries have played any role.

The position of the republics that formally constituted the USSR will first be examined. In this respect, it will prove necessary to differentiate between the legal position of the three Baltic States (Estonia, Latvia, and Lithuania) and that of the other twelve republics. The situation as regards the Yugoslav republics will then be addressed.

The Baltic republics[1]

The position of the republics

In December 1918 the Russian Soviet Federated Socialist Republic (RSFSR), the successor to the Russian Empire, recognized the sovereignty of Estonia, Latvia, and Lithuania. Soon thereafter, the three Baltic States became internationally recognized members of the League of Nations. They remained as such until 1940, when the Soviet Union, taking advantage of the free hand it had secured from Hitler with the conclusion of the German–Soviet Non-Aggression Pact and the secret Molotov–Ribbentrop Accords of August 1939 first occupied and then annexed the Baltic States.

Until recently, the USSR Government insisted that the 1940 incorporation of Estonia, Latvia, and Lithuania into the Soviet Union was consistent with the (political) principle of self-determination. To support this view, the central authorities cited the 21 July 1940 pronouncements issued by the Estonian, Latvian and Lithuanian legislatures approving the incorporation of the Baltic States, despite the fact that the 21 July announcements came immediately after mock-elections conducted in violation of the constitutions and election laws of the Baltic States.[2] The USSR government steadfastly refused to acknowledge that in 1940 it had forced the Baltics to accede to its demands by issuing the following ultimatum: approval or annihilation. It should be noted that most Western States refused to recognize the legal validity of the Soviet incorporation of the Baltic States.[3]

---

[1] See generally B. Meissner, *Die Sowjetunion, die Baltischen Staaten und das Völkerrecht*, Cologne 1956; H. J. Uibopuu, *Die völkerrechtliche Stellung der Baltischen Staaten*, Stockholm 1965; B. Meissner, 'Die Baltische Frage in der Weltpolitik', *Oeffentliches Recht und Politik – Fest. für H. U. Scupin zum 70. Geburtstag*, Berlin 1973, 281–93; R. Yakemtchouk, 'Les républiques baltes en droit international. Echec d'une annexion opérée en violation du droit des gens', 37 AFDI, 1991, 259–89.

[2] See in particular, E. Levits, 'Der Politische Konflikt zwischen den Selbstbestimmungs-bestrebungen und dem sowjetischen Herrschaftsanspruch in Lettland', 14 *Dokumentation Ostmitteleuropa*, 1988, 313 ff.

[3] The position of Australia deserves to be underlined. In 1974 the Australian Government recognized the Soviet Government as the government de jure of those States. In October 1974, answering a parliamentary question, the Prime Minister Mr Whitlam said, *inter alia*: 'I have very thoroughly reviewed this matter, both before the Government decided to recognize the de jure incorporation of the republics of Estonia, Latvia and Lithuania in the Union of Soviet Socialists Republics, and since. There is no question of changing the decision. The decision could be changed by the present Government or any subsequent Australian Government only at the cost of relations

On 24 December 1989 the Soviet central authorities took the first step
in putting an end to the deception that was their annexation of the Baltic

with the USSR. The great majority of countries in the world accept the de jure
incorporation of these States.

Nevertheless, the fact is that no good purpose will now be served in pretending that
these States will again have, as they did only between the two World Wars, a separate
international sovereignty. It is deluding and deceiving people from those countries who
have settled in Australia to give them the impression that any Australian government
would promote the detachment of those countries from the Soviet Union' (6 AYIL,
1978, 230).

In November of the same year the Prime Minister added: '1. Prior to the recognition
of the incorporation of Latvia, Estonia and Lithuania into the Soviet Union as de jure
incorporation there was no extradition treaty in force between Australia and the
U.S.S.R. Australian citizens wishing to visit the three Baltic States had to apply to a
Soviet Embassy or Consulate for a visa, and a person residing in one of the three Baltic
States who wished to enter Australia as a migrant had to comply with the relevant
provisions of Soviet law regarding exit permits and had to apply to the Australian
Embassy in Moscow for migrant visa. Before 1940, Australia had succeeded to extradition treaties with the Governments which controlled the Baltic States up to the time
of the incorporation. After the Soviet Union seized control of the States, these treaties
remained in force in theory, but in practice ceased to have any effect. The Leader of the
Opposition, when Attorney-General, clearly accepted this situation in the debate on
the Extradition (Foreign States) Bill 1966. The recognition of the incorporation as
incorporation de jure thus simply accepts what has been a reality for over thirty years.

2. Recognition does not necessarily imply either approval of the way in which
governmental control was established or of the controlling government's policies; it is
rather an acknowledgement of existing realities.

3. During the period before Australia's recognition of the incorporation of the area
into the USSR Australia had no formal governmental relations with the three governments which as members of the Soviet Union were effectively administering the Baltic
States. Nor did Australia have effective relations with governments in exile. Australia
accepted, however, the de facto situation that the Soviet Government was in effective
control of Lithuania, Latvia and Estonia' (*ibid.*, 230–1).

Following the election of a new Liberal–Country Party Government on 4 December
1975, the new Government decided to withdraw de jure recognition of the incorporation of the Baltic States into the Soviet Union. On 7 April 1976 a Minister
representing the Minister for Foreign Affairs stated the following in the Australian Senate: 'The Commonwealth Government implemented its decision to withdraw de jure
recognition of the incorporation of the Baltic States into the Soviet Union soon after its
assumption of office in December 1975. On 17 December 1975 the Government
instructed the Australian ambassador in Moscow that he and members of his staff
should not in future make official visits to Estonia, Latvia and Lithuania. Mr. R.G.
McComas, who was the honorary consul for Latvia before the previous Government's
decision in July 1974 to give de jure recognition, has been informed that he may resume
his function as honorary consul. It should be observed that the question of recognition
in this connection is not one of the recognition of statehood or of a government, but simply one of title to territory. This Government is thus saying no more than that it does
not accept the legality of the Soviet annexation of the Baltic States. Whatever may have
been said on this subject in the past cannot prevent this Government from making
known its own view of the matter' (7 AYIL, 1981, 432).

States. The Congress of USSR People's Deputies found that the secret Molotov–Ribbentrop accords, which provided for the division of Middle Eastern Europe into two spheres of influence and gave the Soviet Union free reign within its sphere, were contrary to international law and, as such, had no legal basis and were invalid from their inception.[4]

Following this announcement the Baltic republics embarked on a programme to reverse the consequences of the illegal agreements concluded in 1939. On 11 March 1990, the Lithuanian legislature boldly declared its independence from the Soviet Union and adopted legal acts and political resolutions affirming the restoration of the pre-1940 independent Lithuanian State.[5] Latvia and Estonia also issued declarations of independence but these were more cautious in tenor: instead of unilaterally declaring independence, the constitutional authorities approved legislation setting in motion a gradual process of secession from the Soviet Union.[6]

Lithuania, Latvia, and Estonia premised their right to independence on the invalidity of the Soviet Union's secret agreements with Hitler in 1939 and the illegal incorporation of the republics into the Soviet Union in 1940. Characterizing the Soviet Union's forcible occupation and annexation of the Baltic States as international crimes which by their very nature could not possibly give rise to a valid legal title, they emphasized the *de jure* continuity of the pre-1940 Baltic States. Not surprisingly, preferring to ground their action in international law as opposed to Soviet constitutional law, they chose not to invoke Article 72 of the USSR Constitution, which granted each republic an unqualified right to secede from the USSR.

Most remarkably, in a world in which at present every disaffected group seems to assert a right to self-determination, those perhaps most justified in doing so, the Baltic republics, refrained from such a move. Instead they chose to rely solely on the illegality of the 1939 Molotov–Ribbentrop accords and Stalin's violation of the international norms prohibiting the use of force. Although they stressed that the 1940 annexations were contrary to the will of the people, the Baltic legislatures did not invoke in express terms a right to self-determination.

Arguably, two political motives drove Estonia, Latvia, and Lithuania to pursue this strategy. First, by basing their moves toward independence on the illegality of the 1940 annexations, the Baltic republics permitted President Gorbachev to apply different standards to the Baltics than to the

[4] *Keesing's*, 1990, 37258.
[5] *Keesing's*, 1990, 37300.   [6] *Keesing's*, 1990, 37460–1 (Latvia) and 37323 (Estonia).

other Soviet republics pushing for independence. Second, by avoiding the invocation of the international legal right to self-determination and basing independence on the invalidity of the 1939 Molotov–Ribbentrop pact and the *de jure* continuity of the pre-1940 Baltic States, the Baltic leaders constructed a good case against the Soviet referendum scheme adopted on 7 April 1990 (see below). This is important since neither Estonia, with an Estonian population of 64 per cent, nor Latvia, with a Latvian population of 53 per cent, was likely to achieve independence under the 7 April 1990 Soviet law that required approval by a two-thirds majority.[7]

The position advanced by the Soviet Union

The Soviet Union regarded the Baltic republics' declarations of independence or 're-establishment' as lacking any legal validity. It recognized that the Baltics had a constitutional right to self-determination but it insisted that the right was tempered by the 'political, economic, social, territorial, legal, and other problems that arise' when a State secedes from a federation.[8] According to President Gorbachev, the scope of the constitutional right to self-determination turned, in part, on the needs and interests of the Soviet Union and the programme of 'perestroika'. The Soviet government also stressed that any exercise of self-determination must take into account the rights of non-Lithuanian, non-Estonian and non-Latvian Russians living within the republics.

On 7 April 1990 the USSR Supreme Soviet passed a law concerning the procedures for resolving matters connected with a Union Republic's secession from the Soviet Union. This law was never implemented following the rapid disintegration of the USSR. The then Baltic republics were recognized by many States as independent and sovereign in 1990 and re-acquired their political independence.

---

[7] On the Baltic Republics and self-determination, see generally B. Meissner, *Die Sowietunion, die Baltischen Staaten und das Völkerrecht*, Cologne 1956; S. P. Sinha, 'Self-Determination in International Law and Its Applicability to the Baltic Peoples', in *Res Baltica – A Collection of Essays in Honour of the Memory of A. Bilmanis*, Leiden 1968; B. Meissner, 'The Right of Self-Determination after Helsinki and its Significance for the Baltic Nations', 13 Case WRJIL, 1981, 375–384.

[8] Resolution of 15 March 1990 of the Extraordinary Third USSR Congress of Peoples' Deputies, on the Resolutions of 10–12 March 1990 Adopted by the Supreme Soviet of the Lithuanian SSR.

The rights of the Baltic republics under international law

In the case of the Baltic republics, as for instance in that of Palestine, the interesting issue is not whether a right to self-determination exists under international law but how that existing right is to be exercised. The existence of the right is a given, despite the fact that the principle of self-determination did not ripen into a right until the 1960s – more than twenty years after the 1940 invasion. The Soviet Union's forcible acquisition of the Baltic States in violation of the existing prohibition against the use of force, subsequently reinforced by the adoption of the United Nations Charter, later gave rise to a right to self-determination (i.e., the right to be free from foreign occupation or domination) – as soon as a *norm* on this subject evolved in the world community, and in the absence of any *acquiescence* by the whole international community.

Although the existence of the right was certain, the proper means of implementing the right was not. International law did not specify whether the Baltic republics were entitled to secede from the Soviet Union by virtue of a unilateral act, as attempted by Lithuania in March 1990, or whether they were to conclude a settlement with the Soviet Union prior to declaring independence. More specifically, international law was silent as to the issue of whether the acquiescence of the Soviet government was required. On the other hand, the fact that – in spite of the long duration of effective Soviet control over the Baltic republics (fifty years!) – the United States and several other Western States had never acquiesced in the Soviet Union's claims to sovereign title over the Baltic States, preferring instead to recognize the *de jure* continuity of the pre-1940 Baltic States, was suggestive but not determinative of the issue.

It must, however, be emphasized that international law, although deficient in many respects, chiefly as regards precise procedures for exercising self-determination against a foreign occupant (see above, Chapter 6), did offer an important guideline. As I pointed out above (Chapter 5), the legal *principle* of self-determination sets out the core of self-determination by providing that a people must be allowed to express its free and genuine will concerning its future. Taking their cue from this, the Baltic republics held referendums on whether or not to secede from the Soviet Union and achieve independence.[9] In these referendums the

---

[9] A referendum was held in *Lithuania* in February 1991; 90.47 per cent of voters favoured independence (voters had been asked the question: 'Are you in favour of the Lithuanian State being an independent, democratic Republic?'); see *Keesing's*, 1991,

overwhelming majority opted for independent statehood. The Baltic republics can therefore be said to have applied the general principle and its legal implications with much ingenuity. True, no international monitoring of the referendums was provided for, nor was a broader choice of options offered to the populations concerned, than the alternative between seceding or remaining within the Soviet fold. It would nevertheless seem that the populations concerned were enabled to make a real and democratic choice; it is symptomatic that no objection was raised by the Soviet authorities based on alleged abuses or mishandling of the referendums. On the other hand, the central Soviet authorities would not have permitted any international supervision. As for the limited character of the alternatives offered, it is difficult to envisage any further option – save for integration into a confederation of sovereign Baltic States, which was not a realistic prospect at the time.

Rights versus reality

Although the international community agreed that the Baltic Republics had a right to self-determination, support for their rapid move toward independence was limited. At first the Conference on Security and Co-operation in Europe (CSCE) rejected the Republics' petition for fully fledged membership. Poland was one of the few States which, as early as 12 March 1990, supported Lithuania's self-determination, although expressing the hope that this could be achieved peacefully through negotiations.[10] The statement issued on 26 April 1990 by President François Mitterand and Chancellor Helmut Kohl was indicative of the international community's somewhat circumspect approach; the two statesmen affirmed the validity of Lithuania's declaration of independence but nevertheless urged Lithuania to 'suspend' it, as well as the attendant legislation, pending negotiations with the central authorities of the Soviet Union. Mitterand and Kohl noted that the Lithuanian declarations were valid 'because they rest on a universally accepted principle – the self-

---

38014 and 38419. As for *Latvia*, a referendum was held in March 1991; 73.68 per cent of voters favoured independence, which was declared on 21 August 1991 (see *Keesing's* 1991, 38078 and 38419); the voters were asked: 'Are you for a democratic and independent Latvian Republic?'). A referendum was held in March 1991 in *Estonia*; 77.83 per cent of the voters voted yes to the question 'Do you want the restoration of the state of independence of the Estonian Republic?' (*Keesing's*, 1991, 38078, 38419).

[10] *Keesing's*, 1990, 37300.

determination of peoples'[11] – but were unwilling to recognize the re-established State immediately.

The reluctance on the part of Western States to provide strong support for the Baltics undoubtedly stemmed from the widely held belief that a unified democratic Soviet Union was in the interest of the international community. The Mitterand–Kohl statement urging the Baltic republics to negotiate a settlement with the federal authorities was motivated by a desire to facilitate the Soviet Union's gradual transformation from autocracy to democracy. The two leaders, although they were keen to restate their upholding of the principle of self-determination of peoples, did not press for its immediate application. Intent on assisting President Gorbachev in his monumental task of holding the Soviet Union together, France, Germany, and other States were reluctant fervently to support a political and legal principle which, being often invoked by ardent nationalists and separatists, could be perceived as an instrument that would cause dramatic disruption to the fabric of Soviet society.

The case of the Baltic republics neatly illustrates how concerns about 'global balance' and the territorial integrity of the Soviet Union restrained, or at least slowed down, not only the furtherance of, but also international support for, the quest for self-determination.

The other Soviet republics[12]

Unlike the Baltic States, the remaining twelve Soviet republics had no right of self-determination, let alone secession, under current international law. In contrast, such a right was explicitly laid down in Article 72 of the 1977 Soviet Constitution, which, however, had remained a dead letter.[13] It should be added that the law hastily adopted in 1990, providing for the

---

[11] *The International Herald Tribune*, 27 April 1990, 1:6.
[12] On self-determination and the Soviet break up, see generally Halperin, Scheffer, and Small, *Self-Determination in the New World Order*, 27–32; R. McCorquodale, 'Self-Determination Beyond the Colonial Context and its Potential Impact on Africa', 4 AJICL, 1992, 596–9; R. Müllerson, 'Self-Determination of Peoples and the Dissolution of the USSR', *Essays in Honour of Wang Tieya*, Dordrecht 1993, 567–85.
[13] Art. 72 provided that 'Each Union Republic shall retain the right freely to secede from the USSR.' This provision was closely linked to Art. 70(1), whereby 'The Union of Soviet Socialist Republics is an integral, federal, multinational state formed on the principle of Socialist federalism as a result of the free self-determination of nations and the voluntary association of equal Soviet Socialist Republics'. See generally J. Hazard, 'Soviet Republics in International Law', *Encyclopedia*, vol. X, 1985, 418–22.

holding of referendums by the Soviet republics, clearly failed to meet international standards on self-determination.[14]

This law, which purported to implement Article 72 of the Soviet Constitution (see Article 1) made the whole process of possible secession from the Soviet Union so cumbersome and complicated, that one may wonder very much whether it ultimately constituted a true application of self-determination or was rather intended to pose a set of insurmountable hurdles to the implementation of that principle.[15]

It is apparent from its text that the law made it extremely difficult for republics successfully to negotiate the entire secession process. Admittedly, in other respects this law is undoubtedly very significant. For one thing, it was the first piece of national legislation regulating the right of secession in

---

[14] Russian text in *Pravda* (first edn), 7 April 1990.

[15] In short, the Law provided that a Republic could secede if a referendum was first requested by the Republic's Supreme Soviet or by at least one-tenth of the USSR citizens permanently resident on the Republic's territory and possessing the right to vote under USSR legislation (Art. 2(1)). The referendum was to be held by secret ballot no sooner than 6 and no later than 9 months later: Art. 2(3). Provision was made for observers from the USSR, or other Republics or from the United Nations (if the USSR Supreme Soviet deemed it necessary) (Art. 5). Secession required a two-thirds majority of the Republic's electorate: Art. 6(1). Complete independence could, however, only be obtained after a transition period of a maximum of five years, during which time 'matters arising in connection with the Republic's secession from the USSR must be resolved': Art. 9(1). Moreover, a confirmation referendum requiring a two-thirds majority could be requested at the end of the five-year period by the Republic's Supreme Soviet or by one-tenth of the USSR citizens permanently resident on the Republic's territory and possessing the right to vote under USSR legislation: Art. 19(1). If a two-thirds majority in favour of secession was not then reached, the decision on secession was to be regarded as 'repealed' and 'the procedures envisaged by this Law terminated': Art. 19(2).

Even if the required two-thirds majority for secession was reached, this was not the end of the story. Completion of the secession process was subject to ratification by the USSR Congress of People's Deputies, in that the Congress was to adopt 'a resolution confirming the completion of the process for co-ordinating the interests and satisfying the claims of the seceding Republic, on the one hand, and of the USSR, union Republics or autonomous Republics, autonomous formations and ethnic groups referred to in Art. 3(2) of this Law, on the other hand': Art. 20(1). The Law also stipulated that if a referendum in a Republic failed to endorse secession, a new referendum could only be held ten years later (Art. 10).

Furthermore, the Law provided that an autonomous Republic or district within a Republic had the right, subject to referendum, to remain within the Soviet Union should the rest of the Republic choose to secede (Art. 3(1)). Similarly, areas within a seceding Republic populated predominantly by ethnic groups that formed the majority there, and a minority in the Republic, and which did not enjoy regional autonomy, were allowed, subject to a referendum and negotiations, to remain within the Soviet Union (Art. 3(2)).

a detailed way. For another, it made extensive and careful provision for all the legal issues raised by the possible secession of the Republics.[16] In spite of these merits, the law was, however, inadequate, for the reasons mentioned above. It is therefore only natural that it was never applied; instead it was rapidly superseded by the dramatic events in the USSR, that brought about the precipitous collapse of the Federation.

The process of independence by the twelve republics therefore occurred *outside the realm of law, both international and municipal.* It was a *de facto* process precipitated by the political crisis at the centre of the Soviet Union and the correlative increase in the strength of centrifugal forces.

Once again, it is striking to note that most of the twelve Soviet republics also felt it necessary to hold referendums on whether or not to secede from the Soviet Union.[17] This clearly proves that the republics, although lacking any legal claim to secession or independence under international law, *sought a form of legitimation* for their breaking away in the general legal principle of self-determination. They therefore had resort to the practice of referendums, which undoubtedly constitutes a fair and widely used application of that principle.

It should, moreover, be emphasized that other States as well looked upon the progressive dissolution of the Soviet Union from the point of view of the principle of self-determination. This approach was taken, in particular, by the European Community and its Member States. When the Foreign Ministers of the Twelve States met on 16 December 1991 to decide on the stand to be taken in response to the breakaway republics of the Soviet Union and Yugoslavia, they eventually adopted a set of 'guidelines' on the recognition of those republics. Self-determination came into play in two respects. It was firstly formally proclaimed as some form of preamble or general premise. The EC declaration started off with the following words: 'The Community and its member States confirm their

---

[16] See, in particular Articles 12–18 of the Law (Art. 12 deals with State borders and military facilities; Art. 13 with succession to treaties concluded by the USSR; Art. 14 with matters of ownership and financial settlements, as well as the status of territories within the seceding Republic but not belonging to it; Art. 15 with citizenship; Art. 16 with human rights; Art. 17 with matters of extradition; Art. 18 with administrative and criminal cases).

[17] An independence referendum was held in *Georgia* on 31 March 1991 (see *Keesing's*, 1991, 38078), in *Turkmenia* on 26 October 1991 (see *Keesing's*, 1991, 38538), in *Ukraine* on 1 December 1991 (see *Keesing's*, 1991, 38492, 38656), in *Uzbekistan* on 29 December 1991 (see *Keesing's*, 1991, 38657). In *Moldavia* a referendum was announced in June 1991 (see *Keesing's*, 1991, 38492), but was only followed by a declaration of independence on 27 August 1991 (*Keesing's*, 1991, 38373, 38417).

attachment to the principles of the Helsinki Act and the Charter of Paris, in particular the principle of self-determination.' By these words the Twelve intended to emphasize that they regarded the progressive breaking up of the two States as a realization of the *political principle* of self-determination and as a historical process furthered by the concept that each people should freely choose its international political status.

Self-determination also came into play in another, more novel respect. Among the various requirements the nascent Republics were to meet in order for them to obtain recognition,[18] the Twelve put forward the requirement of respect for the 'rule of law, democracy and human rights', as well as the establishment of 'guarantees for the rights of ethnic and national groups and minorities in accordance with the commitment subscribed to

[18] The text of the 'Declaration on the Guidelines on the Recognition of New States in Eastern Europe and in the Soviet Union' is as follows: 'The Community and its member States confirm their attachment to the principles of the Helsinki Final Act and the Charter of Paris, in particular the principle of self-determination. They affirm their readiness to recognize, subject to the normal standards of international practice and the political realities in each case, those new States which, following the historic changes in the region, have constituted themselves on a democratic basis, have accepted the appropriate international obligations and have committed themselves in good faith to a peaceful process and to negotiations.

Therefore, they adopt a common position on the process of recognition of these new States, which requires:

– respect for the provisions of the Charter of the United Nations and the commitments subscribed to in the Final Act of Helsinki and in the Charter of Paris, especially with regard to the rule of law, democracy and human rights;
– guarantees for the rights of ethnic and national groups and minorities in accordance with the commitments subscribed to in the framework of the CSCE;
– respect for the inviolability of all frontiers which can only be changed by peaceful means and by common agreement;
– acceptance of all relevant commitments with regard to disarmament and nuclear non-proliferation as well as to security and regional stability;
– commitment to settle by agreement, including where appropriate by recourse to arbitration, all questions concerning State succession and regional disputes.

The Community and its member States will not recognize entities which are the result of aggression. They would take account of the effects of recognition on neighbouring States.

The commitment to these principles opens the way to recognition by the Community and its member States and to the establishment of diplomatic relations. It could be laid down in agreements' (see 4 EJIL, 1993, 72).

On the criteria set out by the European Community for the recognition of secessionist European States, see generally R. Bieber, 'European Community Recognition of Eastern European States: A New Perspective for International Law?', 86 Proceedings ASIL, 1992, 374–6.

in the framework of the CSCE'. In other words, recognition was made contingent on *democratic rule*, that is, *internal self-determination.*

It should be noted here that this approach was in some respects profoundly innovative, so much so that one could even term it revolutionary. Indeed, by making their recognition of secessionist republics conditional on respect for democracy, the Twelve forcefully affirmed *the close link existing between external and internal self-determination.* They made it clear that they were prepared to endorse the achievement of independent statehood, i.e. external self-determination, only on condition that the breakaway republics fully respected the principle of representative democracy, that is, internal self-determination. For the first time in the world community the inextricable connection and interdependence between the *two dimensions* of self-determination was brought to the fore (this connection had no doubt remained theoretical and abstract in the UN Covenant on Civil and Political Rights, on account of the loose language in which both Article 1 and the various provisions on political rights were couched in the Covenant).

In addition, the Twelve stressed the *link between self-determination and the protection of minorities.* They made it clear that internal self-determination could not be accepted without the full protection of minorities, just as no endorsement could be given to external self-determination unless internal self-determination was realized.

The crisis in Yugoslavia

Yugoslavia, a federation of six republics with a population of 23 million, was formed under Tito's Communist partisan army at the end of the Second World War. Since Tito's death in 1980, the country has been plagued by surging nationalism and separatism and federal authority has steadily diminished. Inter- and intra-republican strife has broken out, the most prominent examples being: the desire on the part of Slovenia, Croatia, Bosnia-Herzegovina, and Macedonia to secede; Serbia's treatment of the nearly 2 million Albanians forming 90 per cent of the population in the Autonomous Province of Kosovo; Serbia's plan to impose customs duties on goods entering Serbia from other Yugoslav Republics and to withhold Serbia's payments to the federal Republic; the demands of the Serbians living in South-Eastern Croatia for an 'autonomous State'. All these claims and actions were compounded by the growing hatred between the three principal ethnic groups (Muslims, Croats, and Serbs), that led to appalling internecine strife and egregious violations of basic human rights. These and other problems led Yugoslavia to civil war and its subsequent break up.

As in the case of the twelve Soviet republics, under international law the six Yugoslav republics had no right to external self-determination. In addition, no such right was proclaimed in the Yugoslav constitution.[19] Interestingly, several provisions of the 1974 Yugoslav Constitution expressly proclaim that Yugoslavia is based upon and actually constitutes an incarnation of the principle of the self-determination of peoples, nations, and nationalities and also pursues self-determination as an objective of foreign policy.[20] However, unlike the Soviet Constitution, that of Yugoslavia does not make specific provision for the right of one of the six constituent republics to secede.[21] In addition, Article 5(4) stipulates that 'The frontiers of the Socialist Federal Republic of Yugoslavia may not be altered without the consent of all Republics and Autonomous Provinces.'[22]

---

[19] See, in particular, B. Bagwell, 'Yugoslavian Constitutional Questions: Self-Determination and Secession of Member Republics', 21 *Georgia Journal International Comparative Law*, 1991, 489 ff. More generally, on the question of Yugoslavia and self-determination, see D. Rusinow, 'Yugoslavia: Balkan Break up?', 83 *Foreign Policy*, Summer 1991, 143–59; M. Weller, 'The International Response to the Dissolution of the Socialist Republic of Yugoslavia', 86 AJIL, 1992, 596–607; Halperin, Scheffer, and Small, *Self-Determination in the New World Order*, 32–8; Bieber, 'European Community Recognition of Eastern European States: A New Perspective for International Law?', 374–8; R. F. Iglar, 'The Constitutional Crisis in Yugoslavia and the International Law of Self-Determination: Slovenia's and Croatia's Right to Secede', 15 *Boston College International and Comparative Law Review*, 1992, 213–39; R. McCorquodale, 'Self-Determination Beyond the Colonial Context and its Potential Impact on Africa', 599–600. See also D. Türk, 'National Minorities in Austria, Italy and in the successor States of the former Yugoslavia', in Ermacora, Tretter, and Pelzl, *Volksgruppen im Spannungsfeld von Recht und Souveranität in Mittel-und Osteuropa*, 48–54.

[20] See e.g., the Preamble ('Introductory Part-Basic Principles'), Principle I, ('The nations of Yugoslavia, proceeding from the right of every nation to self-determination, including the right to secession, on the basis of their will freely expressed in the common struggle of all nations and nationalities in the National Liberation War and Socialist Revolution, and in conformity with their historic aspirations, aware that further consolidation of their brotherhood and unity is in the common interest, have, together with the nationalities with which they live, united in a federal republic of free and equal nations and nationalities and founded a socialist federal community of working people – the Socialist Federal Republic of Yugoslavia, in which, in the interests of each nation and nationality separately and of all of them together, they shall realize and ensure: . . . '.) See also Principle III, Principle VII (Yugoslavia 'shall strive' 'for the right of nations to self-determination and national independence, and for their right to wage a liberation war to attain these aims'), Articles 1, 2, 3, 244–9.

[21] See, however, Bagwell, 'Yugoslavian Constitutional Questions', 508–21.

[22] The 1974 Constitution was amended in 1988 but no right of self-determination was provided for.

It should be added that a draft law on the right to self-determination, hastily adopted by a Committee of the Yugoslav Federal Assembly on 20 January 1992, was never passed by the plenary assembly because it was rapidly overtaken by the dramatic secession of various Republics.[23]

The achievement of independence by Slovenia, Croatia, Bosnia-Herzegovina, and Macedonia can therefore be seen as a revolutionary process that has taken place beyond the regulation of the existing body of laws.

However, just as in the case of the 'Soviet' republics, the Yugoslav breakaway republics deemed it fit to hold referendums before declaring their independence.[24] In addition, the EC 'guidelines' for the recognition of seceding States, referred to above, were also applied.[25]

---

[23] See *Keesing's*, 1992, 38703.

[24] Slovenia voted for independence in a referendum in December 1990 (*Keesing's*, 1990, 37924). On 20 February 1991, the Slovene Assembly adopted almost unanimously a resolution on the 'dissociation of Slovenia from Yugoslavia (*Keesing's*, 1991, 38019). The government announced on 8 May 1991 that it would secede by 26 June 1991 (*Keesing's*, 1991, 38274). Slovenia declared its independence on 25 June 1991.

In Croatia a referendum was held on 19 May 1991: 93.2 per cent of those who went to the polls voted in favour of the proposal that Croatia, as 'a sovereign and independent country which guarantees cultural autonomy and all civic rights to the Serbs and members of other nationalities in Croatia, may with other republics join a confederation of sovereign States' (*Keesing's*, 1991, 38204).

In Macedonia a referendum was held on 8 September 1991: 95 per cent voted in favour of 'a sovereign and independent Macedonia with a right to enter a union of sovereign States of Yugoslavia' (*Keesing's*, 1991, 38420).

In Bosnia-Herzegovina the Parliament declared the Republic's sovereignty on 15 October 1991. As the EC Arbitration Committee had recommended that an independence referendum be held (see below, pp. 000–00), citizens of Bosnia-Herzegovina voted on independence on 29 February and 1 March 1992; 63 per cent of the population took part (the Serb population boycotted the referendum), with 99 per cent of those voting favouring independence (cf. Halpern, Scheffer, and Small, *Self-Determination in the New World Order*, 157).

It should be added that on 11 April 1991 the summit of the presidents of Yugoslavia's six republics produced an agreement to *hold a referendum* on the future structure of the country (ideas for that structure had crystallized into two models: (a) a community of independent and sovereign States, as advocated by Croatia and Slovenia; (b) a united federal State, in which representatives continued to delegate some sovereign rights to a central government; Serbia and Montenegro favoured this solution, while Macedonia and Bosnia-Herzegovina advocated a compromise solution but inclined towards the first option) (see *Keesing's*, 1991, 38163).

[25] On 16 December 1991 the Twelve adopted the following declaration concerning Yugoslavia: 'The European Community and its member States discussed the situation in Yugoslavia in the light of their guidelines on the recognition of new States in Eastern Europe and in the Soviet Union. They adopted a common position with regard to the recognition of the Yugoslav Republics. In this connection they concluded the following:

That which markedly differentiates the achievement of independence by Slovenia, Croatia, Bosnia-Herzegovina, and Macedonia from the independence process of the 'Soviet' republics is that a *monitoring process* was set up within the framework of the 'Peace Conference on Yugoslavia' established by the EC, for the purpose of ascertaining whether the breakaway republics met the requirements set out by the Twelve. The monitoring process hinged on an 'Arbitration Committee' consisting of the presidents of the Constitutional Courts of France, Italy, FRG, Belgium, and Spain. The 'Arbitration Committee' tackled, in its first three 'Opinions', some general legal problems.[26] In so doing the 'Committee' stressed the importance of the 'rights of peoples and minorities' and even defined the norms that provided for these as part of *jus cogens*.[27]

> The Community and its member States agree to recognize the independence of all the Yugoslav Republics fulfilling all the conditions set out below. The implementation of this decision will take place on January 15, 1992.
>
> They are therefore inviting all Yugoslav Republics to state by 23 December whether:
>
> - they wish to be recognized as independent States;
> - they accept the commitments contained in the above-mentioned guidelines;
> - they accept the provisions laid down in the draft Convention – especially those in Chapter II on human rights and rights of national or ethnic groups – under consideration by the Conference on Yugoslavia;
> - they continue to support the continuation of the Conference on Yugoslavia.
>
> The applications of those Republics which reply positively will be submitted through the Chair of the Conference to the Arbitration Commission for advice before the implementation date.
>
> In the meantime, the Community and its member States request the U.N. Secretary General and the U.N. Security Council to continue their efforts to establish an effective cease-fire and promote a peaceful and negotiated outcome to the conflict. They continue to attach the greatest importance to the early deployment of a U.N. peace-keeping force referred to in U.N. Security Council Resolution 724.
>
> The Community and its member States also require a Yugoslav Republic to commit itself, prior to recognition, to adopt constitutional and political guarantees ensuring that it has no territorial claims towards a neighbouring Community State and that it will conduct no hostile propaganda activities versus a neighbouring Community State, including the use of a denomination which implies territorial claims' (see 4 EJIL, 1993, 73).

[26] In the first Opinion, it discussed the question of whether the seceding Republics could succeed to Yugoslavia and, if so, by virtue of which procedures; in the second, it dwelt on the question of whether the Serbian population in Croatia and in Bosnia-Herzegovina had a right to self-determination; the third Opinion dealt with the question as to whether the internal boundaries between the Yugoslav Republics could be regarded as international frontiers. For the text of the Opinion, see 3 EJIL, 1992, 182–5.

[27] See the first Opinion, *ibid.*, 182–3.

In the successive four Opinions the Arbitration Committee made pronouncements on the requests for recognition made by Bosnia-Herzegovina, Croatia, Macedonia, and Slovenia respectively.[28] In all four 'Opinions' the Committee ascertained, in particular, whether or not referendums on independence had been held in each republic, as well as whether each republic had committed itself to respecting the rights of individuals, groups, and minorities. Strikingly, whereas in the case of Croatia, Macedonia, and Slovenia it was found that all the requirements had been satisfied, in the case of Bosnia-Herzegovina it was emphasized that no referendum had been held involving the whole population. Instead, a plebiscite had been held on 10 November 1991 by the 'Serbian people of Bosnia-Herzegovina', which had opted for a 'common Yugoslav State'. Furthermore, on 21 December 1991 an 'Assembly of the Serbian people of Bosnia-Herzegovina' had adopted a resolution for the creation of a 'Serbian Republic of Bosnia-Herzegovina' and on 9 January 1992 had proclaimed the independence of this republic. On 11 January 1992 the Arbitration Committee therefore concluded that 'under these circumstances . . . the expression of the will of the populations of Bosnia-Herzegovina to set up the Socialist Republic of Bosnia-Herzegovina as a sovereign and independent State could not be regarded as fully established'. It went on to say that this appraisal could be modified if 'safeguards' were established by the Republic, 'if necessary by way of a referendum in which all citizens of the Republic were to participate, under international supervision'.

It is apparent from the above that the Arbitration Committee regarded the holding of an internationally monitored referendum involving *the whole population* as an indispensable element for the granting of international recognition of Bosnia-Herzegovina as an independent State. The Committee thus elevated the referendum to the status of a basic requirement for the *legitimation of secession*.

On 29 February and 1 March 1992 a referendum was held; the overwhelming majority of those who took part in the polls voted for independence, although many Serbs boycotted the vote.[29] Subsequently, on 6 April 1992 the Twelve and the EC granted their recognition, followed, the next day, by the United States and Croatia.

---

[28] See the text of these Opinions in 4 EJIL, 1993, 74–84.
[29] See *The Observer*, 26 April 1992, 11, and above, note 24.

Concluding remarks

The birth of new States in the former Soviet Union and Yugoslavia has occurred outside the realm of both municipal and international law – except in the case of the three Baltic republics.

However, the body of international rules on self-determination has had a remarkable bearing on the whole process of secession. Their impact has been twofold, although at different levels. First, self-determination has operated at the level of *political rhetoric*, as a *set of political principles* legitimizing the secession of national States from central, oppressive State structures. Second, self-determination has provided *the legal tools for establishing the demands of the seceding peoples* to achieve independent statehood: referendums have been held in almost all the breakaway republics in order to verify the will of the populations concerned.

The process of the dissolution of the two States and the consequent birth of the new republics is legally relevant in another respect. Third parties, namely the Twelve member States of the European Community have established *general criteria for recognizing the new States*. Among these criteria there have emerged (a) the free expression of the will of the population concerned, by way of plebiscites or referendums and (b) the firm commitment to respect the rule of law, human rights, and the rights of groups and minorities. Thus, the basic requirement of *internal self-determination* has been proclaimed and indeed respect for it, as well as respect for the rights of minorities, have been raised to the status of *sine qua non* conditions before the endorsement of *external* self-determination.

It is well known that in Croatia and Bosnia-Herzegovina, as well as in a few former Soviet republics, secession has rekindled old hatreds and led to *loathsome* bloodshed. The realization of self-determination, instead of gradually unravelling old inter-ethnic enmities and solving deep-rooted conflicts, has triggered a settling of accounts that has been ferociously carried out by force of arms, thus resulting in the negation of the very essence of self-determination. The existing body of law on self-determination cannot be held responsible for these frightening consequences: primary blame must be laid on the momentous errors of the past, the tenacious unwillingness of the different ethnic groups to solve their disputes peacefully, and the astounding inability of the world community to impose peaceful and sensible settlements. Nevertheless, it cannot be denied that international legal rules could prove more helpful, were they more alert to modern exigencies; in the last chapter, I shall endeavour to suggest possible ways to develop current international law.

PART IV

The new trends emerging in the world community

11

Attempts at expanding
self-determination

Introduction

So far, I have discussed some of the international legal instruments such as
the UN Charter or the UN Covenants on Human Rights. I have also
analysed State practice, including some authoritative UN resolutions
(chiefly the 1960 Declaration on Colonial Peoples and the 1970
Declaration on Friendly Relations) which in some respects can be regarded
as a significant element of State practice. This examination has made it
possible to pinpoint the content and scope of the most important treaty
provisions on self-determination, as well as the customary norms (the
principle and rules) on the subject.

It may now be appropriate to consider two international texts which also
deal with self-determination but possess a formal status that is different
from that of the international instruments so far discussed. Neither
document is a legally binding treaty and both have a primarily political and
moral value. The first is the Helsinki Declaration adopted in 1975 by the
(then) thirty-five States constituting the Conference on Security and
Cooperation in Europe (CSCE), the other is the Declaration adopted in
1976 at Algiers by a private group of politicians, trade-union leaders,
representatives of liberation movements, and intellectuals from various
countries.

As is apparent from these brief descriptions, the two texts differ radically
from each other, both in origin and formal status, as well as – as we shall
see – content. Undoubtedly, the former is endowed with much greater
political force and moral weight, since it was solemnly adopted by the
thirty-five governments which undertook to abide by it. In contrast,
the latter text emanates from private individuals not acting in any official

capacity; therefore, it merely constitutes a declaration of the ideals of those individuals – however important the intellectual and moral standing of those individuals may be. It follows that the former document can be of relevance with regard to the possible formation of a new general norm on self-determination, while the latter can only be taken as an expression of the feelings of a segment of public opinion.

In spite of these differences, it is worth examining both texts, for they both improve upon existing international legislation in some respects and to a large extent show the path the world community might take with a view to accommodating the aspirations of peoples and nations in a more satisfactory (or less unsatisfactory) manner than is currently provided for in the internationally binding legal rules.

Following the examination of these two texts, I shall dwell upon some new trends emerging in the world community at a law-making level: trends that are directed towards the gradual formation of a general international rule on internal self-determination. As we shall see, the two aforementioned texts point in the same direction, so that it can be safely argued that they are part and parcel of the new normative tendencies of the international community in the area of self-determination.

The Helsinki Final Act

General

The two situations which the UN Documents consider as giving rise to the right to external self-determination – colonialism and foreign occupation – are almost wholly absent in Europe (and the West generally). The only, arguably 'colonial' situation is Gibraltar, a very controversial and unclear issue that, because of its anomalous character, the world organization has so far been unable to settle (see chapter 9). There are no racist regimes in Europe comparable to those of South Africa or Southern Rhodesia and, with the exception of Cyprus, no forms of alien occupation exist that can be equated with the Israeli occupation of Arab lands. The logical conclusion should be that, to a very great extent, the principle of external self-determination has already been realized in Europe (as well as in the United States and Canada) and so, therefore, it would be pointless to codify and reaffirm it in some sort of 'regional' European instrument. Yet both North America and Europe are rife with cases falling within the scope of a *broader* concept of self-determination. Reference can be made to the

German nation, which in 1975 was still divided into two sovereign States, or to the Irish people, some of whom are now (legally) under British rule in Northern Ireland, to the question of Quebec and the issue of native Indians in Canada as well as the United States. Even more serious is the problem of ethnic, national, or linguistic minorities living in a number of European countries. These minorities clearly raise a question of internal self-determination. They also raise the problem of the limits or justifiable scope of self-determination. The same problem, though in a different context, arose in 1975 with regard to peoples living in authoritarian European States – provided, of course, a more comprehensive concept of internal self-determination is accepted than that reflected in the UN texts.

It is against this background that in 1973 the European States considered the Federal Republic of Germany's proposal that a provision on self-determination be included in the 1975 Helsinki Declaration.

The FRG urged the inclusion of the principle of self-determination with an eye towards facilitating the potential reunification of the two Germanies.[1] Clearly, the FRG was more interested in external self-determination. As the Foreign Minister of the FRG stated in Helsinki in 1973, 'it is the political aim of the FRG to help create a state of peace in Europe in which the German nation can regain its unity in free self-determination'.[2] Following West Germany's footsteps, a few States offered proposals that included the principle of self-determination. The Soviet Union and France advanced formulations that followed traditional lines but were couched in such general terms that they were even applicable to peoples living in sovereign (non-racist) States. Two other countries, Yugoslavia and The Netherlands, proposed innovative formulas that covered situations outside the scope of the UN texts.[3]

---

[1] H. S. Russel, 'The Helsinki Declaration: Brobdingnag or Liliput?', 70 AJIL, 1976, 269.

[2] Doc. CSCE/I/PV.3, 26.

[3] On the principle of self-determination in the Helsinki Declaration, see A. Cassese, 'The Helsinki Declaration and Self-determination', in T. Buergenthal (ed.), *Human Rights, International Law and the Helsinki Accord*, Montclair and New York 1977, 95 ff.; Arangio-Ruiz, 'Human Rights and Non-Intervention in the Helsinki Final Act', 223–31; T. Veiter, 'Das Selbstbestimmungsrecht als Menschenrecht', *Fest. für H.R. Klecatsky*, vol. II, Vienna 1980, 976–80; Arangio-Ruiz, 'Auto-determinazione (diritto dei popoli alla)', 4–5, 9–11.

The 1973 proposals

THE TEXTS OF THE FOUR PROPOSALS

The Soviet proposal included equal rights and the self-determination of peoples among the 'principles of primary significance' which States should strictly observe. However, self-determination was narrowly defined. Although it was heralded as the principle 'in accordance with which all peoples possess the right to establish the social regime and to choose the form of government which they consider expedient and necessary to secure the economic, social and cultural development of their country',[4] this definition only referred to internal self-determination. Even given this narrow definition of the principle, it remained a loose and somewhat ambiguous formulation of internal self-determination. In particular, it did not specify whether self-determination was a right to be implemented merely by the establishment of a sovereign State or whether it was a permanent right of people to political and social change. Furthermore, the Soviet text made no reference to the right of peoples to determine their status free from any outside interference.

It was left to the French to fill in the gaps. The French text, although hardly innovative, was exhaustive. Advancing traditional concepts and formulations, the French proposed:

En vertu de ce principe, tous les peuples ont le droit de determiner leur statut politique *interne et externe en toute liberté et sans ingérence extérieure* et de poursuivre leur développement économique, social et culturel et tous les Etats ont le devoir de respecter ce droit. Les Etats participant considèrent que le respect de ces principes doit guider leurs relations mutuelles comme il doit caractériser les rapports entre tous les Etats.[5]

The French draft was rejected in favour of fresher proposals, in particular, the texts submitted by Yugoslavia and The Netherlands. Departing from the traditional formulation of self-determination, Yugoslavia suggested that:

---

[4] Doc. CSCE/I/3.
[5] Doc. CSCE/II/A/12 (my italics). 'By virtue of this principle, all peoples have the right to determine their own political status, *both internal and external, with complete freedom and without outside interference* and to pursue their economic, social and cultural development. Further, all States have a duty to respect this right. The participating States believe that respect for these principles should govern their relations with one another and should also characterize relationships among all States.'

The participating States reaffirm the *universal significance* of the principle of equal rights and self-determination by peoples for the promotion of friendly relations and co-operation between States in Europe and the world as a whole and *for the eradication of any form of subjugation or of subordination contrary to the will of the peoples concerned.*

They will observe the right of every people freely to determine its political status and to pursue, independently and without external interference, its political, economic, social and cultural development. They will refrain from any forcible or other action denying the equal rights or the right of self-determination of any people.[6]

This definition, which encompasses both internal and external self-determination, is significant for two reasons. First, it places considerable emphasis on the universality of the principle, which, up until that time, had only been stressed by Western countries. Second, the Yugoslav proposal speaks of freedom from any form of (outside) interference. Given that the situations referred to in the UN instruments are an anomaly in Europe, the Yugoslav text addresses more pertinent matters. It refers to situations generally neglected in UN texts. This is made clear first in the sentence referring to the 'eradication of any form of subjugation or of subordination contrary to the will of the peoples concerned'. It is then reiterated by virtue of the statement that all people are entitled to determine their political status 'independently and without external interference'. In addition, all States must refrain 'from any forcible or other action' which would deny the right in question.

The Netherlands proposal contained other innovative elements. It stated:

Each participating State will act in its relations with any other participating State in conformity with the principle of equal rights and self-determination of peoples laid down in the United Nations Charter.

The participating States recognize the inalienable right of the people of every State freely *to choose, to develop, to adapt or to change* its political, economic, social and cultural systems without interference in any form by any other State or *group of States* and with *due respect to human rights and fundamental freedoms.*[7]

This text is striking because it refers to the UN Charter but not to the subsequent developments, for example, those of the Declaration on Friendly Relations. The specifications and also the qualifications of the principle of self-determination embodied in the post-1945 instruments

---

[6] Doc. CSCE/I/PV.3, 26 (my italics).   [7] Doc. CSCE/II/A/8 (my italics).

are therefore set aside. Even more remarkable is the fact that the Dutch proposal, confined to internal self-determination, explicitly states that all people have a right *to change* their political, economic, social, or cultural system free from external interferences (exercised either by a single State or by a group of States). This means that the principle of self-determination is a safeguard against any internal or external attempt to impose the preservation of the status quo. This was forcefully stressed in 1973 by the Foreign Ministers of The Netherlands[8] and Ireland.[9]

This doctrine of self-determination is in clear contrast with the pre-1989 Eastern Bloc view that so far as non-racist sovereign States were concerned, internal self-determination was not relevant because the right of self-determination ceased to apply when a people had attained its own sovereignty. According to the Dutch proposal the right is permanent: it is not destroyed once exercised. Furthermore, The Netherlands proposal establishes an important *link between self-determination and human rights*. The provision mandating that the right to social, political, economic, and cultural change be exercised with due respect for human rights and fundamental freedoms renders self-determination a progressive force: self-determination means the realization of greater respect for human rights. The Dutch proposal was clearly designed to allow the Eastern European countries gradually to evolve towards a less severe form of socialism, free from the Soviet Union's interference.

[8] The Dutch foreign minister observed: 'It can happen that a nation, which at some moment in its history has adopted a certain political or social-economic system, may want to adjust this system to changed circumstances. If in such a situation the peoples' democratic rights to adapt its structures were interfered with, either from within or especially from outside, tensions can build up which might endanger peace and security. The future system of relations in Europe should be flexible enough to allow for changes to occur without necessarily upsetting the international situation'. (Doc. CSCE/I/PV.7, 18 ff.)

[9] The Foreign Minister of Ireland stated: 'The first essential condition for European security as a whole is that each State exercise fair and democratic government capable of peaceful change and evolution in response to the evolving will of the people. Responsible government must have regard to the interests and aspirations of all sections of the community so that all these sections, even if in some cases unenthusiastically at times, can freely give their consent to it. Wherever injustice exists, wherever the rights of individuals are not fully respected, wherever governments are inflexible in response to the popular will, there are sown not only the seeds of internal discord but also the seeds of tension and instability in Europe as a whole. This is a truth which each of our governments has to recognize if we are serious in the pursuit of a genuine and lasting detente on our continent' (Doc. CSCE/I/PV.6 at 83).

THE DISCUSSION OF THE TEXTS

It is not easy to follow the debate that developed on the four proposals outlined above, partly because there are no records of some stages of the discussion and partly because the self-determination issue was closely intertwined with other questions. However, the following observations can be made.

First, a number of States expressed misgivings about the disruptive impact that the principle of self-determination might have on the territorial integrity of States. The majority of the thirty-five participating States have national minorities with which they must contend. Accordingly, many voiced the concern that an unqualified proclamation of the right of self-determination might kindle separatist aspirations to the detriment of national unity. Both Eastern and Western States urged that this danger be guarded against. A general consensus ultimately emerged. *National minorities* had to be excluded from the scope of self-determination; only *entire populations* of sovereign States should be the beneficiaries of the right.

While agreement on this point was quickly reached among most States, Western or Eastern, on other issues the two blocs appeared to be in sharp conflict. As far as external self-determination was concerned, the Soviet Union strongly opposed the Western effort, initiated by the FRG, to insert a clause providing, in general terms, for situations such as the reunification of the two Germanies. The USSR tenaciously held to its thesis that external self-determination only applies to colonial-type situations.[10]

Western and Eastern countries also split on some aspects of internal self-determination. The former advanced the Dutch view: they considered the principle as the basis for gradual, peaceful, and democratic change and as being necessary in order to adapt to internal and international realities in conformity with the will of peoples. In contrast, the Soviet Union and some other socialist States vigorously promoted the view that once a people had chosen a form of government or a certain social structure its right to self-determination was to be regarded as exhaustively exercised. They resisted all attempts to relate the principle of self-determination to peoples who, like those of the thirty-five countries, had already made a choice as to their

---

[10] 'The USSR objected to inclusion of a principle on self-determination in a Declaration enunciated by developed countries on the ground that self-determination has been traditionally associated with the right of colonial peoples to establish their independence' (Russel, 'The Helsinki Declaration').

internal political, social, economic, and cultural status. The Soviet Union strongly opposed the verbs 'adapt' and 'change' contained in The Netherlands proposal, as well as the verb 'choose'. It also found the word 'inalienable' (right), which had been proposed by a number of Western delegations, completely unacceptable.

Another conflict arose with respect to the Yugoslav proposal. The provision condemning 'any form of subjugation or of subordination contrary to the will of the peoples concerned' received some support from Western countries. However, it was firmly opposed by the Soviet Union. Apparently, this State feared that the clause might wreak havoc throughout the Eastern Bloc. The provision was eventually dropped.

Another interesting point about the debates preceding the adoption of the Principles in the Final Act of Helsinki is that some States, which for domestic reasons might have been expected to emphasize the principle of self-determination did not in fact do so. For example, although Spain referred to the situation in Gibraltar during the Helsinki talks, it did not explicitly connect this situation with self-determination. The same is true for Ireland with regard to its discussions concerning Northern Ireland.[11] Similarly, neither Cyprus nor Greece nor Turkey called for self-determination for the people of Cyprus.[12] One possible explanation for these omissions is that they reflect the perceived inapplicability, in actual practice, of self-determination in some cases (Gibraltar, Northern Ireland), while in other cases (that of Cyprus) they are probably indicative of a desire to eschew political polemics, which would have proved sterile in that particular forum.

Principle VIII of the Helsinki decalogue

The text eventually agreed upon reads as follows:

The participating States will respect the equal rights of peoples and their right to self-determination, acting all times in conformity with the purposes and principles of the Charter of the United Nations and with the relevant norms of international law, including those relating to the territorial integrity of States.

By virtue of the principle of equal rights and self-determination of peoples, all peoples always have the right, in full freedom, to determine, when and as they wish, their internal and external political status, without external interference,

---

[11] See, respectively, Doc.CSCE/I/PV.3, 87 and III/PV.4, 40 (Spain) and Doc. CSCE/I/ PV.6, 82 ff. and III/PV.3, 20 (Ireland).

[12] See Doc. CSCE/I/PV.6, 26, PV.7, 29 ff.; Doc. CSCE/III/PV.3, 24; PV.4, 12.

and to pursue as they wish their political, economic, social and cultural development.

The participating States reaffirm the universal significance of respect for and effective exercise of equal rights and self-determination of peoples for the development of friendly relations among themselves as among all States; they also recall the importance of the elimination of any form of violation of this principle.

This formulation applies to both external and internal self-determination. To the extent to which it refers to internal self-determination, it substantially reflects the Western view and, in particular, the Dutch proposal. This being acknowledged, let us now first isolate that which may be considered innovative and then turn to the conservative traits of the formulation adopted in 1975.

THE NOVEL FEATURES OF PRINCIPLE VIII

At the outset, it must be stressed that the principle of self-determination applies to *all peoples*, regardless of whether they live in a sovereign and independent State. At first sight, this seems a mere repetition of the first paragraph of the principle laid down in the UN Declaration on Friendly Relations. However, the Helsinki provision is a marked improvement on the UN instruments. For instance the phrase 'all peoples' takes on a significance wholly absent in the Declaration on Friendly Relations. In the Helsinki Declaration, the definition of self-determination that follows 'all peoples' is focused. It is specific and well-suited for application to the peoples of European States. In addition, the 'always' ('all peoples always have the right') and the phrase 'when and as they wish' ('have the right . . . to determine, when and as they wish, their internal and external political status') ensure that the right of self-determination is considered a *continuing* right: it exists even after a people has chosen a certain form of government or a certain international status. Moreover, the Helsinki Declaration has no clause (comparable to that included in the Declaration on Friendly Relations) that attempts to restrict the principle to sovereign States which have racist regimes or discriminate against religious groups by denying them access to the political decision-making process. The absence of any such qualification bears out the view that, in the Helsinki Declaration, the principle of self-determination has a very wide scope.

There is, moreover, an extrinsic element that confirms that the Helsinki Declaration applies primarily to *peoples living in sovereign States*. The thirty-five States participating in the European Conference intended to put forth principles that would apply in their relations with one another. Thus, the

Helsinki provisions on self-determination must be construed as being relevant *vis-à-vis* the peoples of Europe, in other words, *vis-à-vis* peoples living in sovereign States. The principle in the Helsinki Declaration is addressed primarily, if not exclusively, to these people, not to people under colonial or foreign domination or under a racist regime.

A second important feature of the principle enunciated in the Helsinki Declaration is that it puts the relationship between self-determination and human rights into proper perspective. Paragraph 2 states 'all peoples always have the right, *in full freedom*, to determine . . . their internal and external political status, without external interference '. 'In full freedom,' is not merely the positive expression of the phrase 'without external interference'. It has a separate, distinct, and consequently broader meaning. This becomes clear once one compares the Helsinki text with the 1970 Declaration on Friendly Relations. Paragraph 1 of the Declaration on Friendly Relations states that 'by virtue of the principle . . . all peoples have the right *freely* to determine, without external interference, their political status'. This wording suggests 'freely' actually means 'free from external interference'. In contrast, the wording of the Helsinki Declaration is bold and of broader meaning.

If this textual analysis remains unconvincing, a second more conclusive argument may be advanced. The debates preceding the adoption of the Helsinki Declaration illustrate that the phrase 'in full freedom' reflects the Western view that the right of self-determination cannot be implemented if basic human rights and fundamental freedoms, in particular the freedom of expression and association, are not ensured to all members of the people concerned.[13] A people cannot choose its political status or establish an economic, social, or cultural programme when it is subject to an authoritarian government. 'In full freedom' is intended to express precisely this notion. It grants peoples the right to exercise self-determination free *from internal interference* (i.e., free from oppression by an authoritarian government). By contrast, the expression 'without external interference' denotes freedom *from possible encroachment by third States*.

To sum up, it is submitted that the Helsinki Declaration provides a definition of self-determination that breaks new ground in international relations. The innovative part of the Helsinki Declaration primarily relates to *internal* self-determination. The wording agreed upon by the thirty-five

---

[13] See thereon, A. Cassese, 'The Helsinki Declaration and Self-Determination', in Buergenthal, *Human Rights, International Law and the Helsinki Accord*, 95–9, 102–3.

States embodies the idea that self-determination means the permanent possibility for a people to choose a new social or political regime and to adapt existing social or political structures to meet new demands. As the Prime Minister of The Netherlands remarked in the Helsinki final session in 1975, self-determination, as set forth in the Declaration, 'means that where the people express an opinion on their own destiny their voices shall be reflected in the policy of their governments'.[14]

Hence, the principle of self-determination embodied in the Helsinki Declaration has a distinct *anti-authoritarian and democratic thrust*. One of the champions of self-determination, Woodrow Wilson, had earlier contemplated just such a principle but the democratic elements of self-determination were soon overshadowed, first by paramount considerations of *Realpolitik* and then, after the Second World War, by the ferment that was anti-colonialism. It is to the credit of the States gathered at the CSCE that when they 'revisited' the idea of self-determination in 1975 they chose 'revitalization' over mere reiteration.

A third important feature of the Declaration is that it proclaims for the first time, in express terms, the right to *external* self-determination for the peoples of every signatory State. What is the meaning of this proclamation? It is submitted that the proper interpretation of the clause can only be attained if the following elements are taken into account: (i) as stated above, the peoples referred to in the Helsinki Final Act are the whole populations of each signatory State; (ii) by contrast, no right to self-determination is granted to any minority or ethnic group, as we shall soon see; (iii) furthermore, no right to secession is recognized (see below, pp. 288–9), because territorial integrity is given paramount importance in the Declaration. If all these elements are read in conjunction, it follows that by 'right to external self-determination' is meant the right – bestowed on the whole people of every signatory State – to freely pronounce upon any possible change in the *international status* of the State: in the case where the Government of one of the thirty-five States decides that the territory should be *merged* with that of another State, or that the State should be *incorporated* into another country, or split into two separate sovereign entities, or on any other similar change, it is for the people to have the final say on the matter, through a referendum, plebiscite or by any other democratic procedure. Thus, external self-determination means that no territorial or other change can be brought about by the central authorities of a State that is contrary to the will of the whole people of that State.

[14] Doc. CSCE/III/PV.5, 17.

Plainly, the situation that most countries had in mind when drafting this clause, and that – as we saw above – lay behind the 'Principle on self-determination', was that of the two Germanies. The merger of the two countries was authorized by the Principle on condition that the two peoples concerned freely expressed their wish for reunification (however, as is well known, the dramatic and sudden events that occurred in Eastern Germany did not make it necessary for the peoples of the two Germanies to hold a referendum; nor was a referendum or plebiscite held before the recent splitting of Czechoslovakia).[15]

THE TRADITIONAL FACETS OF PRINCIPLE VIII

As noted above, Principle VIII does not introduce innovations to *all* issues relating to self-determination. It is traditional in at least three respects. First, it recognizes that self-determination must not disrupt the *territorial integrity of States*.[16] The Helsinki Declaration thus

---

[15] On 17 July 1992 the National Council of Slovakia adopted a 'Declaration on the Sovereignty of the Slovak Republic', where it proclaimed the 'natural right of the Slovak nation to self-determination, in keeping with the international agreements and treaties on self-determination'. It seems that, by not mentioning the Constitution in force at the time (enacted in 1968), the Slovak Republic intentionally refrained from referring, at least explicitly, to its preamble, where mention was made of the right to self-determination and it was also added that this right could lead to the 'separation' of each of the two nations making up the Federation of Czechoslovakia. In any event, following the resignation of Mr Havel as Head of the Federation, on 25 November 1992 the Federal Assembly (the Parliament of Czechoslovakia) passed a law on the dissolution of the Federal State and its splitting into two Republics. It should be noted that this law simply provided for dissolution, without the prior holding of any referendum (this was not in keeping with Art. 1 of the Constitutional Law no. 397 of 1991, which explicitly provided that in the case of a proposal for secession by one of the two nations, a referendum must be held). The failure to hold a referendum was regarded as justified on two grounds: first, the 1991 law did not envisage referendums as compulsory but merely made allowance for them; second, in any case, a referendum was made superfluous by the fact that the two Republics concerned readily agreed on the dissolution of the Federal State. As a matter of fact, a series of agreements were concluded by the two Republics on a number of problems, including those of nationality, borders, customs and real property. See generally, C. Saladin, 'Self-Determination, Minority Rights and Constitutional Accommodation: the Example of the Czech and Slovak Federal Republic', 13 *Michigan Journal of International Law*, 1991, 172–217.

[16] Paragraph 1 of the Principle provides: 'The participating States will respect the equal rights of peoples and their right to self-determination, acting at all times in conformity with the purposes and principles of the Charter of the United Nations and with the relevant norms of international law, including those relating to the territorial integrity of States.'

reiterates the safeguard clause of the UN Declaration on Friendly Relations.[17]

Second, the Helsinki formulation implicitly limits the scope of the word 'peoples' with the inclusion of a provision dedicated to the protection of minority individual rights. The wording of this provision suggests that *minorities are excluded from Principle VIII*. Although 'national minorities' could be covered by both Principle VII and Principle VIII, the debates preceding the adoption of Principle VIII make it clear that there was complete agreement that 'national minorities' (and, *a fortiori*, religious, racial, or linguistic minorities) were to be excluded. Extending the scope of Principle VIII to 'national minorities' would mean that minorities have the right to external self-determination and hence the right to secede. Given that many of the signatory States are composed of a variety of national groups, it is natural that their governments would resist any such construction of Principle VIII. They were willing to grant civil rights and fundamental freedoms to individual members of the minority groups but were unwilling to go any further.[18] It appears incontrovertible that the Helsinki Declaration, when it discusses the principle of self-determination, only extends the right to entire populations living in and identifying with sovereign States (for example, Italian or French citizens).

Third, the Declaration perceives self-determination as significant 'for the development of friendly relations' among States. In this, the Helsinki Declaration follows the UN Charter doctrine of self-determination as a

---

[17] On closer examination one might argue that the Helsinki text does show some originality with respect to external self-determination. Respect for territorial integrity is a duty incumbent upon States, not on individuals or peoples. The reference to international rules concerning territorial integrity does not qualify the rights of people to self-determination; it only restricts the actions of States, which are duty-bound neither to support secessionist movements elsewhere nor to take any action likely to impair the territorial integrity of other States. It would follow that, under the Helsinki Declaration, a 'people' can claim a right to secede if they consider secession the only means available to implement their right to self-determination (but that which was stressed above must be recalled: 'peoples' is not synonymous with 'minorities'; the latter are not entitled to self-determination and certainly not to secession). By contrast, the safeguard clause of the Declaration on Friendly Relations is couched in terms that restrict the right to self-determination and oblige States not to interfere with the territorial integrity of non-racist sovereign States.

[18] 'States with militant minorities, such as Canada and Yugoslavia, felt the need for a "balancing element", which was a euphemism for a limit to the application of the principle to national minorities in order to avoid any implication that the principle could be used to bring about the dissolution of federated States comprised of peoples of different nationalities or other minorities.' Russel, 'The Helsinki Declaration', 269 ff.

means for achieving peaceful relations among States and not as a goal in itself.[19]

The Helsinki Principle, the UN instruments and customary international law

At the final session of the Helsinki Conference, the Secretary-General of the United Nations remarked: '[M]embership in the United Nations has surely provided a common point of reference in approaching many of the sensitive issues with which the Conference has dealt.'[20] It is difficult to disagree with this statement. The Helsinki Declaration was conceived as a means of reaffirming and reinforcing among the thirty-five participants the basic tenets of the UN Charter;[21] it gives them a 'new dimension in European space'[22] and 'enhanc[es] their implementation among the participating States'.[23]

While it is true that the Helsinki Declaration 'is in line with the Charter of the UN'[24] and 'does not in any way conflict with or compete with [the principles of the UN]',[25] such statements do not do justice to the Helsinki Declaration's significance. Although it does restate the UN principles, in many respects the Declaration goes further. It elaborates and refines the old principles by adapting them to conditions prevailing in Europe.[26] The

---

[19] One might question if the authors of the Helsinki Declaration simply wished to pay respect to a 'sacred' text, or whether they really intended to subordinate the realization of self-determination to the primary goal of the pursuit of friendly relations among states. Statements made by some delegations to the Helsinki Conference would seem to support the latter interpretation. See, for example, the declarations of the Foreign Ministers of the Netherlands and Ireland, quoted above, notes 8 and 9.

[20] Doc. CSCE/III/PV.1, 5.   [21] *Ibid.*

[22] Greece, *ibid.*, PV.2, 10.

[23] Ireland, *ibid.*, PV.3, 21 ff.

[24] German Democratic Republic, *ibid.*, 25.

[25] Ireland, *ibid.*, PV.3, 21.

[26] The remarks of the President of Finland, made at the conference in 1975, are pertinent in this regard: 'While it is based on the principles and purposes of the United Nations, the Declaration on Principles Guiding Relations between Participating States goes further than the Charter of the world organization, as it applies these principles to the particular conditions of our own continent. Thus it is evident that such harmony of interests prevails in Europe at present that States can state in binding terms the prevailing situation and agree on the manner of further development of the conditions. In consequence, the principles agreed upon by the present Conference are not merely repeating what has been said before but, proceeding from an established basis, recognizing its value, they mean developing a new set of standards to open up new dimensions in the mutual relations of States.' Doc. CSCE/III/PV.4, 34. Although the Finnish representative was speaking about the entire Helsinki agreement, his remarks are particularly true with regard to the principle of self-determination.

Helsinki text articulates a concept of self-determination that is different in many respects from that incorporated in the UN instruments. Recent UN statements tend to follow the Afro-Asian and pre-1989 Eastern Bloc philosophy of self-determination. In contrast, the Helsinki doctrine of self-determination reflects, to a very great extent, some of the basic tenets of the Western view. The Helsinki approach seems well justified, for the Afro-Asian-Eastern Bloc view that self-determination is only relevant where there is colonialism, foreign occupation, or a racist regime unnecessarily limits the principle, rendering it inapplicable in most areas of Europe and North America. Now there are new standards to which States should aspire.

However, what is the exact nature of the interplay between the Helsinki Declaration and the various UN Documents which precede it? Can one argue that the Helsinki Declaration has no bearing at all on the existing international legal norms governing self-determination? Although this question is too complex to be treated in great detail here,[27] the following tentative observations seem to be warranted.

Whenever the Helsinki Declaration does not restate or reaffirm legally binding international rules or principles, the 'code of conduct' it embodies[28] may have three effects.

First, although it cannot be said that disregard of the Helsinki Declaration amounts to an international wrongful act, signatory States are made (politically) *accountable* for non-compliance with the standards of the Helsinki Declaration.

Second, signatory States, because of their adherence to the principles set forth in the Helsinki Declaration, are *precluded from* challenging the validity of the content given to those principles in the Helsinki Declaration. To put the matter another way, the Helsinki Declaration has an estoppel effect as to the principles it defines. Although signatory States are not legally bound by Principle VIII, nevertheless they are estopped from claiming that where self-determination is denied, only UN norms or customary international law apply to the exclusion of the Helsinki Declaration. Nor may they assert that the Helsinki Declaration must be construed in light of the previous existing norms governing self-determination.

Third, the Declaration and the subsequent practice relating to its

---

[27] On this question, see among others, O. Schachter, 'The Twilight Existence of Non-binding International Agreements', 71 AJIL, 1977, 296.

[28] This expression was used by the Soviet Union: Doc. CSCE/I/PV.2, 5; and by the United Kingdom: *ibid.*, PV.5 9 ff.

application can amount to a powerful factor *promoting legal change* in the international community. Indeed, it should not be forgotten that among the thirty-five States there are the (then) two Superpowers. Their behaviour, coupled with that of a significant number of European States (as well as Canada), can gradually lead to a change in the existing customary regulation of the principle of self-determination.

The CSCE follow-up to the Helsinki Final Act

The Helsinki Principle on self-determination was restated, almost literally, in 1989, in the Concluding Document of the Vienna Meeting of the CSCE on the Follow-Up to the Helsinki Conference. The only slight variations with respect to the Helsinki Final Act concerned two points: (i) mention was no longer made of the importance of self-determination for the development of friendly relations among peoples and States and (ii) the principle of territorial integrity was enhanced, so much so that its co-ordination with self-determination might eventually have a negative impact on respect for the right to self-determination. The recent events in Central and Eastern Europe and the fear of an uncontrolled disintegration of existing States under the impulse of the national aspirations of ethnic groups, probably account for this shift in emphasis between the two principles.[29]

---

[29] Principle 4 of the Concluding Document provides that the participating States 'also confirm that, by virtue of the principle of equal rights and self-determination of peoples and in conformity with the relevant provisions of the Final Act, all peoples always have the right, in full freedom, to determine, when and as they wish, their internal and external political status, without external interference, and to pursue as they wish their political, economic, social and cultural development'.

Principle 5 states that the participating States 'confirm their commitment strictly and effectively to observe the principle of the territorial integrity of States. They will refrain from any violation of this principle and thus from any action aimed by direct or indirect means, in contravention of the purposes and principles of the Charter of the United Nations, other obligations under international law or the provisions of the Final Act, at violating the territorial integrity, political independence or the unity of a State. No actions or situations in contravention of this principle will be recognized as legal by the participating States.'

It should be emphasized that Principle 1 provides that 'The participating States reaffirm their commitment to all ten principles of the Final Act's Declaration on Principles Guiding Relations between participating States and their determination to respect them and put them into practice. The participating States reaffirm that all these principles are of primary significance and, accordingly, will be equally and unreservedly applied, each of them being interpreted taking into account the others' (text in A. Bloed, *From Helsinki to Vienna: Basic Documents of the Helsinki Process*, Dordrecht 1990, 184).

It can be argued that the somewhat restrictive attitude taken at Vienna in 1989 was accentuated in 1990, in the 'Charter of Paris for a New Europe' adopted by the Heads of State and Government of the participating States in the CSCE. The relevant provision states

We reaffirm the equal rights of peoples and their right to self-determination in conformity with the Charter of the United Nations and with the relevant norms of international law, including those relating to the territorial integrity of States.

It has been pointed out[30] that, by not sufficiently insisting on the Helsinki doctrine of self-determination and by instead referring to the less liberal doctrine upheld in the UN Charter and current international law, the Paris Charter 'has created unnecessary doubts about the continuing commitment of the CSCE to the right of self-determination'.[31]

More generally, there may probably be some truth in the contention that CSCE instruments subsequent to the Helsinki Final Act appear 'to downplay the significance of this right [to self-determination] altogether. Because it may well open a Pandora's box for many States and because it may complicate rather than solve the issues facing contemporary Europe, it is very likely that the CSCE will focus more attention on minority rights and less on self-determination. But whether political events in some participating States will permit the CSCE this luxury is difficult to predict at this time'.[32]

The seemingly restrictive approach increasingly taken by the CSCE is chiefly motivated by political factors: essentially, the fear that secession in Europe might be promoted by an interpretation of self-determination that is directed towards granting that right not only to the whole people of each signatory State but also to any ethnic group or nationality living in one of these States. We have seen, however, that this interpretation would be unsound, as it is in no way warranted by a proper reading of the Helsinki Final Act.

However, it is suggested that this process in no way detracts from the importance of the very core of the Helsinki doctrine of self-determination, namely the concept of *internal* self-determination for the peoples of each signatory State. Actually, the recent breaking-up of the Soviet 'imperial' system of power and the gradual turning of Central and Eastern European States to democracy is but an application of that concept of self-

---

[30] T. Buergenthal, 'CSCE Human Dimension: The Birth of a System', AEL, vol. I, Book 2, 1990, 196–7.
[31] *Ibid.*, 197.   [32] *Ibid.*, 179.

determination. The concept, therefore, instead of losing ground, has manifested great vitality. Indeed, the Helsinki follow-up process has increasingly emphasized and delved into the notions of democracy and minority rights. One ought not to be oblivious to the fact that in 1975, at the time of the adoption of the Helsinki Declaration, it proved impossible – on account of socialist opposition – to lay down the principle of democracy. As a fall-back, States confined themselves to generically proclaiming internal self-determination. After 1989, however, it was possible to spell out the concept of democracy and, what is more important, to articulate all its basic implications. This rendered the restatement of self-determination superfluous.

This is a point worth emphasizing. The Helsinki process, by increasingly focusing on the *internal* dimension of self-determination, has contributed in an original way to the delineation of *specific criteria* for that *model* of *pluralistic democratic society*, on which internal self-determination must be based. Suffice it to mention in this respect the 'Paris Charter' of 21 November 1990, where the link between democracy, political pluralism, human rights and rule of law is set out in specific and unambiguous terms[33] and the importance for democracy of the provisions on 'periodic and genuine elections' laid down in the Copenhagen document of 1990 is restated.[34] In this connection, attention should be

---

[33] 'Democratic government is based on the will of the people, expressed regularly through free and fair elections. Democracy has as its foundation respect for the human person and the rule of law. Democracy is the best safeguard of freedom of expression, tolerance of all groups of society, and equality of opportunity for each person.

Democracy, with its representative and pluralist character, entails accountability to the electorate, the obligation of public authorities to comply with the law and justice administered impartially. No one will be above the law' (30 ILM, 1991, 194).

[34] See 30 ILM, 1991, 214. The two provisions of the 1990 Copenhagen Meeting of the Conference on the Human Dimension of the CSCE are paras. 6–8.

Para. 6 states that 'The participating States declare that the will of the people, freely and fairly expressed through periodic and genuine elections, is the basis of the authority and legitimacy of all government. The participating States will accordingly respect the right of their citizens to take part in the governing of their country, either directly or through representatives freely chosen by them through fair electoral processes.'

Para. 7 provides that: 'To ensure that the will of the people serves as the basis of the authority of government, the participating States will (7.1) – hold free elections at reasonable intervals, as established by law; (7.2) – permit all seats in at least one chamber of the national legislature to be freely contested in a popular vote; (7.3) – guarantee universal and equal suffrage to adult citizens; (7.4) – ensure that votes are cast by secret ballot or by equivalent free voting procedure, and that they are counted and reported honestly with the official results made public; (7.5) – respect the right of

drawn to the fact that in 1990 at the Paris Conference States went so far as to set up an 'Office for Free Elections' responsible for fostering the implementation of the Copenhagen text.[35] No less important are the provisions of these texts on the right of minority groups: mention can be made in this respect of the relevant provision of the Paris Charter of 1990,[36] of the provisions of the Helsinki Summit Declaration of 10 July

citizens to seek political or public office, individually or as representatives of political parties or organizations, without discrimination; (7.6) – respect the right of individuals and groups to establish, in full freedom, their own political parties or other political organizations and provide such political parties and organizations with the necessary legal guarantees to enable them to compete with each other on a basis of equal treatment before the law and by the authorities; (7.7) – ensure that law and public policy work to permit political campaigning to be conducted in a fair and free atmosphere in which neither administrative action, violence nor intimidation bars the parties and the candidates from freely presenting their views and qualifications, or prevents the voters from learning and discussing them or from casting their vote free of fear of retribution; (7.8) – provide that no legal or administrative obstacle stands in the way of unimpeded access to the media on a non-discriminatory basis for all political groupings and individuals wishing to participate in the electoral process; (7.9) – ensure that candidates who obtain the necessary number of votes required by law are duly installed in office and are permitted to remain in office until their term expires or is otherwise brought to an end in a manner that is regulated by law in conformity with democratic parliamentary and constitutional procedures.'

Para. 8 provides that: 'The participating States consider that the presence of observers, both foreign and domestic, can enhance the electoral process for States in which elections are taking place. They therefore invite observers from any other CSCE participating States and any appropriate private institutions and organizations who may wish to do so to observe the course of their national election proceedings, to the extent permitted by law. They will also endeavour to facilitate similar access for election proceedings held below the national level. Such observers will undertake not to interfere in the electoral proceedings' (30 ILM, 1991, 220–2).

[35] See 30 ILM, 1991, 214–15.

[36] 'We [the participating States] affirm that the ethnic, cultural, linguistic and religious identity of national minorities will be protected and that persons belonging to national minorities have the right freely to express, preserve and develop that identity without any discrimination and in full equality before the law' (30 ILM, 1991, 195). 'Determined to foster the rich contribution of national minorities to the life of our societies, we undertake further to improve their situation. We reaffirm our deep conviction that friendly relations among our peoples, as well as peace, justice, stability and democracy, require that the ethnic, cultural, linguistic and religious identity of national minorities be protected and conditions for the promotion of that identity be created. We declare that questions related to national minorities can only be satisfactorily resolved in a democratic political framework. We further acknowledge that the rights of persons belonging to national minorities must be fully respected as part of universal human rights. Being aware of the urgent need for increased co-operation on, as well as better protection of, national minorities, we decide to convene a meeting of experts on national minorities to be held in Geneva from 1 to 19 July 1991' (*ibid.*, 199).

1992[37] and, in particular, of the setting up of a 'CSCE High Commission on National Minorities' provided for in the same Declaration.[38]

Thus, in actual fact the Helsinki process has considerably contributed to *refining* the concept of internal self-determination, by specifying the criteria for enabling peoples to make really free and genuine choices. At the same time, it has propounded forms and methods of protecting minorities that are more advanced than the traditional ones and could therefore meet many of the requirements advocated by groups and minorities – however, within the framework of sovereign States and without impairing their territorial integrity.

In summary, the recent tendencies within the CSCE in no way diminish the importance of the nucleus of the concept of self-determination proclaimed in 1975 and, indeed, have greatly enriched and expanded the initial proclamations.

The 1976 Algiers Declaration on the Rights of Peoples

The main features of the self-determination provisions

The Algiers Declaration of the Rights of Peoples, adopted in 1976, emanates not from understandings and agreements concluded among sovereign States, but from a group of individuals having no official governmental status: academics, politicians, trade-union leaders and representatives of national liberation movements, all united by a common

---

[37] 'The participating States . . . (24) will intensify . . . their efforts to ensure the free exercise by persons belonging to national minorities, individually or in community with others, of their human rights and fundamental freedoms, including the right to participate fully, in accordance with the democratic decision-making procedures of each State, in the political, economic, social and cultural life of their countries including through democratic participation in decision-making and consultative bodies at the national, regional and local level, *inter alia*, through political parties and associations; (25) will continue through unilateral, bilateral and multilateral efforts to explore further avenues for more effective implementation of their relevant CSCE commitments, including those related to the protection and the creation of conditions for the promotion of the ethnic, cultural, linguistic and religious identity of national minorities; (26) will address national minority issues in a constructive manner, by peaceful means and through dialogue among all parties concerned on the basis of CSCE principles and commitments; (27) will refrain from resettling and condemn all attempts, by the threat or use of force, to resettle persons with the aim of changing the ethnic composition of areas within their territory' (31 ILM, 1992, 1411).

[38] See *ibid.*, 1396–9.

ideological outlook that could be briefly dubbed 'tiers-mondiste'.[39] Thus, it does not carry the same weight, nor have the same legal standing, as resolutions of the United Nations General Assembly or the Helsinki Declaration. The Declaration's 'private' status does, however, have its advantages. The 'lowest common denominator' problem, which typically renders inter-governmental documents imprecise and ambiguous did not come into play during its drafting. Unlike the inter-governmental compromises in the field of self-determination, the Algiers Declaration is forthright and even radical. The message it bears is clear and accessible.[40] There is no place here for the ambiguity and caution of the United Nations Declaration on Friendly Relations of 1970.

Article 7 of the Algiers Declaration states quite openly that the political oppression of a people constitutes the denial of its right of self-determination:

Every people has the right to have a democratic government representing all citizens without distinction of race, sex, belief or colour, and capable of ensuring effective respect for the human rights and fundamental freedoms of all.

---

[39] See A. Cassese and E. Jouve (eds.), *Pour un droit des peuples*, Paris 1978. On self-determination, see in particular the papers by J. Echeverria (95 ff.); E. Jouve (105 ff.); G. Gaja (123 ff.) and A. Bourgi (185 ff.). See also P. Fois, 'La "Dichiarazione universale dei diritti dei popoli" di Algeri', 31 *La Comunità internazionale*, 1976, 491–500; F. Rigaux, 'The Algiers Declaration on the Rights of Peoples', in A. Cassese (ed.), *United Nations Law and Fundamental Rights*, Alphen aan den Rijn, 1979, 211 ff.; R. Falk, 'The Algiers Declaration of the Rights of Peoples', in R. Falk, *Human Rights and State Sovereignty*, New York and London 1981, 184 ff.; T. van Boven, 'The Relation between Peoples' Rights and Human Rights in the African Charter', 7 *Human Rights Law Journal*, 1986, 189–90; I. Brownlie, 'The Rights of Peoples in Modern International Law', in J. Crawford (ed.), *The Rights of Peoples*, Oxford 1988, 11–13; J. Crawford, 'The Rights of Peoples: Some Conclusions', *ibid.*, 174–5; Arangio-Ruiz, 'Autodeterminazione', at 5; Bokatola, *L'Organisation des Nations Unies et la protection des minorités*, 108, 125–6, 206–7, 233.

[40] Although the chief enemy of the freedom of peoples is bluntly (and with a clear political and ideological bias) identified in the preamble as imperialism, the 'normative' context and the whole spirit of the Declaration show that the ultimate 'adversary' is any form of oppressive and authoritarian government – with special emphasis, however, on neo-colonialist oppression, which, in the opinion of the framers of the Declaration, is at present the most dangerous and widespread form of the denial of self-determination. Thus, the Declaration, in Articles 5 and 6, reaffirms the United Nations' anti-colonialist tenet and in Article 6 goes further and sanctions the right of peoples to break free from any colonial or foreign domination whether direct or indirect. It is clear that here the text refers, among other things, to foreign domination through multinational corporations, co-operation between the repressive organizations of various States and economic control of national industries and markets.

Since those drafting the Declaration were not constrained by State interests, they were able to expand the principle of 'internal' self-determination. They clarified and gave teeth to the loose standards stipulated by the United Nations in 1966, in Article 1(1) of the Covenants on Human Rights (laying down the right of peoples to 'freely determine their political status and freely pursue their economic, social and cultural development') and subsequently restated in 1970, in the Declaration on Friendly Relations (where it speaks of a 'representative' government that does not discriminate as to race, colour or creed). It is now forcefully proclaimed that the government must be democratic, that is, not authoritarian and must be able effectively to guarantee the free exercise of human rights. These additional requirements are of basic importance. They put an end to the charade whereby governments dismiss a variety of forms of discrimination and human rights violations by referring to their being a 'representative' institution. Under the Algiers Declaration a government can claim that it represents the people but it can no longer use this as a convenient defence if it flagrantly and systematically denies human rights and fundamental freedoms. Respect for or denial of human rights is in effect the acid test which indicates whether or not a government is respecting the peoples' right to 'internal' self-determination.

The correct relationship between the rights of individuals and self-determination, which was brought to the fore in Helsinki, has thus been fully spelled out. It is not sufficient to state, as does the United Nations, that self-determination is a basic precondition for the enjoyment of the rights of individuals and that an individual cannot fully enjoy his rights and freedoms if the people to which he belongs are subject to colonial rule, foreign domination, or a racist regime. It is necessary to add – with the force and clarity that is found in the Algiers Declaration – that when the rights and fundamental freedoms of members of a people are systematically denied this means that the right to self-determination of that people is also infringed. From this point of view 'internal' political self-determination is *the synthesis and the summa of human rights*. 'Internal' political self-determination does not generically mean 'self-government' but rather the right freely to choose a government, exercising all the freedoms which make that choice possible (freedom of speech, of association, etc.). At the same time, it means the right to see to it that the government, once chosen, continues to reflect the will of the people and is neither oppressive nor authoritarian.

This concept of political self-determination is of course not new, for it has deep liberal-democratic roots. It suffices to recall the comment made in 1957 by Georges Scelle, the prominent French international lawyer: 'Tyranny, absolutism and dictatorship are both a violation of the rights of the individual and an infringement of the right of peoples.'[41] However, the affirmation of this concept in the Declaration transforms it into a libertarian ideal which is not only aimed against certain historically limited forms of authoritarianism but also against those forms of authoritarianism which took root in different areas of the world where colonialism was unknown; for example, in Central and Eastern European countries, at the time when these countries were 'socialist'.

A second salient feature of the Declaration follows from the fact that the 'founding fathers' spoke up in favour of peoples and not in the interests of governments. In the Declaration there is no trace of the obsession with the sovereignty of States and the protection of territorial integrity at all costs, which is typical of inter-governmental texts. Although the formula adopted is reminiscent of the United Nations 'squash-box' clauses which are so loose as to allow for any interpretation, minorities are permitted to secede. Pursuant to Article 21, the rights of minorities must be exercised with full respect for the legitimate interests of the community as a whole and

cannot authorise impairing the territorial integrity and political unity of the State, *provided the State acts in accordance with all the principles set forth in this Declaration.*

Despite the legalistic and convoluted nature of this provision, taken in the general context of the Declaration and in the light of its aims, the 'message' is clear: secession is permissible when the only way to ensure a minority's survival and the survival of its cultural, religious, and political identity is to grant the minority an independent status or permit it to be integrated in another country where it is bound to be afforded better treatment.

If this is the case, what are we to say when a 'hegemonic power' instigates secession in another country for its own economic and political ends? In such cases secession, presenting itself as the liberation of a minority, is in fact a means of alien domination. However, although such cases exist and must be exposed for what they are, in the view of the draftsmen of the Algiers Declaration their existence should not be allowed to impede real attempts to liberate peoples. According to the draftsmen, demands for liberation ought to outweigh appeals for the preservation of territorial integrity.

[41] G. Scelle, 'Quelques réflexions sur le droit des peuples à disposer d'eux-mêmes', in *Grundprobleme des Internationalen Rechts, Festschrift für J. Spiropoulos,* Bonn 1957, 385.

A third characteristic of the Declaration worth emphasizing is that it does not consider self-determination in terms of friendly inter-state relations and as a means for avoiding international tension – it thus takes a quite realistic and non-instrumentalist view of self-determination. It acknowledges that the implementation of self-determination, far from promoting friendly relations, is frequently the cause of tension, discord, and even serious international crises. Where the implementation of the right to self-determination conflicts with the aim of friendly relations among States, the Declaration opts unhesitatingly for the former. This choice is worthy of approbation, for if the price of peace is the freedom of peoples, the peace attained is certain to be a precarious one. 'Negative peace', that is, the absence of armed conflict, should not be allowed to prevail over 'positive peace', that is, the preventive eradication of violence by the realization of 'social justice'.[42]

Finally, it is worth emphasizing the guarantees provided for in the Declaration. Article 28 of the Declaration proclaims the right of peoples

whose fundamental rights are seriously disregarded to enforce them, especially by political or trade union struggle and even, in the last resort, by the use of force.

Article 29 adds that:

liberation movements shall have access to international organizations and their combatants are entitled to the protection of the humanitarian law of war.

Although these two Articles do not go much beyond the United Nations declarations, they grant an authorization to resort to force which is markedly different from the mere 'licence' embodied in the UN texts. Moreover, Articles 22 and 30, which discuss the rights and obligations of the international community *vis-à-vis* the group being persecuted, represent a significant step forward. Taken together they not only provide for, but also mandate, third-party interventions. Article 22 states:

Any disregard for the provisions of this Declaration constitutes a breach of obligations towards the international community as a whole.

Article 30 adds:

The re-establishment of the fundamental rights of peoples when they are seriously disregarded, is a duty incumbent upon all members of the international community.

---

[42] For the concepts of 'positive' and 'negative' peace, see J. Galtung, 'Peace', in D. Sills (ed.), *International Encyclopedia of Social Sciences*, vol. II, New York 1968, 487.

Given these provisions, it would appear that when a State denies a people entitled to claim self-determination the means of achieving it, it abridges two sets of rights, those belonging to the oppressed people and those belonging to all members of the international community, be they States, national liberation movements, or other bodies subject to the international legal order. The international community has a right to insist that a State permit its peoples self-determination and may enforce that right through a variety of political, economic, and military means, on condition that the State providing assistance is not itself controlled by an authoritarian government.

More importantly, the members of the international community not only have a right but also a duty to intervene. The denial of self-determination is held to prejudice the whole international community; accordingly, a denial of self-determination triggers a duty to actively oppose the oppressive State. The Declaration supports the principle of international solidarity among peoples, which authorizes bodies other than States to aid oppressed peoples.

The Algiers Declaration and existing international law

Save for the provisions permitting secession and granting peoples a 'right' to resort to force for the purpose of realizing self-determination, the Algiers Declaration is, by and large, in accordance with the existing rules of international law on self-determination. It does not depart from the international norms governing self-determination but rather sharpens the existing laws, spelling out and elaborating that which is still implicit or evolutive in the body of international legal standards. The drafters hoped that the Declaration would act as a catalyst. They aimed to spur governments and international organizations into clarifying the concept of self-determination and the rules governing its implementation and enforcement.[43]

The Algiers Declaration and the Helsinki Final Act

The Algiers Declaration is more radical than the Helsinki Declaration. It affords minorities rights – including the right to secede – that States,

---

[43] Surprisingly, I. Brownlie ('The Rights of Peoples in Modern International Law', 13) contends that the Algiers Declaration is 'offered as though it were *lex lata*'. For other critical comments on the Declaration by the distinguished British jurist, see also *ibid.*, 11.

to date, have refused to grant. It also insists that peoples have a right to use force, albeit only as a last resort. Furthermore, it obliges States to enforce the right to self-determination. The duty imposed is explicit.

However, despite these differences, the two documents share the same basic premise: a people's ability to achieve internal self-determination turns on the extent to which the individuals who comprise that group are free to enjoy their fundamental human rights. Both documents seek to strengthen and improve international rules governing self-determination by bolstering individual human rights. Recent events in Eastern Europe indicate that this is the correct approach.

The new drive towards the customary recognition of the right to self-determination of the peoples of sovereign states

As I said before, the Helsinki Declaration – as well as, to a minor extent, the Algiers Declaration – are both indicative of a new trend that is emerging in the world community towards wider recognition of *internal* self-determination and have proved themselves instrumental in helping this recognition to gradually take shape.

For many years, one of the fundamental principles of Western countries has been that self-determination of necessity includes the right of the whole population of a sovereign country freely to choose its rulers.

One of the best formulations of this right was propounded in 1984 by the United Kingdom representative, in a statement he made in the Third Committee of the General Assembly. He noted the following:

Self-determination is not a one-off exercise. It cannot be achieved for any people by one revolution or one election. It is a continuous process. It requires that peoples be given continuing opportunities to choose their governments and social systems, and to change them when they so choose. This in turn requires that they should be enabled to exercise other rights set out in the Covenants [on Human Rights, of 1966], such as the rights to freedom of thought and expression; the right of peaceful assembly and freedom of association; the right to take part in the conduct of public affairs, either directly or through freely chosen representatives; and the right to vote and be elected at genuine periodic elections.

Many peoples today are deprived of the right of self-determination, by elites of their own countrymen and women: through the concentration of power in a

302

particular political party, in a particular ethnic or religious group, or in a certain social class. These oligarchies maintain their dictatorship by imposing their own ideologies on the country as a whole; by refusing to seek a genuine popular mandate from their people; and by denying their peoples the opportunity to practise and profess different beliefs. Such systems are generally characterised by oppression and inequality, and sometimes by more violent abuses such as torture, summary executions and disappearances.

My delegation considers that all peoples are entitled to expect the United Nations to protect their right of self-determination, from abuse by their own countrymen as well as outsiders.[44]

This important statement was not isolated; the UK authorities had already advanced the same concept in 1983 with specific reference to the inhabitants of Grenada,[45] and restated it several times afterwards.[46] The same notion was also advanced by other Western countries such as the United States,[47]

---

[44] BYIL, 1984, 432.

[45] See BYIL, 1983, 405 ff.

[46] See BYIL, 1985, 400; 1986, 515 ff.; 1987, 519.

[47] In 1972 the US delegate to the UN General Assembly's Third Committee stated that 'the right of self-determination and independence cannot be limited to one particular area of the world but must be universal. We view self-determination as a continual process whereby peoples may decide, in light of existing conditions, the manner in which they seek to exercise this right. Independence is only one of the several alternatives from which peoples may choose. In some cases, through mutual consent, a decision may be taken by a group to establish relationships with existing States, for example through voluntary incorporation in another State or a special relationship such as commonwealth status. Freedom of choice is indispensable to the exercise of the right of self-determination. For this freedom of choice to be meaningful, there must be corresponding freedom of thought, conscience, expression, movement and association. Self-determination entails legitimate, lively dissent and testing at the ballot box with frequent regularity' (reported in US Digest 1974, 48).

See also the statement made in 1973 by the US delegate to the ICAO Assembly ('We believe all States are obligated to grant equal rights and self-determination to all peoples', US Digest, 1973, 58), the declaration of the US delegate to the 'Committee of 24', in 1974 (US Digest, 1974, 48–9), and the statement of the US delegate to the General Assembly's Third Committee, in 1975 (US Mission to the UN, *Press Release* USUN-114(75), 10 October 1975, 3; ('[A]chievement of self-determination must mark renewed efforts to guarantee human rights and the dignity of the individual, and . . . freedom among nations is incomplete unless there is also freedom within nations'), as well as the eloquent statements made in 1982 and 1983 by the US delegate to the General Assembly's Third Committee (UN Doc. A/C.3/37/SR.13, 6–9; A/C.3/38/SR.16, 19).

The Netherlands,[48] the Federal Republic of Germany,[49] and Australia.[50]

It is also notable that, from the early 1980's, some Western countries increasingly invoked, in international fora, Article 1 common to the two UN Covenants on Human Rights, regardless of whether or not the Covenants had been ratified. In other words, they relied on Article 1 as enshrining a standard of general purport and legal force, that is as a standard transcending the circle of contracting parties to the Covenants. On this score mention can be made of the statement in 1980 by the Dutch representative to the General Assembly's Third Committee. After the adoption of a resolution (later passed by the General Assembly as Resolution 35/35 A of 14 November 1980) he stated that The Netherlands had cast a negative vote because, among other reasons, the resolution

seemed to imply that only those peoples which had not yet attained independence could exercise that right [to self-determination], which did not do full justice to the concept of self-determination as laid down in Article 1 of the Covenants on Human Rights.[51]

A similar position, with respect to another resolution (for which they had voted), was taken by the delegates of the Federal Republic of

48 See NYIL, 1977, 160; 1982, 179.
49 See *Zeit.*, 1982, 532; 1985, 743. In 1982, the delegate of the FRG stated in the Third Committee of the General Assembly that: 'The right of self-determination could only be realized if a nation was given the opportunity, in an on-going process of decision-making, to choose freely between political alternatives in referendums and elections. In that way, each individual participated in the exercise of that right. It followed that a nation could be said to have realized the right of self-determination if individual citizens could fully enjoy their fundamental rights and freedoms, such as freedom of speech, freedom of information, freedom of assembly and association as well as the right to move freely within their own country and to leave any country, including their own' (A/C.3/37/SR.5, 13, para. 47).
50 In 1988, in submitting the Second Periodic Report on the implementation of the Covenant on Civil and Political Rights, to the UN Human Rights Committee, the Australian delegate stated the following: 'Australia considered that the right of self-determination was not fully exercised by simply gaining independence after a colonial era. It interpreted self-determination as the matrix of civil, political and other rights required for the meaningful participation of citizens in the kind of decision-making that enabled them to have a say in their future. Self-determination included participation in free, fair and regular elections and the ability to occupy public office and enjoy freedom of speech and association' (*Report of the Human Rights Committee to the G.A.*, 1988, UN Doc. A/43/40, para. 428).
51 UN Doc. A/C.3/35/SR.34, 4, para. 14.

Germany,[52] Austria, and Greece.[53] An even stronger case for the application of Article 1 was made in 1988 by the delegate of the Federal Republic of Germany to the General Assembly's Third Committee. He pointed out that:

The right to self-determination had far broader connotations than simply freedom from colonial rule and foreign domination. Article 1 of both the International Covenant on Civil and Political Rights and the International Covenant on Economic, Social and Cultural Rights defined the right to self-determination as the right of all peoples freely to determine their political status and freely to pursue their economic, social and cultural development. The question as to how peoples could freely determine their status and development was answered in article 25 of the International Covenant on Civil and Political Rights. The right to self-determination was indivisible from the right of the individual to take part in the conduct of public affairs, as was very clearly stated in Article 21 of the Universal Declaration of Human Rights. The exercise of the right to self-determination required the democratic process which, in turn, was inseparable from the full exercise of such human rights as the right of freedom of thought, conscience and religion; the right of freedom of expression; the right of peaceful assembly and of association; the right to take part in cultural life; the right to liberty and security of person; and the right to move freely in one's country and to leave any country, including one's own, as well as to return to one's country.

It was a sad fact that the genuine democratic process, which was the essential prerequisite for the exercise of the right to self-determination, had been undermined, perverted and even openly abolished time and again in many parts of the world and in the name of various totalitarian ideologies.[54]

As we shall see, these and other statements, initially only made by Western countries,[55] now enjoy a wide measure of support from the former socialist States, also because of the fact that these States now advocate – even outside the United Nations framework – concepts laid down in the two UN Covenants on Human Rights (see above, Chapter 3), as well as

[52] *Ibid.*, 9, para. 66 (the resolution was later passed by the General Assembly as Res. 35/35 B, adopted on 14 November 1980).

[53] *Ibid.*, 10, paras. 74 and 77 (the Austrian and Greek delegates, however, did not explicitly mention Art. 1 of the Covenants).

[54] A/C.3/43/SR.7, 16–17, paras. 76–77. See also the British statement reported above, in BYIL, 1984, 432.

[55] See also the statement made in 1988 by the UK delegate in the UN Commission on Human Rights, in BYIL, 1988, 441–2. In addition, see the various statements made in the UN General Assembly, on behalf of the Twelve Member States, by the holders of the Presidency of the European Community: the UK, on 15 October 1986 (EPC *Bul.*, 1) Denmark, on 5 October 1987 (*ibid.*), Greece, on 10 October 1988 (*ibid.*), France, on 9 October 1989 (*ibid.*), Italy, on 9 October 1990 (*ibid.*).

in such important political documents as the Helsinki Declaration of 1975 (see above). Furthermore, as we have just seen, currently all the former socialist States are deeply involved in the Helsinki follow-up process and subscribe – at least in theory – to the standards there emerging on democracy as a concept that requires political pluralism, representative institutions, the separation of powers, the rule of law, and respect for fundamental human rights including those of minority groups.

A further important development can be discerned in the fact that the 'Vienna Declaration on Human Rights' adopted by consensus on 25 June 1993 by 160 Member States of the UN takes up the saving clause of the 1970 UN Declaration on Friendly Relations without however including the qualification relating to 'race, creed or colour': it is now stated that a 'representative Government' is a Government 'representing the whole people . . . without distinction of any kind'.[56] This implies that distinctions other than those based on racial or religious considerations are *contrary* to the right to self-determination; in other words, self-determination means the right freely to determine the 'political status' of the country and in particular to have equal access to government *without any political, social, economic, racial or ethnic discrimination*: in short, it means *pluralistic representative democracy.*

The contention could therefore be warranted that at the present time a customary rule on the subject is *in statu nascendi*, that is, in the process of formation.[57]

---

[56] 'All peoples have the right of self-determination. By virtue of that right they freely determine their political status, and freely pursue their economic, social and cultural development.

Taking into account the particular situation of peoples under colonial or other forms of alien domination or foreign occupation, the World Conference on Human Rights recognizes the right of peoples to take any legitimate action, in accordance with the Charter of the United Nations, to realize their inalienable right of self-determination. The World Conference on Human Rights considers the denial of the right of self-determination as a violation of human rights and underlines the importance of the effective realization of this right.

In accordance with the Declaration on Principles of International law concerning Friendly Relations and Cooperation Among States in accordance with the Charter of the United Nations, this shall not be construed as authorizing or encouraging any action which would dismember or impair, totally or in part, the territorial integrity or political unity of sovereign and independent States conducting themselves in compliance with the principle of equal rights and self-determination of peoples and thus possessed of a Government representing the whole people belonging to the territory without distinction of any kind' (A/Conf. 157/23, para 2).

[57] According to Thierry, 'L'évolution du droit international', 159–60, 169–71, 'le droit des peuples est en voie d'être considéré comme celui des peuples de décider du régime

However, one ought to be aware of the stumbling-blocks which lie in the way of the birth of this emergent customary rule. The main point to be stressed is that so far most *Third World countries* have taken an attitude that does not show a convinced and consistent acceptance of the concept that national government should be based on the consent of the governed, expressed at periodic, free, and genuine elections. Admittedly, some elements of international practice tend to support the view that this acceptance has taken place. To this effect, one can refer to various resolutions adopted by UN bodies with the support of developing countries. Thus, for example, particular importance can be attached to GA resolution 43/157 of 8 December 1988 and resolution 45/150 of 21 February 1991 on 'Enhancing the effectiveness of the principle of periodic and genuine elections': they state, among other things, that 'periodic and genuine elections are a necessary and indispensable element of sustained efforts to protect the rights and interests of the governed' and that 'determining the will of the people requires an electoral process which accommodates distinct alternatives [and which] provides an equal opportunity for all citizens to become candidates and put forward their political views, individually and in co-operation with others'. Furthermore, on 17 December 1991 the UN General Assembly passed Resolution 46/137 which set up a procedure for authorizing the monitoring of national elections and endorsed the Secretary-General's decision to create an office to act as a 'focal point' for the purpose of ensuring 'consistency in the handling of requests of Member States organizing elections'.

Mention can also be made of a number of resolutions adopted by various UN bodies on specific countries. By way of illustration, one can recall the string of General Assembly and Security Council resolutions, adopted with the support of developing countries, on *Kampuchea*: there the concept is clearly spelled out that the right of the Kampuchean people to self-determination can only be exercised through free elections under international scrutiny.[58] Furthermore, mention can be made of the resolutions passed by the General Assembly on *Myanmar* (formerly called Burma): for example, Resolution 46/132 of 17 December 1991 and Resolution 47/144, of 18 December 1992. In both of these the General Assembly stated the importance of taking steps toward 'the establishment

politique au sein de l'Etat. Il devient alors un droit à la démocratie. L'évolution en ce sens est peu avancée dans l'ordre mondial mais elle est perceptible en Europe, particulièrement à la lumière des textes adoptés sous le signe de la CSCE' (at 160).

[58] See above, pp. 94–7.

of a democratic State' and urged the national authority 'to allow all citizens to participate freely in the political process'.[59]

One can also recall the various resolutions concerning the democratic process in Latin America adopted by UN bodies, in particular on Nicaragua,[60] Haiti,[61] and Guatemala[62], as well as a few resolutions passed by the UN Commission on Human Rights, notably those on Albania,[63] and on Romania.[64]

Finally, reference can be made to a string of resolutions adopted by the Ministers of Foreign Affairs or the General Assembly of the Organization of American States, some of which are of a general nature and concern the role of the democratic process,[65] others dealing specifically with Haiti.[66]

---

[59] Mention should also be made of the strong support for the democratic manner in which the people of Myanmar were realizing their right to self-determination, expressed by the Twelve Member States of the European Community. See, e.g., the declaration in the UN General Assembly, made by the Italian Presidency on 8 October 1990 (Doc. 90/335, in 6 *EPC Bul.*, 1990, 371).

[60] See GA Res. 44/10 of 23 October 1989, para. 7; 45/15 of 20 November 1990.

[61] See GA Res. 45/2, of 10 October 1990; 45/257, of 21 December 1990; 46/7, of 11 October 1991; 46/138, of 17 December 1991; 47/20, of 24 November 1992.

[62] See Res. 1987/53, of 11 March 1987 and 1990/80, of 7 March 1990, passed by the Commission on Human Rights.

[63] See Resolutions 1991/76, of 6 March 1991 and 1992/69, of 3 March 1992, where emphasis is laid, among other things, on 'the need to guarantee the free expression of will of the electors . . . and, in particular, the right of all Albanian citizens to form their own political parties, to stand for election, and to vote'.

[64] See Resolution 1992/64, of 3 March 1992, which, among other things, 'welcomes the steps taken to establish in Romania a democratic and pluralist system of government based on respect for human rights and the rule of law'.

[65] See in particular, the 1959 Santiago Declaration, of the Fifth Meeting of Consultation of Ministers of Foreign Affairs (in *The Inter-American System. Its Development and Strengthening*, 1966, 370 ff.); see also the resolutions adopted on 18 November 1983 (AG/Res. 666, in *Human Rights Law Journal*, 1983, 474); 9 December 1985 (AG/Res. 778, in *Inter-American Yearbook of Human Rights*, 1985, 1238; on 15 November 1986 (AG/Res. 837, *ibid.*, 1986, 478); on 19 November 1988 (AG/Res.950, *ibid.*, 1988, 1046); on 8 June 1990 (AG/Res. 1063, in *Actes y documentos – Organizacion de los Estados Americanos*, 1990, 109 ff.); on 8 June 1991 (AG/Res. 1124, *ibid.*, 1991, 4 ff.); on 19 May 1992 (AG/Res. 1143, in *Proceedings, Organization of American States*, 1992, 8); on 23 May 1992 (AG/Res. 1182, *ibid.*, 1992, 9). See also the Declaration of Nassau, adopted on 19 May 1992 (AG/Doc. 1, in *Actes y documentos. Organizacion de los Estados Americanos*, 1992, 1 ff.).

[66] See in particular, the resolutions of the Permanent Council of the OAS of 7 December 1987 no. 489 (in *Inter-American Yearbook on Human Rights*, 1988, 678), of 29 June 1988 no. 502 (*ibid.*, 1988, 530 ff.); the resolution adopted on 8 June 1990 by the OAS General Assembly (AG/Res.1048, in *Actes y documentos – Organizacion de los Estados Americanos*, 1990, 52 ff.) and the resolutions adopted by the Ministers of Foreign Affairs no. 3/92, of 17 May 1992 (in 86 AJIL, 1992, 667 ff.).

All this vast array of declarations and pronouncements of international bodies, *made with the support of developing countries*, should not however blind us to their *limitations*.

First of all, these resolutions have often not been matched by State behaviour: we are therefore here faced with elements (or fragmentary expressions) of *opinio juris* unattended by corresponding State practice, or *usus*.

Second, in quite a few instances the collective concern with the democratic process in a specific country was motivated by, or at any rate closely linked to, concern with the maintenance of peace or friendly relations in the area: this is no doubt the case for Kampuchea, Nicaragua, Haiti, and Guatemala.

Third, in some cases developing countries have not seized upon the opportunity, that historic and political circumstances have offered them, to propound a new concept of peoples that is more alive to current demands. This, for instance, holds true for the African Charter on Human and Peoples' Rights, whose content on the matter under discussion is deliberately and disappointingly vague,[67] and in particular does not specify that the right of peoples to self-determination includes a right to democratic governance.

Fourth, in some cases developing countries have also taken a general position that is blatantly inconsistent with their support for other resolutions that stress the importance of the democratic process. This holds true, in particular, for the UN GA Resolution 45/151 of 18 December

---

[67] M. K. Addo ('Political Self-Determination within the Context of the African Charter on Human and Peoples' Rights', 32 *Journal of African Law*, 1988, 182–193) strongly argues that the *African Charter* upholds a broad notion of self-determination, including the right of peoples of sovereign States to have access to central and legal government activity; he also stressed that this right is a continuing right, 'one which is not successfully consummated by decolonization and the vanishing of racist régimes' (192). K. M'Baye ('Les droits protégés et les procédures prévues par la Charte africaine des droits de l'homme et des peuples', in G. M. Palmieri (ed.), *La Charte africaine des droits de l'homme et des peuples*, Padua 1990, 45–6) instead rightly stresses that the notion of peoples in the Charter 'has remained vague'.

On the Charter, see also R. Gittleman, 'The African Charter on Human and Peoples' Rights – A Legal Analysis', 22 *Virginia Journal of International Law*, 1982, 667 ff.; U. O. Umozurike, 'The African Charter on Human and Peoples' Rights', 77 AJIL, 1983, 902 ff.; van Boven, 'The Relations between Peoples' Rights and Human Rights in the African Charter', especially 190–4; R. M. D'Sa, 'The African Charter on Human and Peoples' Rights: Problems and Prospects for Regional Action', 10 AYIL, 1987, 101 ff.; R. Degni-Segni, 'L'apport de la Charte Africaine des droits de l'Homme et des Peuples au droit international de l'homme', 3 AJICL, 1991, 706–15.

1990, which to some extent undermined or at least greatly narrowed down the impact of the aforementioned GA Resolution 45/150 on 'Enhancing the effectiveness of the principle of periodic and genuine elections'. Indeed, resolution 45/151 strongly emphasized the principles of 'national sovereignty' and 'non-interference' and proclaimed that 'it is the concern solely of peoples to determine methods and to establish institutions regarding the electoral process, as well as to determine the ways for its implementation according to their constitutional and national legislation'.

This, and similar stands taken or promoted by developing countries, as well as the authoritarian bent one can discern in the actual behaviour at home of quite a few Third World States, should sound a note of caution against the contention that a fully fledged general rule on internal self-determination is about to evolve and suggest the utmost prudence as regards its emergence. All one can safely submit is that a broad segment of the world community is willing to support the crystallization of such a rule, while another segment has not yet shown a similar attitude. Probably, some time is needed before the contention becomes warranted that a customary rule has taken shape.

Be that as it may, one cannot pass over in silence the negative or even hostile attitude to the birth of such a rule, taken by India – although with specific regard to the content of Article 1 of the UN Covenants.[68] This attitude could be viewed as that of a 'persistent objector' to the emergence of a general rule.[69]

---

[68] See above, pp. 60–1.

[69] The above remarks should explain why I cannot share the view authoritatively and forcefully set out by T. M. Franck in his brilliant article 'The Emerging Right to Democratic Governance' (86 AJIL, 1992, 46 ff.). According to Franck, democracy, as an international means of validating governance, is on the way to becoming a 'global legal entitlement', 'based in part on custom and in part on the collective interpretation of treaties'. This new legal entitlement that is in the process of formation is the result and culmination of three 'related generations of rule-making and implementation': the *set* of norms on *self-determination*, that on *freedom of expression* and the set on the *right to free and open elections*. These sets of norms are the *building blocks* on which the legal entitlement to democracy is founded (*ibid.*, especially at 47, 52, 77, 90).

T. M. Franck's main propositions have been taken up, or opposed, by a group of scholars: see G. H. Fox, 'The Right to Political Participation in International Law', in 86 Proceedings ASIL, 1992, 249–53, as well as the remarks by K. Engle (*ibid.*, 253–7), C. Grossman (*ibid.*, 257–61) and T. Carothers, 'Empirical Perspectives on the Emerging Norm of Democracy in International Law' (*ibid.*, 261–7). See also M. H. Halperin, D. J. Scheffer, and P. L. Smale, *Self-Determination in the World Order*, Washington, DC 1992, 60–5 and Oeter, 'Ueberlegungen zur Debatte um Selbst-bestimmung, Sezessionsrecht und 'vorzeitige' Anerkennung', 760–3.

To sum up, there is room for believing that a new general rule on internal self-determination is in the process of formation. Under this customary norm, the whole people of every State would have the right freely to choose its rulers, through a democratic and pluralistic process and in particular by means of free and genuine elections. This right would be an ongoing one, that is to say permanent in character: it would by no means be a 'once and for all' right.

However, an important caveat is necessary: one should not be blind to the fact that the birth of such a general rule, while undoubtedly constituting a great advance in the international community, might prove of scant legal value, if this rule is not accompanied by some sort of new international mechanism – be it general or specific – for monitoring its implementation and its effective observance by States. By itself, the rule would impose an obligation *erga omnes* (that is, an obligation incumbent upon every State towards all other members of the international community); correlatively, the rule would bestow upon any other international subject a *claim* to demand compliance with its prescriptions. However, so long as some new supervisory and enforcement machinery is not set up in the world community, the rule could only rely on the implementation institutions currently available in the international community. Thus, at the level of customary law, all States would have the right to call upon a certain State breaching the rule to put a stop to such non-compliance; in cases of persistent violation, they would be entitled to take peaceful countermeasures.

All this, however, would remain rather theoretical: in actual practice States would rarely take advantage of these rights, or, if they would, they would primarily do so on account of political motivations. Plainly, the existence of a despotic regime in a State situated in another continent is not of such direct relevance to other States as to prompt them to take formal steps with a view to the implementation of internal self-determination. They would only take action if motivated by some special and direct

---

To our minds, the various elements of State practice and behaviour we have underscored in the text above, as well as the general attitude of many developing countries, justify the view that we are a far cry from the emergence of a customary rule on democracy. Furthermore, if such a rule were to emerge, it would more properly be cast in the form of a rule on internal self-determination, for two reasons: first, in this way it would merely constitute an *expansion* of Art. 1 common to the UN Covenants; secondly, the self-determination 'mould' would facilitate the norm-creating process because the rule would more easily insert itself into a general *framework* (that of self-determination) that is already widely accepted in the world community.

concern. Furthermore, even in the remote case of a genuine concern by a State for humanitarian considerations, how can it be ensured – in the absence of compulsory fact-finding and adjudicatory bodies – that the unilateral finding by this State that another State is breaching the rule under discussion is well-founded? In short, this general rule would either remain devoid of any practical implementation, or might lend itself to possible abuses or manipulation.

So much for the 'anorganic' or customary level of interstate relations. Things are only slightly better if one moves to the level of the 'organized international community'. The record of international organizations (for example, the United Nations, or such regional bodies as the Organization of American States, the Organization of African Unity, the CSCE or the European Community) no doubt shows that they tend to channel and organize the concern of individual member States for the realization of self-determination; what is even more important, they usually act as a filter by which extreme and direct political motivations are played down and also fulfil a sort of fact-finding task. Nevertheless, these organizations are also subject to political concerns and are therefore conditioned by the political or ideological trends emerging within them. Moreover, when they decide to act, their means of action often prove rather ineffective, unless the situation in the target State amounts to a threat or a breach of the peace.

The conclusion is therefore warranted that the possible birth of the general rule under discussion, if unattended by a general or specific system for ensuring compliance with international law, will possess a primarily ethical, political and psychological value. The rule will prove of undisputed significance merely as a general standard by which to gauge the conduct of States and accordingly legitimize or delegitimize their internal regimes, at the international level.

PART V

General stock-taking

12

Recapitulation and conclusion

Merits and failings of the present body of international law

The political principle and its different meanings

The point of departure of this enquiry has been the realization that self-determination was first proclaimed, at the national and international level, as a political guideline for State action. Propounded by the French Revolution and then strongly supported, albeit in differing versions, by such statesmen as Lenin and Wilson, self-determination was intended to brush aside the old, State-oriented approach prevailing in international dealings. Under this approach, the world community consisted of potentates: the sovereign States, each of them primarily concerned with the interests of its political elites. Relations between international subjects in actual fact amounted to relations between ruling groups which took into account the interests of their nationals only when these were threatened by foreign Powers, and only so long as the protection of those interests was of some relevance to the ruling elite concerned.

By contrast, self-determination meant that peoples and nations were to have a say in international dealings: sovereign Powers could no longer freely dispose of them, for example by ceding or annexing territories without paying any regard to the wishes of the populations concerned. Peoples were also to have a say in the conduct of domestic and foreign business. Furthermore, peoples and nations were entitled to be free from any external oppression, chiefly in the form of colonial rule.

Clearly, this set of principles was directed toward undermining the very core of the traditional principles on which international society had rested since its inception: dynastic legitimation of power, despotism (albeit in increasingly attenuated forms), and international dealings based on agreements between rulers only. Self-determination suddenly introduced a new criterion in order to judge the legitimacy of power in the international setting: respect for the wishes and aspirations of peoples and nations. This struck at the very heart of the traditional arrangements. Self-determination also eroded one of the basic postulates of the traditional international community: territorial sovereignty. Territorial sovereignty meant that every international subject was to pay full respect to any other power wielding authority over a territory and the population living there, regardless of how it had acquired its territorial title (whether by conquest, hereditary succession, or barter with another sovereign ruler), regardless both of the way the King treated his subjects and their desires and aspirations. By promoting the formation of international entities based on the free wishes of the populations concerned, self-determination delivered a lethal blow to multinational empires. By the same token, it sounded the death knell for colonial rule. In short, the redistribution of power in the international community, advocated by self-determination, introduced a highly dynamic factor of change that deeply undermined the status quo. The US Secretary of State, R. Lansing, was therefore right when in 1919 he wrote that the 'phrase' so deeply cherished and so warmly advocated by President Wilson was 'simply loaded with dynamite' and went on to point out that the 'fixity of national boundaries and of national allegiance, and political stability would disappear if this principle was uniformly applied'. Further, he rightly raised some crucial questions: 'What effect will it have on the Irish, the Indians, the Egyptians, and the nationalists among the Boers? Will it not breed discontent, disorder and rebellion? Will not the Mohammedans of Syria and Palestine and possibly of Morocco and Tripoli rely on it? How can it be harmonized with Zionism, to which the President is practically committed?'[1]

It should be emphasized that self-determination, in the guise of a political principle, was advanced in at least *five different versions* (see above, pp. 32–3, 90–1). It was first of all propounded as a basic criterion to be used in the event of territorial changes of sovereign States: the population concerned should have a right to choose which State to belong to, either through plebiscites or referendums. Self-determination was further advocated as a democratic principle calling for the consent of the governed in any sovereign State: the people should always have the right freely to choose their own rulers. Self-determination was also proclaimed as an

[1] Lansing, *The Peace Negotiations – A Personal Narrative*, 1920, 96 ff.

anti-colonialist principle; its obvious aim was to disrupt colonial empires and redistribute power in the international community on the basis of the idea of equality among nations, thereby assisting in the emergence of new international subjects consisting of those peoples which had previously been subjected to colonialist rule. Self-determination was also invoked as a principle of freedom for nations or ethnic, cultural, or religious groups constituting minorities in sovereign States. These nations or groups ought to have the right freely to choose their internal or international status, including the right to secede from the State in order to set up a new, independent State, or to join groups existing in another State. More recently, self-determination has been conceived of as a basic prohibition on the invasion and occupation of territories by a foreign Power.

What notion of self-determination has been upheld in international law? The present legal regulation of self-determination

The main task I have undertaken in this enquiry has been to determine the extent to which the various versions of self-determination propounded by political philosophy have developed into international legal standards.

As one would have expected, the dogma of State sovereignty has constituted a powerful bulwark against the full acceptance of the principle into the body of international legal rules. This should not be surprising, given that the transformation of the political principle into a set of international norms presupposed the radical undermining of State sovereignty and a dramatic reshaping of the present framework of the world community. The acceptance of the principle into the realm of law has therefore been *selective* and *limited* in many respects.

To grasp the reasons behind this state of affairs, one should examine the current legal status of the principle against the background of three basic facts.

First, most members of the international community, both old States and newly independent countries, are multinational or multiracial agglomerates; suffice it to recall that, as has been pointed out recently,[2] on the African continent only four sovereign States (Swaziland, Lesotho, Botswana, and Somalia), certainly not ranking among the most powerful, contain ethnically homogenous populations. In a world in which the main actors are domestically so heterogeneous, it is difficult to expect that these

---

[2] A. Guelke, 'International Legitimacy, Self-Determination and Northern Ireland', 11 *Review of International Studies*, 1985, 41.

actors – which are at the same time the world legislators – should pass legal rules empowering domestic disruption, secession or at any rate norms that could fuel or exacerbate ethnic or racial conflict. By the same token, it should not come as a surprise that it is precisely those States which benefited from the principle of self-determination when they liberated themselves from colonial rule, which now rank among the staunchest supporters of a strict interpretation of self-determination. It would therefore seem that most Member States of the world community have heeded the warning issued as early as 1952 by a leading champion of human rights, Eleanor Roosevelt, who, speaking as a US delegate, stated that:

Just as the concept of individual human liberty carried to its logical extreme would mean anarchy, so the principle of self-determination given unrestricted application could result in chaos.[3]

Second, a sizeable group of member States of the international community are made up of authoritarian entities, which pay scarce regard to the aspirations and wishes of their populations. Given these characteristics of the domestic structure of many international subjects, it would be naive or disingenuous to think that these same subjects should accept strict, clear, and detailed legal rules imposing full respect for the free choice of their people.

Third, the distribution of economic, political, and military power in the world community clearly shows that power increasingly tends to concentrate in the hands of few international actors and that the remaining States must of necessity side with one of them, or even become their policy 'tributaries'. This state of affairs makes it increasingly impractical for relatively small nations or groups to be viable, if they attain political independence. It follows that independent statehood has become a myth. However, although it is increasingly cherished and pursued in the present international setting, this myth, once achieved, exposes politically independent groups to a host of problems relating to their very economic, political, and military survival.

If one bears in mind the above remarks, the limited and selective way international law has incorporated self-determination can easily be accounted for.

---

[3] E. Roosevelt, 'The Universal Validity of Man's Right to Self-Determination', 27 *Dept. St. Bul.*, 8 December 1952, 919. A few years later, the US representative in the UN General Assembly, W.B. Wise, stated that 'self-determination carried to a logical but absurd extreme would in fact threaten the very existence of most of the States members of the United Nations' (40 *Dept. St. Bul.*, 2 February 1959, 173).

First of all, States have consistently opposed the formation of any international legal rule granting the right to internal or external self-determination to ethnic or national groups, religious or cultural minorities. On account of the continued prevalence of racism in the international community and the consequent need to fight against it, States have however made allowance for one exception: racial groups living in a sovereign country are entitled to internal self-determination, that is, to be equally represented in the national ruling bodies and therefore to take part in the national decision-making process without suffering any adverse discrimination. This right does not however include an unqualified legal entitlement to secession: territorial integrity still prevails, even in this area, except for some special circumstances.

Second, the existence of many authoritarian or despotic regimes in the world community has so far prevented the emergence of a fully fledged customary rule of international law, granting the peoples of all sovereign States the right to internal self-determination, that is, the right freely to choose their rulers. Self-determination, in this liberal-democratic version, has however been proclaimed in the two 1966 UN Covenants on Human Rights. At the level of treaty law – which, however, has a narrower scope of application than customary law – the principle of the consent of the governed has thus entered the world community stage (albeit with important limitations, which I shall return to on pp. 337–41).

Thus, self-determination appears firmly entrenched in the corpus of international general rules in only three areas: as an anti-colonialist standard, as a ban on foreign military occupation and as a standard requiring that racial groups be given full access to government.

More specifically, there now exists in the body of international law both a *general principle*, serving as a basic, overarching guideline and a set of specific *customary rules* dealing with individual issues (the rules on the external self-determination of colonial peoples, of peoples under foreign occupation, and on the internal self-determination of racially discriminated groups denied equal access to government). These rules specify, with regard to certain areas, the general principle referred to above. The role of the principle is to cast light on borderline situations and to serve as a general standard for the interpretation of both customary and treaty law. The principle therefore transcends, and gives unity to, the individual customary rules. The primary role and meaning of this principle is to set out the *essence* of self-determination; self-determination, as the International Court of Justice put it in the *Western Sahara* case, 'requires a free and genuine expression of the will of the peoples concerned'.[4] In other words, the principle lays down the *method* by which States must reach decisions concerning peoples: this is by heeding their freely expressed will. In contrast, the principle neither points to the various specific areas in which self-determination should apply, nor to the final goal of self-determination (internal self-government, independent statehood, association with or integration into another State). As I pointed out above (see Chapter 5), it is no coincidence that the thrust of self-determination can be chiefly found in a *principle*, while there exist only few *specific customary rules* on the matter. It is indeed typical of the current state of the international community that in those areas where deep political and ideological disagreements prevail, but which need, however, some sort of legal regulation, only general principles evolve: unlike rules, which are fairly specific in content and normally do not lend themselves to contradictory interpretations, principles are loose, sweeping, and do not prescribe any given conduct in precise and unequivocal terms.

The task of specifying at least some of the points left open by the principle is fulfilled – albeit to a varying extent, as we have seen above – by the various customary *rules* relating to such specific areas as the self-determination of colonial peoples, of peoples under foreign occupation and of racial groups living in sovereign States. It should be added that both the principle and customary rules have acquired such a major legal standing in the world community as to have become considered as part of *jus cogens*, that is, peremptory norms of international law.

Alongside this body of customary norms, there exists an important piece of international legislation: Article 1, common to the two 1966 UN Covenants on Human Rights.

The historical and political background of the present international regulation of self-determination

Before summarizing the principal features of the legal principle and rules on self-determination that have evolved in the world community, as well as their co-ordination with other international legal principles, it would be appropriate briefly to trace the historical and political underpinnings of the body of international law on self-determination. This scrutiny, albeit brief, should help us to understand better the rationale behind the existing law.

It is no coincidence that self-determination was first advocated at the

---

[4] ICJ, Recueil 1975, 32.

international level during and after the First World War, the world's first global conflict (which, although it was fought out in Europe, actually involved all the then protagonists of the international community, that is, the countries of Europe and the United States). It is only natural that, faced with the need for the redistribution of power in the world community, which was consequent upon the downfall of three empires (the German, Austrio-Hungarian, and Ottoman) and the rise and installation in Russia of a revolutionary regime, the leading Powers of the time should search for new guiding principles. However, in spite of the stature and charismatic role of the two statesmen who proclaimed self-determination (Lenin and Wilson), traditional tenets eventually got the upper hand: self-determination not only did not mature into a legally binding norm, but also failed in actual practice to play any major role in the redesigning of authority in the international community. The world leaders, while basically adhering to traditional doctrines, only accepted – as a fall-back solution – the concept of minority rights and consequently set about recognizing in a number of international treaties the rights to be granted to minority groups living in sovereign States. I have tried above (see Chapter 2, pp. 23–7) to show briefly how even this limited regime ended in failure.

Again, it should not be surprising that it was after another general and dramatic upheaval in the whole international community: the Second World War, that self-determination was again advocated as an important policy guideline, more consonant than traditional doctrines with the new requirements of the day. This time, however, one of the new leading Powers, the Soviet Union, managed to get the founding fathers of the new world constitution, the UN Charter, to enshrine the principle. On account of the strong opposition of the colonial Powers, the principle was eventually couched in very moderate language: it only meant self-government, and in addition did not impose any direct and immediate obligation on member States, but simply enunciated one of the goals to be pursued by the Organization (see above, Chapter 3). Furthermore, colonial empires were not dismantled; on the contrary, institutional devices were set up for their maintenance and gradual evolution (see Chapters 11–13 of the UN Charter).

Nevertheless, the floodgates had been opened and the new doctrine soon became one of the driving forces of the international community. In the 1950s developing and socialist States seized upon self-determination as an anti-colonial doctrine to drive a powerful wedge into colonial empires. This marked a strong departure from, if not a break with, the moderate concept of self-determination embodied in the UN Charter. As a consequence, a set of rules on the self-determination of colonial peoples soon evolved (see above, Chapter 4, pp. 71–89). By the same token, the condition of racial majorities, like those blatantly discriminated against in Southern Rhodesia and South Africa, led the majority of States to propose, and the Western countries to accept, the gradual formation of rules on the internal self-determination of racial groups denied equal access to government. Following the Six Day War in the Middle East and the Israeli occupation of the Arab territories, the same majority of Third World and socialist countries was instrumental in developing international rules on the right to self-determination of peoples under the military occupation of foreign Powers. All these rules fleshed out the moderate and loose concept of self-government, set out in the UN Charter, by turning it into a sweeping entitlement for colonial peoples to achieve independent statehood (as well as, for racial groups, to gain access to government, and for peoples in militarily occupied territories to achieve freedom from outside domination). In short, in the post-Charter era self-determination was rapidly and dramatically given a new lease of life, thus becoming one of the crucial standards of behaviour, at international level, in the decolonization period.

Western countries, after first playing an essentially passive role (they had mainly tried to curb the revolutionary thrust of the principle advocated by the other countries, thereby circumscribing its impact on the existing body of international law), took the offensive in the 1960s and vigorously propounded two important postulates that were closely bound up with each other: first, that self-determination should be a universal doctrine, not essentially confined to colonial countries; second, it should primarily concern the internal structure of States and, in particular, should require that the authority of rulers be based on democratic consent.

As a result of Western insistence on these concepts, they were eventually upheld in the two 1966 UN Covenants on Human Rights. However, because of the opposition of other States (but also the lukewarm attitude of some Western Powers), the relevant provision of the Covenants (common Article 1) lacked teeth: for one thing, the provision itself was couched in rather general and loose terms, whereas one would have expected incisive and forceful legal commands; for another, the substantive provisions of the Covenant on Civil and Political Rights (on freedom of thought, association, participation in the conduct of public affairs, etc.), to which Article 1 implicitly adverted, were themselves somewhat woolly and at any rate lent themselves to markedly conflicting interpretations; on top of that, one ought to note that the supervisory machinery that should safeguard the implementation of Article 1 of the Covenant on Civil and Political Rights has failed (at least thus far) to ensure full respect for the right of self-determination (see above, pp. 62–5, 145–6). It would however be fallacious to conclude that the adoption of common Article 1 was a Pyrrhic victory for the West: for the first time a powerful concept was enshrined in inter-national legal rules, a concept destined to have a snowball effect as soon as the climate of international relations changed. Indeed, the break up of the Soviet 'empire' and the gradual opening of Central and Eastern European countries to democratic doctrines, as well as the implementation of the same doctrine in Latin America are now setting the stage for both the revitalization of Article 1 common to the two Covenants, and the gradual crystallization of a customary norm proclaiming internal self-determination as a principle of democratic governance (see above, pp. 302–12). Thus, self-determination, instead of withering away with the demise of colonialism, is showing its resilience and indeed is even acquiring a new lease of life.

We shall see in the following pages that a rethinking of self-determination, in order to reorient it in a manner more attuned to the current exigencies of the world community, might prove conducive to an even greater enhancement of self-determination – without, however, this enhancement resulting in imperilling the 'positive values' of the current international community.

Merits of the present law

If the present legal regulation of self-determination is considered against the political background of the world community, it appears that it is in some respects less unsatisfactory than is claimed by so many com-mentators. Three main points must be made.

First, while before 1945 the various members of the international community could afford to take decisions without making allowance for the wishes of peoples and international dealings ultimately consisted of relations between potentates, since the adoption of the UN Charter self-determination has gradually acquired the status and force of a set of general and legally binding guidelines for the action of sovereign States.

Secondly, this corpus of international legal standards considerably enhances the status of various classes of peoples: (i) colonial peoples, (ii) peoples under foreign military occupation, (iii) racial groups living in sovereign countries, (iv) the whole population of sovereign States (but this only occurs at treaty level). For these categories, self-determination means the freedom to choose one's own international status or, as the case may be, the right to be rid of a foreign occupant, or the right to have a representative government which does not deny racial groups access to government, or the right to freely choose one's rulers.

These peoples have thus gained a legal foothold in international relations. Subject to the serious limitations that have been emphasized in Chapter 6, they also have some sort of international 'remedy' available in the case of the forcible denial of their rights. What is even more important, in the case of international breaches of the right to self-determination, third-party States are legally entitled to 'intervene' and to call the responsible State to account.

In short, in spite of all the failings of the present legal regulation and the consequent fragility and precariousness of the status of peoples in the world community, a major advance cannot be denied: at least liberation movements representing peoples entitled to self-determination are no longer passive objects of States' conduct on the international scene. This conclusion is inescapable, although the standing of those peoples is still controversial and many traditional members of the world community are not willing to promote them to the rank of legal subjects proper.

Third, self-determination has also had a significant impact on the most traditional segment of international law, namely the acquisition, transfer, and loss of title over territory. It has cast doubt on traditional legal titles such as colonial conquest and acquisition by cession of sovereignty over overseas territories. In addition, as a result of the principle under discussion no valid legal title can any longer be acquired in the case of the annexation of territories in breach of self-determination. Self-determination also prevents States from regarding as *terra nullius* territories inhabited by organized collectivities lacking the hallmarks of State authority, in such cases where territories are abandoned by the sovereign State previously wielding authority over them. Finally, self-determination renders null and void treaties providing for the transfer of territories without including any prior and genuine consultation of the population involved.

Fourth, in the area of the use of force, self-determination has had a twofold impact. On the one hand, it has *extended* the general ban on force, in that it has brought about the prohibition of the resort to force by States against racial groups in their territory who are denied equal access to government. On the other hand, self-determination has resulted in the granting to liberation movements of a legal licence to use force for the purpose of reacting to the forcible denial of self-determination by a

324

colonial State, an occupying Power or a State refusing a racial group equal access to government (this licence amounts to a *derogation* from the customary ban on the use of force, referred to above).

It is thus apparent that self-determination has been one of the principles that have greatly contributed to the emergence of new trends in the world community and indeed have brought about the passage from the 'Westphalian model' to the 'UN Charter model' of international relations.

The alleged flaws of the law

Many commentators have harshly attacked the present legal regulation of self-determination, claiming that (i) it fails to pay regard to the basic aspirations of nations and minorities, or that (ii) it is strongly one-sided and biased, for it only takes account of the political and ideological demands of some groups of States (those with anti-colonial leanings) and totally neglects the requirements of 'representative democracy', or that (iii) it is made up of a set of rules that are deliberately ambiguous and imprecise and, in particular, do not define their 'beneficiaries', that is, the peoples to which they address themselves, nor provide guidelines as to the modes of implementing self-determination. As a consequence, those rules are open to differing interpretations, much to the detriment of the basic requirement of legal certainty.

While some of these criticisms are sound, and these will be examined shortly, at least two are questionable.

First, it is fallacious to contend that the present legal regulation is ideologically biased, in that it ultimately means *anti-colonialism*. This contention, put forward by a number of legal commentators,[5] fails to note that, as we have seen above (in Chapters 3 and 4), international customary

---

[5] See Emerson, 'Self-Determination Revisited', 25–63 ('In its immediately present incarnation, the loudly proclaimed right of all peoples to self-determination must actually be read to mean that all overseas colonial peoples have a right to be liberated from the overlordship of their alien white masters . . . Far from being a universal and easily available right, the right of self-determination has in fact only on rare occasions been made available to certain peoples under special circumstances' (p. 63) 'What emerges beyond dispute is that all peoples do *not* have the right of self-determination: they have never had it, and they never will have it' (p. 64); Rigo Sureda, *The Evolution of the Right of Self-Determination*, 95 ff., 352–6; Blum, 'Reflections'; Nguyen Quoc, Daillier, and Pellet, *Droit international publique*, 489–96. A forceful plea for not limiting self-determination to colonial situations was made by C. Eagleton, 'Excesses of Self-Determination', 31 FA, 1953, 592–604. That the decolonization process has not made self-determination obsolete is asserted, among others, by S. Prakash Sinha, 'Is Self-Determination passé?', 12 Columbia Journal of International Law, 1973, 260–73.

law also confers a right to (external) self-determination on peoples oppressed by a foreign Power in occupation of the territory in which they live, while treaty law (Article 1 common to the two 1966 UN Covenants on Human Rights) grants to the entire population of each Contracting State both the right to internal self-determination and the right to be free from colonial domination and foreign occupation. Admittedly, between the 1950s and the 1960s, much emphasis was put in the international community on the anti-colonial dimension of self-determination. This was to a large extent due to the need to dismantle colonial empires: the concept of self-determination and the attendant legal instruments were used by the developing and the then socialist States as one of the tools for attaining this objective. This, however, in no way detracts from the expansion of the principle to other areas. Fortunately, Western States did not remain silent and, by vociferously insisting on the universality of the principle, actually caused its legal ramifications to be extended to other peoples than those under colonial rule.

The second criticism to which exception should be taken, is the contention that the present legal regulation *does not define the 'units of self-determination'*, that is, the peoples entitled to the right. This drawback, according to some commentators (e.g. Emerson, Pomerance, Schwebel, and Müllerson)[6] is just one of the volatile aspects of the content of self-determination.

Admittedly, nowhere in international law can one find a definition of the 'peoples' enjoying the right at issue. However, can such a definition be legitimately expected from international legal rules? It is well known that there is much controversy in historical literature and in the writings of political scientists about the meaning of the terms 'people', 'nation', 'ethnic groups', and so on.[7] Given the great confusion existing in this area and the broad differences of opinion, why should States try to agree upon

---

[6] Emerson, *Self-Determination Revisited in the Era of Decolonization*, 63, ('Since there are no rational and objective criteria by which a "people" in the large and in the abstract can be identified, it [the right to self-determination] introduces an incalculably explosive and disruptive element which is incompatible with the maintenance of a stable and organized society'); M. Pomerance, *Self-Determination in Law and Practice*, 14–23; S. Schwebel, in Proceedings ASIL, 1990, 172; R. Müllerson, *ibid.*, 174.

[7] For recent scholarly writings on this matter, see in particular K. Deutsch, *Nationalism and Its Alternatives*, New York 1969; H. Seton-Watson, *Nations and States*, London 1977; E. Gellner, *Nationalism and the Two Forms of Cohesion in Complex Societies*, London 1982; A. Smith, *The Ethnic Origin of Nations*, Oxford 1986; A. Margalit and J. Raz, 'National Self-Determination' 87 *Journal of Philosophy*, 1990, 439–61; Y. Tamir, 'The Right to National Self-Determination', 58 *Social Research*, 1991, 565–90.

legal definitions that would inescapably be exceedingly vague and controversial, and would accordingly lend themselves to highly subjective interpretations? To provide a legal definition in this volatile area would simply lead to bad legal draftsmanship.

It should be added that the lack of formal legal definitions does not entail that the interpreter cannot deduce such definitions from the context of the existing legal framework.[8] Indeed, it is easy to infer such definitions. It is apparent from the set of rules on self-determination, which have been referred to above (Chapters 3–5), that the notion of 'people' to which they advert is sufficiently clear. Some of them refer to 'colonial peoples', that is, to peoples living in territories under colonial rule. Others refer to 'peoples under foreign domination', that is, to the populations living in territories subjected to foreign military occupation. Others refer to racial groups living in sovereign States. Others (Article 1 common to the two 1966 UN Covenants on Human Rights) also refer to the whole population of each Contracting State.

It is thus clear that, albeit indirectly and perhaps somewhat obliquely, international legal rules do indeed specify the 'units of self-determination' to which they grant an international right.[9]

The real flaws

Undisputedly the current legal regulation of self-determination exhibits a number of lacunae, ambiguities, and loopholes. Since these have already

---

[8] On the various conceptions of the 'self', see C. Economides, 'Le droit des peuples à disposer d'eux-mêmes', 10 *Revue hellénique de droit international*, 1957, 296–98; Arzinger, *Das Selbstbestimmungsrecht im allgemeinen Völkerrecht den Gegenwart*, 240–76; Johnson, *Self-Determination within the Community of Nations*, 112–34; J. F. Guilhaudis, *Le droit des peuples à disposer d'eux-mêmes*, 36–66; Crawford, *The Creation of States in International Law*, 84–102; G. S. Swan, 'Self-Determination and the United Nations Charter', 22 *Indian Journal of International Law*, 1982, 271–3; N. Berman, 'Sovereignty in Abeyance: Self-Determination and International Law', 7 *Wisconsin International Law Journal*, 1988, 84–94; Demetriadou, 'To What Extent is the Principle of Self-Determination a Right?', 3327–9; B. Kingsbury, 'Self-Determination and "Indigenous Peoples"', 86 Proceedings ASIL 1992, 384–5.

[9] It is therefore not necessary, except perhaps for extreme cases, to draw upon the criterion suggested by I. Brownlie (*Treaties and Indigenous Peoples*, 48–9: 'In practice the question of the definition of a unit of self-determination is resolved by the process of recognition . . . Such recognition may take the form of a pattern of individual acts of recognition by other States or of a resolution of the General Assembly of the United Nations, or of a regional organization, such resolutions being essentially collective acts of recognition. The Palestinians have been recognized as a people in a long series of UNGA resolutions.').

been pointed to in the course of the present enquiry, they shall now simply be summed up.[10]

First of all, current international law is *blind to the demands of ethnic groups, and national, religious, cultural, or linguistic minorities.*[11] Not only does international law refrain from granting any right of internal or external self-determination to these groups, but it also fails to provide any alternative remedy to the present plight of so many of them. In short, and to put it in R. Falk's words, international law takes a 'statist view of self-determination'.[12] Of course, political stability and the territorial integrity of States are important values that need not be disregarded. Indiscriminately granting the right to self-determination to all ethnic groups and minorities would bring about a major disruption of international relations, a serious threat to peace and the fragmentation of States into a myriad of entities that would often be unable to survive. One should therefore tread cautiously in this area and appreciate the concern of States for their stability and integrity. On the other hand, one cannot fail to note that international law could provide a host of contingency solutions which, while not undermining the international legal order, would be likely to pay regard to the aspirations of those groups and minorities that suffer from discrimination and oppression.

---

[10] For a scathing attack on the present 'law of self-determination', see Pomerance, *Self-Determination in Law and Practice*, especially 9–76. This author sums up her criticisms by stating that 'the "New U.N. Law of Self-Determination" ignores the complexities of the self-determination conundrum and proffers deceptively simple solutions and sham universality' (at 74). As is apparent from that which was stated above, in the text, I share only in part Pomerance's objections to the present 'law of self-determination'.

[11] For the sake of clarity, I shall point out that I share the view held by a number of commentators (see, e.g., C. Tomuschat, 'Status of Minorities under Art.27 of the UN Covenant on Civil and Political Rights', in Chandra (ed.), *Minorities in National and International Laws*, 40–1) that the concept of 'national group' or 'national minority' is broader than that of 'ethnic group' or 'ethnic minority'; the former encompasses groups which, in addition to some objective characteristics (specific cultural ties, a common historical origin, possibly some distinctive racial features), also meet a subjective criterion, i.e. the consciousness of their ethnic identity and the political wish 'to become masters of their own fate'.

As for the concept of 'minority' the best and most accepted definition is that suggested by F. Capotorti ('Minorities', in 8 *Encyclopedia*, 1985, 385) namely 'a group which is numerically inferior to the rest of the population of a State and in a non-dominant position, whose members possess ethnic, religious or linguistic characteristics which differ from those of the rest of the population and who, if only implicitly, maintain a sense of solidarity, directed towards preserving their culture, traditions, religion or language'.

[12] R. Falk, 'The Rights of Peoples (In Particular Indigenous Peoples)', in Crawford, *The Rights of Peoples*, 24–7.

This basic flaw of international law can be better discerned if one moves to a higher level of generalization, by placing the legal regime of self-determination within the overall context of the approach to non-State entities taken by the world community.

From this viewpoint the legal regulation of groups, minorities, and peoples turns out to be singularly skewed and inconsistent. National, ethnical, racial, or religious groups living within sovereign countries are strongly protected by law only if they are menaced with destruction or if members of the group are killed. Genocide is an anathema to the world community, which has both customary rules and an all-important Convention (of 1948) at its disposal in order to fight against this odious phenomenon.[13]

When compared with the legal ban on genocide – so important, although not put into practice – the legal regulation of the 'daily life' of minorities and peoples is even less satisfactory. Minorities and groups are indeed protected against racial discrimination (both by a customary rule on the matter and by the UN 1965 Convention) but not as groups; only *members* of racial groups are legally entitled to demand the suppression of any discriminatory measures. As for ethnic, religious or linguistic minorities and indigenous populations, they are not protected by customary law at all; only Article 27 of the UN Covenant on Civil and Political Rights takes account of minorities and an ILO Convention (revised in 1989) protects indigenous populations.[14] Once again, Article 27

---

[13] However, if one moves from legal condemnation to the actual action of member States of the international community against genocide, one is struck by the impotence or inertia of States and intergovernmental organizations when faced with grave instances of genocide. All too often they remain unperturbed, as is borne out by the recent massacre of the Hutus by the Tutsis in Burundi and of the Kurds by Iraq. Although there have been reactions by some States in the latter instance, they have been strikingly cautious and appear to have been primarily motivated by the use of chemical weapons for the perpetration of genocide, rather than by the fact of the genocide itself. See the presidential communiqué published on 7 September 1988 in *Le Monde*, at 5. See also *Le Monde*, 10 September 1988, 28; *The International Herald Tribune*, 10–11 September 1988, 1–2.

[14] On indigenous populations in general, see G. T. Morris, 'In Support of the Right of Self-Determination for Indigenous Peoples under International Law', 29 *German Yearbook of International Law*, 1986, 277 ff., especially 311–16; R. L. Barsh, 'Indigenous Peoples: An Emerging Object of International Law', 80 AJIL, 1986, 369 ff,; H. Hannum, 'New Developments in Indigenous Rights', 28 *Virginia Journal of International Law*, 1988, 649–78; Hannum, *Autonomy, Sovereignty and Self-Determination*, 74–103; R. Falk, 'The Rights of Peoples (in Particular Indigenous Peoples)', in Crawford (ed.), *The Rights of Peoples*, 17 ff.; G. Nettheim, '"Peoples and Populations" – Indigenous Peoples and the Rights of Peoples', *ibid.*, 107 ff.; R. Stavenhagen, *The*

does not protect the minority as such but only its individual members.[15] Furthermore, it only protects the maintenance of the cultural, linguistic, or religious identity of the group; it does not secure for the group a right to pursue its expansion and development. It does not, in other words, grant 'dynamic' rights.[16] (These sorts of rights are only conferred on racial groups: as we have seen, the principle of self-determination requires that the governments of sovereign States are 'representative' of the various racial groups, that is, it grants them equal access to government.)

The overall picture is then clear; groups living in sovereign States are (in theory) strongly protected only against that most extreme of measures: genocide. Otherwise, they are only ensured the right to maintain their identity, that is, to survive as a group (with the exception of racial groups, which can also demand access to government).

A second flaw of the international legal regime of self-determination is that it ultimately *lacks universality*. To be precise, one can only regard as having a universal scope the general *principle* referred to above (which, as was pointed out, enunciates the essence of self-determination, namely the need always to have regard to the freely expressed and genuine will of the populations concerned). Aside from this principle, customary rules only grant the right to three specific classes of peoples (those under colonial rule or foreign occupation and racial groups denied equal access to government). Hence, they fail to confer the right under discussion on *all peoples* of sovereign States. This right is only bestowed upon the peoples of the States that are parties to the two 1966 UN Covenants on Human Rights.

Thirdly, even in the area where it does provide some sort of legal regulation, the body of international rules on self-determination is *marred*

Ethnic Question – Conflicts, Development and Human Rights, Tokyo 1990, 93–119; Brownlie, *Treaties and Indigenous Peoples*, 55–75; Kingsbury, 'Self-Determination and "Indigenous Peoples"', 383–94; B. R. Howard, 'Human Rights and Indigenous Peoples: on the Relevance of International Law for Indigenous Liberation', 35 GYIL, 1992, 105–50; C. M. Brölmann and M. Y. A. Zieck, 'Indigenous Peoples', in Brölmann, Lefeber, and Zieck, *Peoples and Minorities in International Law*, 187–220. On the 1989 ILO Convention, in particular see N. Lerner, *Group Rights and Discrimination in International Law*, Dordrecht, Boston, and London 1991, 107–10; see also R.L. Barsh, 'Revision of ILO Convention no. 107', 81 AJIL, 1987, 756–62.

[15] The best writings on Art. 27 are by F. Capotorti, *Study on the Rights of Persons Belonging to Ethnic, Religious and Linguistic Minorities* (UN Doc. E/CN.4/Sub.2/384, Rev. I, 1979); see also 'Minorities', in 8 *Encyclopedia*, 1985, 385 ff.) and by C. Tomuschat, 'Status of Minorities under Article 27 of the UN Covenant on Civil and Political Rights', in Chandra, *Minorities in National and International Laws*, 31 ff. See also below, note 32.

[16] For a survey of the various views on this issue, see Lerner, *Group Rights and Discrimination in International Law*, 15–16.

with imperfections. Thus, we have seen above (pp. 71–4) that the rule on the external self-determination of colonial peoples does not include any freedom of choice for ethnic groups living in a colonial country (only the colonial people as a whole can opt for independence or association or integration with another country). Furthermore, strictly speaking, the wishes of the populations concerned must only be ascertained by means of a plebiscite or referendum when the population seems inclined to opt for association or integration with another State. As for the rule on the right to the external self-determination of peoples under foreign domination, a major flaw lies in the fact that the rule fails to specify the procedures for exercising self-determination and the options available to the 'occupied' people. This failure turns out to be most unfortunate in cases where foreign occupation is not the result of aggression or the legal status of the occupied territory is uncertain. In these instances the simple withdrawal of the Occupying Power may not be sufficient for the exercise of self-determination (a case in point is the question of the Arab Territories occupied by Israel). Essentially, international rules do not provide satisfactory guidelines for precisely these kinds of complicated situations.

Also the rule governing the right to the internal self-determination of racial groups is marred by some major deficiencies. First of all, it does not set strict requirements specifying what is needed for a government to be 'representative' in order to fulfil the obligation to respect self-determination. Secondly, it does not specify the means for attaining self-determination, nor does it envisage any other options than the participation of representatives of a racial group in national government. As was emphasized in Chapter 4, the major flaw of this rule is that it crystallized with regard to two specific historic situations (Southern Rhodesia and South Africa) where the racial group (which in fact constituted the majority) was denied access to government. Consequently, the rule is only directed to this sort of situation. It does not provide any satisfactory solution for those situations where a racial group, although it is free to elect its representatives to the central government, claims that more than that is needed to protect its cultural and racial identity and promote its full development.

In addition, treaty law is also far from perfect. Thus, Article 1 common to the two 1966 UN Covenants on Human Rights, in which the right of the population of each Contracting State to enjoy internal self-determination is laid down, does not set strict requirements for determining when the non-observance of the right by a State amounts to a breach of self-determination. To put it differently, and to emphasize again the point we have already underscored above, the 'democratic principle' or the 'rule of the governed' enshrined in Article 1 is couched in rather nebulous wording. This wording, combined with the loopholes contained in the provisions of the Covenant on Civil and Political Rights concerning the democratic process, makes it possible for Contracting States to bypass the prescriptions on self-determination.

More generally, it should be pointed out that both customary and treaty law on *internal* self-determination have little to say with respect to the possible modes of implementing democratic governance. Nor do they provide guidelines on the possible distribution of power among institutionalized units or regions. Still less do they furnish workable standards concerning some possible forms of realizing internal self-determination, such as devolution, autonomy, or 'regional' self-government.

Fourthly, the present international legal regulation of self-determination is sometimes frustrated by the existence of other rules that prevent its application in some specific areas. Thus, as was pointed out above (see Chapter 9), the rule on *uti possidetis juris* enjoins that States, when achieving independence, must retain the borders they had either when they were under colonial rule, or (as was stated in 1992 by the Arbitration Committee set up by the Peace Conference on Yugoslavia in its Opinions nos. 2 and 3), when they were part of a federated State. It follows that the populations living along or close to these borders are denied the right freely to choose the State to which they intend to belong. In this case, overriding geopolitical considerations eventually result in the thwarting of self-determination.

A fifth major deficiency of the present legal regulation of self-determination is that it is not assisted by an effective enforcement machinery or at least a significant body of *remedial measures* capable of implementing the right. Customary international law does not grant peoples any right proper to take remedial action in the event of gross breaches of self-determination however, by not prohibiting liberation movements from resorting to armed violence in the case of the forcible denial of self-determination and by indirectly endorsing this resort to violence, international law grants a licence to use force (see above, pp. 150–5, 197–8). As for treaty law, the UN Covenant on Civil and Political Rights and its Optional Protocol may be interpreted (and indeed have so far been interpreted by the UN Human Rights Committee) as not conferring on peoples, or the representatives of peoples, the right to submit to the UN Human Rights Committee 'communications' on alleged violations of self-determination. As a consequence, so far Article 1 of the

Covenants has not been regarded as attended by any means of vindicating the right it lays down. This shows that although international law grants a legal right proper to some classes of peoples or groups, this right remains to a large extent theoretical because it still lacks the support of any accompanying remedial action on behalf of the holders of the right. In the last resort, it is thus for *third States* to intervene in the event of gross breaches of self-determination. At this level, international law is very generous; since norms on self-determination impose obligations *erga omnes*, any third State is legally entitled to demand fulfilment of such obligations. In reality, however, States very seldom make use of this legal possibility in bilateral relations and instead prefer to promote diplomatic and political action, if any, within international fora such as the United Nations. The rich potential of the legal rules is thus very often left unexploited. The same holds true for *jus cogens;* although general legal standards on self-determination possess the status of peremptory norms, so far no specific action has ever been taken at the international level to rely upon self-determination as *jus cogens.*

The co-ordination of self-determination with the other fundamental legal principles of the world community

It is appropriate now to see how the principle of self-determination and the general rules that specify it co-ordinate with the seven other basic principles governing international relations.[17] In this connection, a distinction should be made between those principles with which self-determination cannot be easily harmonized because they enshrine values that are radically at odds with it and those principles which can instead – in most cases – smoothly interact with it because they substantially express values that are 'on the same wave-length' as self-determination.

The former class includes the principle of sovereignty and that of non-interference in the internal or external affairs of other States. These two principles are the obvious product and reflection of the old world community framework, the so-called 'Westphalian model'. They intend to sanction and safeguard the status quo. It is therefore only natural that they

---

[17] On these principles, see Cassese, *International Law in a Divided World*, 126 ff. On the co-ordination of self-determination with other international principles, see Graefrath, *Zur Stellung der Prinzipien im Gegenwärtigen Völkerrecht*, 7 ff.; Kröger (ed.), *Völkerrecht*, Vol. I, 110–29; Pomerance, *Self-Determination in Law and Practice*, 43–62; Arangio-Ruiz, 'Autodeterminazione (diritto dei popoli alla)', 6–7; Gayim, *The Principle of Self-Determination*, 84–7.

are on a collision course with self-determination, which reflects the 'UN Charter model'. Indeed, as I said above, self-determination, in that it sets out an international standard for the legitimacy of States based on the free choice of peoples, undermines the status quo and loudly proclaims the need for change in international relations.

The latter class of principles includes the prohibition of the threat or use of force, the peaceful settlement of disputes, respect for human rights, international co-operation and good faith. All these principles are the product of the new trends which emerged after the Second World War and denote the innovations introduced into the world community as a result of the establishment of the United Nations. Since they basically exhibit the same hallmarks as self-determination (they all reflect the dynamic tendencies of the new international order), they are more readily harmonized with it.

Let us now examine the extent to which self-determination can be co-ordinated, if not reconciled, with the two fundamental principles of the traditional international community intended to safeguard territorial integrity and political stability: State sovereignty and non-interference.

As far as the dimension of State sovereignty that is relevant to self-determination is concerned, it cannot be denied that it has firmly resisted the powerful pressure of self-determination. This is apparent from the following: (i) no right of secession has been granted to nations, ethnic groups, or minorities; (ii) no right has yet been conferred by general international norms on the whole population of sovereign States freely to decide by whom they should be ruled: 'consent of the governed', a continuing right that peoples might have exercised against the government of the State where they live, has been perceived as too dangerous for the present fabric of the world community. In short, the relationship between the whole population of a sovereign State and its government is still regarded by customary international law as coming within the purview of its domestic jurisdiction; (iii) the right to external self-determination, which entails the possibility of choosing (or restoring) independence, has only been bestowed upon two classes of peoples (those under colonial rule or foreign occupation), based upon the assumption that both classes make up entities that are inherently distinct from the colonialist Power and the occupant Power and that their 'territorial integrity', all but destroyed by the colonialist or occupying Power, should be fully restored; (iv) in the case of the accession of colonial peoples to independence (or of association with or integration into another State), no right has been granted to the ethnic groups making up those peoples freely to choose their international status.

334

Independence (or association or integration) has been granted to the colonial people as a whole, regardless of its possible ethnic components. Furthermore, (v) pursuant to the *uti possidetis* principle, colonial boundaries may not be changed. The few inroads into State sovereignty that self-determination has been able to make have been limited: first, States are duty-bound to grant racial groups living in their territory equal access to government; second, in the case of territorial changes brought about by the agreement of the States concerned, these States must always consult the populations concerned, to ascertain their free will by means of referendums or plebiscites. In cases in which the expression of the free and genuine will of these populations is not permitted, the treaty providing for territorial change is contrary to *jus cogens* and can therefore be subsequently declared null and void at the request of one of the contracting parties. Clearly, these minor erosions of State sovereignty resulting from the application of self-determination are not of striking relevance.

In contrast, self-determination has been able to narrow greatly the scope of non-interference. The latter principle has been remarkably compressed, in that whenever a people has a claim to self-determination under the relevant legal regulation, third-party States are legally entitled to raise the issue both in bilateral negotiations and within international fora. They can discuss the matter with the State concerned and also make proposals and appeals with a view to the prompt realization of the right to self-determination. These *démarches* cannot be rejected as amounting to an undue interference into the domestic or international affairs of the 'target' States. Furthermore, third-party States have the right to call to account, before the appropriate international bodies, those States which grossly infringe upon the right under discussion. In addition, third-party States are entitled to provide any assistance (economic, humanitarian, and political), short of military aid, to liberation movements struggling for self-determination. It is evident that the right of some classes of peoples is no longer the exclusive concern of the State involved but has instead become recognized as an issue of international concern.

Let us now move to the co-ordination of self-determination with the class of 'new' fundamental principles of international law.

As for the principle banning the threat or use of force, in some respects it is simply strengthened by self-determination. This holds true for the customary rule on the right to self-determination of peoples under foreign military occupation. In the case of such occupation, the occupying Power usually invades the foreign territory in breach of the fundamental ban on the use of force (this applies, for example, to the cases of Afghanistan,

335

Kampuchea (Cambodia), Cyprus, Lebanon, and Kuwait). In these cases the occupation is therefore *simultaneously* a (continuing) breach of the ban on the use of force and of the rule on self-determination. Furthermore, self-determination corroborates and expands the general ban on force in that it prohibits States from using force in order to deny a racial group equal access to government (see above, pp. 194–7). This is a major achievement: it is the first time that international law has enjoined States to refrain from using force *on their own territory*, against *a part of their own population*. International rules go even further, in that they not only ban resort to force for denying self-determination, but also prohibit the denial of self-determination through *coercive mechanisms or measures* short of military force (see above, pp. 196–7). It should be added that States are duty-bound to refrain from giving military or economic assistance to Powers forcibly denying self-determination to an oppressed people or racial group.

In other respects, self-determination might instead constitute an exception to the prohibition on the use of force provided for in general international law. However, the attempt made in the 1960s and 1970s by developing and 'socialist' countries to advance in this direction in order to provide for a derogation from the aforementioned ban in favour of liberation movements fighting on behalf of colonial or 'occupied' peoples or racial groups in sovereign countries, did not succeed. The staunch opposition of Western, as well as a number of Latin American countries, prevented the formation of a general rule granting a legal right proper to liberation movements to wage war (as well as the right of third-party States to provide military assistance or even to send troops to help liberation movements). Liberation movements meeting certain requirements were simply granted, under strict conditions, a mere *licence* to use force to repel the *forcible* denial of self-determination by the oppressive Power (see above, pp. 150–5, 197–8).

Three other principles, namely, on the peaceful settlement of disputes, on co-operation, and on good faith, provide guidelines for the proper implementation of the right to self-determination. They make it incumbent upon States involved in disputes concerning self-determination to avoid armed conflict and instead resort, in good faith, to direct negotiations or mediation or conciliation. The three principles thus point to the path to be taken, especially when the inherent intricacies of history and politics make factual circumstances so complicated that they do not lend themselves to clear-cut and easy legal solutions. In these cases co-operation, use of peaceful means of settlement and good faith must be the overriding considerations for the States concerned.

Good faith, however, plays a further and important role by itself. Pursuant to this principle, when States hold plebiscites, referendums, etc., with a view to determining the free will of the peoples concerned, they must give these peoples a fair chance to make a genuine choice. It follows that States must refrain from moving populations from the relevant territory, before the holding of the plebiscite or referendum. Similarly, they must refrain from altering the body of the population by moving in peoples before the 'test'. In short, States must not artificially alter the constituency before the referendum or plebiscite is held. By the same token, good faith enjoins States to offer the population concerned a proper choice between various alternatives. In other words, the options provided to the population must not be so artificial, rigid or limited as *de facto* to result in that population making a fictitious choice or even making no real choice at all (for example, by providing totally unrealistic options, or creating a situation in which it is a foregone conclusion that a proposal will be turned down by an overwhelming majority).

Let us finally discuss the principle which is closest to self-determination, namely that of respect for human rights. Plainly self-determination is the *summa* or synthesis of individual human rights because a people really enjoys self-determination only when the rights and freedoms of all individuals making up that people are fully respected. On a different level, the enjoyment of individual rights presupposes the realization of (external) self-determination because if a people is oppressed by a colonial or occupant Power, individuals cannot really be free to exercise their basic rights and freedoms. Thus, it is clear that the two principles supplement and strengthen each other; respect for one of them must perforce go hand in hand with compliance with the other.[18]

Emerging normative trends

As opposed to the somewhat disheartening legal situation, emphasized above (pp. 327–33), one should, however, point to a significant trend in the general legal regime of self-determination that is emerging in the world community.

Indeed, with regard to internal self-determination the general legal principle is gradually expanding in scope and purport. As was stressed

---

[18] On the link between self-determination and human rights, see in particular J. Charpentier, 'Le droit des peuples à disposer d'eux-mêmes et le droit international positif', 2 *Revue québécoise de droit international* 1985, 195 ff., especially 209–13.

above, the general principle that has evolved as a result of the 'codification' of existing practice by virtue of the 1970 Declaration on Friendly Relations, coupled with the consequent practice of States, is confined to granting the right of self-determination to racial groups denied equal access to government. However, there are a number of new factors that need to be mentioned: the increasing ratification by States of the UN Covenants (which confer that right on the whole people of each Contracting State),[19] the subscription by thirty-five States (European, and the US and Canada) to the 1975 Helsinki Declaration (which explicitly grants the right of self-determination to all peoples)[20] and its follow-up Declarations;[21] the attitude taken in 1991–2 by the European Community and the Twelve Member States towards the seceding Republics of the Soviet Union and Yugoslavia[22] and, in particular, the great emphasis laid by the Twelve on respect for democracy and the rights of minorities (that is, the implementation of *internal* self-determination) as a *condition* for the international endorsement and legitimation of independent statehood (that is, the attainment of *external* self-determination); the spread of democratic governance to many Latin American countries, coupled with the formal upholding of the principles of democracy by both these States and other developing countries in other continents. All these factors are clear indications of an important trend: States are increasingly accepting the idea that internal self-determination should have a much broader purport and consequently apply to the people of each sovereign State as well. The fact that pronouncements of States to the contrary are isolated[23] seems to bear out the contention that customary law is in the process of changing and will thus in the future gradually come to coincide – on this specific point – with treaty law (i.e., the Covenants). This normative development is of course of great importance. However, as I stated above (Chapter 6 and Chapter 11, pp. 145–6 and 311–12), one should be aware that so long as new (general or specific) monitoring mechanisms are not set up in the world community, this new rule, if and when it crystallizes, may turn out to be 'toothless'.

---

[19] As at 31 July 1993, 122 States had ratified the two Covenants. See UN Doc. St/HR/4/Rev.8.

[20] See A. Cassese, 'The Helsinki Declaration and Self-determination', in Buergenthal, *Human Rights, International Law and the Helsinki Accord*, 93.

[21] See above, pp. 264–73.

[22] See above, Chapter 10.

[23] For the position of India and Canada, see above, Chapter 3.

The existing law on self-determination and the new tribalism

It is common knowledge that we are currently witnessing a dangerous resurgence of nationalism in the world community. The wave of nationalistic and ethnocentric feelings that has recently swept Europe, but can also be discerned in Latin America, North America, and some African and Asian countries, is undermining consolidated State structures and triggering secessionist movements (but the most conspicuous instances are the former States of the Soviet Union and Yugoslavia). One is left with the impression that the traditional multi-ethnic State, that has for centuries constituted the mainstay of the world community, has become effete and is probably doomed to demise. The term 'tribalism', which has become fashionable in political discourse,[24] or 'micronationalism',[25] seems appropriate to depict the current situation.

Let us therefore ask ourselves three questions. First, have the international legal norms on self-determination contributed to fuelling this new tribalism or micronationalism? Second, are they capable of putting a stop to the centrifugal and disruptive tendencies of this tribalism? Third, if in the negative, are they at least responsive to the demands of 'micronationalism', or, in other words, are they in a position to furnish satisfactory solutions to the quest for independence of ethnic groups and nations currently striving to establish their standing in the world community?

The answer to the first question is not difficult. We have seen so far that the international body of legal norms on self-determination does not encompass any rule granting ethnic groups and minorities the right to secede with a view to becoming a separate and distinct international entity. The claims and demands of modern 'tribes' do not therefore find any basis in *legal norms*. Nevertheless, national and ethnic groups do find support in, and indeed vociferously rely upon, the tenets of *political philosophy* underpinning international legal standards (or, alternatively, they

---

[24] See for instance *The International Herald Tribune*, 2 July 1993, 1:5 (asserting that the expression 'new tribalism' is the brain-child of Joseph S. Nye Jr, former Director of Harvard's Centre for International Affairs and currently head of President Clinton's National Intelligence Council). See also the brilliant essay by T. M. Franck, 'Postmodern Tribalism and the Right of Secession', in Brölmann, Lefeber, and Zieck, *Peoples and Minorities in International Law*, 3–21, as well as the comments of R. Higgins, *ibid.*, 29–35.

[25] See B. Boutros Ghali, 'UN Multilateralism: a Cure for Ugly New Nationalisms', *The International Herald Tribune*, 21–22 August 1993, at 6.

invoke what the ordinary man in the street erroneously considers to be self-determination). In this respect, one should bear in mind what was stated in the Introduction to this book (Chapter 1) about the inherent ambivalence of the (political) concept of self-determination, its Janus-like nature or, in other words, the fact that this concept may be both radical and progressive and, at the same time, subversive and threatening. In the present stage of development of the world community, it would seem that it is rather the subversive and threatening feature of self-determination that is coming to the fore, at the political level. One may well conclude that the fears held out in the 1970s by Elmer Plischke,[26] that self-determination might unleash 'a Frankenstein of unrestrained proliferation and fragmentation', have come true.

Let us now establish whether international norms are capable of stemming the tide of nationalistic demands of ethnic groups. The answer is a blunt no. As we saw above (pp. 118–20, 122–4), international law does not ban secessionism: the breaking away of a nation or ethnic group is neither authorized nor prohibited by legal rules; it is simply regarded as a fact of life, outside the realm of law, and to which law can attach legal consequences depending on the circumstances of the case (for instance, law may impose the withholding of the recognition of the new entity if this entity has come about in gross breach of human rights; or may make its recognition contingent upon formal and actual respect for the rights of individuals and minorities). It follows that the restraining influence of legal rules is very limited indeed. Nor have institutional settings (such as the United Nations, the CSCE, the European Union) proved so far capable of exercising a decisive impact on the centrifugal forces at work in the world community.

Let us now turn to the third question: are international legal standards in a position to provide constructive solutions designed to avert the fragmentation of the international community in myriads of tiny States? Once again, the answer is bound to be in the negative. For, international law is ill-equipped to deal with a large-scale phenomenon that is totally different from decolonization (which is the only mass phenomenon it has had to cope with so far). International legal rules are too rigid and rudimentary to prove alert to the new wave of tribalism and secessionism. In particular, they are unmitigatedly geared to self-determination as a form of acquisition (or recovery) of independent statehood by colonial or

---

[26] E. Plischke, 'Self-Determination: Reflections on a Legacy', 140 *World Affairs*, 1977–8, at 52.

militarily occupied peoples, and, at the same time, exceedingly unresponsive to the needs of ethnic or racial groups (except for one category: that of those racial groups which are denied equal access to government).

All the above shows that there is at present a strong need for rethinking the concept of self-determination and suggesting possible avenues for the future development of the law in this area.

From *lex lata* to *lex ferenda*: a blueprint for action

The starting point

THE FAILINGS OF UN ACTION

Undisputedly, the generic and embryonic concept of self-determination adopted in the UN Charter has, over the years, gained precision and potency in its external dimensions. The UN has promoted the self-determination of peoples living under colonial or foreign domination and peoples oppressed by racist regimes, with considerable results. The Organization has dismantled the colonial system and, by politically isolating racist regimes, forced changes therein. In addition, the UN has contributed to the resolution of at least some of the situations involving foreign military occupation. The UN has also consistently affirmed that self-determination in the political sphere cannot be dissociated from economic self-determination.

The work of the United Nations has, however, been marred by the inability of the Organization to solve some particularly difficult issues, which are still unresolved and might further degenerate. Furthermore, the UN action has been one-sided. The Organization has disregarded those situations which – when considered in the light of a more comprehensive concept of internal self-determination – denote a complete negation of the right of self-determination of the peoples involved. By and large it has taken scant interest in minority groups severely oppressed by governments and has so far turned a blind eye to authoritarian regimes which systematically deprive peoples of fundamental rights.

This state of affairs can be easily understood if not condoned with respect to the period (1945–65) after the Second World War, when the paramount concern was the dismantling of the colonial scheme. However, now that almost all non-self-governing territories and former colonies have acquired independence this state of affairs can be considered deplorable.

THE CURRENT CONTEXT OF THE INTERNATIONAL COMMUNITY

Before embarking upon the task of propounding a few suggestions for the improvement of the existing situation, it is also necessary to emphasize briefly certain features of the present international setting that are germane to our subject matter.

First, as I have already stressed in the preceding pages, nobody can deny that the 'political' and 'popular' (as opposed to the legally accurate) conception of self-determination is having disruptive effects on the traditional setting of the world community and indeed might even act as a sort of earthquake, if unchecked. The contagious effects of nationalism or tribalism, seen as an ideological approach that draws heavily upon some political versions of self-determination, may progressively disrupt the fabric of traditional multinational States not only in Europe but also elsewhere.

Second, it is a fact that all the ethnic groups that are at present striving for independent statehood suffer from what a great international lawyer, Georges Scelle, termed as early as 1958 'obsession with territory'.[27] He perceptively pointed out that the 'personification' of sovereign States has totally obscured the concept of common good and transformed joint resources or amenities into exclusive property. Hence a 'bodily or proprietary conception' (*conception corporelle ou propriétarienne*) of territory: this plot of land, this part of sea, this area of air space must belong to us; we must appropriate them. All this, according to Scelle, is but the natural upshot of a statist approach (*mentalité gouvernementale*) and of the 'chaos of sovereignties', against which Scelle opposes the need for a gradual trend towards integration in a universal society and the appearance of actual solidarity.[28] One may find Scelle's universalistic approach naive and probably utopian. The fact remains, however, that Scelle was fundamentally right in his proposition that the present statist obsession with territory is an aberration and that 'to get hypnotised by State territory and territorial sovereignty (*s'hypnotiser sur le térritoire étatique et la souveraineté territoriale*) to the extent of elevating them to the obsessive and passionate preoccupation of rulers and national resources' is simply 'to go against

[27] G. Scelle, 'Obsession du territoire', in *Symbolae Verzijl*, The Hague 1958, 347–61.
[28] *Ibid.*, 357–8 ('peut-être pourrait-on concevoir que cette mentalité [gouvernementale] doive changer progressivement avec le mouvement d'intégration de la société universelle et l'apparition, non pas certes d'une solidarité affective qu'il n'est guère raisonnable de demander ni aux gouvernements – ni même aux peuples –, mais d'une solidarité de fait qui s'impose dans l'intérêt seul des rapports entre individus', *ibid.*, 358).

progress and peace'.[29] Even a cursory look at the present condition of the world community suffices to confirm the validity of Scelle's reflections: ethnic groups struggling for independent statehood wrongly believe that possession of exclusive authority over a territory will solve all their problems; they do not even consider the possibility of attaining the satisfaction of their aspirations within the context of existing State structures, under changed internal conditions and subject to the scrutiny of broad international frameworks.

Third, the natural consequence of the new nationalism or tribalism, were it to continue along its present lines, would be, first, the dangerous spread of dramatic conflicts and, by the same token, the proliferation of a myriad of mini-States. Both phenomena would prove exceedingly disruptive to the present international setting. Anarchy – indeed greater anarchy than at present – would become inevitable and with it political and armed clashes. This would lead to the gradual evaporation of the budding elements of democracy in the world community and the creation of a small concert of Great Powers that would of necessity dominate international relations in an authoritarian manner.

Fourth, on the other hand it cannot be denied that too many ethnic and other groups are currently suffering from unbearable discrimination and oppression: their demands must be met. The fundamental tenet enshrined in the preamble of the Universal Declaration of Human Rights ('it is essential, if man is not to be compelled to have recourse, as a last resort, to rebellion against tyranny and oppression, that human rights should be protected by the rule of law') also applies, *mutatis mutandis*, to ethnic and other groups. It is therefore imperative to suggest solutions that reconcile full respect for group rights with a modicum of peace and stability and the maintenance of the present system of multinational States.

In the following pages a tentative (and modest) attempt will be made to delineate some solutions that might prove both workable and helpful.[30]

---

[29] *Ibid.*, 361.

[30] Suggestions for improving the present legal regulation of self-determination have already been put forward by a number of authors. Most of them start from the assumption, which I share, that international legal rules should grant rights and a satisfactory protection to groups without however undermining existing States. See in particular, R. Bernhardt, ' Federalism and Autonomy', in Dinstein, *Models of Autonomy*, 23–8; Y. Dinstein, 'Autonomy', *ibid.*, 291–303; G. Sacerdoti, ' New Developments in Group Consciousness and the International Protection of the Rights of Minorities', 13 IYHR, 1983, especially 132–46; Hannum, *Autonomy, Sovereignty, and Self-Determination*, 453–77; Thürer, 'Das Selbstbestimmungsrecht der Völker – Ein Ueberblick', 134–7; Oeter,'Ueberlegungen zur Debatte um Selbstbestimmung, Sezessionsrecht und

General stock-taking

A plea for a four-pronged strategy

PUTTING EXISTING INTERNATIONAL LEGISLATION INTO EFFECT WITH REGARD TO SOME OUTSTANDING QUESTIONS

It is submitted that if the international community intends to revitalize self-determination so as to come to grips with some crucial problems besetting various areas of the world, it is necessary to act boldly on various fronts. States and international organizations should become aware that only *long-term policies* initiated simultaneously at different levels and in various directions may lead to the hammering out of international legislation capable of actually solving some of the most acute problems of our time.

A first line of action should no doubt aim at utilizing the existing legal rules with a view to settling all the outstanding issues of self-determination to which reference has been made above. While the questions of Western Sahara and Palestine are eventually likely to find a solution thanks to a number of different factors, for other issues no solution consonant with self-determination is in the offing. In this respect, some 'colonial' issues such as Gibraltar and the Falklands/Malvinas and issues related to foreign occupation, in particular those of East Timor, stand out as particularly intractable.

Clearly, each of the States involved in these situations should make a sustained effort to engage in serious negotiations with the other party or parties concerned. Nationalistic sentiments, deep-rooted traditional

'vorzeitige' Anerkennung', 763–75; Bokatola, *L'organisation des Nations Unies et la protection des minorités*, 167 ff.; C. Tomuschat, 'Self-Determination in a Post-Colonial World', in Tomuschat, *Modern Law of Self-Determination*, 1–20; P. Thornberry, 'The Democratic or Internal Aspect of Self-Determination, with Some Remarks on Federalism', *ibid.*, 101–38; A. Eide, 'In Search of Constructive Alternatives to Secession', *ibid.*, especially 161–76; A. Rosas, 'Internal Self-Determination', *ibid.*, especially 232–52; J. Salmon, 'Internal Aspects of the Right to Self-Determination: Towards a Democratic Legitimacy Principle?' *ibid.*, especially 265–82; H. Hannum, 'Synthesis of Discussion', in Brolmann, Lefeber, and Zieck, *Peoples and Minorities in International Law*, 333–9; G. Alfredsson, 'Minority Rights: Non-Discrimination, Special Rights and Special Measures', in Ermacora, Tretter, and Pelzl, *Volksgruppen im Spannungsfeld von Recht und Souveränität in Mittel- und Osteuropa*, 149–57; F. Matscher, 'Der Entwurf einer "Europäischen Konvention zum Schutze der Minderheiten" des Europarats-Kommission "Democracy through Law"', *ibid.*, 255–63; F. Ermacora, 'Erfahrungen und Perspektiven eines übernationalen Garantiesystems für Volksgruppenrechte sowie Möglichkeiten und Chancen eines europäischen Garantiesystem für Volksgruppen', *ibid.*, 317–24.

beliefs, and myopic political outlooks only pay dividends in the short run. The pursuit of *short-term interests* should therefore be set aside and substituted with *long-term policies* that are attuned to the exigencies of peace and international law. If each party becomes aware that the prolongation of the existing situation is only bound to exacerbate problems and fuel new conflicts, and that consequently it is necessary to engage in a constructive trade-off, realistic solutions can be found, based on the fundamental principle that the free and genuine expression of the populations concerned should always constitute the touchstone for any issue of self-determination. The necessity to reckon with sovereign States and international organizations in order to have any prospect of solutions is self-evident: realistically, the key to any problem lies in the hands of those entities which wield power in the world community. Although, as has repeatedly been pointed out, international rules clearly lay down an obligation on States to enable the peoples concerned to make a free choice about their destiny, it remains true that those peoples have no effective means available (except for resort to armed violence, a highly regrettable and dangerous option) to impel States to implement self-determination.

Political will on the part of the States concerned and constant pressure by third-party States, as well as international organizations, may turn out to be the only means for making international legal rules effective and operational.

Moreover, all the resources of treaty interpretation should be used to change gradually the restrictive approach taken by the UN Human Rights Committee as regards the right of peoples to invoke Article 1 of the UN Covenant on Civil and Political Rights, under the Optional Protocol. As I pointed out above (see Chapter 3), one may well wonder whether a liberal interpretation could not be placed upon Article 1 of the Protocol to this effect. For instance, individuals could at the same time be allowed to complain of alleged breaches of the Covenant's political rights (e.g., the right of association, the right to take part in free elections) and Article 1 of the Covenant. In other words, individuals could be allowed to claim that infringements of their political rights also amount to serious violations of the right of the whole population to self-determination. This, among other things, would lead the Committee to pronounce not only upon the application of the specific provision protecting political freedoms, but also, and more generally, on the way the democratic process in the State complained of is being implemented. Thus, the Committee's scrutiny would take on a broader scope and could consequently result in the final 'views' of the Committee having greater impact on domestic systems.[31] In addition, individuals acting as 'representatives' of the population could claim that Article 1 is being breached by a State, although the actual complainant is not directly and immediately a victim of such breaches, or is not the sole victim.

PROMOTING THE CRYSTALLIZATION OF RULES *IN STATU NASCENDI* ON THE INTERNAL SELF-DETERMINATION OF PEOPLES OF SOVEREIGN STATES

We have seen above (Chapter 5) that the approach to internal self-determination taken by the world community has been decidedly narrow and excessively cautious. It has reflected a willingness to support established governments, regardless of those ruling regimes' respect for, and implementation of, the right of peoples freely to choose their rulers.

The only exception to this prevailing attitude has been Article 1 common to the two 1966 UN Covenants on Human Rights which, however, has so far been construed in a strict way.

As was noted above (see Chapters 5 and 11 and pp. 337–8 of this Chapter), there are however signs that the international community's approach is gradually shifting towards greater respect for, and commitment to, the principle of the internal self-determination of peoples of sovereign States. There are grounds for holding the view that a customary rule on internal self-determination as a right of the whole population of a sovereign State is currently taking shape in the international community. For the rule fully to evolve, it is of course necessary to wait for further State practice and pronouncements from international bodies showing

---

[31] Mention should be made of J. Crawford's apposite remarks: 'Although the right of self-determination is vested in a group, it is quite possible for action to be taken with respect to individuals which constitutes a violation of the rights of the group. In certain circumstances it is arguable that those individuals might have a secondary or at least procedural right, on which they can themselves rely notwithstanding that it has its origin in a collective right to self-determination. For example action by a government in detaining or imprisoning the acknowledged leader of a people claiming a right to self-determination could well constitute a violation of that right, and it would seem an unnecessarily rigid insistence on the notion of collective rights to prevent the individual complaining in such circumstances' ('The Rights of Peoples: Some Conclusions', in Crawford, *The Rights of Peoples*, 165–6). The author, however, subsequently limits the scope of these comments by adding that 'this issue could conceivably arise under the African Charter' (166, note 18), thereby implicitly excluding their application to the UN Covenant.

that most, if not all, Member States of the world community consider themselves to be bound by such a rule. Allowance will also have to be made for the position of possible 'persistent objectors' to the nascent rule.

As soon as it is possible to argue that the rule has come into being, it will of course be crucial to establish whether it has the same content as the provision of Article 1 common to the UN Covenants covering internal self-determination, or instead provides more detailed regulation. I pointed out above (see Chapter 3) that the model of representative democracy underpinning the Covenant on Civil and Political Rights is rather loose and that this is reflected in the similarly loose content of the right to internal self-determination, laid down in Article 1 of the Covenant. Bearing this shortcoming in mind, it will be important to determine whether the better and clearer model of democracy reflected in the various CSCE documents and in a number of recent pronouncements by Western States will have a direct bearing on the emergent customary rule. In particular, it is crucial to see whether the rule, in addition to providing for a *continuing* right of peoples to choose and to change their rulers, also provides that peoples are granted the right to make a *free and genuine choice* concerning their political and economic regime, by being able to exercise all the civil and political rights that make it possible for a given people really to choose between various political and economic alternatives or options. Should the customary rule eventually have this content, its scope might have a knock-on effect on the Covenants in that it could gradually lead to an interpretation of Article 1 that is more geared to a *pluralistic* concept of *representative* democracy.

Whatever the content of the rule that will eventually evolve, it is evident that the rule will not play a major role as long as States or the United Nations do not set up some sort of monitoring device capable of inducing compliance with it. It is suggested that a major advance could be made if two steps are taken at the implementation level. First, some appropriate international fora or machinery should be set up whereby third States might put forward claims demanding the implementation of the right by other States; second, some international standing should be given to the representatives of the peoples at issue, to enable them to put forward claims for the realization of their right. So long as these practical steps of an organizational nature are not taken, the rule will only benefit from the present general system for enforcing international norms. As the rule is destined to impose obligations *erga omnes*, any State will be entitled to demand its compliance by other States, as well as being able to take the appropriate peaceful countermeasures in the event of serious violations. It stands to reason that, given the present structure of the world community, this legal regulation is unlikely to be effectively acted upon.

DEVELOPING NEW RULES FOR THE INTERNAL SELF-DETERMINATION OF ETHNIC GROUPS AND MINORITIES

General: the need to rethink self-determination and emphasize its 'internal' dimension
The major international instruments adopted so far by States (the UN Covenant on Political and Civil Rights, the UN Declaration on Friendly Relations and the Helsinki Final Act) all hinge on a *fundamental and sharp dichotomy between the self-determination of peoples on the one side and the protection of minorities, on the other.* States have been at pains to emphasize that the two issues are quite distinct in nature and also as far as their international regulation is concerned. No link or bridge between the two has been envisaged. On the contrary, any possible connection has been adamantly rejected as a dangerous muddling of two topics belonging to two different worlds.

Hitherto the protection of minorities[32] has been envisaged either as a

---

[32] On the question of minorities and self-determination see in particular: I. L. Claude, Jr, *National Minorities, and International Problem*, Cambridge, Mass. 1955, especially 6–55 and 110–212; C. A. Macartney, *National States and National Minorities*, 2nd edn, New York 1968, especially 179 ff.; J. Robinson, 'International Protection of Minorities, A Global View', IYHR, 1971, 61 ff.; B. Whitaker, 'Minority Rights and Self-Determination', in D. P. Kommers and G. D. Loesher (eds.), *Human Rights and American Foreign Policy*, Notre Dame, Ind. 1979, 63 ff.; G. Sacerdoti, 'New Developments in Group Consciousness and the International Protection of the Rights of Minorities', IYHR, 1983, 116–46; N. Lerner, 'From Protection of Minorities to Group Rights', IYHR, 1988, 101 ff.; M. N. Shaw, 'The Definition of Minorities in International Law', 20 IYHR, 1990, 13–43; F. Capotorti, 'Are Minorities Entitled to Collective International Rights?', 20 IYHR, 1990, 351–7; G. Herczegh, 'La protection des minorités par le droit international', *Acta juridica Academiae Scientiarum Hungaricae*, 1990, 215–46; F. Ermacora, 'Rights of Minorities and Self-Determination in the Framework of the CSCE', *The Human Dimension of the Helsinki Process. The Vienna Follow-Up Meeting and its Aftermath*, Dordrecht, Boston, and London 1991, 197–206; H. Hannum, 'Contemporary Developments in the International Protection of the Rights of Minorities', 66 *Notre Dame Law Review*, 1991, 1431–48; H. Isak, 'Self-Determination and the Protection of Minorities', in *Tipologia e protezione delle minoranze in Europa* (Atti del Colloquio internazionale delle minoranze in Europa, Trieste 3–4 novembre 1990), Quaderno no. 4, La Comunità internazionale, Padua 1991, 85–93; P. Thornberry, *International Law and the Rights of Minorities*, Oxford 1991; R. Bilder, 'Can Minorities Treaties Work?', in Y. Dinstein (ed.), *The Protection of Minorities and Human Rights*, The Hague 1992, 59–82; J. Helgesen, 'Protecting Minorities in the Conference on Security and Co-operation in Europe (CSCE) Process', in A. Rosas and J. Helgesen, *The Strength of Diversity – Human Rights and Pluralist Democracy*, Dordrecht, Boston, and London 1992, 159–86; Bokatola,

fall-back solution for self-determination (this, as was noted above in Chapter 1, happened after the First World War, when the treaties on minorities were conceived of as a substitute for the Wilsonian concept of self-determination), or as an attenuated manner of taking into account the aspirations of groups by supplementing the right of peoples to self-determination with the loose protection of some minorities. In this way both the concept of minority protection and of self-determination have been upheld; both, however, in a neutralized or emasculated form.

It is evident that the political underpinning of this position is the fear that minorities, by invoking self-determination, might claim a right of secession. This is because self-determination is still primarily conceived of as a means for achieving independent statehood.

If one starts from this assumption, it is clear that States will never depart from their present intransigence. As regards this position, it is sufficient to consider again the three basic facts which were referred to above: most members of the international community are multinational or multi-ethnic agglomerates; the majority of existing States are authoritarian entities which pay little attention to the aspirations of their populations; the economic and security interests of small or weak States compel them to enter into associations and alliances with the major international players. Since most sovereign States – the legislators responsible for the development of international law – are heterogeneous, the international community undoubtedly will continue to reject any proposals subsequently likely to empower individual sectors of their populations and to threaten their territorial integrity; secession is thus certain to remain an anathema. Finally, the multifarious economic and security problems which small nations or groups would face if constituted as sovereign States makes it questionable whether, even if groups were able to achieve independence, they would be able to maintain it.

These observations suggest that both the concept of self-determination and of minority rights must be reorientated. It is submitted that the approach so far taken by States and international organizations is wrong. It is further claimed that it is possible to take an alternative approach

---

L'Organisation des nations Unies et la protection des minorités, especially 167 ff. See also F. Matscher, 'Der Entwurf einer "Europäischen Konvention zum Schutze der Minderheiten" der Europarats-Kommission "Democracy through Law"', in Ermacora, Tretter, and Pelzl, *Volksgruppen im Spannungsfeld von Recht und Souveranität in Mittel. und Osteuropa,* 255–63; E. Weiss, 'Volksgruppenschutz im Rahmen der KSZE', *ibid.,* 280–90; P. Blair, 'Der Entwurf einer 'Europäischen Charta der Regional – und Minderheitensprachen' des Europarates', *ibid.,* 291–7.

consisting of *rethinking and constructively welding together the two notions of the self-determination of peoples and the protection of minorities and ethnic groups*. This, it is claimed, would not disrupt the fabric of States but rather result in the enhancement of the claims and aspirations of groups.[33]

It is the contention here that any expansion in the scope of self-determination to include ethnic minority groups and others at present not entitled to claim self-determination must be accompanied by a broadening of the concept of self-determination itself (which by the same token also entails a broadening of minority protection). The tenacity with which States guard their own (and other States') territorial integrity forces this conclusion. As long as self-determination is perceived primarily as a right to independent statehood it will remain more a source of conflict than a substantive component in the settlement of disputes.[34] States will continue to oppose with force peoples invoking their right to self-determination, characterizing the members of liberation groups as terrorists intent on dismembering the country. At the same time, those entitled to self-determination will lean towards rigidity and intransigence; convinced that the right to self-determination entitles them to absolute independence, they will be reticent to negotiate if sovereignty does not immediately appear in the offing. All too often, invoking a legal right renders the right holder less flexible and receptive to compromise.

In short, if the aim must be to promote the international protection of all those groups to which at present international law denies any legal standing, the emphasis must be laid on the right to *internal* self-determination. Self-determination today ought primarily to be considered

---

[33] On the issue see the apposite remarks of Thürer, 'Das Selbstbestimmungsrecht der Völker – Ein Ueberblick', 134–7; Thürer, 'Self-Determination', 475. See also Gusy, 'Von der Selbstbestimmung durch den Staat zur Selbsbestimmung im Staat', 405–10; Oeter, 'Ueberlegungen zur Debatte um Selbstbestimmung, Sezessionsrecht und 'vorzeitige' Anerkennung', 763–75. D. Z. Cass, 'Rethinking Self-Determination: A Critical Analysis of Current International Law Theories', 18 *Syracuse Journal of International Law and Commerce*, 1992, 38–40; A. Eide, 'In Search of Constructive Alternatives to Secession', in Tomuschat, *Modern Law of Self-Determination*, especially 161–176.

[34] Among the authors who actually conceive of self-determination as equivalent to independent statehood, a few stand out: Y. Z. Blum, 'Reflections on the Changing Concept of Self-Determination', 10 ILR, 1975, 509–10; and Y. Dinstein, 'Self-Determination and the Middle East Conflict', in Alexander and Friedlander, *Self-Determination: National, Regional and Global Dimensions*, 250–1; Alexander and Friedlander, 'Collective Human Rights of Peoples vis-à-vis Minorities', in Chandra, *Minorities in National and International Laws*, 77–8. In contrast, I. Brownlie ('The Rights of Peoples in Modern International Law', in Crawford, *The Rights of Peoples*, 6) rightly stresses that self-determination includes a variety of 'models'.

a principle mandating the recognition of group rights and regional autonomy. Its value is as the protector of collective rights: it is the counterpart of individual human rights. Accordingly, self-determination should be conceived as a basis for the development of *alternative constitutional frameworks*, affording those with a right to self-determination a meaningful measure of autonomy. In addition, self-determination ought to be considered as affording disadvantaged groups a right to *positive action*.

If the concept of self-determination thus comes to represent a range of choices and options rather than solely the 'ultimate goal' of independence, the gap between legal right and political reality could be considerably narrowed. Self-determination, divisive by its very nature, would still mean a contest for power, control and authority. However, envisioned as a concept permitting a range of solutions, it would render the gulf between States and the groups asserting their rights easier to bridge. If a right to self-determination also meant something less than a legal right to sovereignty, the concept – which generally fuels nationalist and separatist movements – might actually quell nationalism which, if carried to the extreme, can cause immense suffering.

Looking upon minority protection within the framework of internal self-determination: the link between the two concepts
The suggestion that one should consider the possibility of better protecting minorities within the framework and from the perspective of internal self-determination means basically two things.

First, a satisfactory treatment of minorities is based on the imperative condition that *internal self-determination for the whole population* should first be realized. That the whole population of the State where minorities live be granted the continuing right freely to choose its rulers through a democratic process is a (necessary, but not sufficient) pre-condition for full respect of the rights of minorities. This fundamental concept was recently spelled out in the Report of the CSCE Committee of Experts on National Minorities, adopted on 19 July 1991.[35]

---

[35] Section II(2) of the Report stipulates that the States participating in the CSCE process 'Emphasize that human rights and fundamental freedoms are the basis for the protection and promotion of rights of persons belonging to national minorities. They further recognize that questions relating to national minorities can only be satisfactorily resolved in a democratic political framework based on the rule of law, with a functioning independent judiciary. This framework guarantees full respect for human rights and fundamental freedoms, equal rights and status for all citizens, including persons belonging to national minorities, the free expression of all their legitimate

Second, to view the protection of minority and other groups from the vantage point of internal self-determination entails that *it is for the minority group to declare what type of protection it seeks*: autonomy, regional self-government, participation in the national decision-making process, etc. As we have seen, self-determination chiefly means the right of the population concerned to freely express its wishes about its destiny. It follows that the choice among the various alternative ways of safeguarding its basic rights primarily belongs to each minority group and should not be imposed from outside, by central authorities. The choice ought to be made by the people concerned, although of course it needs afterwards to be endorsed by the national authorities, or, in the event of disagreement, negotiated and agreed upon with those authorities. Interestingly, this idea has recently been put forward, although in a rather attenuated manner, by the 1991 CSCE Meeting of Experts on National Minorities.[36]

The means of achieving self-determination for ethnic groups and minorities:
strengthening positive action and participatory rights and granting a wide measure
of autonomy

If for ethnic groups and minorities the most realistic and appropriate way of achieving basic safeguards is through internal self-determination, it is opportune to see by what means this objective can be pursued. It is suggested that there exist two possible means by which to reconcile the need for groups and minorities fully to develop their potential within the framework of internal self-determination: via the requirements of territorial integrity and the political stability of sovereign States.

It is common knowledge that the present legal regime regarding minorities (which aims at the preservation of their separate identity and the prevention of forced assimilation by enabling members of minorities to enjoy their own culture, to speak their own language, and to practise their own religion) is insufficient. It is a fact that most minorities live in under-privileged conditions. States should therefore take *positive action* so as to

---

interests and aspirations, political pluralism, social tolerance and the implementation of legal rules that place effective restraints on the abuse of governmental power' (text in 30 ILM, 1991, 1692 ff., at 1695).

36 Section III(1) of the Meeting's Report stipulates that 'Respecting the right of persons belonging to national minorities to effective participation in public affairs, the participating States [in the CSCE process] consider that when issues relating to the situation of national minorities are discussed within their countries, they themselves should have the effective opportunity to be involved, in accordance with the decision-making procedures of each State' (text in 30 ILM, 1991, at 1696).

redress the balance and compensate for past injustices. This action might consist in granting groups all the financial and other means, as well as the relevant rights, that would enable them not only to maintain their cultural identity but also to fully promote their development at various levels (cultural, economic, political, etc.).[37]

Furthermore, whenever the groups and minorities concerned show that they are interested in fully taking part in the political, economic, and social life of the whole nation, States should grant them *participatory rights*, that is, rights that afford and guarantee participation in the national decision-making process.[38] This would allow those groups and minorities to become integral parts of State life by securing some representation in the various branches of government at both local and national level – while, however, maintaining and developing their own identity.[39]

---

[37] The need to broaden the present protection of minorities by providing for affirmative action is advocated by a number of commentators. See, e.g., R. Hauser, 'The Right of Self-Determination and Protection of Minorities', in Chandra, *Minorities in National and International Laws*, 97–9; I. Brownlie, 'The Rights of Peoples in Modern International Law', in Crawford, *The Rights of Peoples*, 3–7; Brownlie, *Treaties and Indigenous Populations*, 37–45; Lerner, *Group Rights and Discrimination in International Law*, 34–7, 163–7.

[38] It should be noted that in 1992, in discussing before the UN Human Rights Committee its 3rd Periodic Report concerning the implementation of the Covenant on Civil and Political Rights, Colombia stressed among other things the development of participatory rights. The Colombian delegate stated the following: 'Although there was no tradition in Colombia of direct participation in decision-making, two direct national referendums had been held, the first to decide whether a Constitutional Assembly should be held and the second to decide on the membership, powers and procedures of the Constitutional Assembly.' (*Report of the Human Rights Committee to the G.A.*, 1992, UN Doc. A/47/40, para. 377). Committee members were gratified by this attitude ('the Committee expresses satisfaction that the approach taken by Colombia to the right to self-determination of peoples has been in line with the development of participatory democracy and that Colombia is making real efforts to achieve full equality for minority groups' (*ibid.*, para. 391).

[39] On participatory rights, see, among others, V. van Dyke, *Human Rights, Ethnicity and Discrimination*, Leiden 1985, 36–7; Lerner, *Group Rights and Discrimination in International Law*, 35–6. See also, V. van Dyke, 'Self-Determination and Minority Rights', 13 *International Studies Quarterly*, 1969, 343–69.

The CSCE Committee of Experts on Minorities, quoted above, sets out an extremely interesting list of measures which States should take. Section IV(1) and (2) provides as follows: 'The participating States will create conditions for persons belonging to national minorities to have equal opportunity to be effectively involved in the public life, economic activities, and building of their societies.

In accordance with paragraph 31 of the Copenhagen Document, the participating States will take the necessary measures to prevent discrimination against individuals, particularly in respect of employment, housing and education, on the grounds of belonging or not belonging to a national minority. In that context, they will make

If, by contrast, groups and minorities prefer to emphasize their own development without necessarily becoming part of the national decision-making process, States should grant them extensive *personal and territorial autonomy*, that is, a broad measure of self-government in political,

provision, if they have not yet done so, for the effective recourse to redress for individuals who have experienced discriminatory treatment on the grounds of their belonging or not belonging to a national minority, including by making available to individual victims of discrimination a broad array of administrative and judicial remedies' (ILM, 1697).

Section IV(7) stipulates the following:

'Aware of the diversity and varying constitutional systems among them, which make no single approach necessarily generally applicable, the participating States note with interest that positive results have been obtained by some of them in an appropriate democratic manner by, *inter alia*:

- advisory and decision-making bodies in which minorities are represented, in particular with regard to education, culture and religion;
- elected bodies and assemblies of national minority affairs;
- local and autonomous administration, as well as autonomy on a territorial basis, including the existence of consultative, legislative and executive bodies chosen through free and periodic elections;
- self-administration by a national minority of aspects concerning its identity in situations where autonomy on a territorial basis does not apply;
- decentralized or local forms of government;
- bilateral and multilateral agreements and other arrangements regarding national minorities [. . .]
- creation of government research agencies to review legislation and disseminate information related to equal rights and non-discrimination;
- provision of financial and technical assistance to persons belonging to national minorities who so wish to exercise their right to establish and maintain their own educational, cultural and religious institutions, organizations and associations;
- governmental assistance for addressing local difficulties relating to discriminatory practices (e.g., a citizens relations service);
- encouragement of grassroots community relations efforts between minority communities, between majority and minority communities, and between neighbouring communities sharing borders, aimed at helping to prevent local tensions from arising and address conflicts peacefully should they arise; and
- the encouragement of the establishment of permanent fixed commissions, either inter-State or regional, to facilitate continuing dialogue between the border regions concerned.

The participating States are of the view that these or other approaches, individually or in combination, could be helpful in improving the situation of national minorities on their territories' (ILM, 1698–9).

Furthermore, Section V(1) states:

'The participating States respect the right of persons belonging to national minorities to exercise and enjoy their rights alone or in community with others, to establish and maintain organizations and associations within their country, and to participate in international non-governmental organizations' (*ibid.*).

economic, cultural, and religious matters.[40] Groups and minorities located in specific territorial areas should be granted the power to set up regional or local government structures endowed with legislative and enforcement powers and with the authority to take decisions regarding land and natural resources, social services, police and security matters, culture and education, and more generally the promotion of minority rights and interests. The power to impose local duties and indirect taxes on members of the group could also be envisaged. Autonomy would not undermine State sovereignty because, firstly, some matters would be reserved to the central authorities (for example, foreign affairs and defence) and, secondly, there should exist some sort of central power of supervision designed to ensure that the exercise of autonomous powers by minorities and groups does not run counter to the basic principles of the State Constitution.

It should be noted that, although the concept of autonomy is still vague and imprecise, there already exist in many countries instances of self-government that have proved to be workable and capable of reconciling the conflicting needs of minorities and the demands of State integrity. Spain's experiment with regional autonomy in the post-Franco period suggests the merits of this approach. The 1982 'Ley organica de armonizacion del proceso autonomico', based on an agreement concluded by the Spanish Government and the major opposition party the year before, provided for the achievement of extensive regional autonomy.[41]

---

[40] See Dinstein, *Models of Autonomy*. Generally, on autonomy, see L. B. Sohn, 'The Concept of Autonomy in International Law and the Practice of the United Nations', 15 *Israel Law Review* 1980, 180–90; R. Lapidoth, 'Some Reflections on Autonomy', *Mélanges P. Reuter*, Paris 1981, 379–89; D. Sanders, 'Is Autonomy a Principle of International Law?', 55 NTIR, 1986, 17–21; Hannum, *Autonomy, Sovereignty and Self-Determination*, 123 ff., especially 453–78; H. J. Steiner, 'Ideals and Counter-Ideals in the Struggle over Autonomy Regimes for Minorities', 66 *Notre Dame Law Review* 1991, 1539–60; O. Bring, 'Kurdistan and the Principle of Self-Determination', 35 GYIL, 1992, 157–169.

[41] It is interesting to note that in 1985, on the occasion of the discussion of the Second Spanish periodic report on the implementation of the UN Covenant on Civil and Political Rights, members of the UN Human Rights Committee asked the Spanish representatives questions concerning the actual degree to which the Autonomous Communities of Spain were self-governing. The Spanish delegate, in his reply, 'stressed that the Spanish Constitution had been adopted by an overwhelming majority in a referendum in 1978 and that his Government felt that it had fully carried out its obligation with respect to the right of self-determination of the Spanish people. He noted, with respect to the status of the Autonomous Communities, that they were authentic political entities with their own executive and legislative institutions sharing responsibilities with the State in their areas of competence, which were defined by the Constitution and the Constitutional Court. The 17 Autonomous Communities, which

The apparent success of this programme has resulted in an abatement of separatist sentiments in the region that witnessed the greatest turmoil, the 'Basque Country'. Indeed, the strong showing of the moderate Basque Nationalist Party and their governing partners, the Socialist Party, in the elections of 28 October 1990 in the autonomous Basque region was widely regarded as a rejection of radical separatist sentiments.[42]

Similarly, the granting of autonomy to South Tyrol, pursuant to the 1946 Agreement between Italy and Austria, has proved successful, in spite of the slowness with which Italy has implemented its international commitments. As I mentioned in Chapter 7, in 1992 Austria and Italy agreed that the set of domestic measures adopted by Italy for the granting of complete autonomy to the German-speaking minorities put an end to their dispute. On that occasion the Austrian Foreign Minister, Mr Mock, stated the following to the UN General Assembly:

Austria and Italy have thus been able to show to the community of nations a good example [of] how to resolve an ethnic conflict and how to guarantee and protect the rights and the identity of minorities.

The measures taken do indeed promise to provide a safe basis for the cultural, economic and social development of the German and the Ladin speaking ethnic group in South Tyrol, because they have sufficient legal safeguards on national and international levels.[43]

It should be added that the Italian Foreign Minister pointed out, in his speech to the UN General Assembly on 27 September 1991, that Italy had

made up the Spanish State, had had certain powers transferred to them from the central Government through a complex process which had now been practically concluded as far as most of them were concerned' (*Report of the Human Rights Committee to the G.A.*, 1985, UN Doc. A/40/40, para. 479).

[42] See Hannum, *Autonomy, Sovereignty and Self-Determination*, 263–79.

[43] Statement made in October 1992. Full text delivered by the Austrian Mission to the UN. The Minister went on to state that: 'The resolution of this controversy was greatly facilitated by a positive development in the political atmosphere of all parties involved, in particular by [the] strengthening of confidence between the State authorities and the ethnic groups. Although the protection of ethnic groups is clearly a dynamic process, the minority has to be assured that the Italian Republic will respect its different identity and maintain the laws and regulations which have been created for the promotion of the ethnic groups. Furthermore the minority must be ensured that its cultural ties based on common ethnic affiliation beyond the Italian frontier will also in the future not be impeded. If such confidence exists the State will acquire the loyalty of the minority. It will also create an atmosphere conducive to better and intensified cooperation across the borders.'

It should, however, be stressed that neither Mr Mock (in the parliamentary debate in Austria that took place on 5 June 1992) nor some political groupings in South Tyrol/Alto Adige seem to exclude a future invocation of self-determination.

constructed in this area a 'model of autonomy' which, when completed, could synthesize in a felicitous manner both 'the demands for self-determination and the needs of integration'.[44] The importance of the settlement reached on the South Tyrol/Alto Adige issue also lies in the existence of 'international safeguards' (namely, the right of Austria to submit to the International Court of Justice any dispute with Italy concerning the implementation of the 1946 De Gasperi–Gruber Agreement). Indeed, satisfactory protection of ethnic groups must of necessity include, in addition to domestic measures designed to grant full autonomy or other freely chosen or agreed upon forms of self-government, *international monitoring mechanisms*.[45]

Other forms of realistic and acceptable autonomy have already been realized in other countries, such as Denmark (in the case of Greenland) and the United States (in the case of Puerto Rico). In addition, it has been contended that the solution agreed upon in 1984 concerning Hong Kong constitutes a useful model for dealing with disputed territories.[46] Other models are in the process of being developed: reference can be made, for instance, to the granting by Australia of broad rights to aboriginal peoples.[47]

---

[44] For the text of the statement, see 74 RDI, 1991, 770.

[45] Some authors have also advocated a 'federal' solution for self-determination: see I. Brownlie, 'The Rights of Peoples in Modern International Law', in Crawford, *The Rights of Peoples*, at 6; C. Tomuschat, 'Bewährung, Stärkung, Ausgestaltung. Zur Künftigen Menschenrechtspolitik Deutschlands in den Vereinten Nationen', 39 *Vereinte Nationen*, 1991, at 9; C. Tomuschat, 'Self-Determination in a Post-Colonial World', in Tomuschat, *Modern Law of Self-Determination*, 13–14. A contrary view is taken by O. Kimminich, 'A "Federal" Right to Self-Determination?', *ibid.*, especially 89–100.

[46] See the remarks by R. E. Lutz, J. V. Feinerman, and H. Hannum in Proceedings ASIL, 1986, 349–53, 353–9 and 364–8 respectively. See also E. M. Amberg, 'Self-Determination in Hong Kong: A New Challenge to an Old Doctrine', 22 *San Diego Law Review*, 1985, 839–58; Hannum, *Autonomy, Sovereignty and Self-Determination*, 129–50; A. M. Han, 'Hong Kong's Basic Law: The Path to 1997, Paved with Pitfalls', 16 *Hastings International Comparative Law Review*, 1993, 321–42.

[47] In 1988, the Australian delegate stated the following in the Third Committee of the UN General Assembly: 'The original inhabitants of Australia, the Aboriginals and Islanders, had lived on Australian soil for some 40,000 years. For too much of the past 200 years, they had suffered discrimination, cruelty and oppression. Over the past 20 years, since a constitutional amendment had given his Government power to legislate for Aboriginals and Islanders, progress had been made in redressing those wrongs. Federal Governments, assisted by state and territory governments, had taken special measures to accelerate access by Aboriginals and Islanders to government services and to provide a base for their economic and social equality. Although they were entitled to all the legal rights and freedoms enjoyed by other Australians, in practice many of them remained seriously disadvantaged; the Government was therefore pursuing major initiatives to

It should be added that the examples pointed to here are intended to be merely illustrative of the various possibilities open to States: they have a whole range of solutions, formulas, and devices at their disposal. To mention just another example, it is worth recalling that in its Opinion no. 2, the Arbitration Committee set up in 1991 by the EC Peace Conference on Yugoslavia, after stating that the Serbian populations of Croatia and Bosnia-Herzegovina did not have a right to self-determination but were entitled to enjoy all the fundamental rights laid down in international instruments for individuals and minorities, pointed out that these rights might include the right to be granted the nationality of their own choice.[48] This innovative concept could constitute a further element capable of contributing to the solution of the question of ethnic groups and minorities.

Although, as has just been said, it is for States and international fora to

enable Australia's indigenous people to decide their own future and assume a full role in Australian society. In 1988 it had provided a total of $A 671.6 million for special programmes for Aboriginals and Islanders in the fields of housing, education, training and community development. His Government had adopted a state-by-state approach to Aboriginal land rights, taking into account the differences between the six Australian states and the varied needs of Aboriginal people. All but one of the state governments had taken action to provide secure land title for Aboriginal people and some 12 per cent of Australia was now held by Aboriginal communities under various forms of secure title. In 1987, it had been announced that there would be a fundamental restructuring of the government machinery responsible for policy development and programme administration in regard to Aboriginals and Torres Strait Islanders so as to enable them to manage their own affairs. A new Aboriginal and Torres Strait Islander Commission was to be created in 1989. His Government was also committed to improving the position of Aboriginals and Islanders in the criminal justice system; in 1987 the Federal Government had established a Royal Commission to study and report on the high incidence of Aboriginal deaths in custody since 1980; it had also promoted urgent measures in states to prevent further deaths in custody. The colonizers of the Australian continent had operated under the fallacious rule of *terra nullius*, which had wiped out the rights of the indigenous people to their land, its sacred places and the protection of their culture. Modern-day Australians had a responsibility to recognize the dispossession of the indigenous people and redress the wrongs of the past. In June 1988 it had been agreed that a treaty should be negotiated between the Aboriginal people and the Government on behalf of all the people of Australia, and in August 1988 a motion had been passed jointly by the two Houses of the Australian Parliament affirming the entitlement of Aboriginals and Islanders to self-management and self-determination subject to the Constitution and laws of Australia' (UN Doc. A/C.3/43/SR.7, 5 ff., paras. 15–18).

See also the landmark decision delivered on 3 June 1992 by the High Court of Australia in the *Mabo and others v. State of Queensland* case, in 107 *Australian Law Reports* 1993, 1 ff. (recognizing the native title of aboriginals over the lands of the Murray Islands and, in many ways, even restructuring the government–aboriginal relationship).

[48] See 3 EJIL, 1992, 183–4.

show vision, imagination, and flexibility, the contention can be made that two basic standards ought to inspire their action.

First, a pragmatic, case-by-case approach should be taken. Plainly, solutions should be adjusted to the specific conditions of each country and minority, in the light of the unique historical, economic, cultural, and political context of each case. States and international organizations should endeavour to formulate constitutional and administrative arrangements suitable to the specific circumstances of each individual case.

Second, States should endeavour to act, as far as possible, within the framework of international organizations or fora. The possibility of discussing and negotiating burning domestic issues within international institutions often helps to defuse conflicts and dissensions and facilitates the reaching of solutions that are acceptable to all the parties concerned. Moreover, international bodies should be given the authority to oversee the implementation of the constitutional schemes agreed upon by the parties, so as to ensure that the beneficiaries of these schemes are not subsequently denied their rights.

ALLOWING FOR THE EXCEPTIONAL GRANTING OF EXTERNAL SELF-DETERMINATION TO ETHNIC GROUPS AND MINORITIES, SUBJECT TO INTERNATIONAL CONSENT AND SCRUTINY

Starting from the assumption that the essence of self-determination lies not in the final shape in which self-determination is achieved, let alone in actual independent statehood, but in the method of reaching decisions (based on the need to pay regard to the freely expressed will of peoples), we have so far argued that future legal developments of self-determination should tend to enhance internal self-determination as a way of solving the problems of democracy and respect for the needs and aspirations of ethnic and national groups and minorities.

Allowance should nevertheless be made for exceptional cases where factual conditions render internal self-determination impracticable. When, in a multinational State, armed conflict breaks out and one or more groups fight for secession, it may be that it is too late to plead for a peaceful solution based on internal self-determination. Similarly, when the central authorities of a multinational State are irremediably oppressive and despotic, persistently violate the basic rights of minorities and no peaceful and constructive solution can be envisaged, it seems difficult to imagine that those central authorities would be willing to grant autonomy, or participatory rights.

As was seen in Chapter 2, the possibility of secession in such cases was envisaged as early as 1920–1, at the time of the League of Nations. In 1920 the International Commission of Jurists foresaw cases of 'manifest and continued abuse of sovereign power' by a State against 'a section of the population' and clearly implied that under such circumstances minority protection would no longer be workable.[49] More boldly, in 1921 the International Commission of Rapporteurs, basing its views on the concept that self-determination embodies 'the idea of justice and liberty', explicitly admitted that 'the separation of a minority from a State of which it forms part' could be considered 'an altogether exceptional solution, a last resort when the State lacks either the will or the power to enact and apply just and effective guarantees'.[50] These concepts should be taken up and revitalized – subject to a set of conditions designed to avoid dangerous repercussions for the international community.

In the aforementioned two sets of cases, one might thus envisage the intervention of the international community with a view to promoting some sort of independent statehood for the minorities at issue. A case in point, regarding the first category, is that of Yugoslavia. As is well known, in 1991 the member States of the European Community promoted, with the support of the CSCE, the setting up of a political forum, the Peace Conference on Yugoslavia, for the settlement of the questions raised by the civil strife in that State. In addition, an Arbitration Committee was called upon to decide on several delicate legal issues linked to the will of a number of republics to secede from the State. Once it became clear that the process of secession could no longer be stopped, the Conference formulated a number of conditions to be met before the recognition of the independent statehood of the seceding republics. These standards included respect for human rights and the rights of minorities, as well as compliance with a number of other international commitments. Under these strict requirements, not all republics wishing to secede have been regarded as eligible for international independent status.[51]

In the case just referred to, international bodies have thus worked as a powerful filter for the purpose of ensuring that separatist aspirations are only realized subject to a set of stringent requirements. Admittedly, the

[49] See above, p. 31, note 57.
[50] See above, p. 31, note 58.
[51] For the text of the EC Declaration of 16 December 1991 setting out the above-mentioned requirements, see above, pp. 270–1, note 25. For the text of some of the Opinions delivered by the Arbitration Committee, see 3 EJIL, 1992, 182–5 and 4 EJIL, 1993, 74–91.

distressful situations that have subsequently evolved in Croatia and Bosnia-Herzegovina are likely to beget pessimism as to the effective capability of international mechanisms to come to grips with, and contribute to the solution of, serious problems of nationality, ethnic minorities, and secession. However, the conditions in the former Yugoslavia are uniquely intricate and complex, on a number of historical, political, and military grounds. Hence, what appears an intractable problem there is likely to prove less arduous to resolve in other cases. With regard to less complex cases, it would seem that international bodies should monitor the continued fulfilment of general requirements by the new States recognized as independent (the consequences that one would expect to accompany a failure to adhere to those requirements might include withdrawal of recognition, economic sanctions, banning from membership of the European Union or even from entering into association agreements with the European Union for a certain number of years, etc.).

Solutions are also difficult in the case of minorities which, for a number of reasons (military oppression by the central authorities, lack of organization, etc.) have not yet set in motion a *de facto* process of secession. In such cases, where armed conflict has not broken out, it is harder for the international community to intervene. The only recent instance of international intervention for the protection of a minority group is that envisaged, albeit in loose terms, by Resolutions 688 and 689 adopted in 1991 by the UN Security Council as regards the repression of the Kurds by Iraq. On the strength of either of these resolutions – or, arguably, of Resolution 678 (authorizing the Allies to restore peace and security to the area) – allied intervention by American, British, and French troops took place. However, this case[52] is quite exceptional, if only because the allied intervention occurred in the aftermath of an international armed conflict in which Iraq was the vanquished party. In any event, the intervention was short-lived and did not result in a resolution of the problem.

It therefore seems more realistic to envisage the possibility of international bodies intervening only at the diplomatic and political level, in order gradually to promote peaceful solutions acceptable to the State concerned. One possible way out could consist of promoting a *confederation*

---

[52] See thereon P. Malanczuk, 'The Kurdish Crisis and Allied Intervention in the Aftermath of the Second Gulf War', 2 EJIL, 1991, 114 ff.; R. Zacklin, 'Les Nations Unies et la crise du golfe', in B. Stern (ed.), *Les aspects juridiques de la crise et de la guerre du Golfe*, Paris 1991, 72–4; Corten and Klein, *Droit d'ingérence ou obligation de réaction*, 223–30. See also, Halperin, Sheffer, and P.L. Small, *Self-Determination in the New World Order*, 38–44.

or some sort of *international association* between the seceding nation and the State or other States, or membership of the breakaway nation in a *regional organization.*

This or similar solutions would be in keeping with the new trends currently emerging in the world community towards both greater political and economic integration at the 'supranational' level and, at the same time, the growing emphasis on the ethnic and cultural distinctiveness of groups, at the 'intrastate' level. This 'apparent paradox of a simultaneous movement toward integration and transnational co-operation on the one hand, and towards decentralization – a phenomenon evident not only in Western Europe but throughout the industrialized and industrializing world' has already been emphasized by political scientists.[53] They have rightly underlined that the increasing aversion toward anonymity, cultural standardization, and homogenization brought about by the modern process of industrialization stimulates 'a growing desire for identification and membership in a community more distinct and culturally homogenous than national society'. At the same time, there is a growing need for transnational co-operation and the setting up of international frameworks transcending the State. These seemingly contradictory trends result in a weakening of the traditional nation-State, which is gradually losing its authority and legitimacy. This might, to some extent, assuage the fears of States that the loosening up of the central structure of authoritarian States could lead to the falling apart of existing poles of power in the world community, hence to international anarchy.

Given the present condition of the world community, it appears, however, that it will take some time before the prospect of multilateral 'intervention' in this area becomes a reality. Clearly, sovereign States, especially those having authoritarian regimes, will strongly oppose any international action aimed at alleviating the plight of oppressed ethnic groups, nations, and minorities. The world community is faced here with a challenge that it must, however, take up, in order to defuse explosive situations that might easily degenerate and pose a serious threat to international peace and stability.

---

[53] See S. Rokkan, 'Dimensions of State Formation and Nation-Building: A Possible Paradigm for Research on Variations within Europe', in C. Tilly (ed.), *The Formation of National States in Western Europe*, Princeton 1975, 562–600; E. Gellner, *Nationalism and the Two Forms of Cohesion in Complex Societies*, London 1982, 165–87; G. Majone, 'Presentation of Cultural Diversity in a Federal System: the Role of the Regions', in M. Tushnet (ed.), *Comparative Constitutional Federalism: Europe and America*, Westport, New Zealand 1990, 67–76 (the citations above, in the text, are from Majone's paper).

It is within this context that one might envisage some sort of viable and realistic solution for groups living in authoritarian multinational States. At the instigation, and with the co-operation, of the international community it would perhaps be possible to devise *transnational structures* allowing groups to achieve some independent political and economic status, always, however, within international or transnational frameworks (associations, confederations, and other international unions). In addition, the State authorities from which the group would acquire independence or autonomy should be allowed to participate in these international frameworks (on condition that their presence should not be perceived by the groups as oppressive or paralysing).

A word of caution about the proposed strategy and some alternative solutions

One should not be blind to some flaws inherent in the approach suggested above. It must be frankly admitted that this approach – using the spirit of self-determination to address the current problems which have manifested themselves in Europe and elsewhere – has serious limitations. In some respects the proposed solutions entail a conceptual return to the minority regimes of the end of the First World War: not full self-determination realized in statehood, but more or less limited forms of autonomy. The recent experience in former Czechoslovakia and former Yugoslavia demonstrates that the granting of regional autonomy or minority rights can easily fuel the state of mind which leads to a breaking up of, or breaking away from, the State. It is thus likely that, with all the commitment to minority rights expressed in transnational instruments, the architects of the new international order will be as suspicious of regional autonomy or minority rights as were their predecessors in the earlier incarnation of self-determination.

But the limitations referred to above are even deeper and go beyond contingent political circumstances. Autonomy and minority-based regionalism are poor options or no option at all in at least two circumstances: first, when the number of minorities increases to an extent that regional autonomy becomes non-functional; and second, when the minorities are not situated in a geographically coherent area but are spread all over the State's territory. The end of the Cold War and the various manifestations of regional integration, notably in Europe, will render these problems more acute. It is against this background that we can touch upon some of the deepest conceptual and political problems of self-determination.

As was pointed out in Chapter 1, together with its radical and subversive traits, self-determination also possesses some highly regressive features and, in the evolution of the international order, it also turned out to be a potentially reactionary concept. After all, the basic underpinning of self-determination is constituted by two of the hallowed 'articles of faith' of international legal doctrine: (i) the centrality of the ethno-national 'self' as the principal subject of self-determination and (ii) the idea that the ethno-national territorial State is the bedrock of the entire world order and therefore constitutes the principal goal and vindication of the right at issue. This should not be surprising if one recalls the historical origins of self-determination discussed in the opening chapters of this book. Translated from law – via political theory – to social consciousness, this creates a belief which asserts that France belongs to the French, Germany to the Germans, Britain to the Britons, etc. Although, admittedly, there have been, and are, many tolerated exceptions, the fact remains that the ethno-culturally coherent territorial State is still regarded as the linchpin of the present inter-state system.

Only if one bears these concepts in mind, can one understand some of the deeper contradictions, or even pathologies, of self-determination which go beyond its international and internal dimension of 'political subversion' which was alluded to in the introduction.

When the ethno-national State is confronted with 'permanent' inhabitants who are not part of the dominant national culture, this is regarded as a crucial 'problem'. Often, one of the two following options is chosen: either to regard them as long-term aliens – accorded at best fundamental human rights, but with few if any civil and political rights – or to exact, as a price for full political and civil integration, their 'naturalization'; that is complete cultural assimilation. This, of course, contradicts, so far as a minority is concerned, the very values which self-determination seeks to promote.

A third option consists of adopting the forms of autonomy proposed above. It is now clear that this solution is really informed by the spirit of self-determination: it recognizes the separate ethno-cultural identity of the minority and seeks a political and territorial solution to it. In the arena of self-determination, autonomy and minority regimes present for the ethno-national State an *ersatz* or fall-back solution. Although these solutions more or less recognize the national and cultural identity of the minority, they do not bring to fruition the full potential of self-determination for regional minorities (indeed, autonomy is not independence). Moreover, they enhance the frustration of those minorities which, being scattered over the whole State territory, cannot enjoy limited autonomy.

Perhaps the best solution is neither to embrace some form of utopian cosmopolitanism nor to assume an attitude that decries ethno-cultural differences. Too much richness would be lost if diverse cultural expression could not find expression. What deserves, instead, careful consideration is the need for separation of *ethno-cultural differences* from the *State* as a political entity. Thus, the next stage in the evolution of self-determination, the most radical stage of all, might be one in which States would increasingly become polities belonging to their citizens defined in 'civic' terms rather than in 'ethno-national' terms. The separation of 'State' and 'nationality' would imply that within the 'non-national' or truly 'multi-national' State – that is, the State that belongs to all its citizens – citizens would be free to group themselves around their cultural heritage and symbols (just as in the liberal secular State, where everybody enjoys full religious freedom, whatever the religion or the religious group to which he or she belongs). Naturalization would then involve a commitment to a 'plural constitution' and immigration policies would be functional and not dependent on nationality. To some States, like the United States, this would not formally mean much of a shift; to others like, for example, Germany this approach would constitute a radical shift in the self-image of the society and the State.

This, of course, is a way of thinking more than a blueprint. Admittedly, the problems of multicultural co-existence, even in a non-national State, would be legion. However, it is suggested that the concepts just outlined might stimulate a new generation of younger scholars and policy makers to rethink even the most fundamental, seemingly axiomatic, premises of that central concept – self-determination – which has overshadowed so much of this century.

Index of names

366

Index of names

Index of names

Gaja, G., 172, 174, 180, 297
Gaja, R., 104
Galtung, J., 300
Gattini, A., 104
Gayim, E., 28, 41, 99, 178, 333
Gellner, E., 326, 362
Genscher, H.-D., 228
Gess, K. N., 99
Ginther, K., 166
Gittleman, R., 309
Goodman, E. R., 44
Gorbachev, M., 260, 261, 264
Gordon Levin, N., Jr, 21
Gorelick, R., 194
Gotlieb, Y., 232
Gourion, D. B., 234
Graefrath, B., 44, 45, 109, 129, 158, 202, 333
Graf Huyn, H., 45
Graf zu Dohna, B., 109
Green, L. C., 127, 231
Grenville, J. A. S., 37
Gros Espiell, H., 75, 93, 135
Grossman, C., 310
Guarino, G., 120, 143, 194
Guelke, A., 317
Guilhaudis, J. F., 13, 41, 45, 99, 111, 122, 127, 223, 232, 327
Gusy, C., 71, 101, 146, 350

Hachey, T. H., 46
Halperin, D., 57
Halperin, M. H., 264, 269, 310, 361
Han, A. M., 357
Hannikainen, L., 135
Hannum, H., 25, 28, 123, 329, 343, 348, 355, 356, 357
Harper, E., 250
Hasbi, A., 166, 202
Hauser, R., 353
Havel, V., 288
Hazard, J., 264
Helgesen, J., 348
Henkin, L., 47, 57, 61, 132, 146
Heraclides, A., 122
Héraud, G., 59
Herczegh, G., 129, 348
Higgins, R., x, 80, 122, 126, 252, 339
Hill, C., 17
Hitler, A., 258
Hoffman, P., 75, 208, 223
Horowitz, D. L., 113
Hossein, A. I., 236
House, E., 25, 26
Howard, B. R., 330
Hu, C. Y., 47
Hughes, A. D., 96

Hula, R. C., 37
Hussain ibn Ali, Sheriff of Mecca, 232, 233

Iglar, R. F., 269
Iovane, M., 86
Isaak, R., 19
Isak, H., 348
Islam, M. R., 122, 194

Jennings, R. Y., 127, 187, 190, 192
Jiménez de Arechaga, E., 111, 118, 153, 172
Johnson, C. D., 109, 111
Johnson, H. S., 46, 76, 132, 327
Jouve, E., 297
Juste Ruiz, J., 59

Kamanu, O. S., 122
Kaur, S., 127
Keynes, J. M., 141
Kimminich, O., 75, 194, 357
Kingsbury, B., 327, 330
Kiss, A., 129, 135
Kiwanuka, R. N., 59
Klabbers, J., 192
Klein, E., 48, 135, 166, 184, 194, 361
Knight, D. B., 231
Kohl, H., 94, 263
Kommers, D. P., 348
Koteswara Rao, M., 68
Krishnan, M. V., 44
Kröger, H., 15, 44, 129, 151, 166
Kunz, J. L. 74

Lamberti Zanardi, P. L., 198
Lansing, R., 22-5, 316
Lapidoth, R., 355
Lapierre, J., 252
Lattanzi, F., 41, 48, 194, 198
Lauterpacht, H., x, 186, 190, 231
Lawrence, P., 223
Lazarus, C., 166, 168
Leben, C., 155, 183
Lefeber, R., 45, 113, 122, 192, 194, 330, 339, 344
Lenin, V. I., 6, 13-19, 21, 24, 33, 44, 315, 321
Lerner, N., 44, 330, 348, 353
Lévasque, R., 248
Levie, H. S., 208
Lévi-Strauss, C., 113
Levitin, M. J., 194
Levits, E., 258
Levkov, I., 44
Linares, A., 109
Loebl, E., 45
Loesher, G. D., 348
Lombardi, A. V., 70, 75, 166,

Index of names

Index of names

Index of names

Index of subjects

Index of subjects

Index of subjects